All in One®

Computer Applications

CBSE Class 9

Focused Theory ▪ Practice Exercise ▪ Sample Papers

Author
Neetu Gaikwad
(B.Tech, MBA)

arihant
SUCCESS AND NOTHING LESS

ARIHANT PRAKASHAN

(School Division Series)

ADMINISTRATIVE & PRODUCTION OFFICES

Regd. Office

'Ramchhaya' 4577/15, Agarwal Road, Darya Ganj, New Delhi -110002

Tele: 011- 47630600, 43518550; Fax: 011- 23280316

Head Office

Kalindi, TP Nagar, Meerut (UP) - 250002, Tel: 0121-7156203, 7156204

SALES & SUPPORT OFFICES

Agra, Ahmedabad, Bengaluru, Bareilly, Chennai, Delhi, Guwahati, Hyderabad, Jaipur, Jhansi, Kolkata, Lucknow, Nagpur & Pune.

PO No : TXT-XX-XXXXXXX-X-XX

Published By Arihant Publications (India) Ltd.

For further information about the books published by Arihant, log on to www.arihantbooks.com or e-mail at info@arihantbooks.com

Follow us on

PRICE ₹300.00

PRODUCTION TEAM

Publishing Managers
Mahendra Singh Rawat & Keshav Mohan

Cover Designer
Rakesh Rawat

Inner Designer
Ankit Tyagi

Project Head
Shruti Aggarwal

Page Layouting
Ravindra Kumar

Proof Reader
Sumit

Index *cum* Study Planner

Studied | Revised | Exam ready

One Book- Endless Features

to Help you Succeed

Chapter Checklist

At the start of each chapter, all the topics of the chapter have been listed , so that students may know what they are going to study.

CHAPTER

01

Computer System Organisation

Chapter Checklist

Characteristics of a Computer
Components of a Computer
Input Devices

A computer is an electronic device that manipulates information or data according to the set of instructions, i.e. programs. It has the ability to store, retrieve and process the data. It is used to type documents, send E-mails and browse the Internet. It is also used to handle spreadsheets, accounting, database, presentations, games and many more.

Characteristics of a Computer

The characteristics of a computer are as follows

Accuracy Computer operates with very high degree of accuracy and can do 100% error free calculations. It does not get exhausted to the extent of making mistakes.

Speed Computer is generally known for its speed. It can process data very fast at the rate of millions of instructions per second. Units of speed is measured in micro seconds, nano seconds and pico seconds.

Diligence Unlike human beings, a computer is free from monotony, tiredness, lack of concentration etc and can do work for hours without creating any errors.

Simplified Theory

Each chapter contains the necessary study material well supported by Definitions, Facts, Figures, Flow Charts, etc.

The needed instruction for processing and any kind of intermediate results are also stored in primary memory. Another kind of memory is referred as secondary memory of a computer system. This unit is used to permanently store data.

Register

It is an internal part of CPU which is used to store intermediate results obtained during the execution of instructions.

Boxed Matter

Information in the boxes is given to focus important points related to the concept.

Gigo

- The first **keyboard** was invented in 1868 by Christopher Sholes.
- The first **joystick** was created in 1926 by CB Mirick.
- The first **image scanner** developed for use with a computer was a drum scanner. It was built in 1957 at the US National Bureau of Standards by a team led by Russell A Kirsch.
- The **first computer mouse** was invented by Douglas Engelbart at Stanford Research Centre in 1960s.
- The first ever touchscreen was developed by EA Johnson in 1960s.

GIGO

Random and Important Facts that enhance the knowledge about particular topic.

One Book- Endless Features

to Help you Succeed

Illustrative Figures

To make the concepts completely visible, illustrative diagrams have been given at various place.

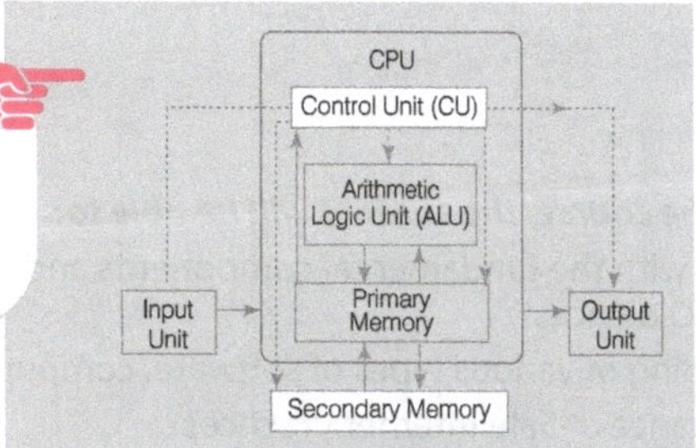

Components of a computer

Exam Practice

To make students completely prepared for examination, this Exercise contains Exam Pattern Questions. This exercise covers all types of questions, like; MCQs, Application Oriented Questions, Assertion-Reason, VSA, SA & LA Type Questions.

Exam Practice

Multiple Choice Questions

1 A computer is free from tiredness, monotony, etc., reflects which characteristic?
(a) High speed (b) Versatile
(c) Accuracy (d) Diligence

Ans. (d) Unlike human beings, a computer is free from monotony, tiredness, lack of concentration etc, and can work for hours without creating any errors. This characteristic of computer is known as diligence.

2 It is responsible for all numerical and logical calculations.
(a) CPU (b) CU (c) MU (d) ALU

Ans. (d) ALU is a digital circuit in which numerical and logical operations are defined.

8 .... is a medium size scanner which has rolling drum to scan your documents.
(a) Drum (b) Handheld
(c) Flatbed (d) Roller

Ans. (a) Drum

9 Large amount of cheques are processed by using
(a) OCR (b) MICR
(c) OMR (d) All of these

Ans. (b) Large amount of cheques are processed by the MICR (Magnetic Ink Character Recognition). It can read characters that are printed using a special magnetic ink. It is mostly used in banks.

Chapter Summary

Summary of chapter given at the end of each chapter helps to revise the chapter quickly at the time of examination or routine school tests.

SUMMARY

- Computer is an electronic device that stores and manipulates information.
- Computer itself is a combination of different types of separate electronic device, i.e. input device, processing unit and output device.
- An input device is any hardware device that sends data to a computer, allowing you to interact with and control the computer. e.g. keyboard, mouse, joystick, light pen, scanner, web camera etc.
- A keyboard is an external input device usually includes alphabetic, numerical and common symbols used to type data.
- Scanner is a device that reads or copies information or images into a computer.
- OMR technology scans a printed form and reads predefined positions and records where marks are made on the form.
- An output device is any peripheral device that receives data from a computer usually for display, projection or physical reproduction. e.g. monitor, printer, plotter, speaker etc.
- A monitor (also called visual display unit) looks like a television and it displays alphanumeric and graphic output.
- Printer is an output device that prints paper documents.
- CPU is the brain of the computer which performs basic arithmetical and logical operations of the system.

Sample Question Papers

To make students practice of examination in real sense, there are 3 Sample Question Papers at the end. All these Sample Questions Papers are exactly prepared on the latest syllabus & pattern of examination.

SAMPLE QUESTION PAPER 1

A Sample Question Paper for CBSE Class 9th

Computer Applications

Instructions

1. This question paper has 5 Sections A-E.
2. All questions are compulsory. However, internal choices have been provided in some of the questions.
3. Section A has 12 questions carrying 1 mark each.
4. Section B has 7 Short Answer (SA-I) type questions carrying 2 marks each.
5. Section C has 4 Short Answer (SA-II) type questions carrying 3 marks each.
6. Section D has 1 Long Answer (LA) type question carrying 4 marks.
7. Section E has 2 Source-based/Case-based/Passage-based questions carrying 4 marks each.

Time : 2 hours *Max. Marks : 50*

Section A

$(12 \times 1 = 12)$

1. Interactive combination of text, graphics, images, audio, video etc., is known as
(a) data (b) information (c) multimedia (d) internet

Latest Course Structure

Learning Outcomes

After the completion of the course, the student will be able to:

1. Familiarise themselves with the fundamental components and functions of computer systems, memory, storage devices, and I/O devices.
2. Develop an understanding of various types of software, computer networks, and multimedia.
3. Understand the importance of Safe Internet Practices
4. Create and edit documents, spread sheets, and presentations.
5. Perform basic data manipulation using spread sheets.
6. Animate text and pictures using presentation tool

Distribution of Marks and Periods

Unit No.	Unit Name	Marks
1.	Basics of Information Technology	20
2.	Cyber Safety	15
3.	Office Tools	15
4.	Lab Exercises	50
	Total	**100**

UNIT I Basics of Information Technology

- Computer Systems: Characteristics of a Computer, Components of a Computer System – CPU, Memory, Storage Devices and I/O Devices
- Memory: Primary (RAM and ROM) and Secondary Memory.
- Storage Devices: Hard Disk, CD ROM, DVD, Pen/Flash/Drive, Memory Stick
- I/O Devices: Keyboard, Mouse, Monitor, Printer, Scanner, Web Camera
- Types of Software: System Software (Operating Systems, Device Drivers), Application Software including Mobile Applications
- Computer Networking: Types of networks : PAN, LAN, MAN, WAN, Wired/Wireless Communication, Wi-Fi, Bluetooth, Cloud Computers (Private/Public)
- Multimedia: Images, Audio, Video, Animation

UNIT II Cyber-Safety

- Safely Browsing the Web and Using Social Networks: Identity Protection, Proper Usage of Passwords, Privacy, Confidentiality of Information, Cyber Stalking, Reporting Cybercrimes
- Viruses, Malware and Adware

UNIT III Office Tools

- Introduction to a Word Processor: Create and Save a Document.
- Edit and Format Text: Text Style (B, I, U), Font Type, Font Size, Text Colour, Alignment of Text. Format Paragraphs With Line and/or Paragraph Spacing. Add Headers and Footers, Numbering Pages, Grammar and Spell Check Utilities, Subscript and Superscript, Insert Symbols, Use Print Preview and Print a Document.
- Insert Pictures, Change the Page Setting, Add Bullets and Numbering, Borders and Shading and Insert Tables – Insert/Delete Rows and Columns, Merge and Split Cells
- Use Auto-format, Track Changes, Review Comments, Use of Drawing Tools, Shapes and Mathematical Symbols.
- Presentation Tool: Understand the Concept of Slide Shows, Basic Elements of a Slide, Different Types of Slide Layouts, Create and Save a Presentation and Learn About the Different Views of a Slide Set – Normal View, Slide Sorter View and Hand-outs
- Edit and Format a Slide: Add Titles, Subtitles, Text, Background, and Watermark, Headers and Footers, and Slide Numbers.
- Insert Pictures from Files, Create Animations, Add Sound Effects and Rehearse Timings.
- Spreadsheets: Concept of a Worksheet and a Workbook, Create and Save a Worksheet.
- Working with a Spreadsheet: Enter Numbers, Text, Date/Time, Series Using Auto Fill; Edit and Format a Worksheet Including Changing the Colour, Size, Font, Alignment of Text; Insert and Delete Cells, Rows and Columns. Enter a Formula Using the Operators (+,-,*, /), Refer to Cells and Print a Worksheet.
- Use Simple Statistical Functions: Sum (), Average (), Max (), Min (), If () (Without Compound Statements); Embed Charts of Various Types: Line, Pie, Scatter, Bar and Area In a Worksheet.

Lab Exercises

- Browser settings for a secure connection.
- Working with the operating system: Navigation of the file system using a mouse and keyboard.
- Word processing: create a text document; create a letter, report and greeting card.
- Create a text document with figures in it. It should describe a concept taught in another course.
- Discuss the following in a text document about the basic organisation of a computer: CPU, memory, input/output devices, hard disk.
- Create a text document in an Indian language other than English.
- Create a presentation.
- Create a presentation with animation.
- Include existing images/ pictures in a presentation.
- Animate pictures and text with sound effects in a presentation.
- Create a simple spreadsheet and perform the following operations: min, max, sum, and average.
- Create different types of charts using a spreadsheet: line, bar, area and pie.

Breakup of Marks for the Practicals

S.No.	Unit Name	Marks
1.	Lab Test **(30 marks)**	
	Word processing Handling Spreadsheets Creating Presentations	10 10 10
2.	Report File + viva **(10 marks)**	
	Report file : 4 Documents each with a Word Processor, Spreadsheet and Presentation Tool	8
	Viva Voce (Based on the Report File)	2
3.	Project (that uses most of the concepts that have been learnt) **(10 Marks)**	10
	Total Marks	**50**

CHAPTER

01

Unit I

Computer System Organisation

Chapter Checklist

- Characteristics of a Computer
- Components of a Computer
- Input Devices
- Output Devices
- Computer Memory
- Limitations of a Computer
- Applications of a Computer

A computer is an electronic device that manipulates information or data according to the set of instructions, i.e. programs. It has the ability to store, retrieve and process the data. It is used to type documents, send E-mails and browse the Internet. It is also used to handle spreadsheets, accounting, database, presentations, games and many more.

Generally, computer is the combination of hardware and software, which converts data into information.

Computer system

Terms Related to Computer

Hardware It is the collection of physical elements that constitute a computer system. e.g. Input devices, output devices, CPU, floppy disk, hard disk, CD, DVD etc.

Software It is a set of programs and procedures. It tells the hardware, what to do and how to accomplish a task. e.g. Web browsers, Word processors etc.

Data It is an unprocessed raw facts and figures like numbers, text, images etc.

Processing It is the sequence of actions taken on data to convert it into information.

Information It is the meaningful content that is extracted from data after processing. e.g. 2 + 2 = 4 here, 4 is the information.

Characteristics of a Computer

The characteristics of a computer are as follows

Accuracy Computer operates with very high degree of accuracy and can do 100% error free calculations. It does not get exhausted to the extent of making mistakes.

Speed Computer is generally known for its speed. It can process data very fast at the rate of millions of instructions per second. Units of speed is measured in micro seconds, nano seconds and pico seconds.

Diligence Unlike human beings, a computer is free from monotony, tiredness, lack of concentration etc and can do work for hours without creating any errors.

Automaticity It means that once the program is loaded in the memory of the computer system, the operations which are instructed by the program are performed one after the other without any human interference.

Versatility Computer is highly versatile in nature. It fits into different fields of human endeavour ranging from business, education, technology, engineering, law, commerce, agriculture, medicine, sports etc. It can perform different types of tasks which are provided in a logical way to execute.

Large Storage Capacity Data can be stored electronically in considerably less space which can be retrieved in a fraction of the time when needed. A limited amount of data can be stored temporarily in primary memory of computer. For permanent storage of data, secondary storage devices are used.

Plug and Play Computer has the ability to automatically configure a new hardware and software component.

Components of a Computer

A general purpose computer has three main components which are as follows

1. Input/Output Unit 2. Central Processing Unit (CPU)
3. Memory Unit

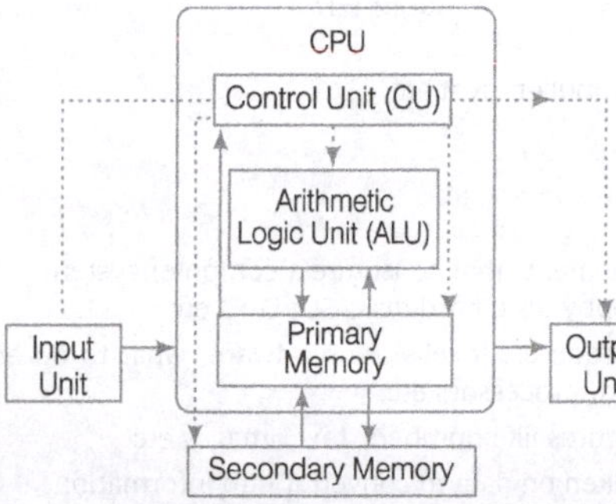

Components of a computer

Input Unit

Data and instructions must enter the computer system before any computation that can be performed on the supplied data.

The input unit that links the external environment with the computer system performs this task. It enters input in the form that depends upon the particular device used.

Output Unit

The job of an output unit is just the reverse of an input unit. It supplies information and results of computation to the outside world. Thus, it links the computer with the external environment.

Central Processing Unit (CPU)

It is the hardware within a computer system that carries out the instructions of a computer program to perform the basic arithmetical, logical and input/output operations of the system. CPU is also known as **brain of the computer**. The speed of CPU depends upon the type of microprocessor used and it is measured in MegaHertz (MHz).

Microprocessor

It is fabricated on a single IC (Integrated Circuit). IC is a piece of silicon, composed by thousands of transistors.

The **first chip**, **Intel 4004**, was made by Intel in 1971 *by scientist Ted Hoff and engineer Federico Faggin*. Some of the popular microprocessors are i7, i5, i3, Core2 Duo Intel, Dual Core, Pentium IV etc.

Two typical components of a CPU are as follows

Arithmetic Logic Unit (ALU)

In computing, an ALU is a digital circuit that performs arithmetical and logical operations. It is a fundamental building block of the CPU of a computer.

Most ALUs can perform the following operations

- **Arithmetic operations** (addition (+), subtraction (–), multiplication (*) and division (/)).
- **Logical operations** (AND, NOT, OR, XOR)

- **Bit-shifting operations** (shifting or rotating a word by a specified number of bits to the left or right, with or without sign extension).
- **Comparison operations** (=, <, <=, >, >=)

Control Unit (CU)

It coordinates the input and output devices of a computer system. It fetches the instructions which are given in the form of microprograms and directs the operation of the other units by providing timing and control signals.

CU is the circuit that controls the flow of data through the processor and coordinates the activities of the other units within it. It acts like human nerves system, which does not process data but behaves as a central unit for other data-manipulating components. So, it is also known as **nerve centre** of a computer system.

Memory Unit/ Storage Unit

This unit is responsible to store programs or data on a temporary or permanent basis. It has primary memory and secondary memory. The input data which is to be processed is brought into main memory before processing.

The needed instruction for processing and any kind of intermediate results are also stored in primary memory. Another kind of memory is referred as secondary memory of a computer system. This unit is used to permanently store data.

> **Register**
>
> It is an internal part of CPU which is used to store intermediate results obtained during the execution of instructions.

Input Devices

It is a hardware device that sends data into the computer system. These devices are used to input (or enter) data and instructions into the computer system. All instructions are accepted by the CPU through electrical pulses from various kinds of input devices.

Some of the input devices are explained as follows

Keyboard

It is the most commonly used input device which uses an arrangement of buttons and keys. Both data and program can be entered into the computer through the keyboard. It is an essential device for interactive processing because user can easily issue commands to receive the data response immediately on the computer screen.

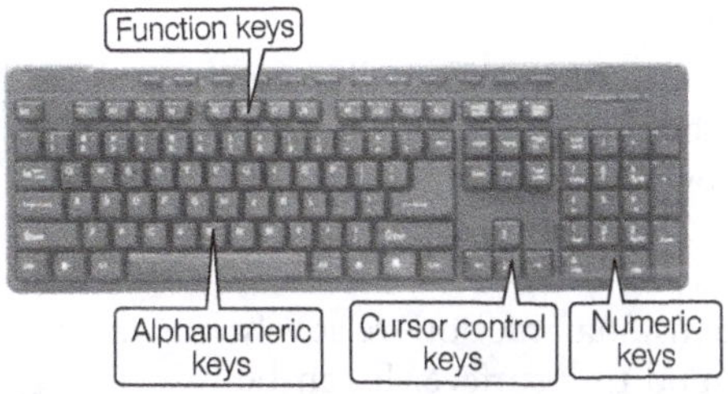

Layout of a keyboard

Types of keys on keyboard are as follows

- **Alphanumeric keys** All of the letters and numbers on the keyboard are A-Z and 0-9.
- **Punctuation keys** Such as comma(,), period(.), semicolon(;), brackets(), parentheses and so on.
- **Special keys** Such as Control key, Arrow keys, Caps lock key, Delete key, Alt key, Shift key etc.
- **Function keys** Keys labeled from F1 to F12. These keys have different meaning depends on running program.
- **Cursor Control keys** Include four directional (left or right, up or down) arrow keys that are arranged in a inverted T formation between the alphanumeric and numeric keypad.

Advantages of a Keyboard

(*i*) Way of entering text and numbers into computer is quite simple and easy.

(*ii*) Available in variety of formats, such as multimedia and simple.

(*iii*) Keyboards have special keys that perform special functions.

Disadvantages of a Keyboard

(*i*) For entering some specific type of data (e.g. pictures, diagrams, voice, video etc), keyboard is not much useful.

(*ii*) Very slow while selecting menu options or various objects displayed on the screen.

(*iii*) Sometimes, it is needed to use number of keys or combination of specific keys to perform some task.

> **Pointing Device**
>
> It is used to communicate with the computer by pointing to the locations on the monitor. Pointing device can also be used for:
>
> - sending command signals to the computer.
> - selecting items on the screen.
> - selecting commands from commands menu.
> - drawing graphics, sketches etc.
>
> Some commonly used pointing devices are mouse, trackball, joystick, light pen, graphics tablet, touch screen and touch pad.

Mouse

It is a pointing device that allows to control the movement of a pointer (also known as **mouse pointer**) on screen. It performs various functions by detecting two-dimensional motion relatively to its supporting surface. It can be of different types like wired mouse, wireless mouse, optical mouse, mechanical mouse etc. Generally, it has two buttons, i.e. a **right button** and a **left button**. It also includes a **scroll wheel** between the buttons to scroll up and down the application window and their contents also.

Wired mouse

Wireless mouse

Different types of mouse are as follows

- **Mechanical mouse** In this type of mouse, movement of a cursor on the screen is relative to the movement of the ball available at the bottom of the mouse.
- **Optical mouse** It uses a Light Emitting Diode (LED) and photodiodes to detect movement.
- **Laser mouse** It uses Infrared Laser Diode instead of a normal LED.
- **Wireless mouse** It communicates with the computer *via* radio waves (often using bluetooth hardware and software), so that a cord is not needed (but such mouse needs internal batteries).

Advantages of a Mouse

(*i*) Ideal for pointing objects/options.
(*ii*) Most familiar and easy to use.
(*iii*) Works very well for navigating a Graphical User Interface (GUI).

Disadvantages of a Mouse

(*i*) Need a flat space close to computer.
(*ii*) Wired mouses can't easily be used with a laptop, notebook or palmtop computers.

Joystick

It is also a pointing device like the mouse, which consists of a stick that pivots on a spherical ball on its base.

Joystick is similar to mouse except that the movement of cursor on screen stops working as soon as user stop moving the mouse. But with a joystick, the pointer continues moving in the previously pointing direction.

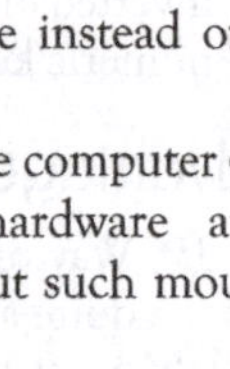
Joystick

Commonly, joysticks are used for playing computer games like **flight simulators** but, occasionally used for **CAD/CAM** (Computer Aided Design/Computer Aided Manufacturing) systems and other applications. Some joysticks have a third degree of freedom, i.e. the stick can be twisted in clockwise or anti-clockwise direction.

Advantages of a Joystick

(*i*) It is more comfortable and functional.
(*ii*) It gives a better gaming experience for racing or flying style computer games.
(*iii*) It is easy to learn and use.

Disadvantages of a Joystick

(*i*) Movement is offered only in forward, backward, left or right directions at a time.
(*ii*) Some players find it more difficult to control it, instead of using a mouse.
(*iii*) Not compatible with most computers.

Light Pen

It is a pointing device shaped like a pen which is connected to a Visual Display Unit (VDU). The tip of the light pen contains a light sensitive element which is placed against the screen, detects the light from the screen, enabling the computer to identify the location of the tip of pen on the screen. It is also used to draw images on the screen.

Light pen

Advantages of a Light Pen

(*i*) Easy to use.
(*ii*) Helpful to indicate locations on a computer screen with CAD.
(*iii*) Useful to instruct the computer to shape, size, position and color of different sections.

Disadvantages of a Light Pen

(*i*) Not very much accurate while drawing.
(*ii*) Expensive compared to alternate pointing device like mouse.
(*iii*) It can be easily damaged.

Graphics Tablet

A graphics tablet (or digitisers, digitising tablet, tough tablet or simply tablet) is an input device that consists of an electronic writing area and a special pen that works with it.

Graphics tablet

A graphics tablet allows artists to create hand- made images and graphical images with motion and action, similar to the way, a person draws images with pencil and paper. The pen of the graphics tablet is pressure sensitive, so pressing harder or softer can result in brush strokes of different width. When user draws anything on the tablet with the special pen, the drawing appears on the screen.

The tablet and pen can also be used like a mouse to move the cursor and click. It may also be used to capture data or handwritten signatures.

Advantages of a Graphics Tablet

(*i*) Beneficial for graphics artist like photographers.
(*ii*) Useful for drawing, painting and editing projects.
(*iii*) Provides better quality images.

Disadvantages of a Graphics Tablet

(*i*) Slower than paper drawing.
(*ii*) Useful for line diagrams only.
(*iii*) Screen damage risk is high.

Touch Screen

It is an electronic visual display that detects the presence and location of a touch within the display area. The term touch screen generally refers to touching the display of the device with a finger or hand.

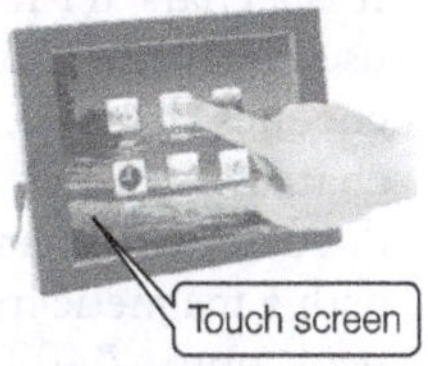

Touch screen sends a signal to the computer. This signal gives the location on the screen, which has been touched. It is quick and simple to use.

There are different types of touch screens available with electronic devices like capacitive touch screen, resistive touch screen. Generally, smartphones have a high-resolution capacity touch screen like gorilla glass.

It is pressure sensitive and activated by finger or stylus. It works as

- **Touch sensor** It is a clear glass panel with a touch responsive surface.
- **Controller** A small PC card translates information in the form which can be understand by the PC easily.
- **Software driver** It allows to work with existing software.

Advantages of a Touch Screen

(*i*) It is simple and user friendly.
(*ii*) It provides fast access to all types of digital media.
(*iii*) It ensures that no space is wasted as the input device which is completely integrated into monitor.

Disadvantages of a Touch Screen

(*i*) Although it is user friendly, it cannot be used to enter large amount of data.
(*ii*) Its system cost is about two or three times of the amount of an existing keyboard display.
(*iii*) It often requires you to navigate through several layers of menus which can make finding something difficult.
(*iv*) Touchscreens are difficult to read under the sun, low precision and low battery life.

Touchpad (Trackpad)

It is a specialised surface that can translate the motion and position of a user's finger to a relative position on the screen. This is a common feature of laptop computers and also used as a substitute of a computer mouse, where desk space is scarce. The sensors of touchpad only react through fingertip, not through a pencil or other object. There are usually two buttons next to the touchpad which works like a left and right button of the mouse.

Advantages of a Touchpad

(*i*) Useful for laptops, when using a mouse is not practical.
(*ii*) The pad's position is fixed compared to the keyboard, unlike with a traditional mouse.
(*iii*) Very short finger movements are required to move the cursor.

Disadvantages of a Touchpad

(*i*) Takes practice and skill to control the position of the cursor using the touchpad.
(*ii*) Gloves cannot be worn, i.e. in a clean room or industrial environment, where gloves need to be worn.
(*iii*) Moist, sweaty or callous fingers can disrupt the signals picked up by the sensors.

Trackball

It is designed for computers, generally serves as mouse replacement. It is primarily used to move the cursor on the screen. It has a ball on its top which can be rolled with fingers and the internal rollers sense the motion, which is transmitted to the computer.

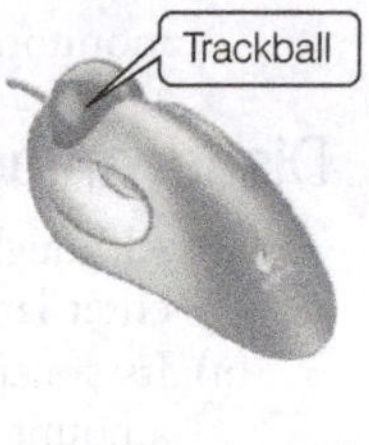

Trackballs are common on CAD workstations and sometimes seen on computerised special purpose workstations, such as the radar consoles in an air-traffic control room or sonar equipment on a ship or a submarine.

Advantages of a Trackball

(*i*) It has the advantage over the mouse that the body of trackball remains stationary on the user's desk.

(*ii*) Even the largest trackball takes less work surface space than it is required to effectively use the smallest mouse.

(*iii*) Modern trackballs allow a user to control cursor movements with finger tips or thumb. They are much more precise than the hand and wrist movement required to move a mouse.

Disadvantages of a Trackball

(*i*) It is physically larger than mouse (even though they required less space to use) so, it is harder to find a selection of trackballs.

(*ii*) It is typically expensive because it is manufactured in lower volume.

Scanner

It is a device that allows a user to take an image or a text and convert it into a digital file, allowing the computer to read or display the scanned object.

Scanner

Scanner can be used for storing the documents in their original form that can be modified and manipulated later on.

Scanner comes in a variety of size from hand-held models to desktop models which are as follows

- **Hand-held scanners** They are very small which can be held in a hand. These are less expensive and less wide. Hence, in order to scan a single page image, multiple passes are required. But, their handiness is a major advantage of it.
- **Flatbed scanners** They are large and more expensive scanners that create higher quality of images. These scanners have a flat surface on which the printed image to be scanned is placed (similar to the way a page is placed on a photocopier). They can scan a page in a single pass.
- **Drum scanners** They are medium size scanners with a rolling drum. The sheet is fed through the scanners so that the drum rolls over the entire sheet to be scanned (just as the sheets are fed in a fax machine).

Advantages of a Scanner

(*i*) Easy to use and install.

(*ii*) Gives the copy of a document in digital format.

(*iii*) Works like a photocopy machine.

Disadvantages of a Scanner

(*i*) Quality of digital image depends on the quality of original image.

(*ii*) Easily broken if get hit.

(*iii*) Too big to carry around.

MICR (Magnetic Ink Character Recognition)

It is a character recognition technology which is primarily used by the banking industry to facilitate the processing of cheques. This technology allows the computers to read characters (such as account numbers) on printed documents. Characters are printed in special typefaces with a magnetic ink (that contains Iron Oxide). MICR can read upto 2,400 documents/min. The MICR coding system contains 14 characters (4 special symbols and 10 decimal digits). So, it can recognise these 14 characters only. The type font E-13B, a standard typographical style, is used to print the characters or identification marks.

Format of a cheque

Advantages of a MICR

(*i*) It decreases the margin of error.

(*ii*) Document can still be read after being folded or split.

(*iii*) Provides high security.

Disadvantages of a MICR

(*i*) MICR readers and encoders are expensive.
(*ii*) The system can only accept few characters.
(*iii*) Time consuming standards.

- The **first keyboard** was invented in 1868 by Christopher Sholes.
- The **first joystick** was created in 1926 by CB Mirick.
- The **first image scanner** developed for use with a computer was a drum scanner. It was built in 1957 at the US National Bureau of Standards by a team led by Russell A Kirsch.
- The **first computer mouse** was invented by Douglas Engelbart at Stanford Research Centre in 1960s.
- The first ever touchscreen was developed by EA Johnson in 1960s.

OCR (Optical Character Recognition)

It is used to translate scanned images of handwritten, typewritten, printed text or special type font printed on conventional paper with conventional ink into machine-encoded text.

Functioning of an OCR

OCR is widely used to convert books and documents into electronic files, to computerise a record-keeping system in an office or to publish the text on a Website.

OCR uses **photoelectric devices** to scan the characters being read and convert the reflected light patterns of the data into the binary data suitable for computer input.

Type font for OCR

The normal speed of an OCR is 1500 to 3000 characters per second. The technology is being developed for greater accurate recognition which is also known as **Intelligent Character Recognition** (ICR).

Advantages of an OCR

(*i*) Increases efficiency and effectiveness of the office work.
(*ii*) Ability to scan the characters accurately depends on how clear the writing is.
(*iii*) Much faster than manual entering of large amount of text.

Disadvantages of an OCR

(*i*) Not 100% accurate.
(*ii*) Expensive and difficult maintenance.
(*iii*) Limited number of characters are offered by it.

OMR (Optical Mark Recognition)

It is used to capture human marked data from document form such as surveys and tests. One of the most familiar applications of OMR, is the checking of optical answer sheets in multiple choice questions. It uses high intensity to read the marks or symbols.

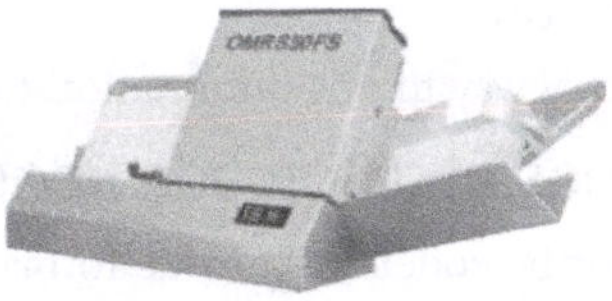
Optical mark recognition

Advantages of an OMR

(*i*) There is a large number of documents to justify designing and printing them.
(*ii*) The user can only make marks and cannot write any information.
(*iii*) Its scanning is easy to implement and support.

Disadvantages of an OMR

(*i*) Document for mark reader are complicated to design.
(*ii*) It is difficult for a computer to check marked data.
(*iii*) The person putting the marks on the document has to follow the instructions which are provided to them.

Barcode Reader

A barcode is a machine readable representation of information in the form of stripes of dark and light ink.

0816430026192

Barcode

Barcode reader is an input device used for reading printed barcodes (Universal Product Code) available on product to be sold. A barcode reader emits a beam of light, which reflects off the barcode image. A light sensitive detector in the barcode reader identifies the barcode image by recognising special bars at both ends of the image.

Barcode reader

Once code is identified, it is converted into a numeric code. A perfect example of a barcode reader is using it in a super market where barcode scanner reads the price of a product. Software like Wasp, BarCode Pro are used for scanning and printing barcodes.

Advantages of a Barcode Reader

(*i*) Easy, fast and reliable method of input data.
(*ii*) Can read the data even from curved or upside down surfaces.
(*iii*) It is an easy way to put information together.

Disadvantages of a Barcode Reader

(*i*) Data must be coded in barcode format.
(*ii*) Input is limited to a number code.
(*iii*) Scratched barcodes may cause problems.

Microphone (Mic)

We can send sound to the computer through a special manual input device called *microphone* or *mic*. A mic converts the received sound into computer's format, which is called **Digitised Sound** or **Digital Audio**. To convert a voice into digital form, an additional hardware is always needed which is known as **Sound Card**. Sound is used most often in multimedia, where user can make his/her presentation more attractive using recorded narration, music or sound effects. Microphone can be attached to a computer to record sound. Now-a-days, it is being used with speech recognition software. This means that you do not have to type the document, rather just have to speak and the spoken words appear in your document.

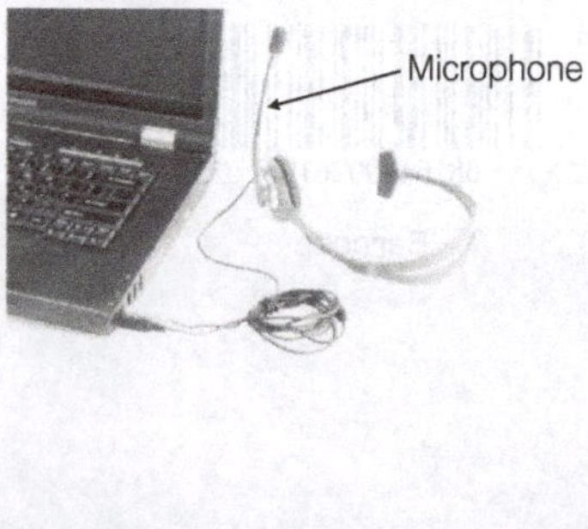

Advantages of a Microphone

(*i*) Useful to input the audio (sounds).
(*ii*) It does not need external power supply.
(*iii*) Greater freedom of movement for the speaker.

Disadvantages of a Microphone

(*i*) Needs specific and additional hardware called **sound card**, must be inserted in motherboard.
(*ii*) The sound quality is low.
(*iii*) The signal may be weak.

Web Camera (Webcam)

It is a digital camera attached to computers and can be used for video conferencing or online chatting etc. It is also able to capture full motion videos. It is connected to a computer that allows the user to view either a still picture or a motion video of a user or other object. Now-a-days, it is embedded into the display with laptops or connected *via* USB or firewire port or Wi-Fi to the computer system. After connecting webcam to a computer, you need to install required software or drivers.

A Webcam attached with computer

Webcam

Advantages of a Web Camera

(*i*) Enables a user to interact with people across long distances.
(*ii*) Both sound and video are used, making the communication better.
(*iii*) Users can use the webcam to save videos and can watch them later or send to others.

Disadvantages of a Web Camera

(*i*) Discourages people to interact face-to-face.
(*ii*) Can be used to film inappropriate/illegal videos.
(*iii*) Hackers can enable webcams even when, the owner is not aware.

Digital Camera (Digicam)

It is a device that stores the pictures or videos in an electronic format instead of film. There are several features that make digital camera a popular choice, when compared to film cameras. Most enjoyable feature is the LCD display on the digital camera.

Digital camera

This display allows users to view and save photo or video after the picture or video has been taken, that means, if you take a picture and don't like the results, you can delete it, or if you like the picture, you can save it and can easily show it to other people.

Advantages of a Digital Camera

(*i*) No need of scanner, as the photograph is directly converted into a digital graphical format.
(*ii*) Inexpensive and fast.
(*iii*) Most digital cameras take both photos and videos. There is no need to buy a separate device to record home movies.

Disadvantages of a Digital Camera

(*i*) Battery consumption can be quite high.
(*ii*) More sensitive to weather changes than film cameras.
(*iii*) Extreme heat, cold or moisture can cause camera to malfunctioning.

Biometric Sensor

It is a device which recognises physical or behavioural traits of an individual. It is mainly used for marking attendance of employees/students in organisations/ institutions. It works with accuracy so, it is widely used for security purpose.

Biometric sensor

Advantages of a Biometric Sensor

(*i*) It minimises the opportunity for ID fraud and punching.
(*ii*) It reduces administration costs for passwords.
(*iii*) It eliminates the problems caused by lost IDs or forgotten passwords.

Disadvantages of a Biometric Sensor

(*i*) It is an expensive security solution.
(*ii*) For people affected with diabetes, the eyes get affected and produce differences in results.
(*iii*) It needs devices of a large size to store biometric information.

MIDI Devices

Musical Instrument Digital Interface (MIDI) is a system designed to transmit information between electronic musical instruments. A MIDI musical keyboard allows a performer to play music, i.e. captured by the computer system as a sequence of notes with the associated timing (instead of recording digitised sound waves).

Check Point 01

1 What is the full form of MIDI?
2 Which pointing device is used to detect the location of a touch within the display area?
(a) Joystick (b) Touch screen
(c) Mouse (d) Touch pad
3 Name the different types of mouse.
4 Who developed the first joystick?

Output Devices

It is a part of computer hardware equipment, used to communicate the results of data processing which are carried out by information processing system (such as a computer), to the outside world. It carries the results of various operations performed by the user. Some of the devices, which are used to display the processed result or output are as follows:

Monitor

A monitor (called a **Visual Display Unit**-VDU) is an electronic visual device used to display the output. The rectangular area of the monitor, its refresh rate and dot pitch, all directly affect the resolution of the display.

Resolution

It refers to the clarity of screen and measured by the number of individual tiny colored dots (known as **pixels**), scattered on the screen. Resolution indicates the number of dots per inch (dpi).

Types of Monitor

The popular types of monitor are as follows

1. **CRT** (Cathode Ray Tube) It works in the same way as a television. It contains an electron gun at the back of the glass tube. This gun fires electrons in a group of phosphor dots, which is coated inside the screen. When electrons strike the phosphor dots, they glow to give the colors.

CRT monitor

2. **LCD** (Liquid Crystal Display) These screens are used in laptops and notebook sized PCs. A special type of liquid is sandwiched between two plates. It is a thin, flat and light weight screen made up of any number of colors or monochrome pixels arranged in front of a light source.

LCD monitor

3. **LED** (Liquid/Light Emitting Diode) It is an electronic device that emits light when electrical current is passed through it. It usually produces red light, but now-a-days LEDs can produce RGB (Red, Green and Blue) light and white light also.

LED monitor

4. **3-D Monitor** It is a television that conveys depth perception to the viewer. It describes an image that provides the perception of length. When 3-D images are made interactive, user feels involved with the scene and this experience is called **virtual reality.**

3-D monitor

Advantages of a Monitor

(*i*) Displays both text and graphic images.

(*ii*) It is available in various sizes like 8", 12", 14", 15", 17", 19" and 21".

(*iii*) Various kinds of monitors are available in black and white or colored.

Disadvantages of a Monitor

(*i*) Only limited amount of information can be displayed at a time.

(*ii*) CRT screens are made up of glass and can be fragile.

(*iii*) CRT monitor has low refreshing ability which is known as **flickering effect.**

TFT (Thin Film Transistor)

TFT and Active-Matrix LCD (AMLCD) is a Liquid Crystal Display (LCD). With active-matrix displays, each pixel is controlled by one to four transistors that can make the screen faster, brighter, more colorful than passive-matrix and capable of being viewed at different angles. Because of this improved technology, active-matrix screens are often more expensive but, have better quality than a passive-matrix screens.

Printer

It is an output device, which produces a hard copy of documents that are stored in an electronic form on physical print media such as paper or transparencies. So, printers are the primary output devices used to prepare permanent documents. The speed of a printer is normally rated either by Pages Per Minute (PPM) or by Characters Per Second (CPS). The quality of the image is determined by the Dots Per Inch (DPI).

Types of Printer

It can be classified into two broad categories which are as follows

1. Impact Printers

These rely on a forcible impact to transfer ink to the print media, similar to the action of a typewriter. There is a mechanical contact between the paper and the print head. The main types of impact printers are as follows

- **Line printer** It is impact shaped character printer, which are capable of printing an entire line at once instead of one or more characters at a time. Printing quality of line printer is not high.

Line printer

- **Drum printer** It is printer technology that is used to form character images around a cylindrical drum as its printing mechanism. When the desired character for the selected position rotated around the hammer line, the hammer hit the paper from behind and pushed it into the ribbon and onto the character.

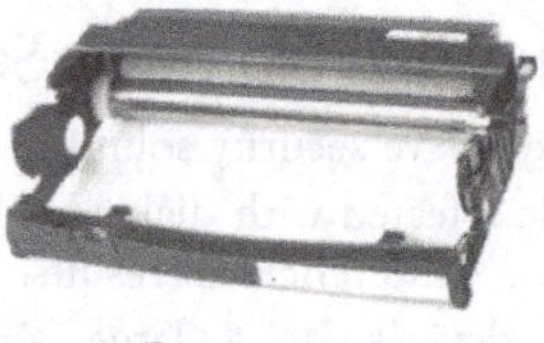

Drum printer

- **Daisy wheel printer** It can print one character at a time. In daisy wheel printer, round disk extends a portion of the wheel making contact with ink ribbon that makes contact with paper for creating the character. This procedure is repeated for each key, when it is pressed. These printers are fitted with unchangeable print heads called **daisy wheels.** To print each character, the wheel is rotated and the appropriate stroke struck against an ink ribbon. It cannot produce high quality print graphics. The speed of daisy wheel printer is about 100 cps.

- **Dot-matrix printer** The term dot-matrix refers to the process of placing dots to form an image. It uses print heads to shoot ink or strike an ink ribbon to place hundreds to thousands of little dots to form text or images. It prints one character at a time. The speed of dot-matrix printer lies between 100 to 600 cps.

  These printers are slow and noisy that are not commonly used for personal computers. They can print multi-layer forms. It can print special characters and graphic and does not have fixed character fonts.

Advantages of an Impact Printers

(*i*) Installation cost is low.

(*ii*) They are robust and can be used in harsh conditions.

(*iii*) It creates the characters by striking on the paper.

Disadvantages of an Impact Printers

(*i*) Print quality is too poor to produce documents.

(*ii*) Printing speed is less than 600 characters per minute.

(*iii*) Cannot produce color copies.

2. Non-impact Printers

These printers much quieter than impact printers as their printing heads do not strike on the paper. Most of non impact printers produce dot-matrix patterns. There is no mechanical contact between the paper and the print head. These printers are comparatively faster and produce high quality output. They can be used for printing text and graphics both in black and white and colored.

The main types of non-impact printers are as follows:

- **Electromagnetic printer** Electrographic or electro-photographic printers are very fast printers which fall under the category of page printers. They can produce documents at a speed of over 20,000 lines per minute, i.e. more than 250 pages per minute. The electrographic technology has developed from the paper copier technology.
- **Thermal printer** These printer paper tends to darken over time due to exposure of sunlight or heat. The quality of produced print is poor. It is widely used in battery powered equipment such as portable calculators.
- **Electrostatic printer** These printers are generally used for large format printing and favoured by large printing shops because of their ability to print fast and making low cost.
- **Laser printer** In this printer, the method of printing is based on principle of electro-photography and use a beam of laser light as a photocopy machine. It is the most expensive printer.

Laser printer

The powdered ink (i.e. toner) is transferred to paper in the form of text/image pattern and then fixed by heat or pressure. When used to print bulk of papers, the laser printer produces the cheapest cost per printout. It has very high resolution from 600–1200 dpi (dots per inch) but, cost of maintenance and repairing is high due to complex equipment set inside the printer. It occupies a lot of space and emits dust particles that can cause respiratory diseases.

- **Inkjet printer** It fires extremely small droplets of ink onto the paper to create impression of text or image. The print-head of inkjet printers, known as **print cartridge**, contains tiny nozzles (50 or more) through which different colored inks can be sprayed onto the paper to form the characters or graphic images.

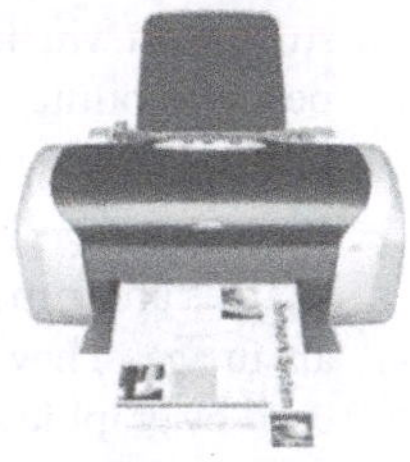

Inkjet printer

Color inkjet printers provide an inexpensive way to print fully colored documents. It has good resolution usually 300–600 dpi and capable of printing in vivid colors but, color printing can take 25-30 seconds for each page.

Inkjet printer is fast as compared to a dot-matrix printer but, slow as compared to a laser printer.

Advantages of a Non-impact Printers

(*i*) Much lower ink cost over time.

(*ii*) Less maintenance.

(*iii*) Much more reliable.

(*iv*) Better for multiuse.

Disadvantages of a Non-impact Printers

(*i*) Cannot print multipart forms.

(*ii*) More costly to replace cartridges for a laser printer.

(*iii*) Harder to use with old PC's.

Plotter

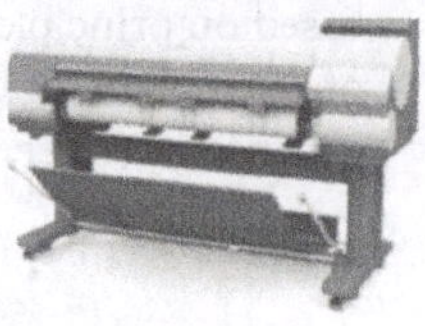

Plotter

It is an output device similar to a printer that uses a pen, pencil, marker or other writing tool to make a design. It is generally used to generate the map of building and shopping malls. It is a computer printing device for printing vector graphics. In the past, plotters were widely used in applications such as CAD and other printing jobs. Though, they have generally been replaced with wide format conventional printers.

Types of Plotter

The types of plotter are as follows

- **Drum plotter** It contains a long cylinder and a pen carriage. The output paper is placed over the drum. The pen is mounted horizontally on the carriage. Both, pen and drum move under the computer's control to produce the desired drawing.
- **Flatbed plotter** It consists of a stationary horizontal flat surface on which paper or any other medium is fixed. The pen is mounted on a carriage that can move along the horizontal and vertical axes.
- **Electrostatic plotter** It marks paper with electrostatic charges and runs it through a developing system to create an image. They produce high quality images which are used by graphic and commercial artists.

Advantages of a Plotter

(*i*) It may print on a wide variety of materials like steel sheet, plywood, aluminium etc.
(*ii*) Large size paper can be used.

Disadvantages of a Plotter

(*i*) Plotters are slower than printers, draw each line separately.
(*ii*) The price of plotters is much higher than the price of printers.
(*iii*) They do not produce very high quality text printouts.

Speaker

Speakers

It is an output device that receives the sound in the form of electric current from the sound card and convert it into sound format which is used for listening to music. Computer speakers (multimedia speakers) are the speakers, which are attached internally or externally to a computer system.

Advantages of a Speaker

(*i*) Very simple to operate.
(*ii*) Useful for alerting computer user even if it is busy.
(*iii*) Very reliable, good sound reproduction.

Disadvantages of a Speaker

(*i*) It can take up a fair amount of desk-space compared to the headphone.
(*ii*) It can distract people around you, therefore disrupt a communal work area.
(*iii*) Limited in frequency response and require multiple speakers to produce full sound spectrum of 20-20,000 Hz.

Headphone

Headphone

It is a pair of small loudspeaker or less commonly a single speaker, held close to a user's ears and connected to a signal source such as an audio amplifier, radio, CD player or portable media player. It is also known as **stereo phones, headsets** or **cans.**

Advantages of a Headphone

(*i*) Both hands are free.
(*ii*) Easier to concentrate on other tasks.
(*iii*) It is comfortable to use.

Disadvantages of a Headphone

(*i*) Extra costs.
(*ii*) Single task oriented, can't do additional tasks.

Gigo

- The first **digital camera** was developed by Steven Sasson in December 1975.
- **Output devices** are used to translate data and information from electrical impulses to human-readable form.
- The output is sent to printer whenever the output is needed in hard copy (printed form). Printers are the primary output devices used to prepare permanent documents.
- The I/O devices are also known as **peripheral devices** like keyboard, mouse, printer etc.

Check Point 02

1. Name three output devices.
2. What is the other name of TFT?
3. Who was developed the first digital camera?
   (a) CB Mirick (b) Russell A. Kirsch
   (c) E A Johnson (d) Steven Sasson

Computer Memory

It is one of the most important element in a computer system, which is the internal or external storage area and holds the data and instructions during the processing in the form of binary numbers. It also relates to many devices and components that are responsible for storing data and applications on a temporary or a permanent basis.

Computer memory can be classified into two types which are as follows

1. Primary Memory

It is also known as **main memory.** It is the internal memory used by computer to hold data, instructions and programs needed at that instant by CPU. It has limited storage capacity and volatile in nature, i.e. it requires constant power supply to motion the current information.

Parameters of Memory

The following terms are most commonly used for identifying comparative behaviour of various memory devices and technologies:

- **Storage Capacity** It represents the size of the memory. The capacity of internal memory and main memory can be expressed in terms of numbers of words or bytes.
- **Access Modes** A memory is comprised of various memory locations. The information from these memory locations can be accessed randomly, sequentially and directly.
- **Access Time** It is the time required between the desired modes for a read or write operation till the data is made available or written at the desired location.
- **Physical Characteristics** In this respect, the devices can be categorised into four main categories, i.e. electronic, magnetic, mechanical and optical.
- **Permanence of Storage** Its permanency is high for future in magnetic or optical materials.
- **Throughput** It defines the amount of information exchanged per unit of time, expressed in bits per second.
- **Cycle Time** It represents the minimal time interval between two successive accesses.

The two types of primary memory are as follows

(a) RAM (Random Access Memory)

RAM is the internal memory that can be accessed (read from as well as written to). This memory is often associated with volatile types of memory.

RAM

It can hold data only on temporary basis because it requires a continuous flow of electrical current. If current is interrupted, data is lost. It is an integrated circuit that enables you to access the stored data in a random order constantly.

The two main forms of RAM are as follows

(*i*) **SRAM** (Static RAM) It is a computer memory that requires a constant power flow in order to hold information. It is more expensive which requires more power, therefore, it is commonly used in cache and video card memory.

(*ii*) **DRAM** (Dynamic RAM) It stores information in a cell containing a capacitor and transistor, these cells must be refreshed with electric impulses in few milliseconds. This process allows memory to keep charge which hold the data as long as needed. Also, it is slower than SRAM.

There are some enhanced versions of RAM, which are as follows

- **EDORAM** (Extended Data Output RAM)
- **SDRAM** (Synchronous Dynamic RAM)
- **DDR SDRAM** (Double Data Rate Synchronous Dynamic RAM)

Advantages of RAM

(*i*) RAM operation is completely silent, there is no moving part.

(*ii*) Uses much less power than disk drives.

(*iii*) Fastest storage medium.

Disadvantages of RAM

(*i*) Volatile in nature.

(*ii*) Limited storage capacity.

(*iii*) Much expensive.

(b) ROM (Read Only Memory)

In ROM, information once stored remain fixed, i.e. it can not be changed. So, it can only be read and used.

ROM

Generally, it contains a set of start-up instructions, i.e. what to do when a computer is turned ON. The contents of ROM remain stored even if power gets turned OFF.

This memory is often associated with non-volatile types of memory. It cannot be altered once the chip has been made.

ROM is further sub divided into several types which are as follows

(*i*) **PROM** (Programmable ROM) It is a computer memory chip capable of being programmed after it has been created. But, once the PROM has been programmed, the information written is permanent, i.e. it can't be erased or deleted.

(*ii*) **EPROM** (Erasable Programmable ROM) It is a computer memory chip on which the written information can be changed by exposing to ultravoilet light. It is just like a small glass circle that exposed the chip that can be re-programmed.

(*iii*) **EEPROM** (Electrically Erasable Programmable ROM) It is a PROM that can be erased and reprogrammed using electricity.

Advantages of ROM

(*i*) Non-volatile in nature.

(*ii*) Design can be easily changed or modified.

(*iii*) Cheaper and more reliable than RAMs.

Disadvantages of ROM

(*i*) More power consumption.

(*ii*) Data is physically encoded in a circuit, so it can only be programmed during fabrication.

(*iii*) It cannot be altered.

Cache Memory

Cache (pronounced cash) memory is extremely fast memory that is built into a computer's CPU, or located next to it on a separate chip. The CPU uses cache memory to store instructions that are repeatedly required to run programs, improving overall system speed.

As the microprocessor processes data, it first looks in the cache memory and if it finds the data there (from a previous reading of data), it does not have to do the time consuming reading of data from larger memory.

2. Storage Devices/Secondary Memory

It is also known as **Secondary Storage** or **Auxiliary Memory**. It is slower and cheaper form of memory, which is a permanent storage device. CPU does not access the secondary memory directly. The contents in it must be first copied into the RAM to get processed. Secondary memory is non-volatile in nature, i.e. the information does not get erased even when power gets switched OFF and data will not be destructed until and unless, the user erases it.

Secondary memory devices include

Magnetic disks	*Optical discs*	*Solid State*
Floppy Disk Drive	CD	Pen/Flash Drive
Hard Disk Drive	DVD	Memory Stick
Magnetic Tape	Blu-ray Disc	

Floppy Disk Drive (FDD)

It is a computer disk drive that enables a user to save data on removable diskettes. This portable storage device is a rewritable media that can be reused number of times. It is made of plastic with magnetic coating on it and round in shape which is covered by square plastic jacket. It is commonly used to move files between different computers. Although, 8" disk drives made available in 1971 were the first real disk drives, the first widely used floppy disk drives were the 4", $5\frac{1}{4}$" floppy disk drives, which were later replaced with $3\frac{1}{2}$" floppy disk drives. However, today these drives are being replaced with CD-R and other writable disc drives and flash drives.

Floppy disk

Note $5\frac{1}{4}$" diameter-floppy has a capacity of 1.2 MB.

$3\frac{1}{4}$" diameter-floppy has a capacity of 1.44 MB.

Advantages of a Floppy Disk Drive

(*i*) Small and light weighted.

(*ii*) Inexpensive and reusable.

(*iii*) Information is retrieved or accessed only sequentially.

Disadvantages of a Floppy Disk Drive

(*i*) Can easily be broken or damaged and not much reliable.

(*ii*) Quite slow to access and retrieve data.

(*iii*) Easily affected by heat.

Hard Disk Drive (HDD)

It is a non-volatile, random access digital data storage device which is used for storing and retrieving digital information using rotating disks (platters) coated with magnetic material. All programs of a computer are installed in hard disk within a particular drive.

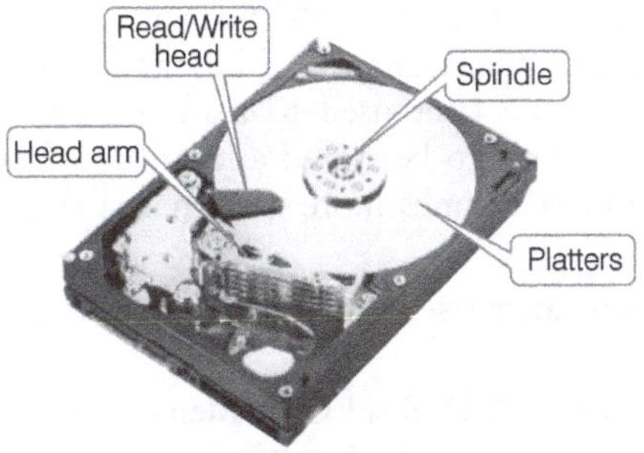

Hard disk drive

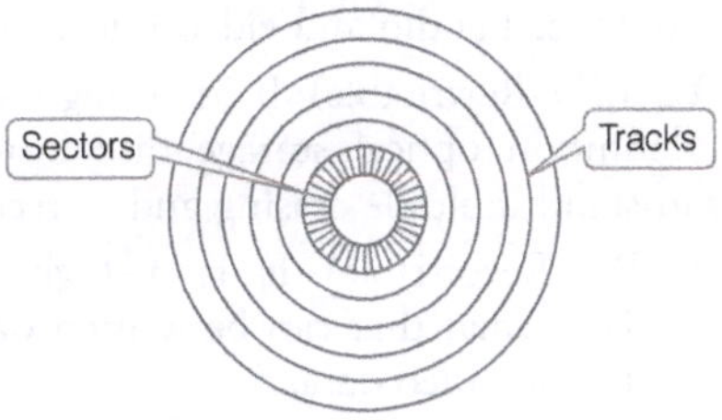

Tracks and sectors

HDD consists of a **spindle** that holds non-magnetic flat circular disks called **platters**, which hold the recorded data. Each platter requires two read/write heads, that is used to write and read the information from a platter. All the read/write heads are attached to a single access **arm**, so that they cannot move independently.The information is recorded in **bands**, each band of information is called a **track.** Each platter has the same number of tracks and a track location that cuts across all platters is called a **cylinder.** The tracks are divided into pie-shaped sections known as **sectors.**

Advantages of a Hard Disk Drive

(*i*) Store and retrieve data much faster than a floppy disk.

(*ii*) Usually fixed inside the computer so don't get lost or damaged easily.

(*iii*) Cheap on a cost per megabyte compared to other storage media.

Disadvantages of a Hard Disk Drive

(*i*) Slower than RAM/ROM.

(*ii*) Cannot easily be transferred to another computer.

Magnetic Tape

It is a storage medium made up of a magnetic material on a large open reel or in a smaller cartridge or cassette (like a music cassette). It is used for those applications that are based on sequential data processing, i.e. it is a sequential data access medium. Due to this (sequential data access) nature, these tapes are not suitable for data files that need to be revised or updated often. It is generally used to store backup data or that type of data, which is not frequently used or to transfer data from one system to another.

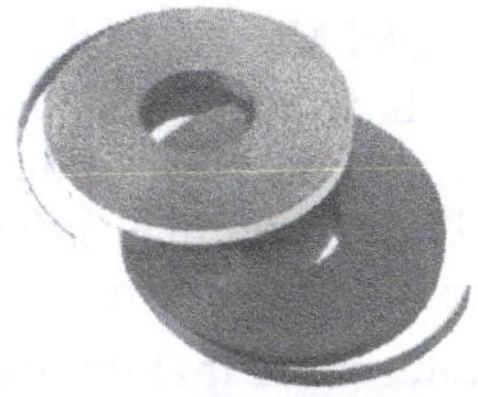

Magnetic tape

Advantages of a Magnetic Tape

(*i*) Tapes can be erased and reused many times.

(*ii*) A large amount of data can be stored in a small storage space.

(*iii*) Tape reels and cartridges are compact and light in weight.

Disadvantages of a Magnetic Tape

(*i*) Sequential in nature, not suitable where data is accessed requires a random order.

(*ii*) Tape ribbon may get twisted due to wrapping, resulting in loss of stored data.

(*iii*) Updating the record is difficult.

Compact Disc (CD)

It is an optical media that is used to store digital data. It is relatively cheap storage device.

Compact disc is categorised into three main types which are as follows

1. **CD-ROM** (CD-Read Only Memory) Data is recorded permanently on the surface of the optical disc through the use of laser. The recorded content cannot be changed or erased by the users. It is also called **WORM** (Write Once Read Many) disc. It is capable of storing large amount of data upto 1GB, although the most common storage capacity is 700 MB.
2. **CD-R** (CD-Recordable) Data can be written on these discs only once. The data once stored in these discs cannot be erased.
3. **CD-RW** (CD-Rewritable) It is an erasable disc, which is used to write data multiple times on a disc by the use of format feature.

Advantages of a Compact Disc

(*i*) Large storage capacity.
(*ii*) Very cheap to produce in large quantities.
(*iii*) It is easy to carry.

Disadvantages of a Compact Disc

(*i*) Have high access time.
(*ii*) It is read only and cannot be updated.
(*iii*) It cannot be used more than once.

Digital Video Disc (DVD)

It is also known as Digital Versatile Disc (DVD) or Super Density Disc (SDD). It is an optical disc storage media manufactured for the first time by Philips, Sony, Toshiba and Panasonic in 1995. It offers high storage capacity than compact disc while having the same dimensions.

Digital Video Disc is categorised into three main types which are as follows

1. **DVD-ROM** (DVD-Read Only Memory) A read-only DVD disc used to permanently store data files. These discs are widely used to distribute large software applications that exceed the capacity of a CD-ROM disc.
2. **DVD-R** (DVD-Recordable) It is a digital optical disc storage format. It is a DVD that can be written once and read arbitrarily many times and typically has a storage capacity of 4.7 GB.
3. **DVD-RW** (DVD-Rewritable) It is a rewritable optical disc with equal storage capacity to a DVD-R, typically 4.7 GB (4,700,000,000 bytes). The smaller **Mini DVD-RW** holds 1.46 GB with a diameter of 8 cm.

Advantages of a Digital Video Disc

(*i*) Superior data storage.
(*ii*) High density and portability.
(*iii*) Sound and picture quality are excellent, making them ideal for storing films with video and sound.

Disadvantages of a Digital Video Disc

(*i*) DVDs do not work in CD drives.
(*ii*) It can be easily damaged by breaking or scratching.
(*iii*) It does not fully support HDTV.

Blu-ray Disc (BD)

It is an optical disc storage medium designed to recapture data normally in DVD format. It contains 25 GB (23.31 GB) per layer space. The name blu-ray disc refers to the blue laser used to read the disc, which allows information to be stored at a greater density. It can hold almost 5 times more data than a single layer DVD.

Blu-ray disc is categorised into four main types which are as follows

1. **BD-ROM** (BD-Read Only Memory) It is a high definition optical disc storage format of the Blu-ray family that consists of pre-recorded data. It can only read audio and video information.
2. **BD-RE** (BD-Rewritable) It is a high capacity, high definition optical storage disc format that can withstand multiple erasing and re-recording.
3. **BD-R** (BD-Recordable) It is a high capacity optical disc format that can be written only once with audio and video data.
4. **BD-RW** (BD-Rewritable) It specifies that PC data on the disc can be re-written many times.

Advantages of a Blu-ray Disc

(*i*) Large storage capacity.
(*ii*) Backwards compatibility.
(*iii*) Mandatory managed copy.

Disadvantages of a Blu-ray Disc

(*i*) Very expensive technology.
(*ii*) Not widely used by the general public.
(*iii*) External blu-ray drives are expensive and unwieldy.

Pen/Flash/Thumb Drive

Pen drives

It is a data storage device that consists of flash memory (USB memory/key memory) with an integrated, Universal Serial Bus (USB) interface. USB flash drives are typically removable, rewritable and physically much smaller than a floppy disk. A USB flash drive or data stick is a portable drive that is same as the size of your thumb that connects to the computer USB port. Today, flash drives are available in various storage capacities as 256 MB, 512 MB, 1 GB, 2 GB, 4 GB, 16 GB, 64 GB etc. It is widely used as an easy and small medium to transfer and store the information from the computers.

Advantages of Pen/Flash/Thumb Drive

(*i*) Data is read/write faster compared to traditional hard disk drives.

(*ii*) It uses little power and have no fragile moving parts.

(*iii*) It also stores data densely compared to many removable media.

(*iv*) It is smaller in size.

Disadvantages of Pen/Flash/Thumb Drive

(*i*) Limited number of write and erase cycles before failing.

(*ii*) Easy to mislay because of its smaller size.

(*iii*) Most flash drives do not have a write protection mechanism.

Memory Stick

It is a physically different form of memory card from SD.

It is an USB based flash memory drive. A family of flash memory cards from Sony designed for digital storage in camera, camcorders and other handheld devices. Capacity of memory stick varies from 4 MB to 256 MB. Its average transfer rate is 2.45 MB/sec, write rate is 1.5 MB/sec, average power consumption is 45 mA and in standby mode is 130 μA. Memory stick comes in various varieties which are as follows

- **PRO** The Memory Stick PRO, introduced in 2003 as a joint effort between Sony and ScanDisk. It has high transfer speed and a maximum storage capacity of 32 GB. All Memory Stick PROs larger than 1 GB support high speed mode.
- **DuO** It is a small flash memory card developed for digital camera, cell phones etc. It is a smaller version of memory stick.
- **MagicGate** It was introduced by Sony in 1994, as a copy-protection technology. It encrypts the data on the device and using MagicGate chips, reader controls over how the files are copied on the device.

Advantages of a Memory Stick

(*i*) It allows more immediate access.

(*ii*) It has relatively large storage space compared to old backup devices.

(*iii*) It is a USB drive thus, it can be used on any computer system.

Disadvantages of a Memory Stick

(*i*) It can be break and lost easily.

(*ii*) These cards may get affected by electronic corruption.

(*iii*) Cannot be attached or read on the computer without proper hardware unlike pen drive.

Primary *v/s* Secondary Memory

Volatile Primary memory is both volatile and non-volatile in nature whereas secondary memory is non-volatile in nature.

Accessible Primary memory is directly accessible by the CPU whereas secondary memory is not.

Position Primary memory is situated inside the CPU but secondary memory may be attached externally or internally.

Storage Space Primary memory has a limited storage space, whereas secondary memory has virtually infinite space to run and stores bulk of data.

Basic Units of Measurement

When user uses a RAM, ROM, Floppy disk, Hard disk etc, the data is measured using some units. In computer terminology, they are called Nibble, Bit, Byte, Kilobyte, Gigabyte etc.

Units of computer memory measurements

- **Bit** (Binary digit) The smallest unit of data. It is either 0 or 1.
- **Nibble** A group of 4 bits or half a byte.
- **Byte** A group of 8 bits. A byte can represent 256 (2^8) distinct values, such as the integers from 0 to 255. Each keyboard character is represented through atleast 1 byte.
- **Kilobyte** (KB) It is actually 2^{10} bytes or 1 KB = 1024 bytes.
- **Megabyte** (MB) It is actually 2^{20} bytes or 1 MB = 1024 KB.
- **Gigabyte** (GB) It is actually 2^{30} bytes or 1 GB = 1024 MB.
- **Terabyte** (TB) It is actually 2^{40} bytes or 1 TB = 1024 GB.
- **Petabyte** (PB) It is actually 2^{50} bytes or 1 PB = 1024 TB.
- **Exabyte** (EB) It is actually 2^{60} bytes or 1 EB = 1024 PB.
- **Zettabyte** (ZB) It is actually 2^{70} bytes or 1 ZB = 1024 EB.
- **Yottabyte** (YB) It is actually 2^{80} bytes or 1 YB = 1024 ZB.
- **Brontobyte** It is actually 2^{90} bytes or 1 Brontobyte = 1024 YB
- **Geopbyte** It is actually 2^{100} bytes or 1 Geopbyte = 1024 Brontobyte.

Limitations of a Computer

Although, a computer is far better in performance than a human being, it fails in certain ways as follows

(*i*) **Lack of decision making power** Computer cannot decide on its own. It does not possess this power which is a great asset for human beings.

(*ii*) **Zero IQ** Computer is dumb machine with zero IQ. It needs to be told each and every step, no matter how minute it is. It cannot think itself.

(*iii*) **No heuristics** Heuristics means learning from past experiences. If a computer commits an error once and similar situation/event occurs again, computer will commit the same error again. It cannot learn from past experience. But, human beings learn from past experience very well.

Check Point 03

1 What is the full form of EDORAM?

2 1 Megabytes is equivalent to

(a) 1024 KB (b) 1024 bytes

(c) 512 KB (d) 1024 GB

3 Write the names of some memory cards.

Applications of a Computer

Now-a-days, computer has been employed in almost all the aspects of professional and personal life of human beings. Some of the areas where computers are being used are as follows

(*i*) **Education** Computer has proved to be an excellent teacher. Educational institutes are using computers in many ways like tele-education, virtual classroom, online classes etc.

(ii) **Science** Scientists have been long users of computer. A new adventure among scientists is the idea of a collaboratory (Internet based collaborative laboratory) in which researchers from all over the world can work together easily even at a distance.

(*iii*) **Industry** Computer is used to control manufacturing systems and continuous running of the machinery. Parameters like temperature, pressure, volume are monitored and controlled by computers. Robotics developed with the help of computers which play a very crucial role.

(*iv*) **Recreation and Entertainment** Computers in recreation and entertainment are the ones that are divided into various categories, i.e. social, communication, sports, music and games. Thus, people look forward to the entertainment for recreation, so that they can reduce their stress and strains of their complex machined like schedules.

(*v*) **Government** Various departments of the government use computers for their planning, controlling and law enforcement activities. e.g. budgets, weather forecasting, income tax department etc.

(*vi*) **Health** Computer plays a very crucial role in this area. Activities like scanning, X-ray, tele-medicine, patient monitoring, patient records and diagnosis etc., are performed with the help of computers.

(*vii*) **Multimedia** It is the field concerned with the computer controlled integration of text, graphics, drawings, animation, audio and any other media, where each type of information can be represented, stored, transmitted and processed digitally.

(*viii*) **Banking** Computers are used in banks to keep the records of customer's accounts. It also provides online accounting facility which includes current balances, deposits, overdrafts, interest charges etc.

(*ix*) **Military Personnel** Computers are used for the crucial tasks like determining the weather, computing the trajectories of missiles, smart weapons etc.

(*x*) **Business** Using a wide range of business software, a company's marketing division can produce sales forecasts and devising new strategies.

(*xi*) **E-Commerce** Traditionally, commerce is seen as the exchange or buying and selling of goods and services, which involves exchange of money and sometimes transportation of goods. Electronic commerce (E-Commerce) that takes place between businesses is referred to as **Business-to-Business** or **B2B**.

(*xii*) **Publication** Computers has made publication process an easy one. Without computer, the different parts of a publication-text, illustrations and graphics must be created individually, then cut out and pasted down to form a page layout.

Different areas of computer applications

SUMMARY

- Computer is an electronic device that stores and manipulates information.
- Computer itself is a combination of different types of separate electronic device, i.e. input device, processing unit and output device.
- An input device is any hardware device that sends data to a computer, allowing you to interact with and control the computer. e.g. keyboard, mouse, joystick, light pen, scanner, web camera etc.
- A keyboard is an external input device usually includes alphabetic, numerical and common symbols used to type data.
- Scanner is a device that reads or copies information or images into a computer.
- OMR technology scans a printed form and reads predefined positions and records where marks are made on the form.
- An output device is any peripheral device that receives data from a computer usually for display, projection or physical reproduction. e.g. monitor, printer, plotter, speaker etc.
- A monitor (also called visual display unit) looks like a television and it displays alphanumeric and graphic output.
- Printer is an output device that prints paper documents.
- CPU is the brain of the computer which performs basic arithmetical and logical operations of the system.
- Primary memory is a computer memory that is accessed directly by the CPU.
- RAM is a type of data storage used in computers that is generally located on the motherboard.
- ROM is a storage medium that is used with computers and other electronic devices.
- Secondary memory refers to storage devices, such as hard drives, floppy disk drives etc.
- Computer has some limitations such as lack of decision-making power, zero IQ, No heuristics etc.
- Some of the areas where computers are being used education, science, multimedia, banks, business, entertainment etc.

Exam Practice

Multiple Choice Questions

1 A computer is free from tiredness, monotony, etc., reflects which characteristic?

(a) High speed (b) Versatile
(c) Accuracy (d) Diligence

Ans. (*d*) Unlike human beings, a computer is free from monotony, tiredness, lack of concentration etc, and can work for hours without creating any errors. This characteristic of computer is known as diligence.

2 It is responsible for all numerical and logical calculations.

(a) CPU (b) CU (c) MU (d) ALU

Ans. (*d*) ALU is a digital circuit in which numerical and logical operations are defined.

3 Which of the following does not represent an I/O device?

(a) Speaker (b) Plotter
(c) Joystick (d) CU

Ans. (*d*) CU is used to coordinate the input and the output devices of a computer system.

4 Control unit is called the .... of a computer system.

(a) heart (b) nerve centre
(c) primary memory (d) All of these

Ans. (*b*) Nerve centre because it controls the overall processing of a computer system.

5 The first computer mouse was invented by

(a) Christopher Sholes
(b) C.B. Mirick
(c) Douglas Engelbart
(d) Russell A Kirsch

Ans. (*c*) The first computer mouse was invented by Douglas Engelbart at Stanford Research Centre in 1960s.

6 Out of the following, whom do you think is the most probable user of a light pen?

(a) Computer Programmer (b) Graphic Designer
(c) Journalist (d) Scientist

Ans. (*b*) Light pen is useful for graphic designer as it is useful for identifying a particular location on the screen.

7 Input device is used to make a digital copy of a photograph.

(a) Graphics Tablet (b) Scanner
(c) MICR (d) OMR

Ans. (*b*) Scanner is an input device that is used to make a digital copy of a photograph. It converts the image or text into a digital file.

8 .... is a medium size scanner which has rolling drum to scan your documents.

(a) Drum (b) Handheld
(c) Flatbed (d) Roller

Ans. (*a*) Drum

9 Large amount of cheques are processed by using

(a) OCR (b) MICR
(c) OMR (d) All of these

Ans. (*b*) Large amount of cheques are processed by the MICR (Magnetic Ink Character Recognition). It can read characters that are printed using a special magnetic ink. It is mostly used in banks.

10 What does OCR stand for?

(a) Optical Character Reader
(b) Optical Character Recognition
(c) Operational Character Reader
(d) Only Character Reader

Ans. (*b*) OCR stands for Optical Character Recognition used as an input device in a computer system.

11 Input device used in evaluating answer sheets by a teacher.

(a) OCR
(b) OMR
(c) MICR
(d) Barcode

Ans. (*b*) OMR (Optical Mark Recognition) is the process of capturing human marked data from document forms such as surveys and test.

12 Which type of monitor works in the same way as a television?

(a) CRT (b) LCD (c) LED (d) 3-D

Ans. (*a*) CRT monitor works in the same way as a television.

13 Dot matrix is a type of

(a) Tape (b) Disk (c) Printer (d) Bus

Ans. (*c*) Dot matrix is a type of impact printer that prints one character at a time.

14 Output device is used to generate the long map of building and shopping malls.

(a) Dot-matrix (b) Inkjet
(c) Plotter (d) Deskjet

Ans. (*c*) Plotter is a computer hardware device similar to a printer that uses a pen, pencil, marker or other writing tools to make a design.

15 Out of these which one is a volatile memory?
(a) ROM (b) RAM (c) Floppy (d) DVD

Ans. (*b*) RAM is a volatile memory that means data remains stored in RAM only when power supply is there and computer is switched ON but as soon as the computer is turned OFF, the contents of RAM get erased.

16 Which of the following is an example of non-volatile memory?
(a) ROM (b) RAM (c) LSI (d) VLSI

Ans. (*a*) Among given options, ROM is the memory that retains its contents even after the interruption of power so, it is a non-volatile memory.

17 .... memory is used to store large amount of information permanently.
(a) RAM (b) ROM
(c) Secondary (d) Primary

Ans. (*c*) Secondary memory is used to store large amount of information permanently.

18 Which of the following statement is false?
(a) Secondary storage is faster
(b) Primary storage is both volatile and non-volatile in nature.
(c) When the computer is turned OFF, data and instructions stored in RAM are erased
(d) None of the above

Ans. (*a*) Secondary memory is the slowest and cheapest form of memory. It cannot be processed directly by the CPU and it must be first copied into RAM.

19 The concentric circles on the floppy disks are further divided into
(a) tracks (b) sectors
(c) cylinders (d) None of these

Ans. (*b*) The concentric circles on the floppy disks are known as tracks. These tracks are further divided into pie-shaped sections known as sectors.

20 Which of the following storage device can be used for storing large backup data?
(a) Floppy disk (b) Hard disk
(c) Magnetic tape (d) None of these

Ans. (*c*) Magnetic tape is used with larger computers such as the mainframe, where huge amount of data is kept stored for longer period of time.

21 The .... offers more than five times the storage capacity of traditional DVDs.
(a) Compact disc (b) Pen drive
(c) Blu-ray disc (d) Ext-DVD

Ans. (*c*) Blu-ray disc can hold almost 5 times more data than a single layer DVD.

22 Pen drive is also known as
(a) Flash drive
(b) Data stick
(c) Thumb drive
(d) All of the above

Ans. (*d*) A USB flash drive, data stick, thumb drive or pen drive is a portable drive that connects to a computer's USB port.

23 The largest unit of memory is
(a) Terabyte (b) Petabyte
(b) Exabyte (d) Geopbyte

Ans. (*d*) Geopbyte is the highest memory measurement unit. It is equal to 1024 Brontobyte, (nearly 2^{100} bytes).

Fill in the Blanks

1 .... is an electronic device that manipulates information or data according to the set of instructions called program.

Ans. Computer

2 .... is the meaningful content that is extracted from the data after processing.

Ans. Information

3 The first chip .... was made by Intel in 1971 scientist Ted Hoff and engineer Frederico Faggin.

Ans. Intel 4004

4 .... is used for playing video games.

Ans. Joystick

5 Scanner is a device that allows a user to convert an image into a .... file.

Ans. digital

6 .... is the light sensitive pointing device.

Ans. Light pen

7 Touch screen is an electronic .... display that can detect the presence and location of a touch within the display area.

Ans. visual

8 .... is used to translate scanned images of handwritten, type written or special type of font printed on a conventional paper.

Ans. OCR

EXAM PRACTICE

9 Examination papers are checked by ....

Ans. OMR

10 .... reads the bar code information.

Ans. Barcode reader

11 The printed information on the paper is called ....

Ans. hardcopy

12 The speed of printer is rated by ....

Ans. cps or ppm

13 The .... prints its output on special heat sensitive paper.

Ans. thermal printer

14 .... printers are based on electro-photography technology to print the data.

Ans. Laser

15 Computer memory is divided into .... and .... memory.

Ans. primary, secondary

16 .... memory is a special memory used for speeding up the transfer of data and instructions in CPU.

Ans. Cache

17 .... memory does not deal directly with the CPU.

Ans. Secondary

18 .... disks are portable but have less storage capacity.

Ans. Floppy

19 .... is an example of secondary memory.

Ans. Magnetic tape

20 .... stands for Compact Disc Read Only Memory.

Ans. CD-ROM

21 .... is the latest optical disc secondary storage device.

Ans. Blu-ray Disc (BD)

22 A .... is a thumb sized gadget that can be used to read, write or erase data as many times.

Ans. pen drive

23 .... memory stick was introduced by Sony in 1994 as a copy-protection technology.

Ans. MagicGate

True or False

1 A computer is a mechanical machine, which is used only for record keeping.

Ans. **False** Computer is an electronic device that has the ability to store, retrieve and process data.

2 A computer follows the rule of IPO (Input Process Output) cycle.

Ans. **True** Computer first takes the input via input devices, process it with the help of the CPU and gives the output through output devices.

3 In CPU, control unit performs the actual processing on the data.

Ans. **False** In CPU, control unit does not perform any actual processing instead it controls and guides the operations like a supervisor.

4 There are 12 function keys on the keyboard.

Ans. **True** The keys at the top of a keyboard marked 'F1' to 'F12' are function keys.

5 A mouse is a pointing device.

Ans. **True** Because it allows the user to control and provide the data to the computer system using physical gestures point, click and drag.

6 The sensors of touchpad can only react to a fingertip.

Ans. **True** The sensors of touchpad can only react to a fingertip that not a pencil or other object.

7 The MICR coding system contains 14 characters.

Ans. **True** MICR's coding system contains 14 characters (4 special symbols and 10 decimal digits).

8 Wasp is an example of OMR software.

Ans. **False** Software like Wasp, Barcode Pro are used for scanning and printing barcodes. It is an example of barcode reader.

9 Barcode reader is an input device to play sound.

Ans. **False** A barcode reader (or barcode scanner) is an electronic device for reading printed barcodes.

10 An LCD monitor allows the user to input information by touching the icons on the screen.

Ans. **False** Because most of the LCD monitors do not come with touch facility where information is provided by touching the icons.

11 Inkjet is a non-impact printer.

Ans. **True** Because there is no physical contact between the print heads and the paper.

12 In Random Access Memory, if current will be interrupted, data will not lost.

Ans. **False** Random Access Memory (RAM) is a volatile memory, if current is interrupted, data will lost.

13 ROM stands for Random Operation Memory.

Ans. **False** ROM stands for Read Only Memory.

14 Secondary storage is also called auxiliary storage.

Ans. **True** Because secondary storage is a part of external memory. It is used to store a large amount of data at less cost per byte than primary memory.

15 The secondary or magnetic memory is a volatile memory.

Ans. **False** The secondary or magnetic memory is a non-volatile memory.

16 The hard disk is hard to format on different systems.

Ans. **False** Hard disk is a secondary storage device which can be formatted on another system using boot sector format option.

17 The data on a CD-ROM is written at the time of its manufacture.

Ans. **False** CD-ROM is a blank storage device which can be written when user wants.

18 The Compact Disc (CD) is a digital storage device.

Ans. **True** Because CD is used to store audio, video, graphical and textual data.

19 A magnetic tape is a direct access storage device.

Ans. **False** It is a non-volatile memory hence, it is not directly accessible by the CPU.

20 Gigabyte is actually 2^{10} bytes.

Ans. **True** Because it is actually 2^{10} bytes or 1 GB =1024 bytes.

Very Short Answer (VSA) Type Questions

1 Name the most commonly used input device.

Ans. Keyboard is the most commonly used input device, which can also be used to type commands directing the computer to perform certain actions.

2 Explain the main advantage and disadvantage of an OCR.

Ans. The main advantage of an OCR is the ability to scan the characters accurately.

The disadvantage of an OCR is limited number of characters offered by it.

3 Why do we use webcam?

Ans. A webcam is basically used for capturing a series of digital images that are transferred by the computer to a server and then displayed to the hosting page.

4 Name the memory (Primary/Secondary)with the following features:

(a) If current is interrupted, data is lost.

(b) Before a program is ready to run, the program is loaded into this memory, which allows the CPU directly access the program.

Ans. RAM because it has above given features.

5 Write any one advantage of cache memory.

Ans. The main advantage of cache memory is that if needed data is found in cache, then CPU does not have to use motherboard's system bus for data transfer and processing gets fast.

6 Which disc is created using laser beam?

Ans. CD-ROM disc is created using laser beam.

7 Give one difference between primary memory and secondary memory.

Ans. The primary memory is volatile and has limited storage capacity, whereas secondary memory is non-volatile and can store huge amount of data.

8 Arrange the following memory units in ascending order of their storage capacities: Kilobyte, Byte, Terabyte, Megabyte, Geopbyte

Ans. The ascending order of memory units is Byte, Kilobyte, Megabyte, Terabyte, Geopbyte.

9 What do you understand by DuO as variety of memory stick?

Ans. DuO is a small flash memory and developed for digital camera, cell phones etc.

10 Define the term byte. Differentiate between a bit and a byte.

Ans. Byte is a unit of measuring computer storage. Binary digit is called bit in short. There are only two binary digits 0 and 1, whereas a combination of 8 bits is called a byte.

Short Answer (SA) Type Questions

1 Distinguish between input unit and output unit.

Ans. Differences between input unit and output unit are as follows

Input Unit	Output Unit
It accepts the data and instructions from outside.	It accepts the result which produced by the computer.
It converts the accepted instructions and data in computer acceptable form.	It converts the results, which are in a coded form to human readable form.
It supplies the converted instructions and data to the computer system for further processing.	It supplies the converted results to the user.

2 Differentiate between OCR and OMR.

Ans. OCR stands for Optical Character Recognition which is used to read characters of special type font that are printed on conventional paper with conventional ink. On the other hand, OMR stands for Optical Mark Recognition which is used to transcribe marks that are marked with a dark pencil or ink on a special pre-printed form (e.g. answer sheet of a multiple choice question paper where a choice of answer can be reflected by shading the appropriate box).

3 Name the device which is used to read the barcode. Explain in short.

Ans. Barcode reader is a device which is used to read the printed code (barcode) from the products to be sold. It contains a light sensitive detector which identifies the values of the bars printed on the product and converts them into a numeric code. This barcode reader technology is used in shopping malls to identify products and generate bills.

4 Which device is used for recognising physical or behavioural traits of an individual. Also, write one advantage of this device.

Ans. Biometric sensor is a device used for recognising physical or behavioural traits of an individual. This device is mainly used for security purpose and for marking attendance of employees/students in organisations/institutions. The major advantage of this device is that it eliminates the problem caused by lost IDs or forgotten passwords etc.

5 Explain LCD. Write the features of an LCD monitor.

Ans. LCD stands for Liquid Crystal Display. These screens are used in notebooks and laptops sized PCs. A special type of liquid is sandwiched between two plates. It is thin, flat and light weight screen made up of any number of colors. Some of the major features of LCD monitors are as follows

(*i*) Reduced radiation
(*ii*) Light weight
(*iii*) Less eyestrain

6 Define the non-impact printers.

Ans. Refer to text on Page No. 11.

7 Which technology is used in laser printers?

Ans. Laser printers are based on photocopy technology to print. They use a laser beam and dry powder ink to produce a high quality dot matrix pattern. They can print graphic images too.

They are ideally used when good quality and large scale printing is required.

8 What are plotter? State their areas of application.

Ans. Refer to text on Page No. 12.

9 Name the storage device whose contents have to be erased completely everytime when a user wants to change or add some data.

Ans. CD-RW (Compact Disc-Rewritable) is a storage device whose contents have to be completely erased everytime when a user wants to change or add some data.
A CD-RW can be written multiple number of times. The data burned on a CD-RW cannot be changed, but it can be erased.

EXAM PRACTICE

Long Answer (LA) Type Questions

1 What are the characteristics of a computer?

Ans. Refer to text on Page No. 2.

2 What are the functional units of a computer?

Ans. The functional units of a computer are as follows

(*i*) **Input Unit** Computer takes data from input devices.

(*ii*) **CPU** (Central Processing Unit) It is the brain of the computer, where most of the calculations takes place.

It consists of

- **ALU** (Arithmetic and Logic Unit) It performs arithmetical and logical operations.
- CU (Control Unit) It extracts instructions from memory, decodes and executes them.

(*iii*) **Output Unit** Gives out results or data through output devices.

(*iv*) **Auxiliary Storage** Secondary storage devices are used to store data and instructions permanently.

3 What is an input device? Explain the input device that is used to convert handwritten text into machine readable format.

Ans. An input device is used to enter data or information into the computer for processing. e.g. keyboard. OCR is an input device used to convert handwritten text into machine readable format. It reads the characters with the help of a light source and photoelectric cells. The technology is being developed for greater accurate recognition which is also known as Intelligent Character Recognition (ICR).

4 Define the different types of scanners.

Ans. Refer to text on Page No. 6.

5 What is MICR? Where is it mostly used? What are the major advantages and disadvantages of MICR as general purpose input medium?

Ans. MICR stands for Magnetic Ink Character Recognition. It is a character recognition technology that can read human unreadable characters that are printed using a special magnetic ink. It is mostly used in banks to facilitate the processing of cheques.

Advantages of MICR are as follows

(*i*) It decreases the margin of errors.

(*ii*) Provides high security.

Disadvantages of MICR are as follows

(*i*) Time consuming standards.

(*ii*) The number of characters that can be recorded with present techniques is very limited.

6 Write two categories of printers. Which type of printers are more speedy and quieter?

Ans. The printers can be classified into two categories which are as follows

(*i*) **Impact printers** In these types of printers, there is a mechanical contact between the paper and the printer head. These can further be classified as-Line printers (which can print a line at a time) and Daisy wheel printers (which can print a character at a time).

(*ii*) **Non-impact printers** In these types of printers, there is no mechanical contact between the paper and the printer head.

The printing takes place with some electromagnetic thermal or laser techniques. The non-impact printers are more speedy and quieter than impact printers.

7 Differentiate between RAM and ROM.

Ans. **Random Access Memory** (RAM) is also called the read/write memory as data can be read and write to it. It is a temporary memory. The contents of the RAM are accessible only as long as the computer is ON. Once the computer is turned OFF, the contents of RAM are wiped out. It stores operating system routines, application programs and the data in current use are kept temporarily.

The types of RAM are SRAM and DRAM.

Read Only Memory (ROM) is a special type of memory whose contents can only be read. It is a permanent memory, so the contents of the ROM are not lost, even when the computer is switched OFF. It is normally used to store the manufacturer's instructions.

The types of ROM are PROM, EPROM and EEPROM.

8 Explain secondary memory. Give some examples of secondary memory.

Ans. Refer to text on Page No. 14-15.

9 Which one of the magnetic storage disks is also known as diskette? Explain it with its advantages and disadvantages.

Ans. Floppy disk drive is also known as diskette or FDD. For brief description with advantages and disadvantages refers to the text on Page No. 14.

10 Differentiate between a flash drive and a memory card.

Ans. Differences between a flash drive and a memory card are as follows

Flash Drive	*Memory Card*
It is a small and portable data storage device.	It is small, re-recordable, easily portable and very light weighted.
It is used to store information and transfer data from one computer to another.	It is commonly used in electronic devices including digital camera, mobile phones etc.
It is available with storage different capacities upto 256 GB.	It is available with storage capacity from 2 MB to 128 GB.

11 Describe the main applications of a computer.

Ans. Refer to text on Page No. 18.

12. A computer is an electronic device that process data and converts into the information according to the set of instructions. This set of instructions are called as programs. Computer main advantages are

It has the ability to store, retrieve and process the data.

It is used by companies now-a-days to make documents by typing using text editors, one can send and receive E-mails and browse the Internet.

In general, computer is the combination of hardware and software. Hardware is a collection of all physical components such as scanner, keyboard, printer, monitor, CPU, etc. While, software comprises the entire set of programs, procedures, and routines associated with the operation of a computer system. There are various characteristics of computers, such as accuracy, diligence, speed, automaticity, etc. The CPU is called as a brain of the computer. It consists with three main components – ALU, MU and CU.

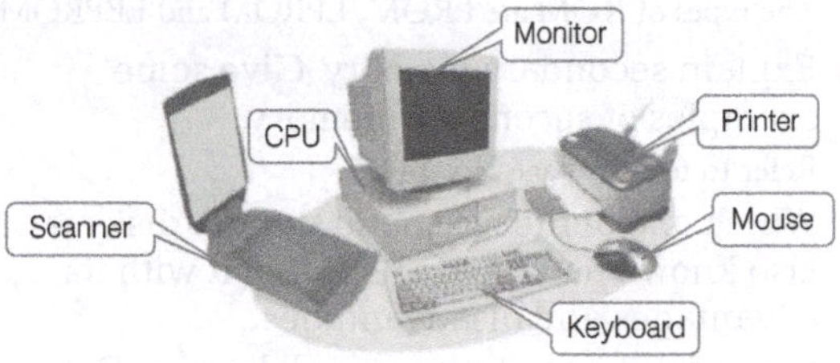

(i) Computer has an ability to
(a) store data (b) process data
(c) retrieve data (d) All of these

(ii) Computer is a combination of hardware and ....
(a) software (b) instructions
(c) flowcharts (d) keyboard

(iii) Which is not a characteristic of a computer?
(a) Accuracy (b) Automaticity
(c) Human like brain (d) Speed

(iv) The .... is called as a brain of the computer.
(a) ALU (b) input (c) CPU (d) output

(v) Computer main task is to convert .... into ....
(a) information, data (b) data, information
(c) data, process (d) process, data

Ans. (i) (*d*) Computer main advantages are – it has the ability to store, retrieve and process the data.

(ii) (*a*) Computer is the combination of hardware and software. Software comprises the entire set of programs, procedures and routines associated with the operation of a computer system.

(iii) (*c*) There are various characteristics of computers, such as accuracy, diligence, speed, automaticity, etc. Hence, human like brain is not a characteristic of a computer.

(iv) (*c*) The CPU is called as a brain of the computer. It consists with three main components – ALU, MU and CU.

(v) (*b*) Computer is the combination of hardware and software, which converts data into information.

13. Drishti, Mohan, Ram, Niti and Harish are Class 9th students and friends. Drishti purchased a new laptop. All friends are exploring her laptop and wants to do the next assignments in her laptop only. They are checking specification of the laptop written on the laptop box. It says it has 1TB hard disk, 4 GB RAM, 2 GHZ processor, keyboard and a screen. Some specification of ROM is also given. Niti is looking for video card and she finds that laptop has no separate RAM for video card. All friends are having various questions in their mind.

(i) The laptop has three type of memory. Which type of memory can be used for storing data permanently?
(a) RAM (b) ROM
(c) Secondary memory (d) Primary memory

(ii) Mohan and Ram are confused with ROM and secondary memory. Ram is asking to Mohan, when ROM can save data permanently, then why do I need to have hard disk? Choose appropriate reason Mohan has specified.
(a) Data on ROM can be written with some specific techniques only.
(b) ROM has a limited size.
(c) ROM data cannot be copied and accessed by users normally.
(d) All of the above

(iii) Drishti is asking to teacher "mam I need to purchase a RAM for my video card in computer. Can you suggest me which RAM I should purchase"?
(a) SRAM (b) DRAM (c) SDRAM (d) Any one

(iv) Harish is confused about the specification 4GB RAM.
(a) It defines the size of RAM in Gega Bytes.
(b) It defines speed of RAM.
(c) It defines the amount of time consumed to access data from RAM.
(d) All of the above

(v) Niti asked a question from Drishti, what is the full form of TB?
(a) Teen Byte (b) Tera Byte
(c) Tetra Byte (d) Tara Byte

Ans. (i) (*c*) Hard disk can be used to store data permanently. As this is a type of secondary memory.

(ii) (*d*) In ROM, information is stored once, and remain fixed which cannot be changed. But in hard disk we can store information and changed it wherever required.

(iii) (*a*) SRAM (Static RAM) is a computer memory that requires a constant power flow in order to hold information. It is more expensive which requires more power, therefore it is commonly used in cache and video card memory.

(iv) (*a*) GB is used a unit to specify size of the memory. Therefore, 4GB is a storage capacity, i.e. size or RAM.

(v) (*b*) The TB is a unit to measure the capacity of a memory. It is called as Tera Byte and 1 TB.

Application Oriented Questions

1 Suhana is to buy a new computer. She wants to use this system in her home as well as in office too. Suggest her a computer that can fulfil her requirements.

Ans. Suhana should buy a laptop as laptops are easily portable computers and easy to use.

2 The usefulness of computers has now become a part of humanity. You cannot imagine life without them.

(*i*) Do computers have weaknesses also. If yes, then give some examples .

(*ii*) Give some use of computers in daily life.

Ans. (*i*) Yes, computers have weaknesses. Some weaknesses of computers are lack of decision-making power, zero IQ and no heuristics.

(*ii*) Computers are used to listen to songs, send E-mail etc. in daily life.

3 A computer is used to type documents, send E-mail and browse the Internet. It is very useful to us.

(*i*) What are the basic parts of a computer?

(*ii*) Write some characteristics of a computer.

Ans. (*i*) Hardware, software, data and information.

(*ii*) Accuracy, speed, diligence and reliability.

4 Koshin, a class IX student, is learning computers. Yesterday her teacher taught a chapter about input devices and gave an assignment. Help her do so.

(*i*) Which of the following statements are true about input devices?

(*a*) Input device is any software device.
(*b*) Input device allows user to interact with computer.
(*c*) Keyboard is an input device.
(*d*) Input devices are not visible.

(*ii*) Name few input devices.

Ans. (*i*) (*b*) and (*c*) statements are true.

(*ii*) Keyboard, mouse, joystick, light pen and touch screen.

5 Identify input/output devices from the clues given below:

(*a*) Transfers typed or handwritten texts, graphs, diagrams and photographs into a digital format.

(*b*) Reads the code number, which is encoded as a series of black and white lines on the product.

(*c*) Checks and marks an examination answer sheet that contains multiple choice questions.

(*d*) Processes the cheque number and code.

(*e*) Produces images on paper such as numbers, alphabets and graphics.

(*f*) Receives sound in the form of electric current from a sound card and then converts it to the sound format.

Ans. (*a*) Scanner (*b*) Barcode reader
(*c*) Optical Mark Recognition (OMR)
(*d*) Magnetic Ink Character Recognition (MICR)
(*e*) Printer (*f*) Speaker

6 Sakshi is preparing a lecture on output device like monitor. Discuss.

(*i*) Give some advantages of the output device 'monitor'.

(*ii*) Write some disadvantages also.

Ans. (*i*) (*a*) Relatively cheap and reliable.
(*b*) Can display text and graphics in a wide range of colors.

(*ii*) (*a*) No permanent copy to keep the results as it will disappear when the computer is switched OFF.
(*b*) Unsuitable for users with visual problems.

7 The computer memory relates to many devices and components.

(*i*) What do you mean by memory?

(*ii*) How many types of memory the computer has?

Ans. (*i*) Computer memory enables a person to retain the information that is stored on the computer.

(*ii*) Computer has basically two types of memory as follows:

Internal memory Main memory units (RAM and ROM) and cache memory.

External memory Secondary memory.

CHAPTER

02

Computer Software

Chapter Checklist

- Classification of Software
  - System Software
  - Application Software
- Programming Language

Software is a set of computer programs, procedures and associated documentation concerned with the operation of a data processing system. Software commonly known as **programs**, consists of all required instructions that tell the hardware how to perform a task. It is not only basic requirement of a computer system but, it makes a computer more powerful and useful.

Classification of Software

Software can be broadly classified into two major categories as follows

1. System software
2. Application software

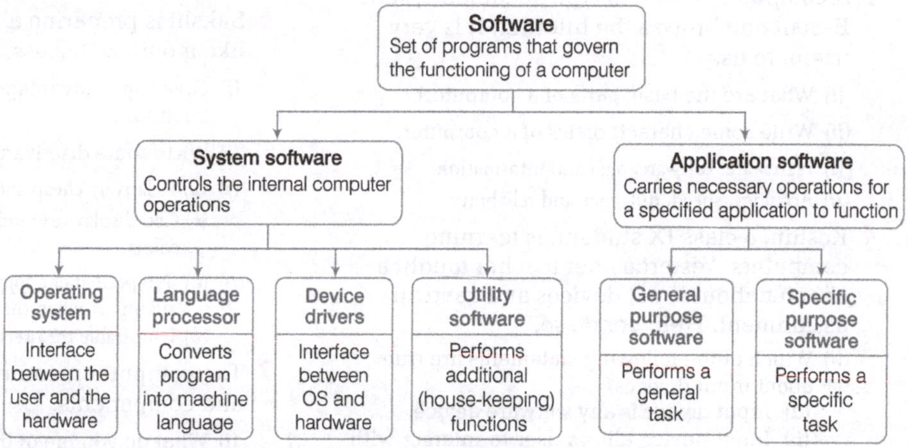

Classification of software

Note The set of instructions which controls the sequence of operations are known as **program**.

1. System Software

All those programs which are used by a computer system either for its activation or internal resource management are called *system softwares*. e.g. software that would transfer the data/instructions from input devices to computer's memory will be a system software. It refers to the programs that control internal computer operations and makes best use of the hardware devices.

System software can further be classified into various categories such as operating system, device drivers, language processors and many more, details of which are as follows

Operating System (OS)

It is a program that acts as an interface between the user and the hardware (i.e. for all computer resources). An operating system is an important component of a computer system, which controls and co-ordinates all other components of it. It activates all devices that make them ready for work. It also performs all internal management functions and ensures systematic functioning of a computer system.

The operating system performs the following functions

- It recognises input from keyboard and sends output to the display screen.
- It makes sure that the programs running simultaneously do not interfere with each other.
- It is also responsible for security, ensuring that unauthorised users cannot access the system e.g. MS-DOS, Windows 95, Windows XP, Windows Vista etc.

BIOS

The Basic Input/Output System (BIOS) is commonly known as **system BIOS**. It is a boot firmware or a small program that controls various electronic devices attached to the main computer system. The initial function of the BIOS is to initialise system devices such as RAM, hard disk, CD/DVD drive, video display card and other hardwares. It sets the machine hardware into a known state that helps the operating system to configure the hardware components. This process is known as **Booting Up the computer**.

Language Processor

It is a system program, which processes a program to make it understandable by the computer, i.e. it converts high level language into machine language. A language processor is also known as **language translator**. A computer system can understand only machine language or binary language. Language processor is extremely difficult to learn for a general programmer and thus, there is a need for some special language that is easy to learn and understand for the programmer in order to interact with the computer system. These special languages or a set of commands are collectively known as **programming languages**.

Some examples of programming languages are C, C++, Java etc.

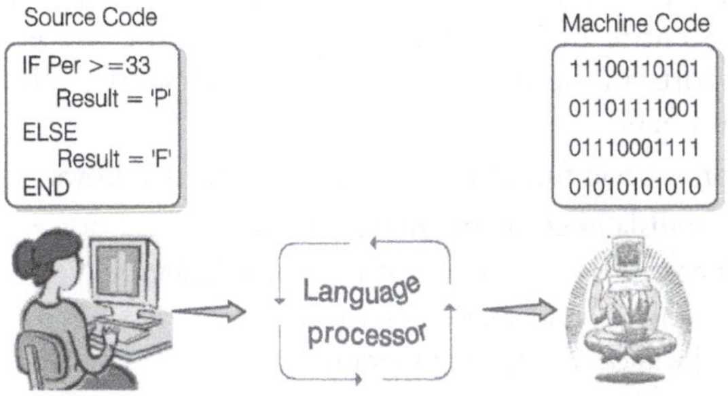

Program translator

Depending upon used programming languages, language processors are divided into three categories which are as follows

(i) Assembler

It converts a program written in assembly language into machine language. Assembly language consists of mnemonic codes, which are difficult to learn and are machine dependent.

Some basic functions of an assembler are as follows

- Replaces mnemonic codes by machine codes.
- Replaces symbolic addresses by numeric addresses.
- Determines machine representation for constants.

(ii) Interpreter

It converts a high level language program into machine language by converting it line-by-line. If there is any error in any line, it stops the execution of the program immediately and reports the user at the same time and program execution cannot resume until the error is rectified by the user.

Interpreter is very useful for debugging and suitable for novice programmer. This is a slow process and consumes less memory space.

Some basic functions of an interpreter are as follows

- Translates one instruction at a time.
- It checks the execution of the instructions line-by-line.
- It does not produce object code.

(iii) Compiler

It converts high level language program into machine language, which can be understood by the processor. For each high level language, the machine requires a separate compiler. A compiler creates a unique object program, i.e. if a source program is compiled, there is no need of that source program because output can be obtained by executing that object program (copy created by the compilation of source code). Compiler converts the entire high level language program in one go and reports all the errors of the program along with the line numbers.

Some basic functions of compiler are as follows

- It translates entire program at a time.
- It converts source code into machine language.
- It provides information on the size of area of main memory to be allocated to the program.

Differences between Compiler and Interpreter

Compiler	Interpreter
Compiler takes entire program as input.	Interpreter takes single instruction as input.
Intermediate object code is generated.	No intermediate object code is generated.
Conditional control statements execute faster.	Conditional control statements execute slower.
Memory requirement is more (since object code is generated).	Memory requirement is less.
Errors are displayed after entire program is checked.	Errors are displayed for every instruction interpreted.
e.g. Compiler in C language.	e.g. Interpreter in Basic language.

Device Driver

The software which is written with the objective of making a device functional, when the device is connected to the computer system is called *device driver* or simply *driver*. A device driver is a system software that acts as an interface between the device and the user or an operating system. All computer accessories like printer, scanner, web camera etc., have their own driver software. This software helps an operating system and other application softwares to communicate with a particular device for optimal use. Devices from different manufacturers work in different ways. e.g. printers from different companies need different drivers to do work.

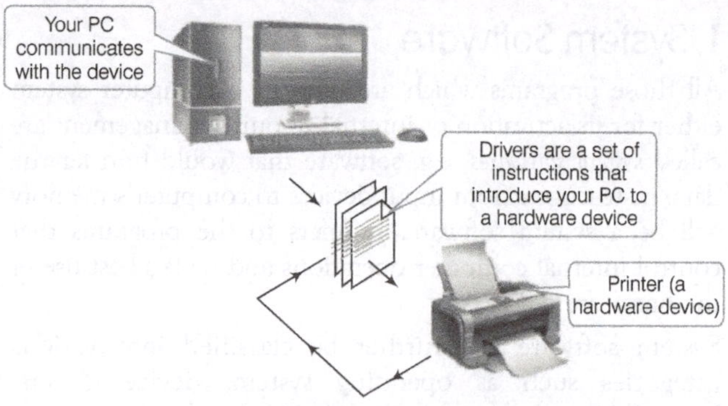

Device driver

When user buys a new hardware, the manufacturer of the hardware provides an installation disk alongwith it. The user simply needs to load that disk into the computer. After this process, that particular device can be used.

Apart from this, drivers can also be downloaded from Internet. But these days, some new operating system like Windows Vista, Windows 7 etc., are already pre-equipped with many device drivers.

So, a user simply needs to plug the device in computer and it works perfectly as its driver is already installed in computer. But, it is possible for some commonly used devices only.

Check Point 01

1. Software commonly known as programs that consist of
   (a) hardware (b) input device
   (c) instruction (d) output device
2. Mention some examples of an operating system.
3. What is the other name of BIOS?
4. Name the types of language processors.

Utility Software (Utilities)

It is a system software designed to help in management and tuning of operating systems, computer hardwares and different application softwares.

A single piece of utility software is usually called a **utility** or **tool**. Utilities are those application programs that assist the computer by performing house-keeping functions like backing up disk or scanning/cleaning viruses.

A utility program carries out some of the common tasks, while using a computer system. Utility software is also known as **service program, service tool** or **utility routine**.

It differs from applications mostly in terms of size, complexity and function. Utility programs are bundled with operating systems. However, these programs are also available in a separate package and that's why they are sometimes considered separate from system software.

Some important utility softwares are disk compression, back up, disk defragmenter, disk checker and disk cleaner, disk partition tool, virus scanner, text editor, debugging tool, file manager, screen saver, encryption/decryption etc.

- Source code is the version of a computer as it is originally written (i.e. typed into the computer) by the programmer.
- Object code is the output of a compiler after it processes source code.

2. Application Software

It is a computer software designed to help the user to perform single or multiple tasks. It acts as a set of instructions, which direct the hardwares to perform specific functions. e.g. accounting software, office suites, graphics software, media players etc.

Application softwares are categorised into two main parts as follows:

(i) General Purpose Application Software

It is a software which is used for any general function. It allows people to do simple computer tasks. General purpose software is sometimes referred to as **GPS**.

e.g. Word Processing Software, Electronic Spreadsheets, Database Management Systems, Desktop Publishing Software, Graphics, Multimedia, Presentation Software etc.

Some common general purpose application softwares are as follows

Word Processing Software

It is a software program capable of creating, storing and printing documents. Unlike the standard typewriter, users are using such Word processors which have the ability to create a document that make changes anywhere in the document. This document can also be saved for modification, later on or to be opened on any other computer using the same Word processor with the help of sharing. Today, the Word processor is one of the most frequently used programs on a computer system.

e.g. MS-Word, WordPerfect, AppleWorks, OpenOffice.org Writer etc.

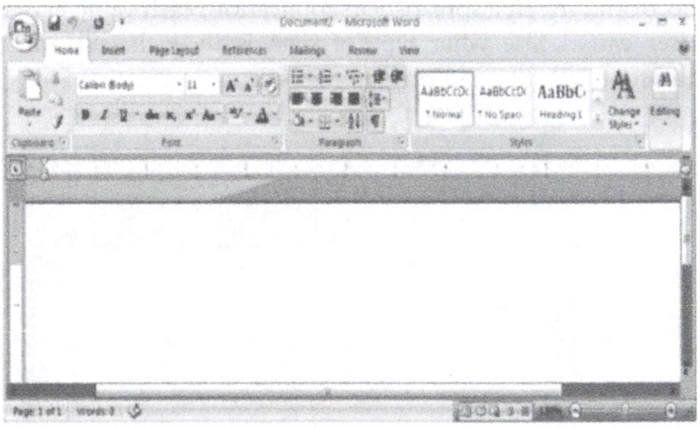

MS-Word window

Presentation Software

It is the practice of showing and explaining the contents of a topic to an audience or learner visually. People in a variety of settings and situations, use presentation software to make their presentations more interesting and professional.

e.g. marketing managers use presentation graphics to present new marketing strategies to their superiors.

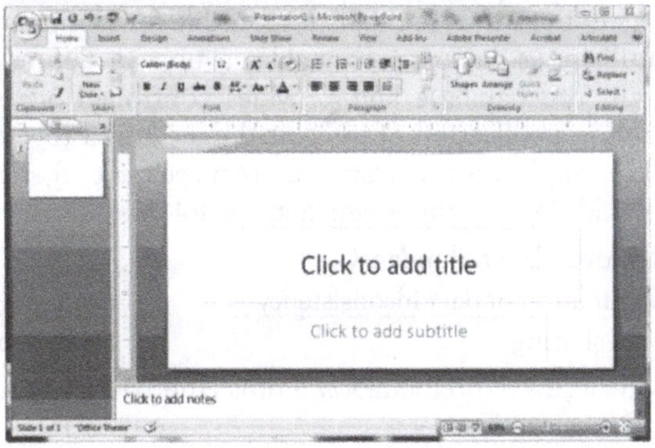

MS-PowerPoint window

Sales people use this software to demonstrate products and encourage customers to make purchases. Students use it to create high quality class presentations e.g. MS-PowerPoint, Corel Presentations, Lotus Freelance Graphics, OpenOffice.org Impress etc.

Electronic Spreadsheets

Spreadsheet applications (sometimes referred to simply as spreadsheets) are the computer programs that accept data in a tabular form and allow a user to create and manipulate spreadsheets electronically. In a spreadsheet application, each value exists in a cell. User can define what type of data is in each cell and how the different cells depend on one another.

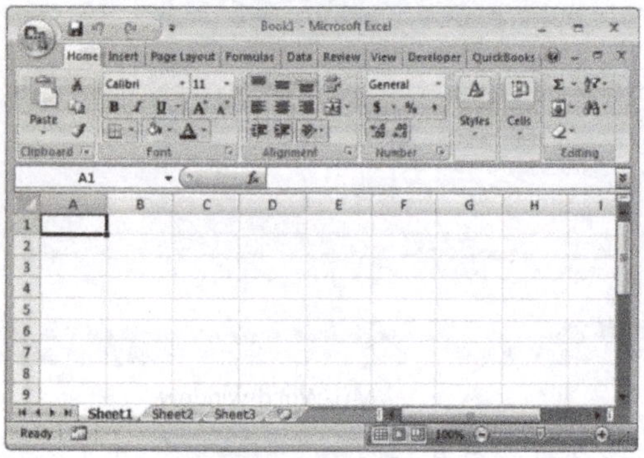

MS-Excel window

A cell is a box in which you can enter a single piece of data. The relationships between cells are called **Formulas** and the names of the cells are called **Labels.**

e.g. MS-Excel, Quattro Pro, Lotus 1-2-3, OpenOffice.org Calc etc.

DataBase Management System (DBMS)

It refers to the software that is responsible for storing, maintaining and utilising a database. It enables a user to define, create and maintain the database and provides controlled access on it. A database is a collection of integrated data stored together to serve multiple applications. Database Management System provides several additional features which are as follows:

- Removes data redundancy
- Elimination of data inconsistency
- Data sharing
- Data integration
- Data security

e.g. MS-Access, Corel Paradox, Lotus Approach, MySQL, OpenOffice.org Base etc.

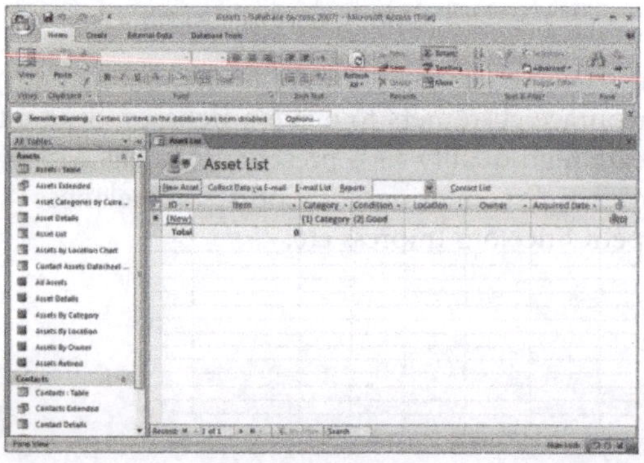

MS-Access window

Desktop Publishing (DTP) Software

It is a tool for graphic designers and non-designers to create visual communications for professional. A complete DTP software involves the combination of type setting (choosing fonts and the text layout), graphic design, page layout (how it fits on the page) and print the document. DTP softwares are used for book publishing, creating leaflets, posters, business cards etc.

e.g. QuarkXPress, Adobe PageMaker, 3B2, CorelDRAW, Corel Ventura, Illustrator etc.

Graphics Software (Image Editing)

It is an application program or collection of programs that enables a person to manipulate visual images on a computer system. In other words, these softwares are used to manipulate images that can be used at home, schools or a business.

Most graphics softwares have the ability to import and export one or more graphic file formats. Typical graphics software enables data to be plotted as line chart, bar chart and pie chart.

e.g. Adobe Photoshop, piZap, Microsoft Publisher, Picasa etc.

Multimedia Software

Multimedia includes a combination of text, audio, images, animations, videos or interactivity content forms.

In simple words, this software allows user to use a mixture of sound, pictures, films and writing is known as *multimedia software*. The term is used in contrast to media which uses only elementary computer display such as text only or traditional forms of printed or hand produced material.

e.g. Flash, Xilisoft Video Converter, VLC Media Player, Nimbuzz etc.

Browser

A browser (or Web browser) is an application software that is used to retrieve, present and traverse the information resources on the WWW (World Wide Web). The information resource is identified by a Uniform Resource Identifier (URI) and may be a Web page, image, video or other piece of content.

e.g. Lynx, Google Chrome, Mozilla Firefox, Microsoft Internet Explorer, Opera etc.

Check Point 02

1 Write any two examples of Word processing software.
2 It is a tool for graphic designers and non-designers to create visual communication.
(a) DTP (b) DBMS
(c) MS-Word (d) MS-Excel
3 This is responsible for storing, maintaining and utilising software.

(ii) Specific Purpose Application Software

It is a type of software, created to execute one specific task. e.g. Hotel Management, Reservation System, Attendance System, Billing System etc. These softwares are called *specific purpose application softwares* because they target or address a very narrow solution to a problem. It may also be created in house and tailored to the specific needs of a user. The type of software developed to meet particular user specified requirements also falls into this category.

Some of the specific purpose application softwares are as follows

Inventory Management System and Purchasing System

It is an attempt to balance inventory needs and requirement to minimise total cost, resulting from obtaining and holding an inventory. **Inventory** is a list of goods and materials available in a stock. Inventory management system is generally used in departmental stores or in an organisation to keep the records of the stock of all the physical resources. Modern inventory management systems must have the ability to track sales and available inventory, communicate with suppliers in real-time, receive and incorporate other data, such as seasonal demand. e.g. Fishbowl, AdvancePro etc.

Payroll Management System

It is used by all modern organisations to encompass every employee of the organisation, who receives regular wages or other compensation. All different payment methods are calculated by the payroll software and the appropriate paychecks are issued. This software can also be used for printing or E-mailing the salary slip of employees.

e.g. Namely, UltiPro etc.

Hotel Management System

It refers to the management techniques used in the hotel sector. It includes hotel administration, accounts, billing marketing, housekeeping, front office or front desk.

e.g. Hotelogix PMS, DJUBO, True Hotel Management, Aatithya HMS etc.

Reservation System or Central Reservation System (CRS)

It is a computerised system used to store and retrieve information and conduct transactions related to air travel, hotels, car rental or other activities. Reservation system is an application software which is commonly seen at railway reservation offices, this software helps the concerned department to automatically check the availability of the seats or berths of any train and on any particular date with an incomparable speed. Today, number of Websites like www.yatra.com, www.makemytrip.com, provide online booking for tourists.

Accounting Software

This system records and processes accounting transactions within functional modules such as accounts payable, accounts receivable, payroll and trial balance. It works as an accounting information system.

There are several types of accounting software as follows

- Accounts payable software
- Bank reconciliation software
- Budget management software etc.

e.g. Tally. ERP9, HDPOS, MARG, ProfitBooks etc.

HR Management System

It refers to the systems and processes at the intersection between Human Resource Management (HRM) and Information Technology (IT). The function of HR department is generally administrative and common in all organisations.

e.g. Effective Staff, Cezanne HR etc.

Attendance System

It is an application software designed to track and optimise the presence of a person/student in an organisation/school. Now-a-days, attendance system can be integrated with customer's existing time/ attendance recording devices like Biometrics/Access cards. Attendance management can be done in two ways as follows

- Biometric integration
- Manual attendance integration

e.g. eTimeTrackLite, Pyramid PTR 4000 etc.

Billing System

It refers to the software that is used to perform the billing process. It handles the tracking of labelled products and services delivered to a customer or set of customers.

e.g. Billing Manager, BillingTracker, kBilling etc.

Programming Language

It is a set of keywords, symbols and a system of rules for constructing statements by which humans can communicate instructions to be executed by a computer. Programming languages are mainly categorised into two parts which are as follows

1. Low Level Languages

These programming languages are more arcane and difficult to understand. It is designed to operate and handle the entire instruction set of a computer system directly which are generally used to write the system software.

e.g. Machine language and Assembly language.

Machine Language

It is the only language understood by the computers. Sometimes, it referred to as **machine code** or **object code** or **binary language**. It is a collection of binary digits (0 or 1) or bits that the computer reads and interprets.

Assembly Language

It is a low level programming language, which is used as an interface with computer hardwares. It uses structured commands as substitutions for numbers, allowing humans to read the code easier than looking at binary codes.

2. High Level Languages

It is an advanced computer programming language that is not limited to one computer, designed for a specific job and is easier to understand.

The main advantage of high level languages over low level languages is that they are easier to read, write and understand. e.g. BASIC, C, FORTRAN, Java and Pascal.

Generations of Languages

- The first generation languages or 1GLs are low level languages like machine language.
- The second generation languages or 2GLs are also low level languages that generally consist of assembly language.
- The third generation languages or 3GLs are high level languages such as C.
- The fourth generation languages or 4GLs are the languages that consist of statements similar to the statements of human language. 4GLs are commonly used in database programming and scripting programming.
- The fifth generation languages or 5GLs are programming languages that contain visual tools, which help to develop a program. A good example of 5GLs is Visual Basic.

Check Point 03

1 What are the types of accounting management?

2 Example of attendance system.

(a) eTimeTracklite

(b) Namely

(c) MARG

(d) Cezanne HR

3 Write few examples of high level languages.

SUMMARY

- Software is a generic term for the organised collection of computer data and instructions.
- Software can be divided into two major categories : System software and Application software.
- Software that contributes to control performance of the computer system and permits the user to use the system more conveniently is termed as system software.
- Some common examples of system software include operating system, device drivers and system utilities.
- System utility programs perform day-to-day tasks related to the maintenance of the computer system.
- Application software is controlled by system software which manages hardware devices and performs background tasks for them.
- Application software can be divided into two major categories : general purpose application software and specific purpose application software.
- Some examples of application software includes Word processors, spreadsheets, accounting programs, desktop publishing, multimedia application etc.
- A programming language is a primary interface of a programmer with a computer. It is an artificial language to express computation that can be performed by a computer.

Exam Practice

Multiple Choice Questions

1 Which one of the following is a set of instructions that tells the hardware how to perform the tasks?
(a) Compiler (b) Software
(c) Hardware (d) CPU

Ans. (*b*) Software is a set of instructions that tells the hardware how to perform the tasks.

2 Operating system is a
(a) application software (b) system software
(c) hardware (d) language

Ans. (*b*) Operating system is a system software that acts as an interface between the user and the hardware.

3 Which software takes control of computer system on startup?
(a) Compiler (b) Operating system
(c) Application software (d) All of these

Ans. (*b*) Operating system takes control of computer system on startup.

4 Which device is used to convert the program written in assembly language into machine language?
(a) Interpreter (b) Compiler
(c) Assembler (d) None of these

Ans. (*c*) Assembler is used to convert the program written in assembly language into machine language because it is a language processor that converts the user defined language into a form which can be easily understood by the computer.

5 Interpreter converts a high level language program into a machine language by
(a) one go mechanism
(b) line-by-line mechanism
(c) group of five lines mechanism
(d) None of the above

Ans. (*b*) Interpreter is a language processor, which converts the high level language program into machine language by using line-by-line mechanism.

6 The language processor which converts high level language into machine language is
(a) assembler (b) compiler
(c) interpreter (d) Both (b) and (c)

Ans. (*d*) Both compiler and interpreter are language processors that converts high level language into machine language.

7 Utility programs include
(a) Virus scanning software
(b) Backup software
(c) Disk defragmenter
(d) All of the above

Ans. (*d*) Utility programs includes virus scanning, backup, disk defragmenter software.

8 Which type of software is designed to perform specific, personal, business or scientific processing tasks?
(a) System
(b) Application
(c) GUI
(d) Compiler

Ans. (*b*) Application software is a computer software which is designed to help the user to perform some specific or personal tasks.

9 Which of the following is not related to a utility software?
(a) Text editor
(b) Antivirus program
(c) Disk compression software
(d) Railway reservation system

Ans. (*d*) Railway reservation system is an example of application software whereas, rest all are software utilities.

10 Which of the following is not related to an application software?
(a) Word processor
(b) DBMS
(c) Operating system
(d) Railway reservation system

Ans. (*c*) Application software is a software which carries out a specific task like Word processor, spreadsheet, DBMS etc. Among the given options, operating system is related to system software.

11 DTP is a tool for graphic designers and non-designers to create visual communications for professional. DTP stands for
(a) Device Transfer Protocol
(b) Desktop Publishing
(c) Device Transfer Programs
(d) All of the above

Ans. (*b*) DTP stands for Desktop Publishing.

12 Assembly language is a low level programming language
(a) makes use of mnemonics to interact with computer system
(b) sometimes referred to as machine code or object code
(c) that is not limited by the computer or for one specific job
(d) used to interact with computer software

Ans. (*a*) Assembly language is a low level programming language that uses mnemonics to interact with computer system.

13 Machine language sometimes referred to as
(a) programming language that is used widely by the programmer.
(b) machine code or object code
(c) programming language that is more easily understood
(d) language that is not limited by the computer

Ans. (*b*) Machine language sometimes referred to as machine code or object code because it is the language which is only understood by the computer as a computer itself is just a machine or an electronic device.

Fill in the Blanks

1 Program is a set of ....

Ans. instructions

2 The software is categorised as .... and .... software.

Ans. system, application

3 .... and .... are system softwares.

Ans. Operating system, language processor

4 .... is a software that controls and manages the hardware.

Ans. Operating system

5 The software that helps the computer in maintaining its performance is called ....

Ans. utility software

6 A .... is a group of related fields.

Ans. database

7 Payroll system and accounting system are the .... softwares.

Ans. applications

8 Programmers use a variety of .... to communicate instructions to the computer.

Ans. programming languages

True or False

1 We cannot work on computer without software.

Ans. **True** Software is a set of programs, which instructs the computer to do a task. We always need a software to work on the computer system.

2 Hardware is operated by system softwares.

Ans. **True** System softwares tell hardwares how to perform a task.

3 Operating system is an application software.

Ans. **False** It is a system software which acts as an interface between the user and the hardware.

4 Interpreter translates whole program at a time.

Ans. **False** Interpreter is a language processor which translates the whole program line-by-line.

5 Device drivers are the part of application software.

Ans. **False** Device drivers are the part of system software, which is used to make interface between the device and the user or the operating system.

6 The set of programs designed to perform user specific tasks is called application software.

Ans. **True** Application software refers to the programs that perform operations for a specified task of a user.

7 MS-Word and MS-Excel are two application softwares.

Ans. **True** MS-Word and MS-Excel are two application softwares because such type of softwares pertain to specific applications and specific task.

8 Assembly language uses mnemonic codes.

Ans. **True** Assembly language uses mnemonic codes to represent each low level machine operation or code.

9 The third generation of languages are low level languages.

Ans. **False** They are high level languages such as C.

Very Short Answer (VSA) Type Questions

1 What is a computer software?

Ans. Computer software is a collection of programs, procedures and related data that provide the instructions for telling a computer what to do and how to do.

2 What do you mean by system software?

Ans. System software refers to the programs that control internal computer operations and make best use of the hardware devices.

3 What do you mean by an operating system?

Ans. Operating system is a program that acts as an interface between the user and the hardware.

4 Which language processor converts an high level language program into machine language at once?

Ans. Compiler is a language processor which converts whole high level language program into machine language at once which can be understood by the processor.

5 In order to use the printer, an operating system will need a special type of software. This software is known as what?

Ans. In order to use the printer, an operating system will need a device driver software.

6 Define a utility software.

Ans. A utility software is a system software designed to help in the management and tuning of operating systems, computer hardwares and different application softwares.

7 Mention some examples of utility software.

Ans. Data compression utilities, virus protection utilities and disk defragmentation utilities.

8 Describe an application software.

Ans. An application software is designed to help the user to perform specific functions.

9 Why do we use spreadsheets?

Ans. A spreadsheet is specially used to organise data in tables and to analyse the tabulated data in desired manner. It allows you to do a lot of calculations.

10 Name the software used to control redundancy from a collection of large amount of data.

Ans. A database is a collection of integrated data stored together with controlled redundancy to serve one or more applications in an optimal fashion.

11 Name the latest attendance recording devices used in an attendance system.

Ans. Biometrics and Access cards.

12 What do you mean by machine language?

Ans. Machine language is the only language that is understood by the computers. It is a collection of binary digits (0 or 1) or bits that the computer reads and interprets.

Short Answer (SA) Type Questions

1 Name the types of software with examples for each.

Ans. There are two types of software, i.e. System software and Application software. Language processors (interpreters, compilers and assemblers), operating systems etc., are the examples of system software. Whereas, payroll system, accounting software etc., are the examples of an application software.

2 Write a short note on BIOS.

Ans. Refer to text on Page No. 29.

3 Which is more beneficial a compiler or an interpreter and why?

Ans. Compiler is more beneficial than an interpreter for translating a high level language program into machine language program because compilation process of a compiler is nearly 5 to 25 times faster than interpreter.

4 What are the functions of an interpreter?

Ans. Refer to text on Page No. 29.

5 Distinguish between compiler and interpreter.

Ans. Refer to text on Page No. 30.

6 What is general purpose application software? Give some examples of general purpose application software.

Ans. General purpose application softwares are those softwares, which are used for any general function. They allow people to do simple computer tasks.

It is sometimes referred to as GPS. e.g. graphics, multimedia, presentation software, desktop publishing software etc.

7 Why do we use reservation system?

Ans. Refer to text on Page No. 33.

8 What is the difference between machine language and assembly language?

Ans. Differences between machine language and assembly language are as follows

Machine Language	Assembly Language
Machine language uses binary digits (0s and 1s) to write a program.	Assembly language used mnemonic codes to write a program in place of binary digits.
It is not human readable language.	It is more human readable language.
It is directly understood by the computer.	It is not directly understood by the computer.
There is no need of any type of language processor.	Assembler is used to translate assembly language into computer understandable language.

9 What are HLLs? Give example of some HLLs.

Ans. Refer to text on Page No. 34.

Long Answer (LA) Type Questions

1 What is an operating system? Explain its functions with an examples.

Ans. Refer to text on Page No. 29.

2 Describe utility software and also define its types.

Ans. Refer to text on Page No. 30-31.

3 Name at least two softwares that could be used to produce a publication such as brochure or newsletter. Explain each.

Ans. A brochure or newsletter can be produced using
(*i*) Word processor (*ii*) DTP software

A Word processor is a general software, which is used for the processing of textual matter and creation of organised and error less documents. However, there are several Word processors, which offer features and utilities similar to DTP software. So, even they can be used for creating professional publications. A DTP software is meant for creating professional publications. It combines the functions of traditional typesetter and a layout artist to produce documents such as newsletters, brochures, leaflets, magazines etc.

4 Explain Database Management System. What are the features of DBMS?

Ans. Refer to text on Page No. 32.

5 Explain any five specific purpose application softwares.

Ans. Refer to text on Page No. 33.

6 What is an accounting software and HR management system? Also, name the types of accounting software.

Ans. Refer to text on Page No. 33.

7 What are the generations of languages? Explain them.

Ans. Refer to text on Page No. 34.

8. The computer has two parts-hardware and software. Hardware needs to be operated by a set of instructions. These sets of instructions are referred to as software. It is that component of a computer system, which we cannot touch or view physically. It comprises the instructions and data to be processed using the computer hardware. The computer software and hardware complete any task together. The software comprises a set of instructions which on execution deliver the desired outcome. In other words, each software is written for some computational purpose. Some examples of software include operating systems like Ubuntu or Windows 7/10, Word processing tool like LibreOffice or Microsoft Word, video player like VLC Player, photo editors like GIMP and LibreOffice draw. A document or image stored on the hard disk or pen drive is referred to as a soft copy. Once printed, the document or an image is called a hard copy.

(i) Hardware can work only with ....
(a) input (b) control
(c) signals (d) instructions

(ii) The computer software cannot be .... physically.
(a) set (b) touch (c) control (d) digital

(iii) Any task of the computer can be completed by .... and .... together.
(a) input, output (b) mouse, printer
(c) hardware, software (d) All of these

(iv) Which is not an operating system software?
(a) Windows (b) DOS
(c) MS-Word (d) Ubuntu

(v) A document stored on pen drive is called as ....
(a) soft copy (b) copy
(c) data (d) All of these

EXAM PRACTICE

Ans. (i) (*d*) To operate the hardware of a computer it requires some set of instructions to be given.

(ii) (*b*) The software part of the computer is a non-physical part, which cannot be touch or view.

(iii) (*c*) Hardware and software are two parts of the computer and any task on the computer can be completed by only these two together.

(iv) (*c*) Except MS-Word all software comes under the category of OS. MS-Word is a general purpose application software.

(v) (*a*) Any data in the form of a document stored on secondary storage such as pen drive or hard disk is called soft copy.

Application Oriented Questions

1 Software is not only the basic requirement of a computer system, it makes a computer more powerful and useful.
Computer systems divide software into two major classes.

(*i*) What is the meaning of the term software?

(*ii*) Name the two major classes of software.

Ans. (*i*) Software is a set of programs that tells the computer to perform a task.

(*ii*) Computer system divides software into two major categories

(*a*) System software

(*b*) Application software

2 Operating system is an important component of a computer system. Various types of operating systems are available.

(*i*) Operating system belongs to which class of software?

(*ii*) What is the need of an operating system?

(*iii*) Why an operating system is important?

Ans. (*i*) System software.

(*ii*) Operating system provides a software platform on which other programs, called application programs are run.

(*iii*) It acts as an interface between the user and the hardware.

3 Reena got an assignment on the topic Word processing software. Help her to solve the assignment.

(*i*) What is Word processing software?

(*ii*) Which type of software is Word processor?

(*iii*) Give some examples equivalent to type of Word processing software.

(*iv*) Give some examples of Word processing program.

Ans. (*i*) Word processing software is an application software that helps to create text based documents. It also processes paragraphs, pages and entire papers.

(*ii*) General purpose application software.

(*iii*) Electronic spreadsheets, database management systems, desktop publishing software, graphics, multimedia and presentation applications.

(*iv*) Microsoft Word, WordPerfect (Windows only), AppleWorks (Mac only) and OpenOffice.org Writer.

4 Mr. X has recently installed a new operating system on his computer

(*i*) Describe the main functions of an operating system.

(*ii*) Name any two utility programs used by an operating system.

Ans. (*i*) Monitors the performance of the system, enables software to communicate with hardware and application softwares to be loaded; gives prompts and error reports to the users.

(*ii*) Antivirus and compression tool.

5 Below is the list of various types of application softwares:

A. Database
B. Desktop publishing
C. Drawing
D. Word processing
E. Spreadsheet

Which one would be the most suitable to use for each of the following tasks?

(*i*) Rotation of shapes

(*ii*) Typing in text for a novel

(*iii*) Using frames to position text and graphics on a page

(*iv*) Replication of cells

(*v*) Carrying out a complex search on two or more criteria

Ans. (*i*) Drawing (*ii*) Word processing
(*iii*) Desktop publishing (*iv*) Spreadsheet
(*v*) Database

CHAPTER

03

Operating System

Chapter Checklist

- Definitions of an Operating System
- Needs for an Operating System
- User Interface
- Characteristics of Modern Operating System
- Some Popular Operating Systems
- Mobile Operating System
- Kernel
- Device Drivers
- File System

An Operating System (OS) is the core software component of a computer system, that manages the **hardware** and **application programs** (e.g. compiler, linker, DBMS, utility program etc). The OS performs all basic tasks in a computer system, such as controlling and allocating memory, prioritising the processing of instructions, controlling input and output devices, networking facilitating and managing files.

An operating system provides a necessary environment and resource for the execution of the application.

Definitions of an Operating System

A collection of softwares or a series of programs which performs various types of functions in order to manage and organise files.

or

A program that is executed by the processor that frequently rejects the control of processor and start controlling all the functions of computer system.

or

A program, which acts as an interface between the user and the hardware (all computer resources).

or

A first program that is loaded into the computer's main memory, when a computer is switched ON.

Needs for an Operating System

The following points describe the needs for an operating system

- The application programs cannot access the hardware resources directly. Therefore, an OS is required to access and use the hardware resources. In a desktop computer, these resources include processor's memory, disk space etc. While on a cell phone, hardware resources are keypad, screen, address book, phone dialer, battery and network connection.

- It provides a stable and consistent way for applications to deal with the hardware without having to know all the details of the hardware devices. This task is important, when more than one of a particular type of computer is using the operating system.
- An OS prepare the computer for taking instructions from the users. Once it is ready to take commands, it converts commands of the user into the machine code, attaches its own input to the commands and then, gives it to the CPU to execute. When we load an OS into computer, it provides us an environment like Command Line Interface (CLI) or Graphical User Interface (GUI). The OS controls and co-ordinates all the activities of a computer system.

History of Operating System

The first operating system used for real work was GM-NAA I/O, produced in 1956 by General Motors Research division for its IBM 704. Through the 1960s, several major concepts were developed for driving the development of OS. The development of **IBM System/360** produced by a family of mainframe computers for which a single operating system **OS/360** was planned. Another key development was the concept of time-sharing. Time-sharing allowed all the users to have the illusion of having exclusive access to the machine. The multi time-sharing system was the most famous OS developed to take advantage of this concept.

By the 1990s, the micro computer had evolved to the point where, extensive GUI facilities, the robustness and the flexibility of operating systems of large computers became increasingly desirable. Microsoft's response to this change was the development of **Windows NT**, which served as the basis for Microsoft's entire OS line starting in the year 1999. Apple rebuilt their OS on top of a Unix core as **Mac OS X** released in 2001.

User Interface

A user interface is also called 'UI' or 'Interface'. It is a set of commands or menus, through which a user communicates with a system. The user interface, regarded as shell, is the layer that actually interacts with the user.

User interface is one of the most important part of any OS because it determines how easily you can make the program.

Two types of user interface are as follows

CUI

A Character User Interface (CUI) or Command Line Interface (CLI) is a mechanism of interacting with a computer system or software by typing commands to perform specific tasks. Programs with character user interface are generally easier to automate *via* scripting. It only uses text types one after another just as commands used in MS-DOS.

GUI

Graphical User Interface (GUI) is a computer program that enables a user to communicate with a computer through the use of symbols, visual metaphors and pointing devices. It is a program interface that takes advantage of the computer's graphic capability to make program easier to use.

In this interface, commands are given to OS by selecting or clicking on the options, which can be identified with the small figures that appear with them. It is best known for its implementation in Apple products.

The Xerox Alto had an early graphical user interface. The Xerox Alto (and later Xerox Star) was an early personal computer developed at Xerox PARC in 1973. It was the first computer to use the desktop metaphor and mouse-driven graphical user interface. Windows, Ubuntu etc., are GUI based operating systems.

GUIs can be found in hand-held devices such as MP3 players, portable media players, gaming devices etc.

Characteristics of Modern Operating System

Some characteristics of modern operating system are as follows

Microkernel Architecture

Provides a communication facility between the client program and the various services that are also running in user space.

Multi-Threading

It is a process, which can be divided into threads, that can run simultaneously. In other words, it is the ability of an OS to execute different parts of a program called **threads**, simultaneously by more than one user at a time.

Thread

It is a dispatchable unit of work. It includes a processor context program counter, stack pointer and its own data storage for the stack. It executes sequentially and is interruptible. Thread is a light weight process. In other words, it is the smallest sequence of program instructions in execution. Threads are managed by OS scheduler.

Process

It is a collection of one or more threads. Each process has its own address in memory, i.e. each process allocates separate memory area. Switching from one process to another requires some time for saving and loading registers, memory maps, updating lists etc.

Symmetric Multi-Processing

In this processing, stand-alone computers with multiple processors that share the common memory and I/O facilities are connected by a communication bus. All processors can perform the same functions.

Object-Oriented Design

It is used for adding modular extensions to a small kernel. Also, it enables programmers to customise an OS without disrupting system integrity.

Gigo

- WAP is a technical standard for accessing information over a mobile wireless network.
- According to Tanenbaum, "SPOOL" is an acronym for simultaneous peripheral operations on line.
- Palm OS is also known as Garnet OS. It was designed for palm handheld computers.
- First Android OS 'Astro' was released by Google on September 20, 2008.

Check Point 01

1 What is the core software component of a computer system?
2 Name the first operating system used for real work.
3 What is the collection of one or more threads?
(a) Process (b) Multi-thread
(c) Microkernel (d) Multiprocessing

Some Popular Operating Systems

Some popular operating systems are as follows

UNIX The first version of Unix was developed in 1969 by Ken Thompson and Dennis Ritchie at AT & T Bell Laboratories. It is primarily used to a server rather than a workstation and should not be used by anyone who does not understand the system.

APPLE MACINTOSH (Mac OS) The Mac OS was introduced in January, 1984 by Steve Jobs and was initially named as System Software, which was later renamed as Mac OS. Most recent version of OS is based on Unix because it has a good graphical interface.

LINUX The first Linux kernel was released on September 17, 1991 by Linus Torvalds. It is an open source software, means anyone can download it and use it without any fees. Linux is similar to Unix in operations. It is difficult to understand by anyone who does not understand the system and can be difficult to learn.

SOLARIS It is a free UNIX based OS developed by Sun Microsystems. The first version of Sun Microsystems was published in 1993 and coined as SunOS.

BOSS (Bharat Operating System Solutions) BOSS GNU/Linux (or simply BOSS) developed by C-DAC (Centre for Development of Advanced Computing) was initially released in 2007 and derived from Debian for enhancing the use of Free/Open Source Software throughout India. BOSS Linux provides GUI to the user.

WINDOWS It is an operating system, based on GUI, developed by Microsoft. Microsoft first introduced an operating environment named Windows on November 20, 1985 in response to the growing interest in GUIs. Over the years, Microsoft has released various versions of Windows OS, some popular versions are as follows

- **WINDOWS NT** (New Technology) The first version of Windows NT was Windows NT 3.1 released in July, 1993 by Microsoft. It is a processor-independent, multi-processing, multi-user operating system.
- **WINDOWS 95** It was developed on August 24, 1995 by Microsoft. It is an operating system based on consumer oriented application. Although, it can run older Windows and DOS applications. It has essentially removed DOS as a underlying platform.
- **WINDOWS 98** It was released on 1998 by Microsoft. It was produced in two main versions, i.e. the first version was plagued with programming errors but the second edition (which came out later) was much better with many errors resolved.
- **WINDOWS 2000** It was released in February 17, 2000 by Microsoft. A better version of the Windows NT OS, that works well both at home and as a workstation in a business.
- **WINDOWS ME** (Millennium Edition) It was released in September, 2000 by Microsoft. An upgraded version of Windows 98 but it has been historically plagued with programming errors, which may be frustrating for home users. It includes Internet Explorer 5.5, Windows Media Player 7.

- **WINDOWS XP** (eXPerience) It was released on October 25, 2001 by Microsoft. It is an OS produced for personal computers. Two versions of Windows XP are Home edition and Windows XP Professional.
- **WINDOWS VISTA** It was released on January 30, 2007 by Microsoft. It offers an advancement in reliability, security, ease of deployment, performance and manageability over Windows XP.
- **WINDOWS 7** It was released on October 22, 2009 by Microsoft. It is an upgrade of Windows XP and Vista. It does not include some standard applications like Windows Movie Maker, Windows Mail etc. Now-a-days, it is the most commonly used operating system.
- **WINDOWS 8** It introduced major changes to the operating system's platform and user interface to improve its user experience on tablets, where Windows was now competing with Mobile OS, including Android and iOS. Windows 8 was released on October 26, 2012 by Microsoft.
- **WINDOWS 10** It was released on July 29, 2015 by Microsoft. It is a personal computer operating system as a part of the Windows NT family of operating systems.

Mobile Operating System

This OS operates on smartphones, tablets and digital mobile devices. It controls mobile devices and its design supports wireless communication and different types of mobile applications. It has built-in support for mobile multimedia formats.

Some popular mobile operating systems are as follows

Android It is a mobile OS developed by Google on September 23, 2008 which is based on Linux kernel. It is basically designed for touch screen mobile devices like tablets, smartphones etc. Now-a-days, it is most common OS used in mobile phones. The latest version of Android is Oreo 8.0.0 which was released on August 21, 2017.

Symbian It is the OS developed and sold by Symbian Ltd. It was released on June 5, 1997. It is an open source mobile OS designed for smartphones. It has been used by many major handset manufacturers including Motorola, Nokia, Samsung, Sony etc. The latest version of Symbian is Nokia Belle which was released in October, 2012.

iOS It is the popular mobile operating system developed by Apple Incorporation. iOS was introduced on June 29, 2007 when the first iPhone was developed. This operating system is commonly used in Apple iPhone, iPod Touch, iPad etc. The latest version of iOS is iOS 11.0.1, which was released on September 26, 2017.

BlackBerry It is the most secure operating system used in leading smartphones developed by BlackBerry company on January 19, 1999. It also supports WAP 1.2. The latest version of Blackberry is BlackBerry OS 10.3.

Windows Phone Windows Phone (WP) is a mobile operating system developed by Microsoft on October 21, 2010 for smartphones as the replacement successor to Windows mobile. Windows Phone features a new user interface derived from the Microsoft developed "Modern" design language (formely known as "Metro"). The latest version of Windows Phone is Windows Phone 8.1 which was released on June 2, 2015.

Check Point 02

1. Name some popular mobile operating systems.
2. Who developed Unix's first version and when?
3. When was Windows 8 released?
   (a) 2012 (b) 2011
   (c) 2013 (d) 2014

Kernel

Kernel is a computer program that manages input/output requests and translates them into data processing instructions. These instructions are available for CPU and other components of a computer system. It is like heart of operating system and plays a vital role in modern OS.

Kernel handles memory and peripheral devices like keyboards, monitors, printers and speakers. It resides in a high system state other than the normal application software. This system state provides a protected memory space and full access to the system hardware. So, system state and memory space is collectively known as the Kernel space.

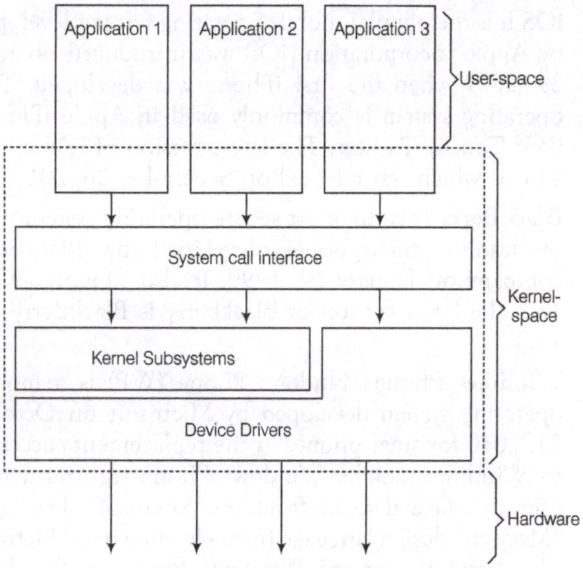

Relationship between Applications, Kernel and Hardware

Kernel controls interrupts. Basically, an interrupt is generated when hardware wants to communicate with the system literally.

Functions of the Kernel

Primary functions of the Kernel are as follows

1. Memory Management

It is one of the most important functions of the Kernel. The Kernel allocates new space whenever a new process gets created and removes old processes from the main memory to create room for new processes.

2. Resource Allocation

The Kernel's primary function is to manage the computer's resources and allow other programs to run and use these resources. These resources are CPU, memory and I/O devices.

3. I/O Device Management

To perform useful functions, processes need access to the peripherals (I/O devices) connected to the computer. These are controlled by the Kernel through device drivers.

A Kernel maintains a list of available I/O devices. A device manager first performs a scan on different hardware buses, such as Peripheral Component Interconnect (PCI) or Universal Serial Bus (USB), to detect installed devices, then searches for the appropriate drivers. The Kernel provides the I/O to allow drivers to physically access their devices through some port or memory location.

4. Inter-process Communication

Kernel provides methods for synchronisation and communication between processes called Inter Process Communication (IPC). There are various approaches of IPC say semaphore, shared memory, message queue, pipe, etc.

5. Scheduling

In a multitasking system, the Kernel will give every program a slice of time and switch from process to process. It will appear to the user as if these processes were being executed simultaneously. The Kernel uses scheduling algorithms to determine which process is running next and how much time it will be given. The scheduling algorithm sets priority among the processes.

6. Process Management

A process defines which memory portions the application can access. The main task of a Kernel is to allow the execution of applications and support them with features such as hardware abstraction.

To run an application, a Kernel first set up an address space for the application, then loads the file containing the application's code into memory, then set up a stack for the program and branches to a given location inside the program, thus finally starting is execution.

7. System Calls and Interrupt Handling

A system call is a mechanism that is used by the application program to request a service from the operating system. System calls include close, open, read, wait and write . To access the services provided by the Kernel we need to invoke the related Kernel functions. Most Kernels provide a C library or an API, which in turn invokes the related Kernel functions. There are few methods by which the respective Kernel function can be invoked using software simulated interrupt or using a gate call or by using a special system call instruction and by using a memory based queue.

8. Security or Protection Management

Kernel also provides protection from faults (error control) and from malicious behaviours (security). One approach toward this can be language based protection system in which the Kernel will only allow code to execute which has been produced by a trusted language compiler.

Types of Kernels

Kernels can be classified into two main categories

1. Monolithic Kernels

Earlier in this type of Kernel architecture, all the basic system services like process and memory management, interrupt handling etc were packed into a single module in Kernel space. This type of architecture led to some serious drawbacks like

- Size of Kernel which was huge
- Poor maintainability, which means bug fixing or addition of new features resulted in recompilation of the whole Kernel which could consume hours.

In a modern day approach to monolithic architecture, the Kernel consists of different modules which can be dynamically loaded and unloaded. This modular approach allows easy extension of OS's capabilities. With this approach, maintainability of Kernel became very easy as only the concerned module needs to be loaded and unloaded every time there is a change or bug fix in a particular module. So, there is no need to bring down and recompile the whole Kernel for a smallest bit of change. Also, stripping of Kernel for various platforms became very easy as we can easily unload the module that we do not want.

2. Micro Kernels

This architecture majorly caters to the problem of ever growing size of Kernel code which we could not control in the monolithic approach. This architecture allows some basic services like device driver management, protocol stack, file system etc, to run in user space. This reduces the Kernel code size and also increases the security and stability of OS as we have the bare minimum code running in Kernel. So, if suppose a basic service like network service crashes due to buffer overflow, then only the networking service's memory would be corrupted, leaving the rest of the system still functional.

In this architecture, all the basic OS services which part of user space are made to run as servers that used by other programs in the system through Inter Process Communication (IPC).

Microkernel servers are essentially programs like any others except that the Kernel grants some of them privileges to interact with parts of physical memory that are otherwise off limits to most programs.

Device Drivers

A device driver is a small piece of software that tells the operating system and other software how to communicate with a piece of hardware.

e.g. printer drivers tell the operating system and by extensions whatever program you have the thing you want to print open in, exactly how to print information on the page.

Sound card drivers are necessary so your operating system knows exactly how to translate the 1's and 0's which comprise that MP3 file into audio signals that the sound card can output to your headphones or speakers. A driver communicates with the device through the computer bus or communicates subsystem to which the hardware connects. When a calling program invokes a routine in the driver, the driver issues commands to the device. Once the device sends data back to the driver, the driver may invoke routines in the original calling program. They usually provide the interrupt handling required for any necessary asynchronous time decedent hardware interface.

Applications of Device Drivers

Because of the diversity of modern hardware and operating systems, drivers operate in many different environments. Drivers may interface with:

- Printers
- Video adapters
- Network cards
- Sound cards
- Local buses of various sorts-in particular, for bus mastering on modern systems
- Low bandwidth I/O buses of various sorts
- Computer storage devices such as hard disk, CD-ROM and floppy disk
- Implementing support for different file systems
- Image scanners
- Digital cameras

Common levels of abstraction for device drivers include

(i) **For Hardware**

- Interfacing directly
- Writing to or reading from a device control register
- Using some higher level interface (e.g. video BIOS)
- Using another lower level device driver (e.g. file system drivers using disk drivers)
- Simulating work with hardware, while doing something entirely different.

(ii) **For Software**

- Allowing the OS direct access to hardware resources
- Implementing only primitives
- Implementing an interface for non-driver software (e.g. TWAIN)
- Implementing a language, sometimes quite high level (e.g. Postscript)

File System

A file is a named collection of related information that is recorded on secondary storage such as magnetic disks, magnetic taps and optical disc. In general, a file is a sequence of bits, bytes, lines or records whose meaning is defined by the files creator and user.

File Structure

A file structure should be according to a required format that the operating system can understand.

A file has various kinds of structure. Some of them can be

- **Simple record structure** with lines of fixed or variables lengths.
- **Complex structure** like formatted document or reloadable load files.
- **No definite structure** like sequence of words and bytes etc.

File Type

File type refers to the ability of the operating system to distinguish different types of file such as text files, source files and binary files etc. Many operating systems support many types of files. Operating system like MS-DOS and Unix have the following types of files:

Ordinary Files

- These are the files that contain user information.
- These may have text, databases or executable program.
- The user can apply various operations on such files like add, modify, delete or even remove the entire file.

Directory Files

- These files contain list of file names and other information related to these files.

Special Files

- These files are also known as device files.
- These files represent physical devices like disks, terminals, printers, networks, tape drive etc.

These files are of two types

- **Character special files** Data is handled character by character as in case of terminals or printers.
- **Block special files** Data is handled in blocks as in case of disks and tapes.

File Access Mechanisms

File access mechanism refers to the manner in which the records of a file may be accessed. There are several ways to access files-

1. Sequential Access

A sequential access is that in which the records are accessed in some sequence. The information in the file is processed in order, one record after the other. This access method is the most primitive one.

2. Direct/Random Access

Random access file organisation provides accessing the records directly. Each record has its own address on the file with the help of which it can be directly accessed for reading or writing. The records need not be in any sequence within the file and they need not be in adjacent locations on the storage medium.

3. Indexed Sequential Access

This mechanism is built up on base of sequential access. An index is created for each file which contains pointers to various blocks. Index is searched sequentially and its pointer is used to access the file directly.

Space Allocation

Files are allocated disk spaces by operating system. Operating systems deploy following three main ways to allocate disk space to files

1. Contiguous Allocation

- Each file occupies a contiguous address space on disk.
- Assigned disk address is in linear order.
- Easy to implement.
- External fragmentation is a major issue with this type of allocation technique.

2. Linked Allocation

- Each file carries a list of links to disk blocks.
- Directory contains link/pointer to first block of a file.
- No external fragmentation.
- Effectively used in sequential access file.
- Inefficient in case of direct access file.

3. Indexed Allocation

- Provides solutions to problems of contiguous and linked allocation.
- A index block is created having all pointers to files.
- Each file has its own index which stores the addresses of disk space occupied by the file.

Check Point 03

1. What is the primary function of Kernel?
2. Which provides the interrupt handling required for necessary asynchronous time?
3. What type of files handle the data in blocks?

SUMMARY

- An operating system or OS is a software program that enables the computer hardware to communicate and operate with the computer software.
- User interface is one of the most important parts of any program that actually interacts with the user.
- GUI is best known for its implementation in Apple products.
- One deficiency of Apple Macintosh is that it can only be run on Apple products.
- Windows 7 does not include some standard applications such as Windows Mail, Windows Movie Maker etc.
- BlackBerry operating system also supports WAP 1.2.
- Kernel is a computer program that is the core of a computer's operating system.
- A device driver is a program that controls a particular type of device that is attached to your computer.
- File system is the way in which files are named and where they are placed logically for storage and retrieval.

Exam Practice

Multiple Choice Questions

1 An operating system manages
(a) memory (b) processor
(c) disk and I/O devices (d) All of these

Ans. (*d*) An operating system manages disk and I/O devices as it is responsible for input from keyboard, mouse etc. It also manages the computer memory, so that each process can run most effectively.

2 An operating system of a computer serves as a software interface between the user and the
(a) hardware (b) peripheral
(c) memory (d) screen

Ans. (*a*) An operating system of a computer serves as a software interface between the user and the hardware.

3 Suppose you have bought all hardware components required for assembling a computer. After assembling the computer system, which will be the very first software to be installed?
(a) Hardware driver
(b) Operating system
(c) Antivirus software
(d) Word processing software

Ans. (*b*) Operating system will be the very first software to be installed after assembling the computer system.

4 A thread is a .... process, which is managed by OS scheduler.
(a) heavy weight (b) multiprocess
(c) inter thread (d) light weight

Ans. (*d*) A thread is a light weight process because it executes sequentially.

5 Which of the following is like a heart of operating system?
(a) Kernel (b) Thread
(c) Process (d) Window

Ans. (*a*) Kernel is like a heart of operating system which plays a vital role in modern OS.

6 Which of the following is not an OS?
(a) Android
(b) Windows
(c) Apple
(d) BOSS

Ans. (*c*) Apple is not an OS while it is the name of a company.

7 Which of the following is/are mobile operating system?
(a) Android (b) Symbian
(c) Both (a) and (b) (d) None of these

Ans. (*c*) Both Android and Symbian are two different mobile operating systems.

8 Oreo 8.0.0 is the version of
(a) Android (b) Symbian
(c) iOS (d) BlackBerry

Ans. (*a*) Oreo 8.0.0 is the version of Android.

9 Identify the option , which is not a function of Kernel in operating system?
(a) Resource allocation (b) Memory management
(c) Process management (d) Programming

Ans. (*b*) Among given options, programming is not a function of Kernel in operating system.

10 .... reduces the Kernel code size and increases the security.
(a) Micro Kernel (b) Monolithic Kernel
(c) Both (a) and (b) (d) None of these

Ans. (*a*) Micro Kernel reduces the Kernel code size and also increases the security and stability of an operating system.

11 Which of the following communicates with the device through the computer bus?
(a) File system (b) Device driver
(c) Kernel (d) Peripheral

Ans. (*b*) A device driver is a small piece of software which communicates with the device through the computer bus.

12 A/An .... is a sequence of bytes organised into blocks.
(a) Object file (b) Source file
(c) Text file (d) Binary file

Ans. (*a*) An object file is a sequence of bytes organised into blocks that are understandable by the machine.

13 Which of the following is/are types of special files?
(a) Character special file (b) Block special file
(c) Both (a) and (b) (d) None of these

Ans. (*c*) Special files are of two types as Character special file and Block special file.

Fill in the Blanks

1 .... is a program that mediates between application programs and hardwares.

Ans. Operating system

2 The .... is regarded as shell, is the layer that actually interacts with the user.

Ans. user interface

3 .... is a program interface that enables a user to communicate with computer through graphics or symbols.

Ans. GUI (Graphical User Interface)

4 Symbian is the operating system developed and sold by ....

Ans. Symbian Ltd

5 The .... is a computer program that is the core of a computer's operating system.

Ans. Kernel

6 The Kernel uses .... algorithm to determine which process is running next.

Ans. scheduling

7 In .... Kernel architecture, all the basic system services were packed into a single module.

Ans. Monolithic

8 Printer drivers tell the .... , how to print information on the page.

Ans. operating system

9 .... refers to the ability of the operating system to distinguish different types of file.

Ans. File type

10 In .... allocation, no external fragmentation.

Ans. linked

True or False

1 Operating system refers to the core software components of a computer system that manages internal operations and hardware.

Ans. **True** Operating system is a set of programs that controls internal computer operations and makes best use of hardware.

2 CPU time, memory space are the examples of system resources.

Ans. **True** System resources include many resources such as CPU time, memory space, I/O address, DMA channel to alert the need of hardware and software.

3 Windows is a graphical user interface.

Ans. **True** In Windows, we can provide commands by clicking on the icons using mouse.

4 System state and memory space is collectively known as the Kernel interrupt.

Ans. **False** System state and memory space is collectively known as the Kernel space.

5 Kernel provides methods for synchronization and communication.

Ans. **True** Kernel provides methods for synchronization and communication between processes called Inter Process Communication (IPC).

6 Random access file organisation provides accessing the records in some sequence.

Ans. **False** Random/Direct access file organisation provides accessing the records directly not in some sequence.

7 Indexed allocation provides solutions to problems of contiguous allocation.

Ans. **True** Indexed allocation provides solutions to problems of contiguous and linked allocation.

Very Short Answer (VSA) Type Questions

1 What is an operating system?

Ans. An operating system is a system software that acts as an interface between the user and the hardware resources. It provides a variety of services to the computer.

2 Which is the first program that loads in a memory?

Ans. Operating system is the first program that loads in computer's main memory, when a computer is switched ON.

3 What is the light weight process?

Ans. Thread is a light weight process. It is the smallest sequence of program instructions in execution that can be managed independently by an operating system scheduler.

4 Is Windows NT a family of an operating system(s)?

Ans. Yes, it is a family of an operating system produced by Microsoft in July 1993. NT stands for New Technology.

5 Name any two commonly used operating system.

Ans. Windows 7 and Windows XP.

6 Who released the first Android OS 'Astro'?

Ans. The first Android OS 'Astro' was released by Google on September 20, 2008.

7 What do you mean by Inter Process Communication?

Ans. Kernel provides methods for synchronization and communication between processes called Inter Process Communication (IPC).

8 Earlier Monolithic Kernel's architecture led some serious drawbacks. Name them.

Ans. (1) Size of Kernel (2) Poor maintainability

9 Write two common level of abstraction for device driver include for hardware.

Ans. (i) Interfacing directly

(ii) Using another lower level device driver

10 Explain sequential access as a file access mechanism in brief.

Ans. A sequential access is that in which the records are accessed in some sequence, i.e. the information in file is processed in order.

Short Answer (SA) Type Questions

1 State any two functions of Kernel operating system.

Ans. Refer to text on Page No. 44.

2 Differentiate between CUI and GUI.

Ans. Differences between CUI and GUI are as follows

CUI	*GUI*
CUI stands for Character User Interface.	GUI stands for Graphical User Interface.
In CUI, user interacts with applications by making use of commands.	In GUI, user interacts with applications by making use of graphics.
Only one task can run at a time.	More than one task can run simultaneously.
A CUI will require less computer resources.	A GUI will require a lot of more system resources because each element that needs to be loaded such as icons, fonts etc.
e.g. MS-DOS	e.g. Windows

3 What do you mean by Linux?

Ans. Linux is an open source operating system, means anyone can download it and use it without any fees.

It is similar to Unix in its working and difficult to understand. It is an OS that controls your computer system.

4 Which OS operates on smartphones and explain any one type of OS?

Ans. Mobile OS is the type of OS, that operates on smartphones, tablets, PDAs or other digital mobile devices. Several types of mobile operating systems available in market are Android, BlackBerry, iOS, Windows Phone etc.

Android is a Mobile OS which is based on Linux kernel and primarily designed for touch screen mobile devices. It provides access to a wide range of useful libraries and tools that can be used to build rich applications. The latest version of Android operating system is Oreo 8.0.0.

5 Kernel is the central module of operating system. Explain.

Ans. Kernel is like heart of an operating system which plays a vital role in modern OS. Kernel is a program that manages I/O requests and translates them into data processing instructions for CPU and other components. It is a part of the OS that loads first and it remains in the main memory.

6 Differentiate between Monolithic Kernel and Micro Kernel.

Ans. Differences between Monolithic Kernel and Micro Kernel are as follows

Monolithic Kernel	***Micro Kernel***
In Monolithic Kernel, both user services and Kernel services are kept in the same address space.	In Micro Kernel, both user services and Kernel services are kept in separate address space.
The Monolithic Kernel is hard to extend.	The Micro Kernel is easily extendible.
To write a monolithic Kernel, less code is required.	To write a Micro Kernel, more code is required.

7 What is file structure?

Ans. Refer to text Page No. 46.

Long Answer (LA) Type Questions

1 Which is used to interface between the user and the hardware?

Ans. An operating system is a system software that acts as an interface between the user and the hardware resources. It controls and co-ordinates the hardware used by various application programs. OS acts as a resource allocator and manager. Since, there are many possible conflicting requests for resources, the OS must decide which requests are allocated resources to operate the computer system efficiently and fairly. An OS is a control program, which controls the user programs to prevent errors and improper use by the computer. It is especially concerned with the operation and control of I/O devices.

Main functions of an OS are as follows

(*i*) Processor management (*ii*) Memory management
(*iii*) File management (*iv*) Device management

2 Explain some of the characteristics of modern operating system.

Ans. Refer to text on Page No. 41-42.

3 Describe a device driver.

Ans. A device driver is a program routine that links a peripheral device to an operating system of a computer. It is essentially a software program that allows a user to employ a device, such as printer, monitor or mouse. It is written by programmers who comprehend the detailed knowledge of the device's command language and characteristics and contains the specific machine language necessary to perform the functions requested by the application . When a new hardware device is added to the computer, such as a CD-ROM drive, a printer or a sound card, its driver must be installed in order to run it.

The driver is the link between the operating system and the peripheral device. If the peripheral device is changed, or if a bug is found in the driver, the driver must also be changed.

To encapsulate the details and unique features of different devices, the Kernel of an operating system is set up to use device driver modules. The device drivers present a uniform device-access interface to the I/O sub system. Each of the different types of I/O devices is accessed through a standardised set of functions-an interface.

A device driver sets the Direct Memory Access (DMA) control registers to use appropriate source and destination addresses and transfer length. The DMA controller is then instructed to begin the I/O operation.

4 What is file access mechanism? Also, explain the ways to access file.

Ans. Refer to text Page No. 46.

5 Operating System (OS) is a program that acts as an interface between the user and the hardware. It is responsible to controls and co-ordinates all other components of the computer. It activates all devices and make them ready for work. It also performs all various functions to make all activities perfect and on time. The main functions of the OS includes

- It recognises input from keyboard and sends output to the display screen and make sure all the connected devices should work properly, called as device management.
- It makes sure that the programs running simultaneously do not interfere with each other, called as process management, this is also called as mutual exclusion .
- OS also responsible for security, ensuring that unauthorised users cannot access the

system, etc . Operating System is of two types- Single user and multi-user. Examples of single user OS are – MS-DOS, Windows 95, etc. Some examples of multi-user OS are – Linux, Ubuntu, etc.

(i) Operating system activates .... and make them ready.
(a) software (b) system
(c) devices (d) buses

(ii) Which is a single user operating system?
(a) Linux (b) Redhat
(c) DOS (d) CentOS

(iii) Choose which is not a function of operating system?
(a) Device management
(b) Process management
(c) Employee management
(d) Memory management

(iv) As per the number of users the OS can be of .... types.
(a) one (b) two
(c) three (d) four

(v) .... is a function of OS in which OS recognise input from keyboard and sends output to the display screen and make sure all the connected devices are working properly.
(a) Process management
(b) Memory management
(c) Device management
(d) Employee management

Ans. (i) (*c*) It is a responsibility of OS to activate all the devices after power ON.
(ii) (*c*) Disk Operating System (DOS) is a first single user operating system.
(iii) (*c*) OS is a system software and its main functions are process management, device management and memory management. Employee management is an application program.
(iv) (*b*) As per number of users OS is of two types – Single user and Multi-user.
(v) (*c*) OS recognise input from keyboard and sends output to the display screen and make sure all the connected devices should work properly, called as device management.

6. Mobile applications which are popularly known as mobile apps, are software programs developed for mobile devices such as smartphones and tablets.
Using these apps the mobile devices becomes miniature powerhouses for completion of various function and fun. Mobile phones generally come preloaded with various mobile apps provided free by the manufacturers or the mobile service providers. But there are various apps which are available only through device specific app stores. We can categorised mobile apps in six categories– Lifestyle apps (covers dating, food, fitness, etc.), Social media apps (facebook, twitter, etc.), Utility apps (reminder, weather, calendar, calculator, etc.), Gaming apps, Productivity apps and News apps. A mobile app is always has a smaller scope in comparison to the websites, means with less functionality.

(i) Mobile apps are .... programs developed for mobile devices.
(a) software (b) hardware
(c) device (d) memory

(ii) Mobile games apps if installed in mobile phone they make mobiles .... of fun.
(a) versatile (b) easy
(c) handy (d) powerhouse

(iii) Some mobile apps comes with device, but there are various apps which are available only through device ....
(a) company (b) user
(c) specific app stores (d) app stores

(iv) There are .... categories of mobile apps.
(a) two (b) four
(c) six (d) five

(v) Mobile apps has .... functionality in comparison to the websites.
(a) more (b) less
(c) maximum (d) min

Ans. (i) (*a*) Mobile apps are software programs specially developed for mobile devices only.
(ii) (*d*) Using these apps the mobile devices becomes miniature powerhouses for completion of various function and fun.
(iii) (*c*) Some mobile apps comes with device, but there are various apps which are available only through device specific app stores. Mobile phones generally come preloaded with various mobile apps provided free by the manufacturers or the mobile service providers.
(iv) (*c*) There are six types of mobile apps- Lifestyle apps, Social media apps, Utility apps, Gaming apps, Productivity apps and News apps.
(v) (*b*) Mobile apps are very precise. These apps has less functionality in comparison to the main websites, so that it can consume less resource and battery.

Application Oriented Questions

1 Suchi has recently installed a new operating system on her computer.

(*i*) Describe the main function of an operating system.

(*ii*) What does command-driven user interface mean?

Ans. (*i*) Monitors the performance of the system, enables software to communicate with hardware, enables applications, software to be loaded; gives prompts and error reports to the users.

(*ii*) Command-driven user interface means CUI, by which a user gives instructions *via* typing command onto the computer.

2 Some features of a specific operating system are given below:

- Free/Open source
- Virus free
- Stable, long running operating system
- Multiple work space

(*i*) Which operating system supports these features?

(*ii*) What is the meaning of multiple workspace?

Ans. (*i*) Linux

(*ii*) With Linux, you get four desktop screens known as workspace.

3 The job of an operating system is to maintain a balance between the CPU and I/O devices in the sense that it has to keep the CPU busy. How is it achieved?

Ans. It is achieved through overlapped processing.

4 The operating system of computers has progressed from a command-driven system to a Graphical User Interface (GUI). Give the reason behind this.

Ans. A GUI allows more information to be communicated to the user through the icons, pictures etc. Icons can make it easier for a user to know what a computer is going to do after providing a command or instruction.

5 Now-a-days, many OS are available, name one Indian OS available free throughout India.

Ans. BOSS is an Indian OS. It is developed by C-DAC derived from Debian for enhancing the use of Free/Open source software throughout India.

CHAPTER

04

Communication Technology

Chapter Checklist

- Network
- Computer Network
- Communication Channels
- Networking Device: MODEM
- Network Protocols
- The Biggest Computer Network: Internet
- Social Networking
- Chat and Instant Messaging
- Mobile Applications
- Cloud Computing

Communication refers "to communicate", i.e. communication held between two (or more) persons or two (or more) systems. Technology has made it easier for people to communicate in a faster, efficient and cost saving means through the introduction of the communication channels. Communication technology involves the hardware equipment, organisation structures and social values by which individuals collect, process and exchange information with other individuals. Using computer for communication, we can transfer information in the form of text, audio or video at any distance just in few seconds or minutes at a very cheap cost. However, for this communication, we need to establish connection among the computers involved in communication which is called a **network.**

Network

A network can be defined as a group of devices connected to each other, i.e. a network allows the exchange data through connected devices. Thus, a network is a series of nodes interconnected by communication paths. Network can interconnected with other networks and also contain subnetworks.

Networking is a process of exchanging the information and ideas among individuals or groups that share a common interest, i.e. the process of creating a network is called networking. The need for networking is mainly to break the barriers of distance, time and cost. Similarly, interconnecting computers, results in a form of networks of computers.

Computer Network

It is a group of computers connected to each other by a link called **communication channel.** A computer network is formed with the intention of sharing files, resources (e.g. printers, hard disks etc.) and softwares (e.g. Microsoft Word). The best computer network is the Internet.

Needs for Computer Network

When computers were first developed, they are mainly intended for a person to work on their own machine with time, the need to different computer arise in order to exchange information and data among them. Thus, the first computer network was created. More needs are as follows

File and Data Sharing

At a time, file-sharing consisted mostly of saving documents to floppy disks that could be physically transferred to other computers by hand. With networking, files can be shared instantaneously across the network, whether with one user or with hundred users. e.g. employees across departments can collaborate on documents, exchange background material etc.

Resource Sharing

Computer networking also allows the sharing of network resources, such as printers, scanners, dedicated servers, backup systems, input devices and Internet connections. By sharing resources, unique equipment like scanners, printers etc., can be made available to all network users simultaneously without being relocated, eliminating the need for expensive redundancies.

Data Protection and Redundancy

Computer networking allows users to distribute copies of important information across multiple locations, ensuring essential information is not lost with the failure of any one computer in the network. By utilising central backup systems both on-site and off-site, unique documents and data can be gathered automatically from every computer in the network and securely backed up in case of physical computer damage or accidental deletion.

Ease of Administration

Instead of individually upgrading each computer in an organisation, a network administrator can initiate an upgrade from a server and automatically duplicate the upgrade throughout the network. Simultaneously, allowing everyone in the company to maintain uniform software, resources and procedures.

User Communication

Computer networking also allows organisations to maintain complex communication systems.

It also allows users to communicate using E-mail, newsgroups, video conferencing etc.

Distributed Computing Power

In computer networks, we can distribute tasks across multiple computers throughout the network, by breaking complex problems into hundreds or thousands of smaller operations, which are then parceled out to individual computers.

Each computer in the network performs its operations on its own portion of the larger problem and return its result. Then, all these results are gathered in such a form that impact as the solution of the complex problem and finally are used for the further task.

Network Gaming

A lot of network games are available, which allow multi-users to play from different locations. It is a type of online game, i.e. played through social networks.

Components of a Computer Network

Computers in a network can be linked in two ways as follows

(*i*) They can be connected directly *via* cable. In this case, computer network has three components, i.e. sender, communication channel and receiver.

Basic components of a network are as follows:

(*a*) **Sender** The person who sends a message to the other person.

(*b*) **Communication channel** It is the medium, which carries the message sent by the sender and takes it to receiver.

(*c*) **Receiver** The person for whom the message was sent by the sender.

(*ii*) They can be connected using telephone cables. In this case, a data communication device is called **MODEM**. It is required at sender and receiver ends, which we will discuss later.

The following diagram shows the placement of various components within a network:

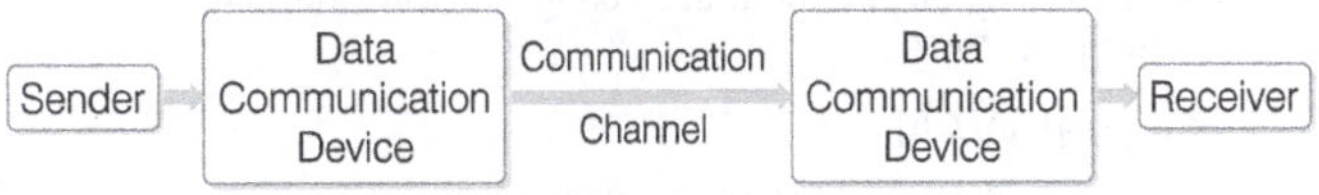

Placement of network components

Hence, in this case, there are five components of a computer network namely, sender, data communication device at sender's site, communication channel, data communication device at receiver's site and receiver.

Types of Computer Network

Networks can be classified on the basis of the geographical area such as LAN, MAN and WAN.

1. Local Area Network (LAN)

A local area network is a computer network covering a small geographical area like a home, office or small group of buildings such as within a school. It is suitable for small sites.

Computers connected to a LAN can share information and peripheral equipments. LAN are widely used to allow resources to be shared between personal computers or workstations. The data rates for LAN ranges from 4 to 16 Mbps with the maximum of 100 Mbps.

2. Metropolitan Area Network (MAN)

A metropolitan area network is a large computer network that usually spans a city or a large campus. A MAN usually interconnects a number of local area networks. So that, resources can be shared LAN to LAN as well as device to device. A MAN can be wholly owned and operated by a private company.

3. Wide Area Network (WAN)

A wide Area Network is a computer network that covers a broad area such as any network whose communication links across metropolitan, regional, national or international boundaries.

WANs are used to connect LANs and other types of network together, so that users and computers in one location can communicate with users and computers in other locations. Mainly WAN is used by business, organisation, governments or by individuals. The biggest example of WAN is Internet.

Enterprise WAN

The computer resources of a single organisation that are located at great distances are connected with the help of enterprise WAN.

Global WAN

The networks of several corporations and organisations are connected with global WAN.

Differences between LAN, MAN and WAN

Basis	LAN	MAN	WAN
Geographical Area	Generally within a building	Within a city	Across the continents
Distance	Upto 5 km	Upto 160 km	Unlimited
Cost	Less expensive	More than LAN but less than WAN	More than MAN
Ownership	Private	Private or Public	Shared across the world
Example	Network within school	Cable TV network within a city	Internet

Personal Area Network (PAN)

PAN is a computer network used for communication among computer and different information technological devices close to one person. Some examples of devices that are used in a PAN are personal computers, printers, fax machines, telephones, PDAs, scanners and even video game consoles. A PAN may include wired and wireless devices. The reach of a PAN typically extends to 10 m. A wired PAN is usually constructed with USB and Firewire connections while technologies such as bluetooth and infrared communication typically form a wireless PAN.

Check Point 01

1 Niharika is a teacher in a school. She sends a leave message to school's principal. Find out the sender and receiver in this example.

2 The CEO of a small organisation is thinking about installing a network so that different departments can share various things. What type of network would be set-up?

(a) LAN (b) MAN

(c) WAN (d) PAN

Communication Channels

Communication channel or transmission media is the link between two computers in which data is transferred between them. Thus, transmission media is a pathway that carries the information from sender to receiver. These are categorised into two types

(*i*) Wired or Guided media

(*ii*) Wireless or Unguided media

Guided media are generally used for establishing LAN and MAN while unguided media are used for WAN.

Wired or Guided Media

In this type of communication channel, as the name suggests, wires or cables are used for connecting two or more computers to transmit data.

It is also called guided media because of the use of cables, signals are guided through a specific path. Since, data signals are bounded, it is also called **bounded media.**

Various types of guided media are as follows

1. Twisted Pair Cable

This is the most common type of communication channel. It consists of two insulated wires twisted around each other and uses copper as a conductor.

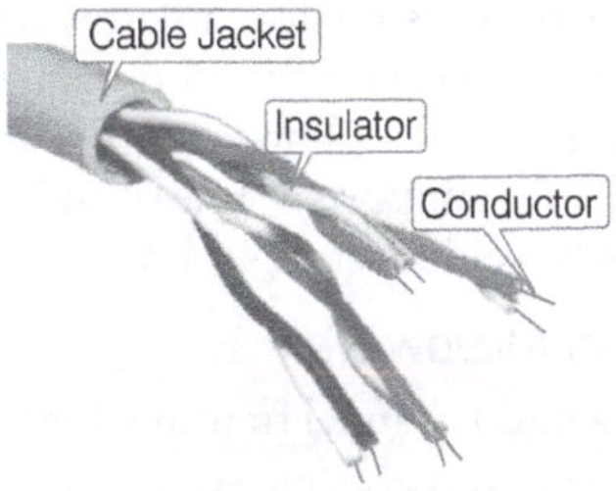

Twisted pair cable

This property of twisted pair cable provides protection against crosstalk and noise.

There are two types of twisted pair cables as follows

(*i*) **Shielded Twisted Pair** (STP) **Cable** This version of twisted pair was created by IBM. It consists of a metal shield covering each pair of insulated wires.

(*ii*) **Unshielded Twisted Pair** (UTP) **Cable** It is the copper media, inherited from telephony, which is being used for increasing higher data rates. It is used in ethernet networks and in telephone systems.

Advantages of Twisted Pair Cable

- It has very light weight.
- Its cost is very low.
- It is easy to install and maintain.
- It supports analog as well as digital transmission.
- It is physically flexible.

Disadvantages of Twisted Pair Cable

- Because of high attenuation, signals cannot be transported over a long distance without using repeaters.
- Data rates supported are 1 Mbps to 10 Mbps.
- Its low bandwidth capabilities make it unsuitable for broadband applications.
- Not a secure medium, it can be easily tapped.

2. Co-axial Cable

It contains two conductors that are parallel to each other, i.e. first is the **inner conductor** or **core conductor** made of solid copper and the second is the **outer conductor**, which serves as a shield against noise. An insulating plastic is placed between the two conductors and this whole setup is covered with a plastic jacket.

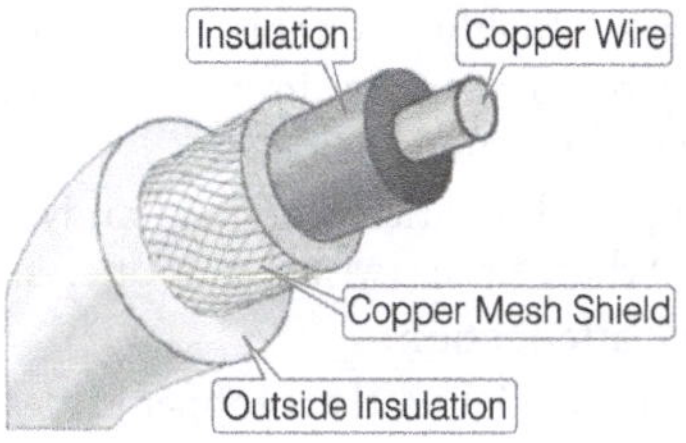

Co-axial cable

Advantages of Co-axial Cable

- Transmission quality of co-axial cable is better than twisted pair cable. It can transmit several channels simultaneously, so these channels are used in cable TV network.
- It can be used for broadband transmission.
- It offers higher bandwidth upto 450 Mbps.

Disadvantages of Co-axial Cable

- More costly than twisted pair cable.
- These are not compatible with twisted pair cable.
- It is difficult to install.
- Failure of the single cable results to fail the entire network.

3. Optical Fibre

These are similar to co-axial cable. It consists of thin strands made up of glass or glass like material, which are capable of carrying light signals from a source at one end to another end.

There are three main parts in optical fibre

(*i*) **Core** It is the section through which the data travels in the form of light. Typically, core has a diameter of 62.5 microns.

(*ii*) **Cladding** It is the covering part of core. Its function is to reflect back the light into the core, as it is a denser medium. Typically, cladding has a diameter of 125 microns.

(*iii*) **Protective Coating** It is the outer cover of cladding for the protection of optical fibre from damage and moisture. It is also called **jacket** or **sheath.** Typically, coating has a diameter of 250 microns.

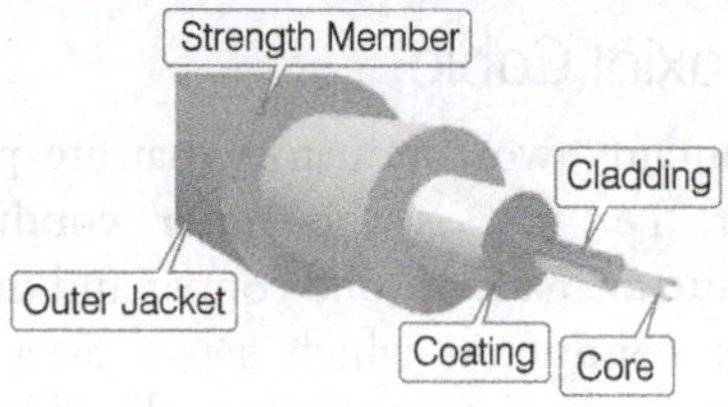

Optical fibre

Advantages of Optical Fibre

- These are highly suitable for harsh industrial environment. These are immune to noise caused by electrical and magnetic fields.
- It can support dramatically higher bandwidths (and hence data rates) than either twisted pair or co-axial cable.
- Less signal attenuation.
- These are much lighter than copper cables.

Disadvantages of Optical Fibre

- These are very difficult to install and maintain.
- They require more protection around the cable than copper cables.
- Propagation of light is uni-directional. For bi-directional communication, two fibres are needed. These are relatively more expensive than other guided media.

4. Ethernet Cable

An ethernet cable is one of the most popular form of network cables used on wired networks. It connects devices on LAN such as PCs, routers and switches. A crossover cable is a special type of ethernet cable specially designed for connecting two computers to each other. By contrast, most ethernet cables are designed to connect one computer to a router or a switch.

A single ethernet cable can extend only limited distances due to their electrical transmission characteristics. RJ-45 is the most commonly used ethernet cable.

Advantages of Ethernet Cable

- It gives fast, secured, reliable transmission across them and external disturbances are very less.
- You can transfer any large data between two or more PC's which are locally connected through ethernet.
- These are robust to noise, thus external disturbances are very less.

Disadvantages of Ethernet Cable

- As the load on ethernet increases, number of collision increases, therefore efficiency decreases.
- It offers non-deterministic service, so it is not suitable for real-time application.
- Higher costs for provisioning in existing building.

Wireless or Unguided Media

This type of communication channel uses waves to transfer data, i.e. no cables are needed to guide the signals. Hence, this is called unguided media. In this, signals are not bounded to any cabling system, therefore, this is also called **unbounded media.**

These can be categorised as follows

1. Long Distance Wireless Media

It supports communication over long distances, i.e. upto thousands of kilometres.

Long distance wireless media are as follows

i. Microwave

In this type of transmission, microwaves are used as an alternative of co-axial cable to transmit data over long distances. It is also known as 802.16. Microwave transmission supports line-of-sight transmission, i.e. signals travel in a straight line.

Advantages of Microwave

- It provides multi-channel transmissions.
- Communication is possible even in difficult terrains.
- Requires fewer amplifiers and repeaters.

Disadvantages of Microwave

- Insecure communication, as the tapping of microwave is easy.
- It is affected by the weather conditions such as rain, thunder, storm etc.
- Cost of maintenance, implementation and design is high.

ii. Radiowave

When two computers communicate by using radio frequencies, then such type of communication is known as radiowave transmission. Radiowaves are omni-directional, i.e. they travel in all directions. It can be classified by frequency and wavelength. When the frequency is higher than 3GHz, it is named as microwave.

Advantages of Radiowave

- They provide enhanced audio volume and clarity.
- They improve accuracy and allow data transmission over long distances. It is cheaper technology.

Disadvantages of Radiowave

- Physical interrupt such as mountains and buildings can prevent or interfere with transmission.
- Any correctly tuned receiver within the range can pick the radiowave signals.
- It is not secured communication medium.

iii. Satellite

Satellites are an essential part of telecommunications systems. They carry a large amount of data in addition to TV signals. When the data is transmitted using satellite then it is said to be satellite communication. A satellite communication consists of an earth station and a satellite at a stationary orbit, which is about 22300 miles above the earth's surface.

A satellite communication is a space station that receives microwave signals from an earth-based station, amplifies the signals and broadcasts the signals back over a wide area to any number of earth-based stations.

Advantages of Satellite

- It covers a very vast area.
- The wired communication is almost impossible and too costly to use across the continents, whereas the satellite communication proves to be the best.
- It is very useful in television transmission.
- Higher bandwidths are available for use.

Disadvantages of Satellite

- Launching satellite into orbit is costly.
- There is atmospheric loss of transmitted signals.
- Interference and propagation delay.

2. Short Distance Wireless Media

It supports communication over a small distance, generally few miles to a few kilometres. The following are the types covered under short distance wireless media:

i. Infrared

This type of wireless media uses infrared light for the transmission of data. Infrared light lies between the visible and microwave portions of the electromagnetic spectrum and is not visible to the human eyes.

Infrared is used for indoor wireless LANs and also use line-of-sight propagation. It cannot pass through solid objects like walls and offers large bandwidth for use.

We cannot use infrared waves outside a building because the sun's rays contain infrared waves that can interfere with the communication.

Advantages of Infrared

- It consumes less power.
- Circuitry cost is less.
- It includes simple circuitry.
- It can be activated with almost any device.

Disadvantages of Infrared

- Line-of-sight is needed for communication.
- Can be blocked by common materials like walls, people, plants etc. This can be used only in enclosed rooms.

ii. Bluetooth

It is a simple, secure and universal wireless communication technology. It refers to a wireless technology that creates small wireless networks, called Personal Area Network (PAN) between PCs and peripheral devices.

The bluetooth wireless technology enables you to establish a wireless communication between any two bluetooth devices, such as mobile phones, laptops, cameras or modem stations without any cables. The data transfer rate over the bluetooth varies from 723 Kbps to 1 Mbps in a short range. The standard specification mandates a minimum range of 100 m (328 feet).

Advantages of Bluetooth

- It can share data without any wire.
- It consumes low power and low processing.
- It is free to use if the device is bluetooth enabled.
- Connecting two different devices using bluetooth is very convenient.

Disadvantages of Bluetooth

- Only short range communication is possible.
- Connection can be lost under certain conditions.
- It can be easily hacked.

iii. Laser

Laser communication is an emerging area of wireless communication system. Due to low noise ratio, it is one of the well suited communication medium for exchange of information. In laser communication, the transmitter and receiver require line-of-sight conditions and it has the benefit of eliminating the need for broadcast rights and buried cables. It is uni-directional.

Laser are wireless connections through the atmosphere. Laser system works similar to fibre optic links, except the beam is transmitted through free space.

Advantages of Laser

- It allows very fast communication between two or more devices than other mode of communications.
- It can provide speed more than 1 Gbps.
- A tiny light detector may allow for superfast broadband communication over interplanetary distances.

Disadvantages of Laser

- It is uni-directional.
- It can be adversely affected by bad weather.
- This can be reduced by multiple number of transmitters.

iv. Wi-Fi

Wi-Fi stands for Wireless Fidelity, has a range of about 100 m and allows for faster rate between 10-54 Mbps. Wi-Fi services have been introduced for providing high speed Internet access at convenient public locations such as Airports, Universities etc.

Wi-Fi is a another name for wireless LAN or WLAN. Home and business networks (private) and public hotspots use it to connect computers and other wireless devices to each other with Internet. Computers and other devices connect to a Wi-Fi network *via* a wireless router or access point. For Wi-Fi to work, we need:

Wi-Fi network

- A broadband Internet connection
- A wireless router
- A laptop or PC having wireless Internet card or external wireless adapter.

Advantages of Wi-Fi

- It can be used while moving within the signal range.
- Network can be created where you cannot lay cable network. It is a wireless connection that can merge together multiple devices.

Disadvantages of Wi-Fi

- It is more costly than wired network.
- Radiation generated by Wi-Fi can effect human health.
- Power consumption is fairly high.

Wi-Fi Hotspot

A hotspot is a site that offers Internet access over a WLAN through the use of a router connected to a link to an Internet service provider. Hotspot may be found in coffee shops and various other public places.

Wi-Fi Router

It is a device that performs the functions of a router but also includes the functions of wireless access point. It does not require a wired link. It can do function *via* WLAN, depending on the manufactures and model.

v. WiMAX

WiMAX stands for Worldwide Interoperability for Microwave Access. It is a wireless transmission of data using a variety of transmission modes.

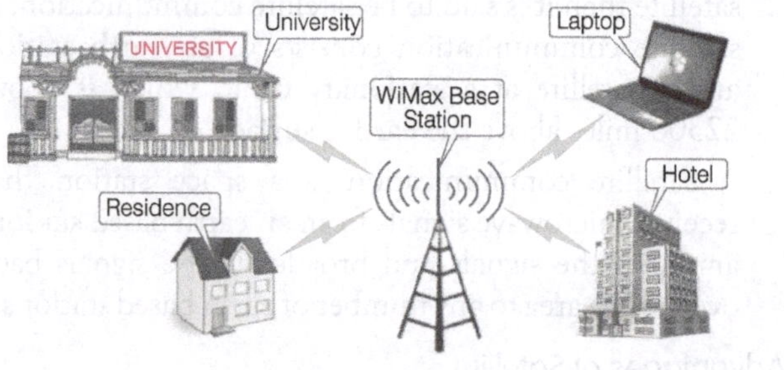

WiMAX network

The technology provides upto 80 Mbps broadband speed without the need of cables over an area of 3-10 miles (5-15 km). Similar to a cell phone tower, WiMAX requires a tower called **WiMAX Base Station.**

The Internet connectivity to an end user is provided through microwave link between the tower and the user-endpoint, known as **WiMAX Subscriber Unit.**

Advantages of WiMAX

- Speed of 10 Mbps at 10 km with line-of-sight.
- Single station can serve hundreds of users.
- It is standardised and same frequency equipment should work together.

Disadvantages of WiMAX

- Line-of-sight is needed for longer connections.
- Weather conditions like rain could interrupt the signal.
- High installation and operational cost.

Differences between Wired and Wireless Communication Channels

Wired Communication Channel	*Wireless Communication Channel*
It is more secure.	More security measures need to be considered for providing security.
It is faster than wireless communication.	It is slower than wired communication.
Technically less difficult to set-up.	Technically more difficult to setup.
More expensive for longer distances.	Less expensive for long distances.
User device cannot be moved.	User device can be moved easily within the wireless range.

Gigo

Some problems that can occurs during data transmission are as follows:

- **Crosstalk** Any disturbance caused by the electric or magnetic fields of one signal in an adjacent circuit or cable is called crosstalk.
- **Repeater** It is a device that is used to expand boundaries of a wired or wireless LAN. Repeater receives the attenuating signals and regenerates them, so that they can travel longer distances.
- **Attenuation** During transmission, the signal strength is reduced and this phenomenon is called attenuation.

Check Point 02

1. Name the cable which is composed of a glass or plastic inner core surrounded by cladding, all encased in an outside jacket.
2. Which transmission would you use that can be setup at no time, if the cost of digging the land for placing the cables is high?
3. Jiya wants to send a picture of events to her sister. She is using bluetooth device for this purpose. What is the range of bluetooth device?
   (a) 50m (b) 500m (c) 100m (d) 25m
4. Mr. Kapoor wants to connect laptop with mobile. Which one is faster channel out of Wi-Fi and WiMAX?

Networking Device: MODEM

MODEM is abbreviated for MOdulator - DEModulator. Modulator converts information from digital mode to analog mode at the transmitting end and demodulator converts the same from analog to digital at receiving end. The process of converting analog signals of one computer network into digital signals of another computer network so that, they can be processed by a receiving computer is referred to as **digitising**. As we know that computer is a digital machine, so it generates digital signals, while our telephone or cable lines, network can carry data in the form of analog signals only.

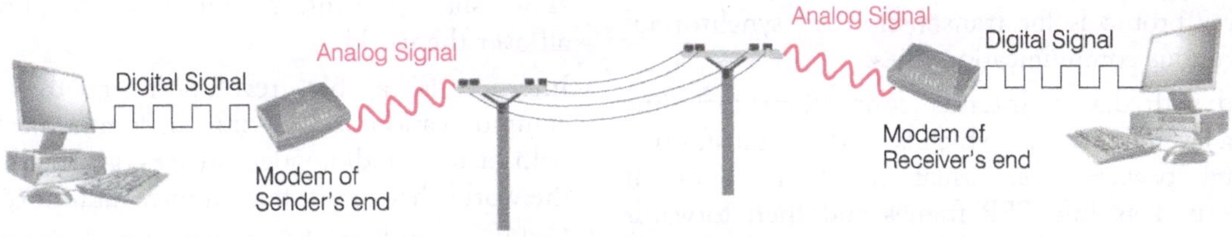

Modulation/Demodulation

Hence, we need a mechanism that can convert digital signals into analog signals at the sender's site and can convert analog signals back into the digital signals at the receiver's site. The data transmitted through modem is measured in bits per second (bps). This measurement gives us the speed of modem.

Analog and Digital Signals

Analog and digital signals are used to transmit information, usually through electric signals. In both these technologies, the information, such as any audio or video, is transformed into electric signals. The difference between analog and digital technologies is that in analog technology, information is translated into electric pulses of varying amplitude. In digital technology, translation of information is into binary format (0 or 1) where each bit is representative of two distinct amplitudes.

Depending upon how your computer is configured and your preferences, you can have an external, internal or PC card modem.

Network Protocols

Protocol refers to the set of rules applicable for a network. The protocol defines standardised format for the data packet to be transmitted through the network.

In a computer network, a protocol allows the setting up of a valid connection, communication and data transferring between two computing end points or computer system. Some of the commonly used protocols are as follows

HTTP (HyperText Transfer Protocol)

HTTP is an application layer protocol. It is widely used protocol. This protocol is used by the world wide web. HTTP defines how messages are formatted and transmitted and what actions web servers and browsers should take in response to various commands. It is a request/response standard between a client (end-user) and a server (website).

e.g. when you enter a URL in your browser, this actually sends an HTTP command to the web server directly to fetch and transmit the requested web page. It is generic, stateless and object oriented protocol.

TCP/IP (Transmission Control Protocol/Internet Protocol)

TCP/IP is the communication protocol for the Internet. It defines the rules, computers must follow to communicate with each other over the Internet. The TCP/IP is a protocol used in E-mail transmission. Infact, it is a set of protocol, i.e. TCP and IP.

TCP/IP is a protocol, which is responsible for finding path for the destination. It also splits the message into several datagrams, if it does not fit in one datagram. Therefore, these datagrams are sent through different alternate paths towards the destination. The TCP makes sure that the datagram arrives at the destination correctly. While IP is responsible for moving packet of data from source to destination. It handles the address part of each packet so that it reaches to the right destination.

PPP (Point-to-Point Protocol)

It is a data link layer protocol, which encapsulates other network layer protocols for transmission on synchronous and asynchronous communication lines.

PPP is used with dial-up Internet connections including ISDN. It is a layered protocol, which is used for transmitting the IP data packets over usual telephone lines. It encapsulates packets into PPP frames and then forwards them to the server over the serial transmission lines. PPP defines the format of frame to be exchanged between devices on one or multiple links and also defines the authenticity of the two devices.

FTP (File Transfer Protocol)

It is a standard network protocol used to transfer files from one host to another over a TCP-based network, such as the Internet.

FTP is based on client/server principle. It establishes two connections between the hosts. One connection is used for data transfer, which is opened and closed for each file transfer and the other for control information, which remains connected during the entire interactive FTP session.

Remote Login (Telnet)

Telnet is a protocol used for creating a connection with a remote computer. Once your telnet client establishes a connection to the remote host, telnet client becomes a virtual terminal, allowing you to communicate with the remote host from your computer. It establishes a connection either with command line client or with a programmatic interface. Telnet provides an error free connection, which is always faster than the latest conventional modems.

Check Point 03

1. Mr. Aman wants to established network over telephone line, which device is required for establishing network connection?
   (a) Modem (b) Repeater (c) Bridge (d) Gateway
2. In digital technology, data is transmitted into which format?
3. Write the name of network that allows controlled access to partners, vendors and suppliers at the same time.
4. Which protocol is known as stateless protocol?

The Biggest Computer Network: Internet

Internet is a network of networks that consists millions of computers connected with each other. Infact, it is the largest computer network of the world. It connects several small, medium, large and all dissimilar networks (heterogeneous) together into a bigger network and allows sharing of information, resources and databases all over the world.

Internet is a big revolution in the world of communication because one can communicate with the help of text, audio, video, images, graphics etc., across the world that too in few minutes and inexpensively.

Unlike, traditional broadcasting media such as radio and television, Internet is not owned by any individual. It contains billions of Web pages created by people and companies around the world. As alternatively, it is referred to as the net or Web. Through Internet, one can also buy and sell goods and services online which can play an important role in their business part.

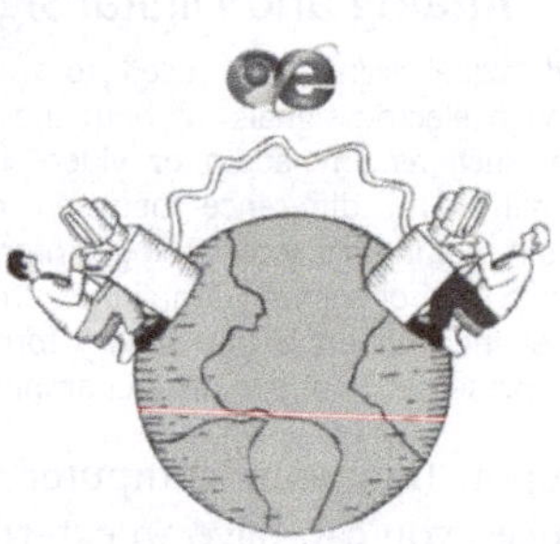

Internet

Uses of Internet

Following are some uses of Internet in today's world

(i) Internet is used for sharing information, data and can also be used to communicate through E-mail, blogs, social networking sites (i.e. facebook), chatrooms, forums etc.

(*ii*) Businesses use the Internet to provide access to complex databases.

(*iii*) Internet is used for providing services like video conferencing, downloading, uploading videos etc.

(*iv*) Internet is used for entertainment and to sell and buy goods and services through E-Commerce.

(*v*) Internet can be used to search information for a project or piece of homework related to any topic, i.e. Internet helps in education.

(*vi*) Internet plays an important role in colleges, i.e. in distributing lecture notes and course materials to students.

Future of Internet : Interspace

Interspace is the most innovative way of interaction available online. It is a client/server system that allows several users to connect or communicate online with real-time sound, movie and text chat in dynamic 3D environments.

Interspace is an application environment for interconnecting spaces to manipulate information such as the Internet is a protocol environment for interconnecting networks for data transmission.

Some Terms Related to Network

Intranet An internal or private network of an organisation that is based on Internet technology and that can be accessed over the Internet is called Intranet.

Extranet It is a private network that uses Internet technology and the public telecommunication system to securely share part of a business's information or operations with suppliers, vendors, partners, customers, or other businesses. An extranet provides various levels of accessibility to outsiders. You can access an extranet only if you have a valid username and password and your identity determines which parts of the extranet you can view.

Server It is a main computer that manages resources connected to a network. Any user on the network can access the resources stored on the server.

Check Point 04

1 Which technique connects several small, medium, large and all dissimilar networks (heterogeneous) together into a bigger network?

2 Which system is a client/server system that allows several users to communicate online with real time in dynamic 3D environment?

3 What is a main computer that manages resources connected to a network?

(a) Server (b) Extranet
(c) Intranet (d) Interspace

Mobile Applications

Mobile applications (also known as mobile apps) are software programs developed for mobile devices such as smartphones and tablets. They turn mobile devices into miniature powerhouses of function and fun. Some devices come preloaded with some mobile app courtesy of their manufacturers or the mobile service providers with which they are associated (for example, Verizon, AT&T, T-Mobile etc.), but many more apps are available through device specific app stores.

Mobile apps are move away from the integrated software systems generally found on PCs. Instead, each app provides limited and isolated functionality such as game, calculator or mobile web browsing. The simplest mobile take PC-based applications and port them to a mobile device. As mobile apps become more robust, this technique is some what lacking.

Mobile App Functions

The purpose of these apps run the approach from utility, productivity, and navigation to entertainment, sports, fitness and just about any others imaginable. Social media is one of the most popular fields of mobile app development and adoption.

In fact, Facebook is the most widely used app across all platforms. Many online entities have both mobile websites and mobile apps. In general, the difference lies in purpose: An app is usually smaller in scope than a mobile website, offers more interactivity.

Six Main Types of Mobile Apps

1. Lifestyle Mobile Apps

Life style apps have come on strong in recent years. A lifestyle app is one that accelerates or supports the individual facts that define your lifestyle. Some common lifestyle mobile apps are

- Fitness
- Dating
- Food
- Music
- Travel

The beauty of these apps is that once they are a part of a user's lifestyle repertoire, they are likely there for good. These are the apps that people turn to on a daily basis to help them find the next new song, restaurant or destination.

They are the apps that help them find themselves, what they like and dislike and where they are top next.

Some examples of lifestye apps are

- Spotify
- TripAdvisor
- Uber

2. Social Media Mobile Apps

Social media apps are some of the most popular types of mobile apps available. We build our social networks and most of us check in with them every day. Facebook alone reports over 1 billion active daily users.

Social media apps have to be fun, fast and continually integrating the expanding features of the social networks they support. Today's society shares more about their day-to-day lives than ever before. For that reason, even apps that don't necessarily fall under the social media category may want to include social sharing functionality.

Some common social media apps are

- Facebook
- Instagram
- Pinterest
- Snapchat

3. Utility Mobile Apps

Utilities are the types of mobile apps that we may use most often without thinking about them as apps. Many of them come pre-installed on your device and serve a single function.

Some common utility mobile apps are

- Reminders
- Calculator
- Flashlight
- Weather

4. Games/Entertainment Mobile Apps

The gaming and entertainment category are huge and as such, very competitive. Games are one of the more obvious mobile app categories and need little explanation. In the most successful games, both the frequency and length of play is high.

Work to make your game as addictive as possible by offering incentives to users who come back every day or a certain number of days in a row.

Some common games apps are

- Angry Birds
- Clash of Clans
- Subway Surfer

5. Productivity Mobile Apps

While productivity may sound like one of the more boring types of mobile apps, it is incredibly popular category. These types of apps help their users accomplish a task quickly and efficiently.

Some common productivity apps are

- Docs
- Sheets
- Wallet/Pay
- Evernote
- Wunderlist

6. News / Information Outlets Mobile Apps

News and information apps are pretty straightforward. They supply their users with the news and information they are looking for in an easy to understand layout that efficiently navigates them to the things they care about most.

Some common news apps are

- BuzzFeed
- SmartNews
- Google News & Weather
- Feedly
- Flipboard
- Yahoo News Digest
- Reddit
- LinkedIn Pulse

Cloud Computing

It provides computing and storage capacity services to heterogeneous community of end recipients. The name comes from the use of clouds as an abstraction for the complex infrastructure it contains in system diagrams.

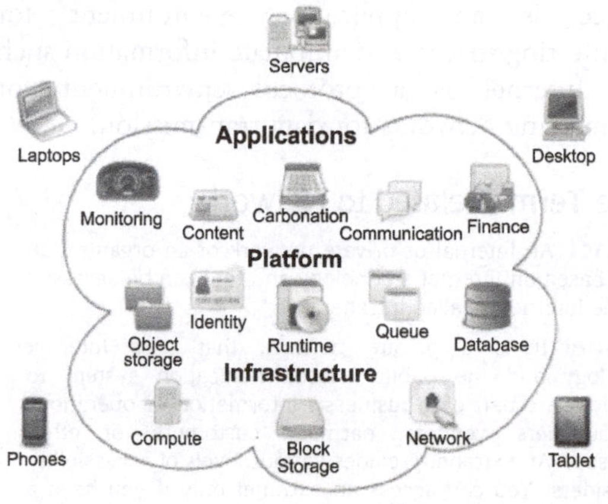

Cloud computing

It entrusts services with a user's data, software and computation over a network. It has considerable overlap with Software as a Service (SaaS).

iCloud

Steve Jobs stood up on 6th July, 2011 at an Apple keynote speech during the Apple World Wide Developers Conference (aka WWDC) and showed Apple's brand new service called iCloud.

Essential Characteristics of Cloud Computing

- **On Demand Self Services** Computer services such as E-mail, applications, network or server service can be provided without requiring human interaction with each service provider.

- **Broad Network Access** Cloud capabilities are available over the network and accessed through standard mechanisms that promote use by heterogeneous thin or thick client platforms such as mobile phones, laptops and PDAs.
- **Resource Pooling** The provider's computing resources are pooled together to serve multiple consumers using multiple-tenant model with different physical and virtual resources dynamically assigned and reassigned according to consumer demand.
- **Rapid Elasticity** Cloud services can be rapidly and elastically provisioned, in some cases automatically, to quickly scale IN OUT and rapidly released to quickly scale In.
- **Measured Service** Cloud computing resource usage can be measured, controlled and reported providing transparency for both the provider and consumer of the utilised service.
- **Multi Tenacity** It refers to the need for policy-driven enforcement, segmentation, isolation, governance, service levels and chargeback/billing models for different consumer constituencies.

Applications of Cloud Computing

The applications of cloud computing are practically limitless. With the right middleware, a cloud computing system could execute all the programs a normal computer could run. Potentially, everything from generic Word processing software to customised computer programs designed for a specific company could work on a cloud computing system.

The applications of cloud computing are as follows

- Clients would be able to access their applications and data from anywhere at any time.
- It could bring hardware costs down. You wouldn't need a large hard drive because you'd store all your information on a remote computer.
- Corporations that rely on computers have to make sure they have the right software in place to achieve goals. Cloud computing systems give these organisations company-wide access to computer applications. The companies don't have to buy a set of softwares or software licenses for every employee. Instead, the company could pay a metered fee to a cloud computing company.
- Servers and digital storage devices take up space. Some companies rent physical space to store servers and databases because they don't have it available on site. Cloud computing gives these companies the option of storing data on someone else's hardware, removing the need for physical space on the front end.
- Corporations might save money on IT support. Streamlined hardware would, in theory, have fewer problems than a network of heterogeneous machines and operating systems.

Types of Cloud Deployments

There are three different ways to deploy cloud computing resources: public cloud, private cloud and hybrid cloud.

1. Public Cloud

Public clouds are owned and operated by a third party cloud service provider, which deliver their computing resources like servers and storage over the Internet. With a public cloud, all hardware, software and other supporting infrastructure is owned and managed by the cloud provider. You access these services and manage your account using a Web browser.

2. Private Cloud

A private cloud refers to cloud computing resources used exclusively by a single business or organisation. A private cloud can be physically located on the company's on-site datacenter. Some companies also pay third party service providers to host their private cloud. A private cloud is one in which the services and infrastructure are maintained on a private network.

3. Hybrid Cloud

Hybrid clouds combine public and private clouds. They bound together by technology that allows data and applications to be shared between them. By allowing data and applications to move between private and public clouds, hybrid cloud gives businesses greater flexibility and more deployment options.

Check Point 05

1 Name any two modes for chatting on the Internet are available.

2 Which type of cloud can be physically located on the company's on-site data center?

(a) Private cloud (b) Public cloud

(c) Hybrid cloud (d) None of these

3 Which mobile apps help the user to accomplish a task quickly?

SUMMARY

- In Information Technology, a network is a series of points or nodes which interconnected by communication paths.
- Computer network is a group of computer systems linked together which are able to communicate and can share files.
- Computer network provides three types of network:
  (i) Local Area Network (LAN) (ii) Metropolitan Area Network (MAN) (iii) Wide Area Network (WAN).
- Communication channel is a medium through which data is transferred from one location to another.
- Wired and wireless are two types of communication channels.
- Twisted pair cable is a type of cable made by putting two separate wires together.
- A cable that consists of a thick copper wire that is enveloped in a cover of insulating material known as co-axial cable.
- Ethernet cables commonly used in a wired network to interconnect the various LAN devices.
- Wireless technology where the information is transmitted using electromagnetic waves over the distance without using wires.
- Some long distance wireless media are: Microwave, Radiowave, Satellite.
- Some short distance wireless media are: Infrared, Bluetooth, Laser, Wi-Fi, WiMAX.
- Bluetooth is a standard for wireless communication providing a secure and convenient connectivity between various devices over short distances.
- Wi-Fi represents a WLAN (Wireless LAN) protocol that helps in communicating data wirelessly within a fixed location.
- A MODEM is a device that enables a computer to transmit data over telephone or cable lines.
- Protocol is the special set of rules that end points in a telecommunication connection.
- Internet is the largest computer network that provides a point access to various online services.
- Social network is a website that brings people together to talk, share ideas and interest.
- Chat is a text-based communication that is live or in real-time.
- A mobile app is a computer program designed to run on a mobile device such as a phone.
- Cloud computing is the on demand delivery of computer power, database storage, application and other IT resources through cloud services.

Exam Practice

Multiple Choice Questions

1 Computer connected with LAN
(a) work fast (b) go online
(c) can E-mail
(d) can share information or peripheral devices

Ans. (*d*) Computer connected with LAN can share information or peripheral devices.

2 A group of computers connected together with the help of cables within an office building is called
(a) PAN (b) WAN
(c) MAN (d) LAN

Ans. (*d*) Using LAN, we can connect computers within a building only.

3 Network formed between computers which are spread across the continents is called
(a) LAN (b) WAN
(c) MAN (d) WLAN

Ans. (*b*) Across the continents, computers can be connected using WAN only.

4 Which of the following uses cables to connect two or more computers?
(a) Transmission (b) Unguided
(c) Guided (d) Radiowaves

Ans. (*c*) In guided media, signals are guided through cables.

5 The .... consists of two conductors, where one is the inner conductor of solid copper (also called the core conductor) and the other is the outer conductor.
(a) Twisted pair cable (b) Optical fibre
(c) Co-axial cable (d) Ethernet cable

Ans. (*c*) Co-axial cable consists of two conductors which are parallel to each other, i.e. inner and outer conductors.

6 Identify the odd term amongst the following.
(a) Microwave (b) Radiowave
(c) Bluetooth (d) Optical fibre

Ans. (*d*) Except optical fibre, all are wireless transmission media.

7 Optical fibres are made up of thin strands of
(a) copper material (b) silver material
(c) glass like material (d) brass material

Ans. (*c*) Optical fibres are made up of thin strands of glass like material.

8 Which type of connector does a Ethernet cable use?
(a) BNC (b) RJ-45
(c) RJ-11 (d) MSAU

Ans. (*b*) RJ-45 is most commonly used to connect computers onto Ethernet based local area network.

9 For using Wi-Fi, which of the following is not required?
(a) An Internet connection (b) Wireless Internet card
(c) Wireless router (d) Bluetooth

Ans. (*d*) Bluetooth is not required for Wi-Fi connection.

10 Modulation and demodulation is performed by
(a) microwave (b) satellite
(c) modem (d) fibre optic

Ans. (*c*) Modulation and demodulation is performed by modem.

11 A modem is connected in between a telephone line and a
(a) computer
(b) serial port
(c) network
(d) communication adapter

Ans. (*a*) Modem is a device that enables computers and other equipments to communicate with each other using telephone lines.

12 Which of the following is not a transmission medium?
(a) Telephone lines (b) Co-axial cable
(c) Modem (d) Microwave

Ans. (*c*) All are communication channel but modem is a device that converts analog signals to digital signals or *vice-versa*.

13 What is the unit used to measure the data which is transmitted through modem?
(a) Bytes per second (b) Band
(c) Bits per second (d) None of these

Ans. (*c*) Bits per second is the unit used to measure the data through modem.

14 Which of the following protocol is also known as Remote Login?
(a) HTTP (b) Telnet
(c) PPP (d) TCP/IP

Ans. (*b*) Telnet is also known as Remote Login, used for creating a connection with a remote computer.

15 What can you do with the Internet?
(a) Exchange information with friends and colleagues
(b) Access pictures, sounds, video clips and other media elements
(c) Find diverse perspective on issues from a global audience
(d) Internet exchange information, access pictures, find diverse perspective on issue from a global audience.

Ans. (*d*) Internet exchange information, access pictures, find diverse perspective on issues from a global audience.

16 A set of rules that governs data communication is
(a) protocol (b) information
(c) HTML (d) E-mail

Ans. (*a*) A protocol is a set of rules that governs the communication between computers on a network.

17 Which part of TCP/IP is responsible for dividing a file or message into very small parts, at the source computer?
(a) TCP (b) IP
(c) Both (a) and (b) (d) None of these

Ans. (*a*) TCP part breaks the messages into smaller packets which are transmitted over the Internet.

18 FTP is referred to as
(a) Force Transfer Protocol
(b) File Transport Protocol
(c) File Transfer Partition
(d) File Transfer Protocol

Ans. (*d*) FTP is a protocol through which Internet users can upload files from their computer to a Website. In which, FTP stands for File Transfer Protocol.

Fill in the Blanks

1 ……….. is the formation of networks.
Ans. Networking

2 ……….. consists of electrical waves.
Ans. Signal

3 The small area network created around a bluetooth device is called……….. .
Ans. PAN (Personal Area Network)

4 Bluetooth is a ………….. wireless connection.
Ans. short range

5 The digital signals to analog signals are carried out by……….., so that data can travel over telephone lines.
Ans. MODEM

6 ……… is called network of networks.
Ans. Internet

7 ……….. is a computer which provides sharing the resources of other computers connected in a network.
Ans. Server

8 In URL http://www.cbse.nic.in/, ……… is a protocol.
Ans. http

9 LinkedIn is an example of ……… website.
Ans. social networking

10 FTP is responsible for downloading ……… from computer network.
Ans. files

11 ……… helps to create and maintain social relationship.
Ans. Social networking

12 ……… could bring hardware costs down.
Ans. Cloud computing

True or False

1 A computer connected to a network is known as stand-alone computer.

Ans. **False** A computer connected to a network is known as host or node.

2 A separate printer will be needed in a network for all connected computers.

Ans. **False** Computers connected to a LAN can share information through a common printer.

3 MANs are the computer networks confined to a localised area such as an office.

Ans. **False** MANs are the computer networks confined to a localised area such as an office.

4 MAN provides communication services upto 5 km.

Ans. **False** MAN provides communication services upto 100 km.

5 Twisted pair cable is suitable for broadband application.

Ans. **False** Twisted pair cable has low bandwidth capabilities while broadband application requires high bandwidth.

6 Microwave transmits signals through open space like radio signal.

Ans. **True** It supports long distance communication through space like radio signal.

7 Microwave transmission is an example of line-of-sight transmission.

Ans. **True** Microwave is the radiowave which supports line-of-sight transmission.

8 Most common example of infrared medium is TV remote.

Ans. **True** TV remote is an example of infrared light for transmission.

9 Bluetooth is commonly used in mobile phones, laptops etc.

Ans. **True** It is a short-range wireless connection. With the help of bluetooth, we can transfer the data from one device to another device.

10 Reduction of signal strength during transmission is called attenuation.

Ans. **True** During transmission, the signal strength is reduced, this phenomenon is called attenuation.

11 The most powerful computer in a typical network is network server.

Ans. **True** A server is a main computer that manages resources to other computers connected to a network.

12 TCP helps in converting the digital singal to analog signal and *vice-versa*.

Ans. **False** The process of converting digital signal into analog singal is called modulation and is done by a modem.

13 We can make groups of our friends and family members on a social networking site.

Ans. **True** Social networking provides various sites like Facebook and Orkut for making groups.

14 Chat rooms are actual rooms, where chat session can take place.

Ans. **False** Chat often occurs in a virtual chat room, which can include different peoples who may or may not know each other.

15 Facebook is a utility mobile app.

Ans. **False** Facebook is a social media app, has to be fun and continually integrating the expanding features.

Very Short Answer (VSA) Type Questions

1 Name the term defined by given below statement:

"A group of computers connected to each other by a link."

Ans. Computer network is defined as a group of computers connected to each other by a link.

2 Two people, one knowing only English and other knowing only Chinese are talking to each other. Can we call it a communication?

Ans. No, because only a meaningful exchange of information between two living beings is called communication.

3 Give few examples of communication technology.

Ans. Telephones, mobiles, fax, Internet etc., are some examples of communication technology.

4 Write down the components of a computer network established between the two offices of a company across the cities.

Ans. The five components will be involved in this computer network, since telephone lines will be used as communication channel.

(*i*) Sender
(*ii*) Data communication device at sender's end
(*iii*) Communication channel
(*iv*) Data communication device at receiver's end
(*v*) Receiver

5 List down the types of computer networks.

Ans. Following are the three main types of computer networks, based upon the geographical area as follows

(*i*) Local Area Network (LAN)
(*ii*) Metropolitan Area Network (MAN)
(*iii*) Wide Area Network (WAN)

6 Which cable networks are used for LAN connections?

Ans. Twisted pair and fibre optic cables are used for LAN connections.

7 What is the importance of communication channel?

Ans. Communication channel is responsible for carrying data in the form of signals from sender to receiver.

8 Give one basic difference between guided and unguided transmission channels.

Ans. In guided transmission media, cables (or wires) are used for communicating data while in unguided transmission, in place of cables, signals travel through air.

9 Why wires in twisted pair cable are twisted around each other?

Ans. Wires are twisted to provide protection against crosstalk and noise.

10 When we transmit signal over a long distance, the intensity of the signal is reduced. What could be the solution for this problem?

Ans. We can use a networking device called repeater, regenerates the feeble signal and transmit it.

11 Write down the name of communication channel used for telephone line and TV.

Ans. Communication channel for telephone line is twisted pair cable and for TV is co-axial cable.

12 Which guided media provides secure transmission amongst all of them?

Ans. Optical fibre provides secure transmission as compared to twisted pair and co-axial cable. As, it is more immune to tapping than copper cables.

13 How is crossover Ethernet cable different from rest of the Ethernet cables?

Ans. A crossover cable is a special type of Ethernet cable specially designed for connecting two computers, whereas most Ethernet cables are designed to connect one computer to a router or a switch.

14 Which wireless technology is commonly used in mobile phones?

Ans. Bluetooth is commonly used as a wireless technology in mobile phones and laptops.

15 Give one major disadvantage of bluetooth.

Ans. Only short range communication is possible using bluetooth.

16 Ramya wants to connect all the computers of her office wirelessly in order to avoid clumsy cables. Which wireless technology would be best suitable for her office?

Ans. Wi-Fi technology would be best suitable for her office to avoid cabling.

17 Define the term Wi-Fi hotspot.

Ans. A hotspot is a site that offers Internet access over a WLAN *via* a router connected to a link from an Internet Service Provider (ISP).

18 Why Internet is called a network of networks?

Ans. Internet is called a network of networks because it connects several large and all heterogeneous networks together into a bigger network.

19 Name any two Internet protocols used by web.

Ans. HTTP and FTP.

20 Distinguish between FTP and Telnet.

Ans. FTP (File Transfer Protocol) facilitates the transfer of files from one point to another while Telnet is a connection protocol that allows a user to connect to a remote server.

21 Name some examples of games mobile apps.

Ans. Angry Birds, Chash of Clans, Subway Surfer.

22 What are two essential characteristics of cloud computing?

Ans. (*i*) On demand self services

(*ii*) Resource pooling

Short Answer (SA) Type Questions

1 Write down any two points of differences between LAN, MAN and WAN.

Ans. Two major points of differences among LAN, MAN and WAN are as follows

Basis	*LAN*	*MAN*	*WAN*
Geographical Area	Generally within a building	within a city	Across the continents
Distance	Upto 5 km	Upto 160 km	Unlimited

2 Write a short notes on LAN and WAN.

Ans. **LAN** A Local Area Network (LAN) is a computer network covering a small geographical area like a home, office or small group of buildings such as buildings in a school. Computers connected to a LAN can share information and peripheral equipments.

WAN A Wide Area Network (WAN) is used to connect LANs and other types of network together, so that users and computers in one location can communicate with users and computers in other locations.

3 In twisted pair cable, two insulated wires are twisted around each other which provides protection against noise. Explain.

Ans. Twisting the cables keep them close together so that, any external magnetic fields must cross both cable at the same time, so the interference created in one cable is cancelled by the almost exact opposite amount of interference in the other.

4 Explain the three main parts of an optical fibre cable.

Ans. The three main parts of an optical fibre cable are as follows

(*i*) **Core** It is the section through which the data travel in the form of light.

(*ii*) **Cladding** It is the covering part of core. Its function is to reflect back the light into the core, as it is a denser medium.

(*iii*) **Protective Coating** It is the outer cover of cladding for the protection of optical fibre from damage and moisture.

5 Compare and contrast the two wireless transmission media; bluetooth and infrared.

Ans. Bluetooth and Infrared both are short range wireless transmission media. This is the only point at which both these data transmission technologies look similar but there is a lot of differences between the two. Infrared is mostly used in TV remotes and there must be a direct line-of-sight between the transmitter and the receiver while on the other hand bluetooth uses a radio frequency which allows transmission through walls and other objects.

6 Explain the term

(*i*) Bandwidth (*ii*) Broadband

Ans. (*i*) **Bandwidth** It is the communication capacity of a network. It refers to the data carrying capacity of a channel or medium.

(*ii*) **Broadband** It is a wide bandwidth data transmission with an ability to simultaneously transport multiple signals and traffic types.

7 Elucidate the following terms

(*i*) PAN (*ii*) WiMAX

Ans. (*i*) **PAN** It stands for Personal Area Network. It is a computer network used for communication among computer and different technological devices close to it. Technologies such as bluetooth and infrared communication form a wireless PAN around the device.

(*ii*) **WiMAX** It stands for Worldwide Interoperability for Microwave Access. It is a wireless transmission of data using a variety of transmission modes.

8 Differentiate between long distance wireless media and short distance wireless media.

Ans. Differences between long distance and short distance wireless media are as follows

Long Distance Wireless Media	*Short Distance Wireless Media*
It supports communication over a long distance, i.e. upto thousand of kilometres.	It supports communication over a short distance, i.e. upto few kilometres.
Microwave, radiowave and satellite communication are long distance wireless media.	Bluetooth, infrared, Wi-Fi, WiMAX are short distance wireless media.

9 When the computer network uses telephone lines as communication channel then MODEM is used as a data communication device. Now, explain the working of MODEM.

Ans. MODEM performs the task of MOdulation at sender's site and DEModulation at the receiver's site. Basically, our computer generates data in the form of digital signals which need to be forwarded to the receiver through telephone lines. Since, telephone lines can carry only analog signals. So, digital signals need to be converted to analog signals at sender's site this is called modulation. At receiver's site, again analog signals should be converted back to the original digital signals, then this is called demodulation.

10 Explain two problems that can occur during transmission of data.

Ans. Two problems that can occur during transmission of data are as follows

(*i*) **Crosstalk** Disturbance caused by the electric or magnetic fields of one signal in an adjacent signal.

(*ii*) **Attenuation** During transmission, the signal strength is reduced, this phenomenon is called attenuation.

11 Write any two uses of Internet.

Ans. Two uses of Internet are as follows

(*i*) Internet is used for communication and information sharing.

(*ii*) Businesses use the Internet to provide access to complex databases.

12 Differentiate between the terms Internet and Intranet.

Ans. Differences between Internet and Intranet are as follows:

Internet	*Intranet*
Access by any individual with dial-up access.	Access by only authorised employees.
Information on Internet could be general, public and advertisement.	Information on Intranet could be specific, corporate and proprietary.

13 What is chatting? Is it necessary to be online while chatting?

Ans. Chatting is the textual or multimedia conversation over the Internet. It is a real-time communication between two users *via* computer. It is widely interactive text based communication process that takes places over the Internet. Yes, it is necessary to be online, while chatting.

14 What is the significance of HTTP?.

Ans. HTTP is a protocol used on Internet. It works in combination with WWW. It allows us to access hypertext documents on WWW. Since, WWW allows us to access or use multimedia files on the Internet and the hypertext files support multimedia.

15 What do you understand by Lifestyle Mobile App?

Ans. Refer to text on Page No. 63.

16 Give the benefits of social networking.

Ans. Benefits of social networking are as follows

(*i*) People sharing views can connect and form a group.

(*ii*) Individuals from all around the world can connect and thereby know about new cultures and languages etc.

(*iii*) It is an easy and cost effective way to reach your consumers and people in your network.

(*iv*) It helps in building credibility amongst the customer.

EXAM PRACTICE

Long Answer (LA) Type Questions

1 Today, computers are being used very widely for communication. Write down some benefits offered by computers when used for communication.

Ans. Refer to topic 'Needs for Computer Network' on Page No. 55.

2 Write down the advantages of networking for an office.

Ans. Various advantages of networking for an office are as follows

(*i*) Using network, we can store our files in many places or computers for data recovery purpose from a disk crash.

(*ii*) It provides sharing of various resources over the network, within the office.

(*iii*) Since, resources are sharable so they can be accessed on any computer by any employee.

(*iv*) Networking supports very fast transmission of data from one system to another.

(*v*) All the application softwares need not be installed on individual system, i.e. they can be centralised and can be accessed by anyone from the central system itself.

3 Explain the given terms with respect to computer networks:

(*i*) File and Data Sharing
(*ii*) Distributing Computing Power
(*iii*) Ease of Administration
(*iv*) Networking
(*v*) Server

Ans. For (*i*), (*ii*) & (*iii*) Refer to text on Page No. 55.

(*iv*) **Networking** Refer to text on Page No. 54.

(*v*) **Server** Refer to text on Page No. 63.

4 Differentiate LAN, MAN and WAN on the basis of following characteristic:

(*i*) Geographical Area
(*ii*) Example
(*iii*) Distance
(*iv*) Cost
(*v*) Ownership

Ans. Refer to text on Page No. 56.

5 When we connect computers in a network using cables then it is called guided media. What are the various types of guided media available? Explain each.

Ans. Three types of cables are used for connecting computers in a network are as follows

(*i*) **Twisted Pair Cable** It consists of two insulated wires twisted around each other and uses copper as the conducting material. This property of twisted pair cable provides protection against crosstalk and noise.

(*ii*) **Co-axial Cable** It contains two conductors, the inner conductor made of solid copper and the outer conductor that serves as a shield against noise. An insulating plastic is placed between the two conductors and this whole setup is covered with a plastic jacket.

(*iii*) **Optical Fibre** It consists of thin strands of glass or glass like material, which are capable of carrying light signals from a source at one end to another.

6 What are the differences between wired and wireless communication channels?

Ans. Refer to text on Page No. 60.

7 What are the types of cloud deployments?

Ans. Refers to text on Page No. 65.

8 What are the dangers associated with social networking?

Ans. Dangers associated with social networking are as follows

(*i*) **Lack of anonymity** Social networking usually requires you to input your name, location, age, gender and many other types of personal information.

(*ii*) **Scams and harassment** Being online you are at risk of facing cases of harassment, cyber stalking, online scams and identity theft.

(*iii*) **Time consuming** If you are new to social networking, learning the process can be very time consuming.

(*iv*) **The illusion of security** The Internet is definitely not secured as social or human hackers can hack one's personal account.

(*v*) **Isolation** Social networking sites do not provide isolation. As, once information is posted to a social networking site, it is no longer private.

9. When group of computers are connected together for sharing of resources, then it is called as computer network. There are various benefits of using computer networks such as – file and data sharing, device sharing, centralised administration of any work, distribution of work, etc. The device sharing also called as resource sharing is the major objective of computer networking. Costly devices such as printers, scanners, dedicated servers, backup systems, input devices and Internet connections can be easily shared with networking among all available network users simultaneously without being relocated. It also eliminating the need for expensive redundancies. Apart from resource sharing networking can protect data from hacking and loss by keeping data at multiple places. Keeping data at multiple places can ensure no loss of data by any accidental deletion or any other situation.

(i) Group of computers connected together for .... of costly devices called as computer network.
(a) creating (b) sharing
(c) adding (d) None of these

(ii) Resource sharing is also called as .... sharing.
(a) human (b) cable
(c) device (d) tab

(iii) The resources can be sharing with only those users who are .... to network right now.
(a) shared (b) connected
(c) sleeping (d) not available

(iv) Data .... can be done, if user keep copies of data at multiple places.
(a) loss (b) connection
(c) backup (d) print

(v) The .... connections can be easily shared with computer network among all available network users at the same time without being relocated.
(a) cable (b) Internet
(c) network (d) data

Ans. (i) (*a*) Group of computers are connected to share costly resources or devices then it is called as computer network.
(ii) (*c*) Resources in terms of computer network are also called as devices.
(iii) (*b*) The resources of the network can be shared with only connected users.
(iv) (*c*) Data backup can be achieved, if data is kept at multiple places.
(v) (*b*) The Internet connection can be easily shared in LAN very easily among all available users.

10. When large number of resources are pool together and can be shared among multiple users on demand in flexi manner anywhere any time can be referred as a cloud environment. There are five essential characteristics of the cloud computing – elasticity, resource pool, network access, measure services and multi tenancy.

There are three deployment models of the cloud – private, public and hybrid. There are limitless applications of the cloud computing. With the right middleware, a cloud computing system could execute all the programs a normal computer could run. The main benefits of cloud computing included data access anywhere any time. Less cost investment in infrastructure and maintenance is required. A company can hire resources from cloud on demand basis and pay as per the utilisation of the resource.

(i) The large number of .... are pooled in cloud.
(a) resources (b) time
(c) task (d) None of these

(ii) Which is a characteristic of the cloud computing?
(a) Public (b) Topacity
(c) Middleware (d) Elasticity

(iii) Which is not a deployment model of cloud?
(a) Private (b) Hybrid
(c) Local (d) Public

(iv) The main benefit of cloud computing is access data .... anytime.
(a) temporary (b) anywhere
(c) onsite (d) None of these

(v) We can save the cost of .... by using cloud computing technology.
(a) data (b) mobile
(c) infrastructure (d) print

Ans. (i) (*a*) The cloud is a pool of large number of resources.
(ii) (*d*) The elasticity is a characteristic of the cloud computing among five essential characteristics.
(iii) (*c*) There are three deployment models of the cloud computing- Private, public and hybrid.
(iv) (*b*) Using cloud computing data can be accessed anywhere anytime.
(v) (*c*) Company can save the cost in infrastructure by using the cloud computing technology.

Application Oriented Questions

1 The following paragraph describes the term computer network.

A computer network is a group of (*i*) .... that are (*ii*) .... to each other for the purpose of (*iii*) ....

A computer (*iv*) .... allows computers to communicate with many other computers and to (*v*) .... resources and information.

Fill in the blanks with words from the list below:

Connected, Computers, Sending, Communication, Network, Share.

Ans. (*i*) computers (*ii*) connected
(*iii*) communication (*iv*) network
(*v*) share

2 Ram and Sita, two persons talking to one another.

(*i*) What are the components of the network?
(*ii*) What is the communication channel?

Ans. (*i*) Components of network are as follows
(*a*) Sender (*b*) Communication channel
(*c*) Receiver

(*ii*) Communication channel is the channel in which two computers can communicate with each other by sending data or sharing information between them.

3 Manoj has to setup a network between his devices at home which included a smartphone, a laptop and a personal computer. What type of network he would be setting up for the same?

(*i*) PAN
(*ii*) MAN
(*iii*) WAN

Ans. Manoj would be setting up a PAN (Personal Area Network) which is best suited for setup involving a computer, a cell phone and/or a handheld computing device such as a PDA.

4 Mr Singh and Mr Tyagi want to send a song from each other. Both having a mobile phone. Both want to send a song through mobile phones. What networking technology is needed to share a song through mobile phone? Describe it.

Ans. Bluetooth technology is used for sharing the data like audio, video etc. Using this technology, users of cellular phones, initiate the sending or receiving data.

In general, having all mobiles and fixed computer devices can be totally coordinated. Thus, Mr Singh and Mr Tyagi can send a song to each other by using a bluetooth technology easily within short time.

5 Ravi has to transfer a photo from his mobile phone to his friend's phone in the same room. Which of the following technologies would let him to do this quickly?

(*i*) Bluetooth
(*ii*) Infrared
(*iii*) Either of the two

Ans. Ravi could use either of the two technologies Bluetooth or Infrared which is supported by both the devices involved. Infrared though slightly faster than Bluetooth has a limitation that it needs a clear line-of-sight between the devices for it to work.

6 Carefully read the following descriptions and identify what is being talked about.

(*i*) It consists of two insulated wires twisted around each other, which provides protection against noise and crosstalk.
(*ii*) Disturbance caused due to interference of one signal's electric or magnetic field into other signals.
(*iii*) It is an omni-directional wireless transmission media. Its range lies between 300 KHz to 10 GHz.
(*iv*) Communication channel that is more secure, faster, easier to set-up but expensive for longer distances and devices once configured cannot be moved.
(*v*) Unique equipments like printers and scanners are available to all the workstations simultaneously.

Ans. (*i*) Twisted pair cable
(*ii*) Crosstalk
(*iii*) Radiowave
(*iv*) Wired communication channel
(*v*) Resource sharing

7 Anila works in a Multinational Company (MNC) and needs to work online from home also. She requires fast Internet connection. Which type of Internet connection in your view would be best suited for her? Apart from browsing on the Internet she will require uploading/downloading of files to/from remote sites. Which protocol will help her to perform this activity?

Ans. Anila should prefer broadband connection. FTP protocol will help her in uploading and downloading of files.

8 As life gets busy, it becomes difficult for everyone to keep track with school and college friends, old colleagues, old neighbours and favourite teachers. It is important to keep in touch with all your near and dear ones.

At times, people sitting miles away doing similar kind of activity or solving similar kind of problems can help you to achieve goals faster by sharing their experience.

Similarly, people belonging to different socio-economic background can change your perspective and can enhance your understanding of various cultures.

(*i*) Suggest any two real-time tools that are suitable for the above mentioned activities.

(*ii*) What is the generic name used for such tools?

Ans. (*i*) Twitter and Facebook

(*ii*) Social Networking

CHAPTER

05

Content Technology

Chapter Checklist

- Data
- Information
- DIKW Pyramid
- Multimedia
  - Components of Multimedia
  - Application Areas of Multimedia
  - Hardware Requirements for Multimedia
  - Software Requirements for Multimedia

The word **content** means the subject matter that can provide something useful knowledge or information to the end user regarding some context. In other words, content is something that needs to be expressed through some medium and that medium could be speech, writing, television, audio CDs, image, article, multimedia etc.

Use of technology for content delivery is called **content technology**. Technology allows instantaneous movement of information from every corner to every point at the same time, i.e. technology has made resources readily available to all.

Data

The raw and unorganised facts that may represent some conditions, ideas or objects is called data. Since, it is unorganised, it does not have any meaning. So, we need to process it, to turn it into something useful. Various forms of data can be alphabets, numbers and alphanumeric, which are described as follows

(*i*) **Numeric data** This type of data consists of ten digits from 0 to 9.
e.g. bank balance, examination score, pincode etc.

(*ii*) **Alphabetic data** It includes letters from A-Z, a-z and blank spaces. This is also called **non-numeric data**. e.g. the name of an employee.

(*iii*) **Alphanumeric data** This type of data consists of alphabets, numbers, special characters and symbols. e.g. the address, password etc.

Information

When raw facts and figures are processed and arrange in some order then they become information, i.e. the data which is accurate, specific, organised for a purpose, presented within a context that gives some meaning that can lead to increase in understanding and decrease in uncertainty is called information. Information helps us in taking decisions. In other words,

Information = Data + Context + Meaning

For the decision to be meaningful, the processed data must qualify for following characteristics

(*i*) **Time** Information should be available when required.

(*ii*) **Accuracy** Information should be in accurate manner.

(*iii*) **Completeness** Information should be complete in every aspects.

e.g. marks obtained by student and student's roll no, separately both are form of data, whereas, when both are combined and organised in the form of report card, it becomes information for student.

Differences between Data and Information

Differences between data and information are as follows

Data	Information
Data is used as input	Information is the output of data.
It is unprocessed facts or figures.	It is processed data.
It does not depend on information.	It depends on data.
It is not specific.	It is specific.
It does not carry a meaning.	It must carry a logical meaning.
It is the raw material.	It is the product.
e.g. each student's height is one piece of data.	e.g. the average height of the class or the student is the information that can be concluded from the given data.

DIKW Pyramid

Data can be viewed at the lowest level from which information and knowledge are derived that means data is the least abstract, information the next least and knowledge the most.

The DIKW pyramid includes all four components (data, information, knowledge and wisdom) in hierarchical level. Representation of DIKW pyramid is given

Knowledge

Information or skill after being transformed into some conceptual framework, so that it can be manipulated and used cognitively is known as knowledge.

Wisdom

The applied knowledge is known as wisdom. That is, alongwith having the knowledge if someone has common sense to know 'when' and 'how' to use that knowledge, it is called wisdom.

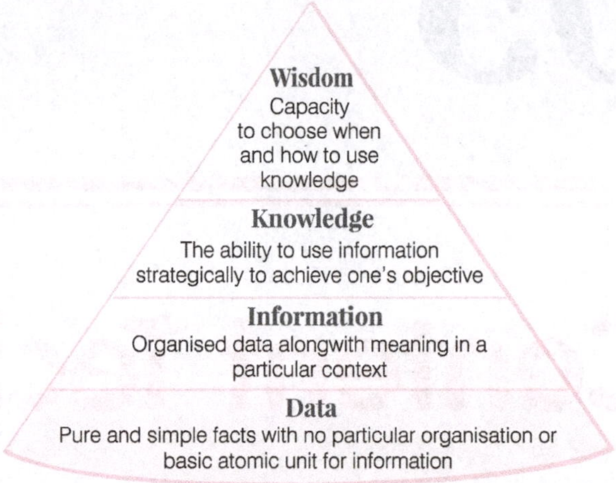

Hierarchical representation

Check Point 01

1 Mr X wants to store the name, age, address of employees. What kind of data is more suitable for address field?

(a) Numeric (b) Alphabetic

(c) Alphanumeric (d) Special Symbol

2 A manager of finance company told his company's director that net profit decreased in the past two months. A finance report of this company is an example of data or information?

3 From the above question, when CBI checks that financial report of this company is correct. This is the ability of knowledge or wisdom?

Multimedia

Any combination of text, graphic art, sound, video and animation to any individual by computer or other electronic means is known as multimedia. Multimedia stimulates the eyes, ears and brain of the person.

Multimedia may be any of the following

(*i*) Text and sound.

(*ii*) Text, sound and still or animated graphic images.

(*iii*) Text, sound and video images.

(*iv*) Video and sound.

(*v*) Multiple display areas, images or presentations, presented concurrently.

Multimedia is a very effective presentation tool. Studies indicate that if a person is stimulated with audio then assumption rate would be upto 20 per cent, with audiovisual. It would be upto 30 per cent with interactive multimedia presentations and assumption rate can be increased upto 60 per cent. Multimedia can be broadly divided into following two categories:

(*i*) **Linear multimedia** This type of content generally progresses without any navigational control for the viewer. e.g. PowerPoint presentation, anime episode.

(*ii*) **Non-linear multimedia** This type of content uses interactivity to control progress. e.g. a video game, hypermedia.

Hypertext

The text containing links to other information is called hypertext. In a hypertext document, when a user clicks on the links, it will navigate him to a different page containing information.

Hypermedia

It is an extension of hypertext, i.e. the content which is not constrained to be text is called hypermedia. It can include graphics, video and sound alongwith text which can be linked with other contents.

Components of Multimedia

Various components of multimedia are as follows

1. Text

Text content is by far the most common media type in computing applications. Most multimedia systems use a combination of text and other media to deliver functionality. Text in multimedia systems can express specific information, or it can act as reinforcement for information contained in other media items.

Multimedia provide many text based languages like XML, HTML, JavaScript. Generally used text formats are TXT, DOC etc. e.g. when Web pages include image elements, they can also include a short amount of text for the user's browser to include as an alternative. In this case, the digital image item is not available.

2. Images

Digital image files appear in many multimedia applications. Digital photographs can display application content or can alternatively form part of a user interface.

Interactive elements such as buttons, often use custom images created by the designers and developers involved in an application. Digital image files use a variety of formats and file extensions. Among them, most common are JPEGs and PNGs. Both of these often appear on Websites, as the formats allow developers to minimise the file size while maximising on picture quality. Graphic design software programs such as Photoshop and Paint allow developers to create complex visual effects with digital images.

3. Audio

Audio files and streams play a major role in some multimedia systems. Audio files appear as a part of application content to aid interaction. Audio formats include MP3, WMA, WAV, MIDI and RealAudio. When developers include audio within a Website, they will generally use a compressed format to minimise download times.

Web services can also stream audio, so that users can begin playback before the entire file is downloaded.

4. Video

Digital video appears in many multimedia applications, particularly on the Web. As with audio, Websites can stream digital video to increase the speed and availability of playback. Common digital video formats include Flash, MPEG, AVI, WMV and Quick Time. Most digital video requires use of browser plug-in to play the video.

5. Animation

Animated components are common within both Web and desktop multimedia applications. It can also include interactive effects, allowing users to engage with the animation action using their mouse and keyboard. The most common tool for creating animations on the Web is adobe flash, which also facilitates desktop applications. Animation formats include SWF, FXG, WNF etc.

Application Areas of Multimedia

Multimedia can be used in a variety of ways. Various application areas of multimedia are as follows

1. Creative Industries

Creative industry refers to a range of economic activities which are concerned with the generation of knowledge and information. Advertising, architecture, art, crafts, design, fashion, film, music, publishing, toys, games etc., all comes under creative industries. In this area, multimedia is found to be very useful for representing information creatively.

2. Entertainment

In present time, multimedia is being heavily used for entertainment purpose. By the use of multimedia, special effects are being added in movies and animations. Multimedia games are becoming very popular among people and kids as their favourite time pass.

3. Business

In business, multimedia is being used in presentations, marketing, advertising, product demos, databases, catalogues, network etc. It is playing major role in making businesses and their products successful. Multimedia is also being widely used in training programs.

4. Schools

The most needy place for multimedia are schools. By using multimedia for explaining a concept, a live and working demonstration can be given to the students in the class itself, so that they can get into the concept and can retain it for longer period of time.

Computer based training courses are being used so that students can get a topic anytime, anywhere without the help of the instructor.

5. At Home

Gardening, cooking, home designing, repairing some home appliances etc., are the areas where multimedia is being continuously used and becoming more popular everyday as a tool in home applications.

6. Public Places

In hotels, railway stations, shopping malls, museums etc., multimedia can provide information and help to the consumers when no one is there to help them.

Hardware Requirements for Multimedia

To develop the system of multimedia, we use the various hardware components as follows:

1. CPU

The CPU, which is recommended for a multimedia computer should be Pentium IV or other advanced chips.

2. Monitor

The multimedia PC should be equipped with a monitor having atleast Video Graphics Array (VGA) card.

The basic advantage of having VGA is that it has a better resolution, thus display will be of better quality for the graphics and pictures.

3. Input-Output Devices

Keyboard and mouse are two important components for any multimedia PC. Apart from this, some commonly used hardware in multimedia are given below

- **Scanner** It allows the input of drawings, photographs or text directly into computer's memory.
- **Microphone** It can be used to allow sound to be entered into a computer's memory.
- **Graphics tablet** It allows the user to draw or trace shapes using pen which will go directly into the computer.
- **Digital camera** Photographs taken using a digital camera can be easily saved to a computer's memory.
- **Speakers** These are required to output the sound for a multimedia presentation.

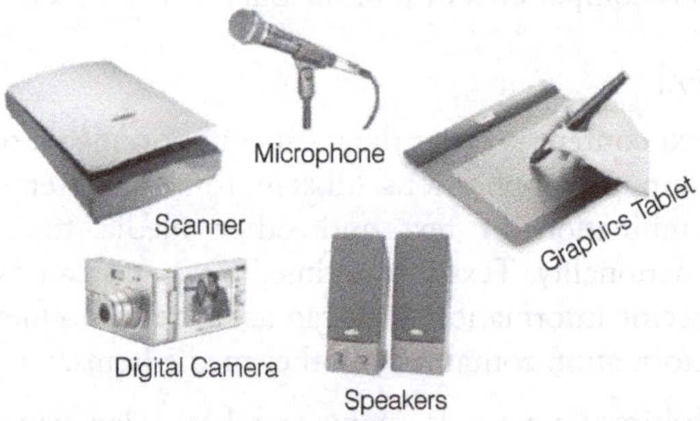

Input-Output devices

4. Sound Card

It is an expansion card or integrated circuit that provides a computer with the ability to produce sound that can be perceived by the user through a peripheral devices like speakers or headphone. If sound of better quality are required, then sound card can be added to the basic machine alongwith speakers and a microphone.

5. CD-ROM

Multimedia uses digitised audio and video, which not only take huge amount of storage space but also require high speed storage media. Also, it can send large amount of data back and forth quickly to keep audio and video playing and recording smoothly.

6. Hard Disk

It is a data storage device used for storing and retrieving digital information. A hard disk with capacity of atleast 100 MB space is required.

7. RAM

RAM stands for Random Access Memory, a type of computer memory that can be accessed randomly. A RAM of capacity atleast 64 MB is needed.

Software Requirements for Multimedia

We can classify multimedia software as system software and authoring *tools* used to develop multimedia applications. These set up the communications between the system resources and the application programs.

Some of the recent softwares used in multimedia industry are as follows

1. Photoshop

It is an industry standard digital imaging software. It uses range from full featured editing of large batches of photos to creating intricate digital paintings and drawings that mimic those done by hand.

2. Adobe Director

It is a multimedia application authoring platform created by macromedia and managed by Adobe System. It allows users to build applications that are built on a movie metaphor, with the user as the "director" of the movie. Adobe director supports both 2D and 3D multimedia projects.

3. Alias/Wavefront

It is a 3D graphic software used to create visual effect for games and movies. This software powers the creative process of users with a range of sketching, modeling, surfacing and visualising tools.

4. Premiere Pro

It is a digital video and post-production tool. It can be purchased and used along, or alongside other applications such as Adobe Photoshop, After Effects etc.

5. Sound Edit

It is a sound capture and editing tool for multimedia. This can be implemented completely or partially as library, as computer application or as a loadable kernel module.

6. Flash Player

It is a vector capture and editing tool for multimedia. It can create fancy introductions, navigation buttons, banners, slideshows, moving text and pretty much anything else which can be needed by user.

7. Front Page

It is a authoring tool for Internet and the WWW. This program offers wide functional opportunities and different tools of optimisation of collective development.

8. Optical Character Recognition (OCR) Software

When you use OCR software with a scanner, text can directly scanned into the computer's memory as a Word processed document. Once the text is scanned into the computer's Word processed then the text can be edited and saved just like any other text you may have typed into the Word processor. It is mostly used in banking area.

9. Voice Recognition Software

This software allows the user to enter text by speaking rather than typing. Voice recognition software used in many industries, including Healthcare, Military, Telecommunications and personal computing etc.

10. Handwriting Recognition Software

It is the ability of a computer to receive and interpret hand written characters, words, symbols, signatures. It may accept direct input as the case with PDA or digitizer.

Check Point 02

1. Manisha is working in animation studio. Choose name any one animation software that is useful for computer animation work.

   (a) SWF (b) FXG
   (c) WNF (d) All of these

2. Sanju's interest in art stream, he wants to make career in multimedia industry. Suggest any two creative industry name for Sanju.
3. Many of large industry areas kept individual's signature for security purpose. Which multimedia software are useful for signature verification?

SUMMARY

- Content is information that is to be expressed through some medium, speech or any of art.
- Content technologies are used for storage and transmission of data, information and multimedia.
- Data is unprocessed facts and figures.
- Information can be considered as an aggregation of processed data.
- Knowledge is usually based on learning, thinking and proper understanding of the problem area.
- Wisdom is the ability to recognise and judge which phase of the knowledge are true, right and applicable.
- Multimedia is the combined use of several media, as sound and full-motion video in computer application.
- Multimedia provides various components such as text, images, video, audio and animation.
- Text is the most widely used and flexible means of presenting information on screen and conveying idea.
- Animation is the creation of artificial moving images to replicate an event.
- Multimedia provides various application areas such as entertainment, business, schools, at home and public places.
- Some hardware equipment which are used by multimedia such as CPU, monitor, input-output devices, CD-ROM, hard disk and RAM.
- Some software which are used by multimedia such as Photoshop, Adobe Director, Flash Player, OCR etc.

Exam Practice

Multiple Choice Questions

1 Data by itself is not useful unless
(a) it is massive
(b) it is processed to obtain information
(c) it is collected from diverse sources
(d) it is properly stated

Ans. (*b*) Data is unprocessed and raw facts. It is not useful unless it is processed to obtain information.

2 For taking decisions, data must be
(a) very accurate
(b) massive
(c) processed correctly
(d) collected from diverse sources

Ans. (*c*) For taking decisions, data must be processed and manipulated correctly.

3 The data which is accurate, specific and organised for a purpose is known as
(a) data (b) multimedia
(c) wisdom (d) information

Ans. (*d*) Data after processing becomes information and it is accurate, specific and organised for a purpose.

4 Raw facts are called
(a) data (b) information
(c) knowledge (d) wisdom

Ans. (*a*) Raw facts represent unorganised form of information called data.

5 Information is
(a) data
(b) processed data
(c) manipulated input
(d) computer output

Ans. (*b*) Information is the processed form of data.

6 Alongwith knowledge, if someone has common sense to know when and how to use that knowledge then it is known as
(a) knowledge (b) internet
(c) wisdom (d) multimedia

Ans. (*c*) Wisdom is applied knowledge and it has a capacity to choose when and how to use knowledge.

7 When the content offers interactivity and users can control the progress of the content, it is called as
(a) linear multimedia
(b) non-linear multimedia
(c) animation
(d) None of the above

Ans. (*b*) Non-linear multimedia uses interactivity to control progress. e.g. video games.

8 Interactive combination of text, graphics, images, audio, video etc., is known as
(a) data (b) information
(c) multimedia (d) internet

Ans. (*c*) Multimedia is a interactive combination of text, animations, sounds, images etc.

9 Which of the following is a component of multimedia?
(a) Text (b) Images
(c) Audio (d) All of these

Ans. (*d*) Text, images, audio all are the components of multimedia.

10 The content like audio, video and animation alongwith text is called
(a) hypertext (b) multimedia
(c) hypermedia (d) None of these

Ans. (*c*) It is an extension of hypertext. Hypermedia can include text, audio, images, sounds etc.

11 Find out the odd one
(a) JPG (b) BMP
(c) WAVE (d) PNG

Ans. (*c*) WAVE is an audio format, rest are image file extensions.

12 What should be the minimum capacity of the RAM for multimedia?
(a) 32 MB (b) 64 MB
(c) 128 MB (d) 512 MB

Ans. (*b*) Atleast 64 MB RAM is needed for multimedia.

Fill in the Blanks

1 Letters, numbers and symbols are the various forms of ....

Ans. data

2 When information is manipulated and used cognitively, it is called ....

Ans. knowledge

3 Capacity to choose when and how to use knowledge is known as ....

Ans. wisdom

4 Multimedia system consists of several ....

Ans. media

5 .... disk drive must be attached to your computer to play multimedia.

Ans. 100 MB

6 Graphics provide an .... impact.

Ans. visual

7 .... is a sequential series of images that create an illusion of motion.

Ans. Animation

True or False

1 Data can be viewed at the lowest level from which information and knowledge are derived.

Ans. **True** Data are raw facts, which after processing is called information and further refinement of information is called knowledge.

2 The raw facts and unorganised form of data is called information.

Ans. **False** Organised form of data is called information.

3 Multimedia has interactivity features.

Ans. **True** Multimedia is an integration of interactive media.

4 Multimedia is an integration of sound, images, text, animation etc.

Ans. **True** Multimedia is a combination of several media like sound, hypertext, image, animation etc.

5 MP3, WMA, WAVE, MIDI are the extensions to audio files.

Ans. **True** All of the above are audio file extensions.

6 You can play your CDs using MS-Paint.

Ans. **False** MS-Paint is not a media player. It is a painting software.

7 You are not required to have a hard disk to run multimedia software.

Ans. **False** Hard disk is required for multimedia software.

8 Optical Character Recognition (OCR) software allows the user to write in his/her normal handwriting.

Ans. **False** Handwriting recognition software allows the user to write in his/her normal handwriting.

Very Short Answer (VSA) Type Questions

EXAM PRACTICE

1 What do you mean by the processing of data?

Ans. The restructuring or reordering of data by people or machine to turn it into some useful information is called processing of data.

2 What do you understand by the term information?

Ans. When data is processed, organised or presented in a given context, so as to make it useful then it is called information.

3 The processed form of data is called information. Describe the further refinement of term information.

Ans. Information after being transformed into some conceptual framework, so that it can be manipulated and used cognitively, is called knowledge.

4 Differentiate between data and information.

Ans. The raw facts are called data while the data after processing is called information.

5 "Multimedia can stimulate the eyes, ears, brain and fingertips of a person." With respect to the given statement explain the meaning of multimedia.

Ans. Multimedia means any combination of text, audio, images, animation or video used for communicating through messages or information.

6 Write down the names of the components of multimedia.

Ans. Components of multimedia are text, audio, video, images and animation.

7 Animated movies, animated games etc, are some common applications of animation. What do you understand by the term animation?

Ans. Animation is a sequential series of still images that create an illusion of motion.

8 How will you distinguish hypermedia from hypertext?

Ans. Hypertext includes only plain text and links while hypermedia is a logical extension of hypertext, which includes graphics, audio, video, alongwith plain text and links.

Short Answer (SA) Type Questions

1 What is content technology?

Ans. Content is information and experiences that may provide value for an end user in specific contexts. Content may be delivered *via* any medium such as the Internet, television and audio CDs, as well as live events such as conferences and stage performances is called content technology. The word is used to identify and quantify various formats and style of information as manageable value adding components of useful media to the target audience.

2 "Information helps us in taking decisions". What should be the characteristics of processed data in order to take meaningful decision?

Ans. For the decision to be meaningful, the processed data (or information) must have the following characteristics

(*i*) **Time** Information should be available when required.

(*ii*) **Accuracy** Information should be accurate.

(*iii*) **Completeness** Information should be complete in every aspect.

3 Explain the meaning of multimedia application.

Ans. An application that uses multiple media sources like text, graphics, audio, video, images, animation or any combination of these is known as a multimedia application.

4 Why is multimedia necessary?

Ans. Multimedia is necessary because it is a very effective presentation tool. When the various elements of multimedia like pictures, animations, sound, video clips are linked together, then these can enhance the thought process of the human brain.

5 Write down any two hardware requirements for multimedia.

Ans. Two hardware requirements for multimedia are as follows

(*i*) The CPU for a multimedia computer should be Pentium IV or other advanced chips.

(*ii*) The multimedia PC should be equipped with a monitor having atleast VGA card.

6 For the creation of multimedia on the PC, we need some softwares, what are they?

Ans. Software requirements for multimedia are as follows

(*i*) Photoshop

(*ii*) Flash

(*iii*) Voice Recognition Software

Long Answer (LA) Type Questions

1 Explain the difference between data and information alongwith the examples of each.

Ans. Refer to text on Page No. 78.

2 Differentiate between the types of multimedia with the help of an example.

Ans. Linear and non-linear multimedia are two different categories that are applicable to the world of multimedia.

Differences between linear and non-linear multimedia

Linear Multimedia	Non-Linear Multimedia
The linear multimedia will go from the start all the way through the end point without any variation.	Non-linear multimedia does not follow the one-way structure and allow free movement around all aspects of the multimedia in any order.
The user has no control over the sequence of events.	The user can control the progress and sequence of multimedia.
It is not interactive.	It is interactive.
e.g. A movie, Documentary	e.g. Game, E-Book.

3 Describe the various components of multimedia.

Ans. Various components of multimedia are as follows

(*i*) **Text** It is the most widely used and flexible means of representing information on screen and conveying ideas. It is not always a good idea to replace text with pictures or sounds, so designer should consider how to present text in an acceptable way and supplementing it with other media.

(*ii*) **Graphics** Today visualisation has become an important part of the communication process and graphical images can be used to add emphasis, direct attention, illustrate concepts and provide a background for the content.

(*iii*) **Audio** It is a very important element of multimedia application as it can enhance your multimedia application a number of ways.

(*iv*) **Video** It provides a powerful impact in a multimedia program. In multimedia applications, now-a-days the digital video is becoming very much popular. These video clips can be edited easily and can be stored like any other computer file.

(*v*) **Animation** It is a process of making a static image look like it is moving. In multimedia, now-a-days animation is being used as 2-D animation and 3-D animation.

4 Write various areas, where multimedia has found its applications in present world?

Ans. Refer to text on Page No. 79-80.

Application Oriented Questions

1 Rinku works in a fruit juice company as the marketing manager. His company has made a new mango juice and Rinku wants to make a presentation on this new fruit juice so that it can attract more and more children towards this. Suggest him some tools for making this presentation.

Ans. Rinku should make an interactive presentation and for this type of presentation nothing could be better than multimedia. He can use various multimedia components for making his presentation interactive.

2 Saurabh wants to insert graphics object in his presentation. Give him names of two graphic objects, which he can insert in his presentation?

Ans. Picture and AutoShapes

3 Give one word for each of the following:

(*i*) An audio file extension.

(*ii*) Ability to use information in a proper way.

(*iii*) Digital image file extension.

(*iv*) Software used for animation.

(*v*) Device used for better quality of sound input or output.

Ans. (*i*) MP3 or WMA or WAVE or MIDI

(*ii*) Knowledge

(*iii*) JPEG or JPG or GIF or PNG or BMP

(*iv*) Adobe Flash

(*v*) Sound Card

EXAM PRACTICE

Unit Test 1

Multiple Choice Questions

1 In computer, system state and memory space is collectively known as ....

(a) Kernel (b) Operating system
(c) Hard disk (d) CD-ROM

2 ....uses blue laser rays to read the data.

(a) Digital video disc (b) Blu-ray disc
(c) Compact disc (d) Hard disk

3 Which of the following is a system software that acts as an interface between the device and the user or the operating system?

(a) Language processor (b) Device driver
(c) Operating system (d) Utility software

Fill in the Blanks

4 Optical fibre consists of ...., cladding and protective coating.

5 .... allows to take sound as input.

6 .... is the technology that is used to create, edit, update, process and manage the digital multimedia content.

True or False

7 The output displayed on the monitor is called hard copy of a document.

8 Xing is the social network for business professionals.

9 The applied form of knowledge is called wisdom.

Very Short Answer Type Questions

10 Raw facts and figure represent, which type of term in content technology?

11 How many types of twisted pair cable?

12 Hotel management, Reservation system, Attendance system software are which type of softwares?

Short Answer Type Questions

13 Differentiate between data, information and multimedia.

14 How are the computers linked with each other in network?

15 What do you mean by private cloud?

Long Answer Type Questions

16 Explain all file types used in file system.

17 Explain the following terms

(i) Computer memory
(ii) Optical storage medium
(iii) Secondary memory

18 Explain general purpose application software.

Application Oriented Questions

19 Shivani works in a MNC and needs to work online from home also. She requires fast Internet connection. Which type of Internet connection in your view would be best suited for her? Apart from browsing on the Internet she will require uploading/downloading of files to/from remote sites. Which protocol will help her to perform this activity?

20 Rohan is researching material for a school project. He has a computer that has a CD-ROM drive and access to the Internet.

(i) Give one advantage of using the Internet rather than a CD-ROM.
(ii) Give one advantage of using a CD-ROM rather than the Internet.

Unit Test 2

Multiple Choice Questions

1 .... is a device that uses telecommunication lines for data transmission.
(a) Drive (b) MODEM
(c) Platform (d) Data

2 Which of the following is not a video file extension?
(a) MP4 (b) JPG
(c) AVI (d) QT

3 Which of the following is a utility mobile app?
(a) Facebook (b) Docs
(c) Weather (d) Subway surfer

Fill in the Blanks

4 .... is the most expensive printer which is based on principle of electro-photography.

5 .... convert and execute machine language to high level language line by line.

6 .... technique needs source device and destination device in line of sight for data transfer.

True or False

7 Networking is needed because it is very cost effective as compared to telephone networks.

8 Utility software is a small program that provides additional capabilities.

9 There are fifteen function keys available on a keyboard.

Very Short Answer Type Questions

10 Which input device is a pointing device shaped like a pen that is connected to a visual display unit?

11 Which technology is helpful in mixing the text, sound, graphics, video, animation etc?

12 Data + Content + Meaning represent, which technical content?

Short Answer Type Questions

13 State the reasons how a Blu-ray disc is superior than a DVD.

14 What is resource allocation as a function of the Kernel?

15 What are the hardware requirements for multimedia? Explain it.

Long Answer Type Questions

16 Explain, how is optical fibre advantage over the other wired media?

17 Define the hierarchical representation from data to wisdom.

18 Define the following terms
(i) Scheduling
(ii) Voice over Internet Protocol
(iii) Modem
(iv) Multimedia
(v) Bluetooth

Application Oriented Questions

19 From the following, identify general purpose software. Place a (✓) mark for the software that comes under this category or a (✗) mark for the software that does not belong to it.
(i) Appleworks
(ii) Lotus 1-2-3
(iii) File Manager
(iv) Tally. ERP9
(v) Disk compression

20 Mr. Praveen has offices in three cities. He wants to connect his computers at various offices. He is unable to decide whether he should go for three LANs for different offices or should also create a WAN connecting these three LANs.

Help him decided by suggesting what should he go for. Support your answer proper justification.

Unit Test 3

Multiple Choice Questions

1 Drum printer prints one .... of text at a time.
(a) line (b) character
(c) serial (d) None of these

2 This runs on computer hardware and serves as a platform for other software to run on.
(a) Operating system (b) System software
(c) Application software (d) All of these

3 Short range (or distance) wireless technology that needs line of sight for transmission of data is........ .
(a) Microwave (b) Satellite
(c) Infrared (d) None of these

Fill in the Blanks

4 .... is the process of passing information from one source to another.

5 .... compries images or hand written document to the computers as an electronic image.

6 The third generation language or 3GLs are high level languages such as......... .

True or False

7 There is no particular hardware and software requirement for multimedia application.

8 The node which transmits data is called a receiver in the network.

9 Computer languages are classified into low level and high level languages.

Very Short Answer Type Questions

10 What do you mean by global WAN?

11 Mention some examples of graphics software?

12 Write anyone advantage and disadvantage of a speaker.

Short Answer Type Questions

13 In which type of cables, copper is used as a conducting material?

14 Explain the differences between system software and application software.

15 List the advantages of CD-RW.

Long Answer Type Questions

16 Explain different types of keys of a keyboard.

17 Give some popular chat sites in brief.

18 Explain the following terms
(i) Computer network
(ii) Twisted pair cable
(iii) Modem
(iv) Internet
(v) Broadband

Application Oriented Questions

19 Ms. Siya is planning to gift an animation digital card to her mother on Mother's Day. She wants to include vector graphics, sound and video. But the size of the movie should be small even if requires additional plug-in to play the movie. Which of the following formats are best suited for this purpose?
(i) GIF
(ii) JPEG
(iii) SWF

20 You have been assigned the task of taking the photographs of the children's day function in the school. After taking the photographs, explain the steps you will perform to:
(i) Save the photographs in a computer as a digital file.
(ii) Generate the hard copies of the selected photographs.

CHAPTER

06

Cyber Safety

Chapter Checklist

- Safely Browsing the Web
- Safely Using Social Networks
- Identity Theft
- Proper Usage of Passwords
- Privacy
- Cyber Stalking
- Reporting a Cyber Crime
- Safely Accessing Websites : Malware

Cyber safety refers to safety in cyber space. It is a wider concept than the commonly used concept in cyber crime. Cyber safety is the safe and responsible use of Information and Communication Technologies (ICT). Various approaches to cyber safety is founded on

- Maintaining a positive approach about the many benefits brought by technologies.
- Encouraging the public to identify the risks associated with ICT.
- Putting in place strategies to minimise and manage risks.
- Recognising the importance of effective teaching and learning programmes.

Safely Browsing the Web

By using a combination of preventative measures and making good choices online you can stay safe when browsing the web. Following are the some precautions for web browsing

Before you Start : Update your Software

Exploiting e-mail and web browsing applications is the most common way hackers and malware try to gain access to devices and your information. Protect yourself before you start browsing the web by making sure that all softwares are up-to-date.

Protect your Web Browser

You can adjust the settings in your web browser to work in a more or less secure way. Most web browsers will give you warnings when they detect you visiting a malicious website. Pay attention to these warnings, they can help protect you from malware, phishing and identity theft.

Learn more about the Security Settings on your Browser

Settings and security models are different for each browsers, visit the following vendor websites to learn more about the security settings in your browser

- Internet Explorer
- Google Chrome
- Mozilla Firefox
- Opera

Safely Using Social Networks

Social networking sites such as Facebook, LinkedIn and Twitter allow users to connect with others to share information such as photos, videos and personal messages.

There are various tips, with the help of these you can protect yourself on social networking sites

- **Be cautious about how much personal information you provide on social networking sites** A common way for cyber criminals to break into your account is by clicking the 'Forget password' link. The answer to your security question could be found in your profile or it could be found in one of your posts. The more information you provide, the easier it is for hacker to steal your identity.
- **Precautions taken when you click on links** Even if these links are in a message from your friend, be cautious when clicking on the link. It could be the case where your friend's account has been hacked. It is sending malicious links to everyone on their contact list.
- **Be selective on who you accept as a friend on your social network** Identity thieves might create fake profiles in order to get information from you. People are not always who say they are.
- **Type the address of your social networking sites directly into your browser** If you click a link that leads you to a social networking website through an e-mail or another website, it may actually be a phishing website. It is design to look like the legitimate website in order to trick users into providing their user name and password. This does not apply only to social networking sites but any links you receive *via* e-mail or any other website.
- **Whatever you post online is permanent** Whatever information you posted on your social networking site is permanent. So, think twice before you post anything on social networking site.
- **Customise privacy settings** Use privacy settings to control who can see various aspects of your personal information.
- **Never use the same password for all your account** This applies not only to social networking sites but to all your online accounts. This ensures that a breach in one of your accounts does not put your other accounts at risk.
- **Be careful when you install third party applications on your social networking sites** Many social networking sites allow you to download third party applications that let you do more with your personal page. However, cyber criminals can make use of these applications to steal your personal information without your knowledge.

Identity Theft

Indentity theft is the act of a person obtaining information illegally about someone else. Thieves try to find such information as full name, maiden name, address, date of birth, passwords, phone number, e-mail and credit card numbers. The thief can then use this information to gain access to bank accounts, e-mail, identify themselves as you.

How Social Media can put you at Risk for Identity Theft

Information such as your full name, date of birth, hometown, interests and hobbies, nature of work etc, post on your profile. Criminals can easily manipulate these details to commit fraud.

You also put yourself at risk for identity theft when you post updates of your activities on your social media accounts.

How to Protect your Information on Social Media Sites

Before deleting your social accounts, you should consider that you can be aware about what you post or provide on your profiles. Here are some points to consider

- Be in control of the information you provide online. Find out how the site will use your information. As much as possible, never allow the site to make your personal information available to third party application developers.
- You should also avoid giving out your credit card number when buying additional apps. This is one way to prevent credit card fraud.
- If you plan on becoming active in social media sites, make sure you provide as little personal information as possible.
- Only invite or accept invitations from people who you know or have met. You should avoid inviting strangers or friends of friends to your network.

Proper Usage of Passwords

Your passwords are the most common way to prove your identity when using websites, e-mail accounts and your computer itself (*via* user account). The use of strong passwords is therefore essential in order to protect your security and identity.

Passwords are commonly used in conjunction with your username. However, on secure sites they may also be used alongside other methods of identification such as a separate pin and / or memorable information.

The Risk of Using Weak Passwords

People impersonating you to commit fraud and other crimes, including

- Accessing your bank account.
- Purchasing items online with your money.
- Sending e-mails in your name.
- Accessing the private information held on your computer.

Choosing the Best Passwords

Do the following to choose the best password

- To create a strong password, simply choose three random words. You can be use numbers, symbols and combination of upper case and lower case.
- Choose a password with at least eight characters.

Don't the following to choose the password

- Your or your family birthdays.
- Your username, actual name or business name.
- The word 'Password'.
- Numerical sequence.
- A single commonplace dictionary word.

Privacy

The right to privacy refers to the concept that one's personal information to be protected from public scrutiny. Privacy is related to the personal information. And, the major issues regarding an individual's right to privacy in the context of computing information is related to the following main information related functions

(*i*) Collecting information
(*ii*) Storing information
(*iii*) Distributing information

The right to privacy also involves decisions related to queries like-what information about an individual or other person must revealed to other, under what conditions and with what safety measures ? Hence, the risk of invading other's privacy is becoming more serious, as the role of information technology in decision-making is increasing day-by-day. With the increase in use of Internet as the means of information transmission, Internet can affect the privacy rights of a person.

A person's Internet usage and transactions done by him / her generates a large amount of information, which provides insights into that person's interests and other vital information. But in order to preserve personal information, it is suggested not to use computers to gather, save or distribute information that exclusively belongs to some other person.

Cyber Stalking

Cyber stalking is a form of cyber crime that takes place online when a criminal uses technology to harass or threaten a person or an organisation. It may include monitoring, identity theft, threats or gathering information that may be used to threaten, embarrass or harass.

Cyber stalking is often accompanied by real time or offline stalking. A stalker may be an online stranger or a person whom the target knows. Cyber stalking is a criminal offense under various state anti-stalking, slander and harassment laws.

Examples of Cyber Stalking

- Uploading personal information such as name, address, social security number or phone number on the Internet.
- Hacking and saving e-mails, text messages and social media posts and using them to harass or blackmail a victim.
- Hacking into the victim's social media account to post offensive material and comments.
- Using the victim's social media account or e-mail to stalk and contact others.
- Creating malicious websites, fake social media profiles and blogs about a victim.

How to Avoid Being Stalked on Social Media

There are various way from which you can avoid being stalked on social media

1. Make your Profile Private

Each social media site allows you to decide what information is shared with the web and what is private or shared with contacts. Take advantage of this feature and easily protect yourself from a stalker. Set your settings to only share information and interact with friends or contacts.

2. Disable Geotagging

Geotagging automatically shows your location from your smartphone. This can be dangerous because a stalker can know where you are. So, you should turn off all location and geotagging services for social media.

3. Hide Your Contacts

If you have a friends list on your social media account, hide it. A stalker may try to reach out to a friend of yours in order to get close to you.

4. Delete Old Accounts

If you have old accounts that are currently inactive, delete them. This is especially important if the sites have personal information or photos of you.

5. Use Security Features

Keep your computer free from threats or breaches in security by installing safety software and a firewall. If you use an account from another computer, log out before you leave.

Reporting a Cyber Crime

The procedure for reporting cyber crimes is more or less the same as for reporting any other kind of offense. The local police stations can be approached for filling complaints just as the cyber crime cells specially designated with the jurisdiction to register complaint. In addition, provisions have now been made for filling of 'E-FIR' in most of the states. The ministry of Home Affairs is also launching a website for registering crimes against women and children only including cyber crimes.

If a police station refuses to register the complaint, a representation may be given to the commissioner of police.

Check Point 01

1 Which refers to safety in cyber space ?

2 Which of the following is not consider to create password ?

(a) Space (b) Numbers

(c) Symbol (d) Alphabet

3 Write one example of cyber stalking.

Safely Accessing Websites: Malware

Malware stands for **Malicious Software**. It is a broad term that refers to a variety of malicious programs that are used to damage computer system, gather sensitive information, or gain access to private computer systems. Malware is an unwanted software that any unauthorised person wants to run on your computer.

These are known as **security threats**. It includes computer viruses, worms, trojan horses, rootkits, spyware, adware etc. Some of them are described below

1. Computer Virus

VIRUS stands for Vital Information Resource Under Siege. Virus is a harmful program, which enters a computer system and starts replicating itself and then corrupts the executable files and folders causing serious damage to the computer system. It may damage or corrupt data, change data or degrade the performance of your system by utilising resources of computer such as memory or disk space.

The virus can also affect or attack any part of the computer software such as the boot block, operating system, system areas, files and application program.

Computer virus needs to be attached with some other programs or executable files to move from one computer to another. In other words, they need host to survive and an external action to activate itself. Thus, virus is a self-replicating computer program which installs itself without user consent. E-mail attachments, games etc. are the examples of programs that generally carry viruses.

e.g. Bomber, Whale, OneHalf, KoKo, Eliza etc.

Some common types of computer virus are as follows

i. Boot Sector Virus

It is also called **Master Boot Record Virus**. A boot sector virus is a computer virus that infects a storage device's Master Boot Record (MBR). A boot sector virus usually infects the computer by altering the boot sector program. Also, boot sector mainly infects the hard disks or the floppies.

e.g. Polyboot.B, AntiEXE etc.

Note The Boot Sector is the first software loaded onto your computer. This program resides on a disk (hard disk, floppy disk or CD). When computer is turned ON, it is automatically loaded and executed. This program then loads rest of the OS into memory. Without boot sector, a computer cannot run software.

ii. Macro Virus

It is a computer virus that infects applications or programs that contain macros like .doc, .xls, .pps etc and causes a sequence of actions to be performed automatically when application is started or something else triggers it. They hide in documents shared through e-mail and networks.

e.g. Melissa.A, Relax, Bablas etc.

iii. File System Virus

It is also called **Cluster Virus** or **Directory Virus**. It infects the directory of your computer by changing the path that indicates the location of a file. It changes the directory, so that when you try to run a program, you first run the virus. e.g. Dir-2 virus

Characteristics of a Computer Viruses

The characteristics of a computer viruses are as follows

(*i*) The ability to replicate itself.
(*ii*) The ability to attach itself to another computer life.
(*iii*) It requires a host program as a carrier.
(*iv*) It is activated by external action.

Symptoms of Computer Viruses Attack

The list of symptoms of computer viruses attack, which indicate that your system is infected with a computer viruses are as follows

(*i*) Odd messages are displaying on the screen.
(*ii*) Some files are missing.
(*iii*) System runs slower.
(*iv*) PC (Personal Computer) crash or restart again and again.
(*v*) Drives are not accessible.
(*vi*) Antivirus software will not run or installed.
(*vii*) Unexpected sound or music plays.
(*viii*) The mouse pointer changes its graphic.
(*ix*) Receive strange e-mails containing odd attachments or viruses.
(*x*) PC starts performing functions like opening or closing windows, running programs on its own.

How Computer Viruses Spread?

Computer viruses can spread through e-mail attachments, application programs on your computer or application programs installed from disk drives.

A computer virus spreads from one computer to another in the following ways

(*i*) Using a local network to access infected files lying on other computer.
(*ii*) Using infected external storage devices such as CD, floppy disk and pen drive.
(*iii*) Surfing suspicious websites on the Internet.
(*iv*) Downloading infected files and gaming software from the Internet.
(*v*) Opening infected e-mail attachments.
(*vi*) Executing an infected file on a computer.

Possible Damages Caused by Virus

The damages caused by a virus, which infect a home computer or a corporate network can be different from insignificant increase in outgoing traffic to the complete network breakdown or the loss of critical data. There are many different effects that viruses can have on your computer, depending on the types of virus. Some viruses can

(*i*) Monitor, what you are doing on computer.
(*ii*) Slow down your computer's performance. Also, can cause the system to hang.
(*iii*) Download illegal files onto your computer without you being able to delete them.
(*iv*) Destroy all data on your local disk, alter data in data files and can destroy specific executable files.
(*v*) Generates IP addresses randomly and sends those IP address automatically.
(*vi*) Effects computer networks and the connection to Internet.
(*vii*) Steal confidential information like password, account number, credit card information by random e-mailing.
(*viii*) Destroys the file allocation table, which leads to the corruption of an entire file system. Thus, arising the need to reinstall the system.
(*ix*) Reduces the available disk space or memory space by creating duplicate files.
(*x*) Creates bad sectors on the disk, destroying parts of programs and files.

Virus Prevention

There are many ways, that a virus cannot be entered into your computer. You can follow these guidelines to prevent a virus attack

i. Do not open unknown attachments in e-mails or do a virus scan after opening them.
ii. Download files only from trusted sites.
iii. Always use an antivirus software program, with both an on-demand and an on-access scanner.
iv. Update your antivirus regularly.
v. Regularly update window.
vi. Always enable the firewall on your computer network.

2. Trojan Horse

A Trojan or Trojan Horse, is a non-self replicating type of malware, which appears to perform a desirable function but instead facilitates unauthorised access to the user's computer system. It is a code hidden in a program such as a game or spreadsheet that looks safe to run but has hidden side effects. When such program runs, the trojan destroys, damages or alter the data in the background while it seems to function as per the user expectation.

Trojans do not attempt to inject themselves into other files like a computer virus. Trojan horses may steal information, or harm their host computer systems. Trojans may use drive by downloads or install *via* online games or Internet-driven applications in order to reach target computers.

e.g. Beast, Sub7, Zeus, ZeroAccess rootkit etc.

How Trojan Horses Spread?

Trojans are generally downloaded with some other program or application. Trojans are also spread through e-mail and exchange of disks and information between computers.

Trojan, itself is a program that does not need a host to embed itself. e.g. A holi wishing executable application, which appears like any other program wishing you 'Happy Holi' but causing great damage in the background.

Possible Damages Caused by Trojan Horses

The damages caused by a trojan horse is similar to that caused by a computer virus. Generally, users are unaware of the damages caused by a trojan horse because it remains hidden and undefected for long periods.

3. Computer Worm

It is a standalone malware computer program that replicates itself in order to spread to other computers. Often, it uses a computer network to spread itself, relying on security failures of the target computer to access it. Unlike a computer virus, it does not need to attach itself to an existing program. Worms squad spread much more rapidly than computer viruses.

Worms generally use such part of operating system, which are automatic and usually work in the background. Worms almost always cause atleast some harm to the network, even if only by consuming bandwidth, whereas viruses almost always corrupt or modify files on a targeted computer. Worms are hard to detect because they are invisible files. e.g. MS-Blaster, Sobig Worm, Melissa Worm etc.

Characteristics of a Computer Worm

The characteristics of a computer worm are as follows

(*i*) Self-contained program and does not require a host.
(*ii*) Activated by creating process.
(*iii*) Able to replicate itself across network links.

How Computer Worms Spread?

Generally, worms are found on computers that are capable of multitasking and connected by a network. Computer worms are self-sufficient viruses that are capable of propagating themselves without the use of another program or involvement of a user.

Possible Damages Caused by Computer Worms

Some computer worms scan passwords and other sensitive information and send these information back to the creator of the computer worm. Sometimes, computer worms can also install trojan horses or viruses that cause damage to the system.

4. Spyware

It is a type of malware that is installed on a computer without the knowledge of the owner in order to collect the owner's private information. Spyware is often hidden from the user in order to gather information about Internet interaction, keystrokes, passwords and other valuable data. Spyware is a general term used to describe software that performs certain behaviours, generally without appropriately obtaining your consent first, such as advertising, collecting personal information, changing the configuration of your computer etc.

e.g. TryMedia, Nuvens, Live PC Care etc.

Impacts of Spyware on your Computer

The various impacts that a spyware can have on your computer are as follows

(*i*) Your PC is start running unusually slow, spyware could be hogging the system's resources.

(*ii*) Ads are popping up even when your browser is not opening or they are addressing you by name.

(*iii*) Your browser's home page has been changed without doing anything.

(*iv*) You have invasive toolbars appearing in your browser.

(*v*) Your anti-spyware and/or antivirus programs are not working correctly. Like viruses, some spyware will sabotage the programs designed to detect and eliminate them.

(*vi*) There is a dramatic increase in Internet traffic, soaking up bandwidth on your Internet connection, making it slow.

Preventions of Spyware

Due to the seriousness of spyware and the harm, it can affect your system and personal information, it is highly recommended you to take the given measures to prevent spyware from overtaking your system

- **Download and install anti-spyware software** Most antivirus applications are effective in identifying different types of malware, including spyware, but may not detect all spyware variants. Once you install the anti-spyware software on your computer, you must keep your anti-spyware application updated to keep up with the latest forms of spyware.
- **Be cautious when web surfing** The best defense against spyware is not to download it in the first place. Spyware is often installed on your computer when you visit an infected or malicious website.

Therefore, you should exercise caution with links to websites from unknown sources. In addition, you should only download programs from trustful websites. When downloading a specific program, ensure that you are not downloading pirated software. Spyware can be distributed by exploits, that promote software piracy.

- **Lookout for pop-ups** Malware can lure you into installing spyware on your computer by prompting you with a pop-up window. If you see an unwanted or random pop-up alert, do not click 'Agree' or 'OK' button to close the pop-up window. This will actually install the malware on your computer. Instead, press Alt + F4 or click on the red 'X' on the corner on the pop-up alert to close the window.
- **Keep current with operating system updates** Important system updates provide significant benefits such as improved security. Just as with any antivirus and anti-spyware software, not keeping up with operating system updates will make your PC vulnerable to the latest malware threats.
- **Harden your browser settings** Updated web browsers may help to prevent exploitation by taking several defensive steps against spyware. Most web browsers will warn you of executable programs and will suggest a safe course of action. In addition to having an updated web browser, ensure that you have properly configured your browser and that all of your plug-ins and add-ons are updated, including Java, Flash and Adobe products.
- **Enable your firewall** Firewalls monitor the network and are capable of blocking suspicious traffic, which can prevent spyware from infecting your system.

5. Spam

It is usually defined as unsolicited e-mail. Spam is an electronic messaging system used by various commercial organisations to send bulk messages to a large number of addresses.

E-mail spam, junk mail or junk newsgroup postings is a widely recognised form of spam.

How to Avoid Spam?

You can use the following guidelines to avoid spam

(*i*) Keep your e-mail address private.

(*ii*) Using appropriate filters to find and alert you about spam.

(*iii*) Use alternate style of writing your e-mail addresses on the web.

(*iv*) Avoiding the use of your true ID when signing-up to various websites.

Some Other Kinds of Cyber Attacks

Adware

These are the kind of unwanted programs which appear on your computer as advertisements.

They harm the network bandwidth, slow down the speed of your computer, change the home page of your computer and reduce the stability and usability of your system.

Phishing

When Internet fraudsters impersonate a business to trick you into giving out your personal information, it is called phishing.

Do not reply to e-mail, text or pop-up messages that ask for your personal or financial information. Phishing is a method of online identity theft.

Password Cracking

The process of attempting to guess or crack passwords to gain access to computer system or network is called password cracking. Crackers will generally use a variety of tools, scripts or software to crack a system's password.

Denial of Service

It is a type of attack on a network that is designed to bring the network to its knees by flooding it with useless traffic. e.g. DOS attacks, there are software fix that system administrators can install to limit the damage caused by the attacks. This type of attack eats up all the resources of a system and the system or application come to a halt.

Sweeper

This is a type of malicious program used by crackers. It is used to erase information from your computer.

Check Point 02

1 It can appear in the form of executable code, scripts, active content and other software. What is it?

2 Which type of virus hides in the documents shared through e-mail and networks?

(a) Boot sector virus (b) Macro virus

(c) File system virus (d) Directory virus

3 A new year wishing executable application, which appears like any other program wishing you 'Happy New Year' but causing great damage in the background. Which type of virus will be behind it?

SUMMARY

- Cyber safety is the safe and responsible use of information and communication technology.
- Identity theft, also known as identity fraud, is a crime in which an imposter obtains key pieces of personally identifiable information.
- Privacy is the ability of an individual or group to schedule themselves or information about themselves.
- Cyber stalking is a criminal practice where an individual uses the Internet to systematically harass or threaten someone.
- Malware is a file or code, typically delivered over a network that infects, explores, steals or conducts virtually any behaviour an attacker wants.
- A computer virus replicates by copying itself to another program, computer boot sector or document and changes how a computer works.
- Computer worm replicates itself over a computer network and usually performs malicious actions.
- Trojan horse is a type of malware that is often disguised as legitimate software.
- Spam is unsolicited bulk messages sent through email with commercial, fraudulent or malicious intent.

Exam Practice

Multiple Choice Questions

1 Cyber safety is the responsible use of

(a) IT (b) ICT
(c) Social networks (d) Passwords

Ans. (*b*) Cyber safety is the safe and responsible use of Information and Communication Technology (ICT).

2 In identity theft, thieves try to find

(a) full name (b) phone number
(c) date of birth (d) All of these

Ans. (*d*) In identity theft, thieves try to find such information as full name, maiden name, address, date of birth, passwords, phone number, e-mail etc.

3 .... stands for Malicious Software, is software designed to infiltrate a computer system without the owner's informed consent.

(a) Blog (b) Attachments (c) Spam (d) Malware

Ans. (*d*) Malware designed to interrupt ongoing computer operations, collect private information and gain unauthorised access to your system resources.

4 Which one of the following is not a malware?

(a) Computer virus (b) Spam
(c) Worm (d) Application software

Ans. (*d*) Application software

5 ....refers to the condition in which your computer stops working.

(a) Hang (b) Virus attack
(c) Hacking (d) None of these

Ans. (*a*) Hang refers to the condition in which your computer or software stops working.

6 Which of the following is not a symptom of a virus attack?

(a) The computer begins to run slowly
(b) Unusual messages and graphics appear on the screen for inexplicable reasons
(c) Some programs or data files on the computer either become corrupt or are difficult to locate
(d) Your data is copied to another location

Ans. (*d*) Your data is copied to another location is not a symptom of a virus attack.

7 A good way to safeguard access to your computer is to protect it.

(a) Deadbolt (b) Copyright
(c) Safemode (d) Password

Ans. (*d*) Password is a good way to safeguard access to your computer to protect it.

8 Which of the following is the first computer virus?

(a) Brain (b) Melissa
(c) Elk Cloner (d) I Love You

Ans. (*c*) Elk Cloner is the first computer virus created by Richard Skrenta.

9 Out of the following, which one will be altered or modified by a computer virus?

(a) Operating system
(b) Speed of network connectivity
(c) Application software
(d) All of the above

Ans. (*d*) All of the above

10 Which one of the following is not a way to get a computer virus?

(a) Through e-mail attachments
(b) Through pen drive
(c) By typing on keyboard
(d) By downloading files

Ans. (*c*) By typing on keyboard is not a way to get a computer virus.

11 The .... at first glance will appear to be useful software but will actually do damage once installed or run on your computer.

(a) worm (b) virus
(c) trojan (d) spam

Ans. (*c*) The trojans are unauthorised programs placed inside a legitimate application.

12 A .... is a virus that is often disguised as a useful computer program.

(a) trojan horse (b) hacker
(c) worm (d) spam

Ans. (*a*) Trojan horse is a virus, i.e. often disguised as a useful computer program.

13 A .... is a software program that is designed to copy itself from one computer to another, without human intervention.

(a) trojan (b) virus
(c) worm (d) spam

Ans. (*c*) A worm is a self-replicating software program. It does not require another program to host it.

14 Which of the following is not an example of worm?

(a) MS-Blaster (b) Sobig
(c) De bumper (d) Melissa

Ans. (*c*) De bumper is a type of trojan horse.

15 Which of the following statements is incorrect in the context of a worm?

(a) It represents a category of malware
(b) It creates infections in a computer
(c) It is self replicating
(d) It cannot travel on its own

Ans. (*d*) Worm is self replicating software and thus, it can travel on its own.

16 A category of software that spies of your computer activities is

(a) De-ware (b) Spyware
(c) Utilities (d) Freeware

Ans. (*b*) Spyware is a category of software that spies computer activities.

17 The electronic equivalent of junk mail is known as

(a) adware
(b) cyber fraud
(c) spam
(d) packets

Ans. (*c*) Spam is an electronic equivalent of junk mail.

Fill in the Blanks

1 ……… are commonly used in conjunction with your username.

Ans. Passwords

2 Geotagging automatically shows your …….. from your smartphone.

Ans. location

3 ……… is the general term to refer to infectious software such as virus, worm, spyware etc.

Ans. Malware

4 A malicious program that is used to remove all information from your computer is known as ……… .

Ans. sweeper

5 A ………… infects the files of the operating system.

Ans. boot sector virus

6 …… and …… are the two types of malware.

Ans. Viruses, worms

7 ……… can decrease the space on hard disks by duplicating files.

Ans. Viruses

8 ……… is a program that appears harmless but actually performs malicious functions.

Ans. Trojan horse

9 …………… is a software program that is designed to copy itself from one computer to another.

Ans. Worm

10 Unlike a computer virus, a ……… can replicate itself automatically.

Ans. worm

11 ………… is a type of malware that is installed on a user's computer and collects information about user without their consent and knowledge.

Ans. Spyware

12 Any crime committed using computers and Internet is termed as ………… .

Ans. cyber crime

True or False

1 A stalker may be an online stranger.

Ans. **True** A stalker may be an online stranger or a person whom the target knows.

2 To create a strong password, you can use a single commonplace dictionary word.

Ans. **False** To create a strong password, you should never use a single commonplace dictionary word.

3 A virus may corrupt or delete data on your computer.

Ans. **True** A virus may corrupt or delete data on your computer.

4 A virus is a harmful program, which one entering a computer, starts creating copies of itself.

Ans. **True** Virus is a malicious program that is designed to make a system sick, just like a real virus.

5 A worm is a self-replicating program which eats up the entire disk space.

Ans. **False** Virus eats up the entire disk space.

6 Spyware is a type of malware but is not capable of collecting personal information.

Ans. **False** Spyware is a type of malware used to collect personal information without his or her knowledge.

7 Adware is a software that posts unwanted advertisements on your computer.

Ans. **True** Adware is a software that is given to the user with unwanted advertisements embedded in the application.

8 Always scan the storage media before connecting it to your computer.

Ans. **True** You should always scan your storage media before connecting it to your computer.

9 Junk e-mails are also called spam.

Ans. **True** E-mail spam, junk mail or junk newsgroup posting is a widely recognised form of spam.

Very Short Answer (VSA) Type Questions

1 What do you mean by cyber safety ?

Ans. Cyber safety refers to safety in cyber space which concept is wider than commonly used concept in cyber crime.

2 Write any two risk of using weak passwords.

Ans. (*i*) Accessing the bank account.

(*ii*) Sending e-mails in your name.

3 What is geotagging ?

Ans. Geotagging automatically shows your location from your smartphone.

4 Define virus.

Ans. A virus is a harmful program, which on entering a computer, starts creating copies of itself. It then attacks by corrupting the executable files and folders saved on the computer.

5 List the different types of computer viruses.

Ans. (*i*) File system viruses (*ii*) Boot sector viruses

(*iii*) Macro viruses

6 Name some forms of malware.

Ans. Worms, Trojan horse, Computer Virus etc.

7 Give some examples of computer worms.

Ans. MS-Blaster, Mellisa worm, SQL Slammer worm are the common examples of worms.

8 Explain denial of service attack.

Ans. A denial of service attack is a type of attack that consumes all the resources of a computer.

9 Privacy deals with personal information. Explain the meaning of term personal information.

Ans. Personal information is the information that identifies you or could identify you. e.g. your name, address etc.

Short Answer (SA) Type Questions

1 What is the proper usage of passwords ?

Ans. The stronger your password, the harder it is to guess. Use special characters like symbols and capital letters when creating your password. Also, don't use common passwords, like your birthday or your child name.

2 What do you mean by cyber stalking ?

Ans. Cyber stalking is a crime in which the attacker harasses a victim using electronic communication, such as e-mail or Instant Messaging (IM), or messages posted to a web site or a discussion group. Cyber stalking messages differ from ordinary spam in that a cyber stalker targets a specific victim with often threatening messages.

3 Write the various tips which help you to protect yourself on social media.

Ans. (*i*) Be selective on who you accept as a friend on your social networks.

(*ii*) Be cautious when you click on links.

(*iii*) Never use the same password for all yours account.

4 How does a virus affect your computer?

Ans. Virus is a software used to infect a computer. After virus code is written, it is buried within an essential programmed. Once the programmed is executed, the virus code is activated and attack copies itself to other programs.

5 Give three guidelines to prevent the virus attack.

Ans. Three guidelines to prevent the virus attack are as follows

(*i*) Avoid the temptation to open unexpected e-mail attachments and downloads from unreliable sources. Resist the urge to double click everything in your mailbox.

(*ii*) In stable reliable antivirus, scanning software and download its updates regularly.

(*iii*) Scan files downloaded from the Internet or other external sources.

6 If your computer attacked by a trojan horse, what damage it may cause?

Ans. If your computer attacked by a trojan horse, it can

(*i*) Steal passwords

(*ii*) Copy sensitive data

(*iii*) Carry out any other harmful operations etc.

7 Write minimum three ways by which a virus can spread to other systems.

Ans. Three ways by which a virus can spread to other systems are as follows

(*i*) When an infected files is copied through network.

(*ii*) When virus file is downloaded from Internet.

(*iii*) When infected file is copied from floppy disk, USB DVD etc.

8 Write any two tips to avoid spams.

Ans. You can use the following guidelines to avoid spam, they are as follows:

(*i*) Keep your e-mail address private.

(*ii*) Using appropriate filters to find and alter you about spam.

9 What are the primary interest of online attackers in spyware?

Ans. Primary interest of online attackers in spyware is using it to steal personal information for financial crimes such as carding and identity theft or to sell that information to someone else who then executes more traditional financial crimes.

10 "Internet can affect the privacy rights of a person." Comment.

Ans. A person's Internet usage and transactions done by him/her online provides a large amounts of information which provides insight into that person's interests and other vital information about the person.

Hacking or tracking of activities of some person without his/her knowledge have become prominent with the increase usage of Internet. Hence, a person with malicious intent can easily invade in some other person's privacy online.

Long Answer (LA) Type Questions

1 Write the various ways from which to avoid being stalked on social media.

Ans. There are various ways from being stalked on social media

- **Hide your contacts** You should hide your contacts because a stalker may try to reach out to a friend of yours in order to get close to you.
- **Use security features** Keep your computer free from threats or breaches in security by installing safety software and a firewall.
- **Disable geotagging** It can be dangerous because a stalker can know where you are. So geotagging should be disable.
- **Make your profile private** Always make your profile private, to protect yourself from a stalker. Set your settings to only share information.
- **Delete an old account** You should delete your old account that are inactive.

2 What are the tips for protecting yourself against identity theft ?

Ans. Refer to text on Page No. 91.

3 What are the common symptoms of a virus attack ?

Ans. Refer to text on Page No. 94.

4 What are the various measures that should be taken to prevent spyware from overtaking your system ?

Ans. Refer to text on Page No. 96.

5 Why is individual's right to privacy important in today's world?

Ans. Recent advances in information technology threaten privacy and have reduced the amount of control over personal data and open up the possibility of a range of negative consequences as a result of access to personal data. A variety of information on individuals is kept in databases. These databases house information, such as social security numbers, credit card numbers, medical histories, family histories and many more. Practically, every organisation has a database full of information on everyone they do business with. The concern with this is whether or not they should be collecting this information, what they will do with it, how secure it is, how accurate it is and to whom it can be sold. Personal data is increasingly made available in online databases, which can be accessed by search engines. The question that concerns is: should personal information, like we discussed, be so readily available to the public? The availability of personal information shows no signs of slowing. Infact, courts and government agencies at all levels are increasingly making public records available online. Some find it troubling given the sensitive information contained in the available documents. For instance, someone filing for bankruptcy must disclose their social security number, their bank and credit card numbers, account balances and even childrens names and ages.

One of the fastest growing crimes has been identity theft. Identity theft is the stealing of another person's social security number, credit card number, or other personal information for the purpose of paying bills, using the personal information to do illegal activities using other person's identity. In some cases, thieves even withdraw cash directly from the victim's bank account. Since, many private organisations and governments keep information about individuals in accessible databases, there is an endless opportunity for thieves to retrieve it and misuse the information.

Application Oriented Questions

1 It is an electronic messaging system used by various commercial organisations to send bulk messages to a large number of e-mail addresses. What is it?

(*i*) E-mail (*ii*) Spam
(*iii*) SMS (*iv*) Adware

Ans. (*ii*) Spam

2 Mohan has downloaded few attachments in his mail to his system from Internet. When he opened those attachments there were multiple copies of the same file opened. After sometime his system got rebooted automatically. He is unable to find out why his system is not responding properly. Can you tell what happened to his system and give him some solutions?

Ans. There is a virus (most likely worm) in Mohan's computer, that has caused damage to data and files on his system. He should install antivirus software, such as Kaspersky, Quick Heal, McAfee etc, as the main defense against online problems. He should take backup of his files regularly.

EXAM PRACTICE

Unit Test

Multiple Choice Questions

1. Which of the following is not a malware?
   (a) Virus (b) Worm
   (c) Human ware (d) Adware
2. The computer threat that delivers unwanted ads to your computer.
   (a) Adware (b) Spyware
   (c) Worm (d) Trojan
3. Never use the same ……… for all your account.
   (a) password
   (b) username
   (c) address
   (d) phone number

Fill in the Blanks

4. The program created for wiping up data of the computer is called …………… .
5. A person who pretends himself as if someone else and does a crime. The crime is known as ………… .
6. User should choose a password with at least …………… characters.

True or False

7. The spyware searches information and sends it out.
8. Flooding the network with bits and jamming the traffic causes denial of service attack.
9. Keeping a copy of the data which can be used when original is lost accidentally in known as spam.

Very Short Answer Type Questions

10. What is meant by spam ?
11. Which refers to the concept that one's personal information to be protected from the public scrutiny ?
12. What is the example of cyber stalking ?

Short Answer Type Questions

13. Differentiate between virus and worm.
14. If the boot sector is infected by the virus, will it affect the working of the computer?
15. How can you report a cyber crime?

Long Answer Type Questions

16. Difference between spyware and trojan.
17. What are the various approaches where cybersafety found ?
18. How to protect your information on social media sites?

Application Oriented Questions

19. Poorvi's computer teacher has asked her to search for virus program on the Internet. Help her to use the Internet to collect information on different virus program available. List out virus program that you discovered during your search and describe them.
20. The process of attempting to guess or crack passwords to gain access to computer system or network is called
    (i) Denial of service (ii) Password cracking
    (iii) Sweeper

CHAPTER

07

Unit III

MS-Word Basics

Chapter Checklist

- Word Processor
- MS-Word 2007
  - Getting Started with MS-Word 2007
  - Creating a New Blank Document
  - Saving a Document
  - Opening and Closing an Existing Document
  - Formatting Text
  - Line Spacing and/or Paragraph Spacing
  - Working with Pictures
  - Page Setting
  - Header and Footer
  - Numbering Pages
  - Correct Spelling and Grammar
  - Using superscript and Subscript
  - Inserting Symbols
  - Printing
- Shortcut Keys for MS-Word

Microsoft Word is a Word processing software package. You can use it to type letters, brochures, newsletters, reports and other documents. It also gives you the ability to use your computer for desktop publishing. In this chapter, you will learn about the basic features of Microsoft Word 2007 that can help you making your documents more attractive.

Word Processor

Word processing software is used for the creation of text based documents. It is a GUI based software used in the Windows environment. A Word processor is a software package that processes textual matter and creates organised documents. In a precise manner, it is an application that is directed by the user, performs Word processing which includes the composition, editing, formatting and sometimes printing of any sort of material. Word processor is different from the conventional typewriter. In this, the document is not printed while typing the text, but it can be stored in computer's memory and displayed on the screen. After completing the typing and verification, user can print the document. There are many software packages available to do the job of Word processing. Some examples of Word processing softwares are AppleWorks, Microsoft Word, StarOffice, TextMaker, WordPerfect, OpenOffice.org Writer etc.

Features of Word Processor

Word processing packages have some features, which are as follows

- You can open and save an existing document and make changes wherever you want. Thus, the saved document can be retrieved whenever required.
- The typed text can be made to appear in any font or style.
- It provides facility of incorporating drawing in the documents, which enhances their usefulness. Mail merge facility enables you to print a large number of letters/documents with more or less similar text. The complete document or a part of the document can be reformatted.
- It allows user to create and include tables in the document.
- A Word processor automatically fits the typed text within the specified left and right margins. This feature is called **word wrapping**.

MS-Word 2007

It is the Word processing software developed and marketed by Microsoft in 2006. It allows you to easily create a variety of impressive and effective documents using features such as formatting text, working with pictures and many more.

Getting Started with MS-Word 2007

Steps to start MS-Word 2007 are as follows

Step 1 Click **Start** button.

Step 2 Click **All Programs.**

Step 3 Then, click **Microsoft Office.**

Step 4 Finally, click **Microsoft Office Word 2007.**

It opens MS-Word with a blank document. By default, the name of the blank document is **Document1.docx,** where .docx is the extension of a MS-Word 2007 file.

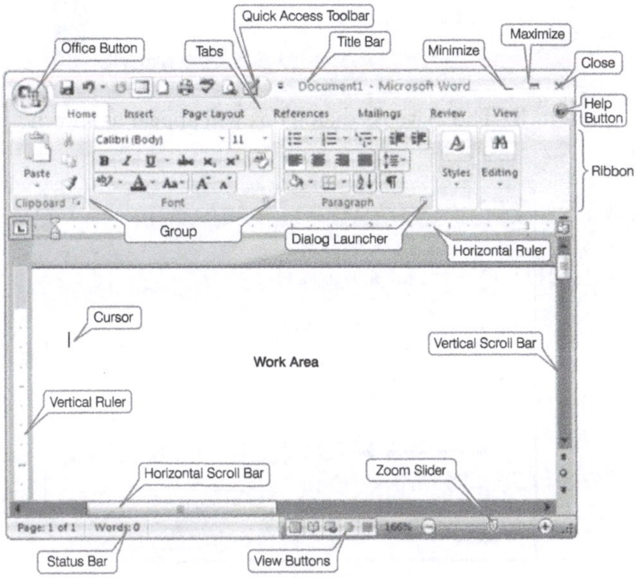

MS-Word 2007 window

The major components of MS-Word 2007 are as follows

Office Button

It is located on the top-left corner of MS-Word window. When the **Office** button is clicked, many of the options such as New, Open, Save, Save As, Print etc, will be found.

Title Bar

It is located at the top of the window and displays the document name. The format of the name displayed on the title bar is **Document name - Microsoft Word.**

Quick Access Toolbar

It is placed to the right of the Office button. It contains shortcut key for commonly used tools like Save, Undo, Redo etc.

Tabs

These are similar to the menu bar of MS-Word 2003. Instead of having drop down menus, MS-Word 2007 creates a Ribbon system, where buttons and commands are grouped under the tabs. Some groups include a dialog launcher button in their lower right corner to bring up the additional options.

Different types of tabs are as follows

- **Home** tab is used to change font, styles, setting of paragraph etc.
- **Insert** tab is used to insert page breaks, tables, illustrations, links, header and footer, text and symbols etc.
- **Page Layout** tab is used to change themes of a page, margin of a page, orientation of a page, insert a page border, column, format paragraph etc.
- **References** tab is used to insert table of contents, foot notes, citations and bibliography, captions, index, mark entry for index etc.
- **Mailings** tab is used to create envelopes, labels, start mail merge, write and insert fields and preview results etc.
- **Review** tab is used for proofing, comments, tracking, comparing the documents etc.
- **View** tab is used to change the outline or draft views, display the ruler or document map, zoom, switch windows etc.
- **Developer** tab is used to visual basic, record macro, protect document and document template etc.

After inserting a picture in MS-Word 2007, a new tab appears namely - **Picture Tools Format.** It includes Adjust, Picture Styles, Arrange and Size groups in it. By using this tab, a user can edit pictures according to his/her need.

Ribbon

In this, there are many buttons/options that are grouped into categories according to tab such as Clipboard, Font, Paragraph, Styles, Editing etc, which are the options of Home tab.

Ruler

It appears on the top and on the left side of the document window. Ruler is used to set tabs, indents and margins for a document. Also, it allows to format the horizontal or vertical alignment of text in a document.

The two types of ruler are as follows

1. **Horizontal ruler** It indicates the width of the document which is used to get left and right margins.
2. **Vertical ruler** It indicates the height of the document, which is used to get top and bottom margins.

Scroll Bar

It is used to view the whole active window by scrolling. There are two types of scroll bars, i.e. horizontal scroll bar and vertical scroll bar.

Status Bar

It is displayed on the bottom of the window which is used to view the information such as page number, current page, current template, column number, line number etc.

Work Area/Work Space

It is the rectangular area of the document window, where you can type the text, insert the pictures etc.

Creating a New Blank Document

Each time when you open MS-Word, a new blank document will appear. However, you will also need to know how to create a new document while an existing document is open.
Steps to create a new blank document are as follows:

Step **1** Click the **Microsoft Office** button.

Step **2** Select **New**, the **New Document** dialog box will appear as shown below:

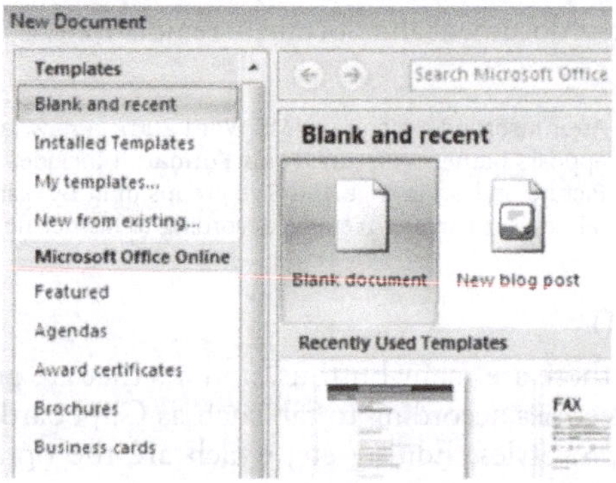

New Document dialog box

Step **3** Select **Blank document** under the Blank and recent section (It will be highlighted by default).

Step **4** Click **Create** button, a new blank document will appear.

Saving a Document

To permanently store a document in the default file format on hard disk, you must have to save the document and assign a name to it.

Use the Save As Command

Steps to save a document in the default file format using Save As command are as follows

Step **1** Click the **Microsoft Office** button.

Step **2** Then, click **Save As → Word Document.**

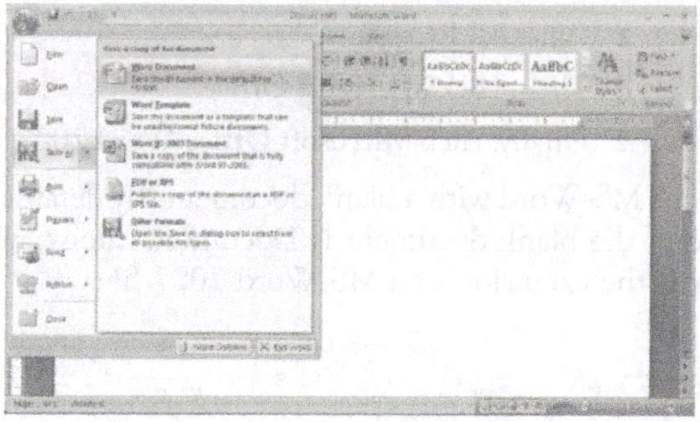

Step **3** The **Save As** dialog box will appear as shown below:

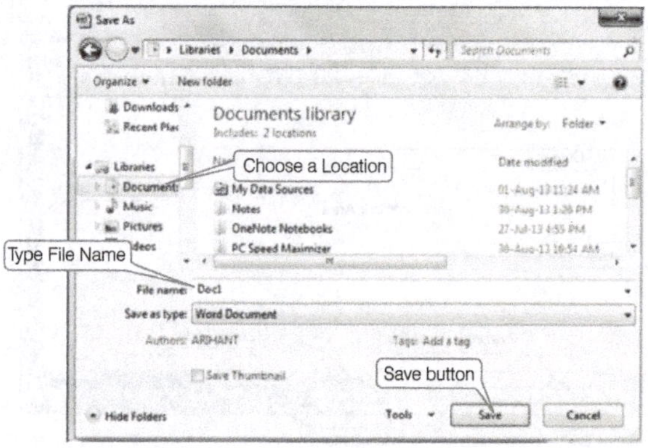

Step **4** Select the **location**, where you want to save the document using the drop down menu.

Step **5** Enter the name of the document in **File name** box.

Step **6** Finally, click the **Save** button.

Save as a Word Template

A **template** is a collection of styles and formatting options. Every document in Word is based on a template. If you create a new blank document, it uses blank template. Using Word Template, save a document as a template that can be used to format new documents.

Steps to save a document as a Word template are as follows

Step 1 Click the **Microsoft Office** button.

Step 2 Select **Save As → Word Template**. The **Save As** dialog box will appear.

Step 3 Select the **location**, where you want to save a template using the drop down menu.

Step 4 Enter the name for the template in **File name** box.

Step 5 Click the **Save** button.

Use your template when creating new documents

Step 1 Click the **Microsoft Office** button.

Step 2 Select **New**, the **New Document** dialog box will appear.

Step 3 Under **Templates,** click on **My templates...** A **New** dialog box will appear.

Step 4 Select an existing template and click on **OK** button.

Step 5 A new document will open as in template format.

Save as a Word 97-2003 Document

Steps to save a document as a Word 97-2003 are as follows

Step 1 Click the **Microsoft Office** button.

Step 2 Select **Save As → Word 97-2003 Document**. The **Save As** dialog box will appear.

Step 3 Select the **location**, where you want to save a document using the drop down menu.

Step 4 Enter a name for the document in **File name** box.

Step 5 Click the **Save** button.

Save as a PDF or XPS

Steps to save a document as a PDF or XPS are as follows

Step 1 Download the PDF extension

(a) Click the **Microsoft Office** button.

(b) Select **Save As → Find add-ins for other file formats.** This will open your web browser to the Microsoft site.

(c) Follow the given instructions on the Microsoft site for downloading the PDF extension.

Step 2 Click the **Microsoft Office** button.

Step 3 Select **Save As → PDF or XPS**. The **Publish as PDF or XPS** dialog box will appear.

Step 4 Select the **location**, where you want to save the document using the drop down menu.

Step 5 Enter the name of the document in **File name** box.

Step 6 Click the **Publish** button.

Use the Save Command

Steps to save a document using Save command are as follows

Step 1 Click the **Microsoft Office** button.

Step 2 Save the document in its current location with the same file name.

Differences between Save and Save As

"Save" means the file gets saved under its current name, in whatever folder it was saved before or in the default folder of that computer whereas "Save As" gives you the opportunity to save the file under a different name and in another folder. "Save As" allows you to save the updated version with a new name while at the same time preserving the old version.

Check Point 01

1 OpenOffice.org Writer and AppleWorks are the examples of which software?

2 What is the name of blank document by default in MS-Word 2007?
(a) Document. word (b) Document1. docx
(c) Document. docx (d) Doc. docx

3 What is the use of Quick Access Toolbar?

4 In how many ways, you can save a document?

Opening and Closing an Existing Document

After saving a file, you can open the same file any time for further changes or updations to be made, save the changes made and then, close it.

Steps to open an existing document are as follows

Step 1 Click the **Microsoft Office** button and click **Open** and then, an **Open** dialog box will appear.

Step 2 Locate the folder in which the file is stored.

Step 3 Type the name of the file, which you want to open and then, click the **Open** button.

Steps to close an active document are as follows

Step 1 Click the **Microsoft Office** button.

Step 2 Click the **Close** button.

Formatting Text

To create and design effective documents, you need to know how to format text, in order to make your documents more appealing and formatted to draw the reader's attention.

Format Font Size

Steps to format the font size of text are as follows

Step 1 Select the **text** that you want to modify.

Step 2 Click the **drop down** arrow next to the Font Size box in the Font group on the Home tab. The Font Size drop down menu will appear.

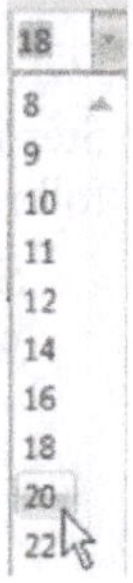

Step 3 Move your cursor over the various font sizes. A live preview of the font size will appear in the document.

Step 4 Choose the **font size** that you want to use.

Format Font Style

Steps to format the font style of text are as follows

Step 1 Select the **text** that you want to modify.

Step 2 Click the **drop down** arrow next to the Font Style box in the Font group on the Home tab. The Font Style drop down menu will appear.

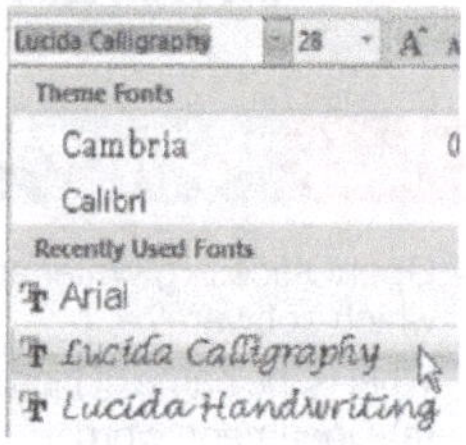

Step 3 Move your cursor over the various font styles. A live preview of the font style will appear in the document.

Step 4 Choose the **font style** that you want to use.

Format Font Color

Steps to format the font color of text are as follows

Step 1 Select the **text** that you want to modify.

Step 2 Click the **drop down** arrow next to the Font Color box in the Font group on the Home tab. The Font Color menu will appear.

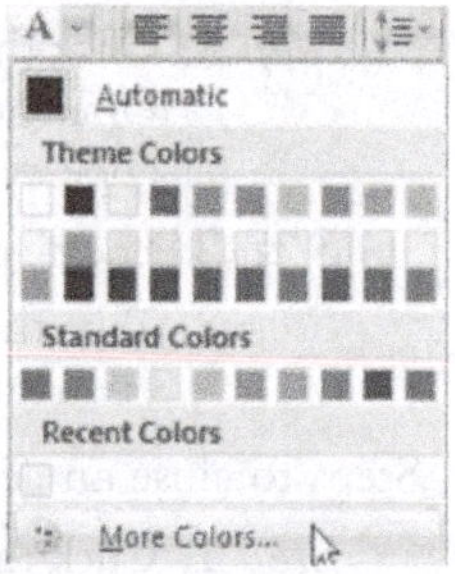

Step 3 Move your cursor over the various font colors. A live preview of the font color will appear in the document.

Step 4 Choose the **font color** that you want to use.

Note Your color choices are not limited to the drop down menu that appears. You can select **More Colors** ... option at the bottom of the list to access the Colors dialog box. Choose the color that you want and then, click **OK**.

Use Bold, Italic and Underline Commands

Steps to bold, italic and underline the text are as follows

Step 1 Select the **text** that you want to modify.

Step 2 Click the **Bold**, **Italic** or **Underline** button in the Font group on the Home tab.

Change the Text Case

Steps to change the text case, i.e. lowercase, uppercase are as follows

Step 1 Select the **text** that you want to modify.

Step 2 Click the **Change Case** option from the Font group on the Home tab.

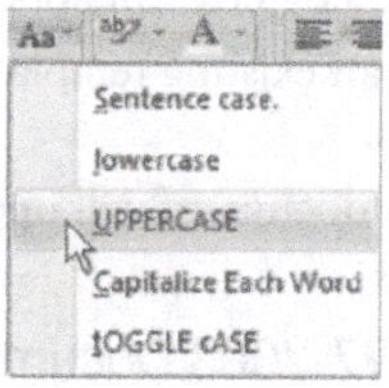

Text Case Options	Description
Sentence case	Changes the first letter of every sentence in uppercase.
lowercase	Changes the whole selected text in lowercase letters.
UPPERCASE	Changes the whole selected text in uppercase letters.
Capitalize Each Word	Changes first letter of every word in capital case.
tOGGLE cASE	It toggles whole selected text, i.e. changes each capital letter into lowercase and each small letter into uppercase.

Step 3 Select one of the text case option from the list as per the requirement.

Change Text Alignment

The text layout within a paragraph with respect to document margins is called *text alignment*. Steps to change the text alignment in a document are as follows

Step 1 Select the **text** that you want to modify.

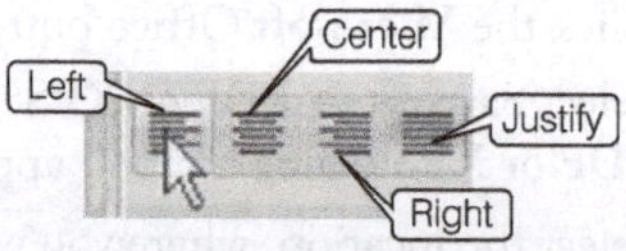

Step 2 Select any one of the four alignment options (i.e. Left, Right etc) from the Paragraph group on the Home tab.

Command Tab	Description
Align Text Left	Aligns all the selected text to the left margin.
Center	Aligns all the selected text to an equal distance from the left and the right margins.
Align Text Right	Aligns all the selected text to the right margin.
Justify	Aligns all the selected text equal from both the sides and lines up equally to the left and the right margins. Traditionally many books, news letters and newspapers use full-justification.

WordArt

It is a gallery of text styles that you can add to your documents to create decorative effects, such as shadowed or mirrored (reflected) text. You can also convert existing text into WordArt.

Line Spacing and/or Paragraph Spacing

It is an important part of creating effective documents that lies in the document design. Line spacing or paragraph spacing is measured in lines or points, which is referred as **leading**. When you reduce the leading, you automatically bring the lines of text closer together. Increasing the leading will increase space between the lines, allowing for improved readability.

Format Line Spacing/Paragraph Spacing

Steps to format the line or paragraph spacing are as follows

Step 1 Select the **text** or **paragraph** that you want to format.

Step 2 Click the **Line spacing** in the Paragraph group on the Home tab.

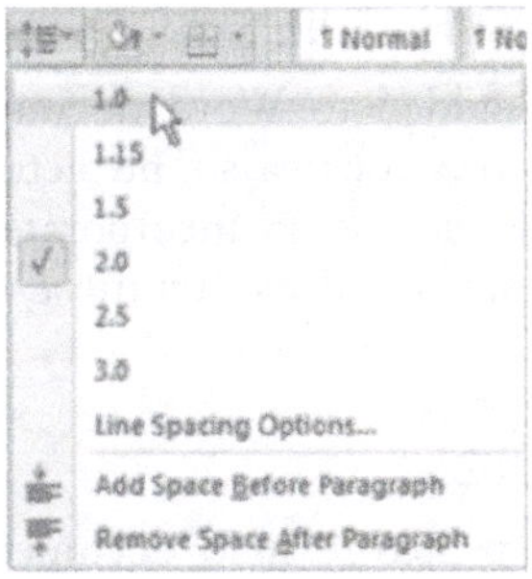

Step 3 Select any **Spacing** option as per the requirement.

or

Select **Line Spacing Options...** . The **Paragraph** dialog box will appear as shown below:

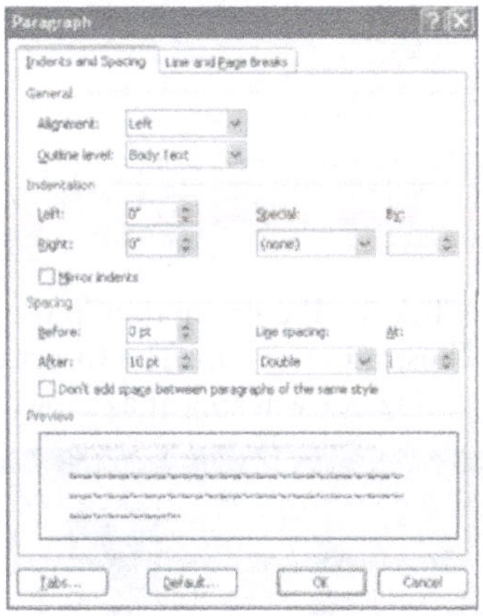

Paragraph dialog box

Step 4 Use the **Line spacing** drop down menu to select a spacing option (i.e. Single, Double, Multiple etc).
Modify the **Before** and **After** points to adjust line spacing as needed.

Step 5 Then, click **OK**.

Compare, how spacing can affect the appearance of text

Summary
Tech-Savvy, solutions-oriented professional with experience in all aspects of office management, administration, and support. Multi-tasking team-player with knowledge of training solutions and database management.

Default spacing

Summary
Tech-Savvy, solutions-oriented professional with experience in all aspects of office management, administration, and support. Multi-tasking team-player with knowledge of training solutions and database management.

Single spacing

Summary
Tech-Savvy, solutions-oriented professional with experience in all aspects of office management, administration, and support.

Double spacing

Working with Pictures

Pictures can be added to Word documents and then, formatted in various ways. The picture tool in MS-Word makes it easy to incorporate pictures into your documents and modify those images in an innovative way.

Insert a Picture

Steps to insert a picture in a document are as follows

Step 1 Place the insertion point, where you want to place the picture.

Step 2 Select the **Insert** tab.

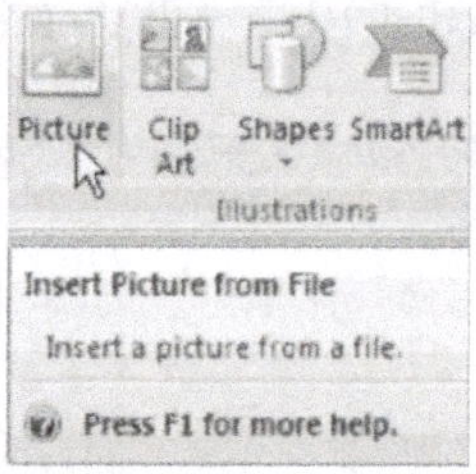

Step 3 Click the **Picture** option in the Illustrations group. The **Insert Picture** dialog box will appear as shown below:

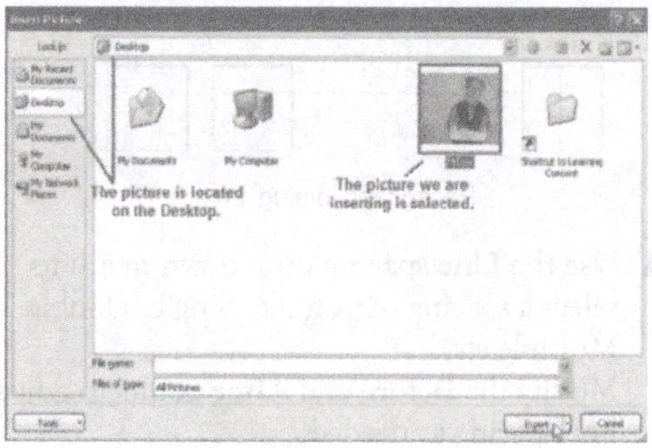

Insert Picture dialog box

Step 4 Select the **picture**.

Step 5 Click **Insert** button and then picture will appear in your document.

Wrap Text Around a Picture

Steps to wrap text around a picture in a document are as follows

Step 1 Select the **picture**.

Step 2 Select the **Picture Tools Format** tab. (This tab appears only after insertion of a picture).

Step 3 Click the **Text Wrapping** in the Arrange group.

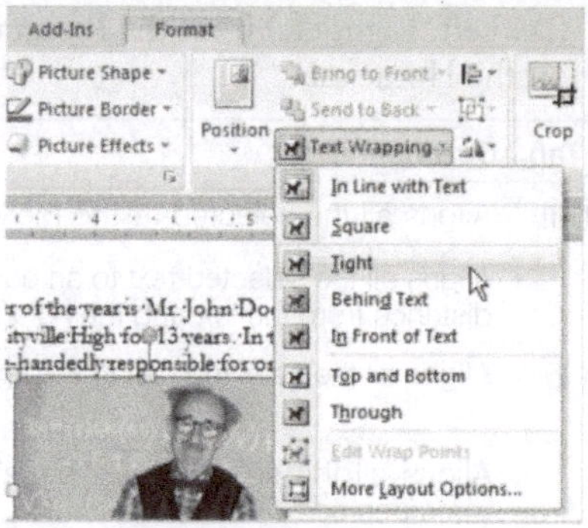

Step 4 Select any one option from the drop down list. In this example, we will select **Tight**.

Step 5 Move the picture around to see how the text wraps for each setting. The Position button has pre-defined text wrapping settings. The Position button is placed to the left of the Text Wrapping button.

Step 6 Click the **Position** button and a drop down list of Text Wrapping options will appear. Move your cursor over the various text wrapping styles. A live preview of text wrapping will appear in the document.
If you cannot get your text wrapped the way you wish, select **More Layout Options...** from the **Position** menu. You can make more precise changes from the **Advanced Layout** dialog box that appears.

Crop a Picture

Steps to crop a picture in a document are as follows

Step 1 Select the **picture**.

Step 2 Click the **Picture Tools Format** tab.

Step 3 Click the **Crop** button from **Size** group. The black cropping handles appear around the picture.

Step 4 Click and move a handle to crop the picture.

Step 5 Corner handles will crop the picture proportionally.

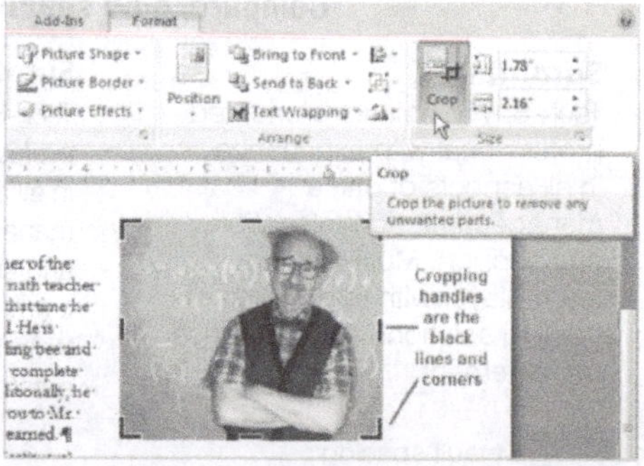

Compress a Picture

Steps to compress a picture in a document are as follows:

Step 1 Select the **picture.**

Step 2 Click the **Picture Tools Format** tab.

Step 3 Click the **Compress Pictures** in the Adjust group. A **Compress Pictures** dialog box will appear as shown below

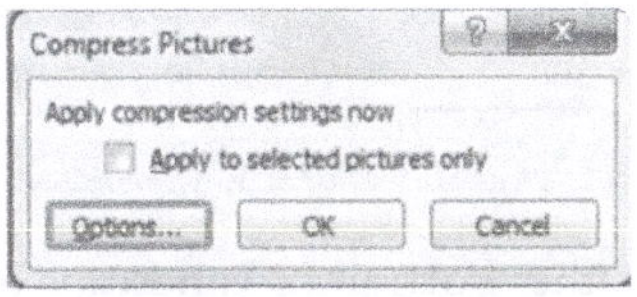

Step 4 Click the **Options...** button to access the **Compression Settings** dialog box as shown below:

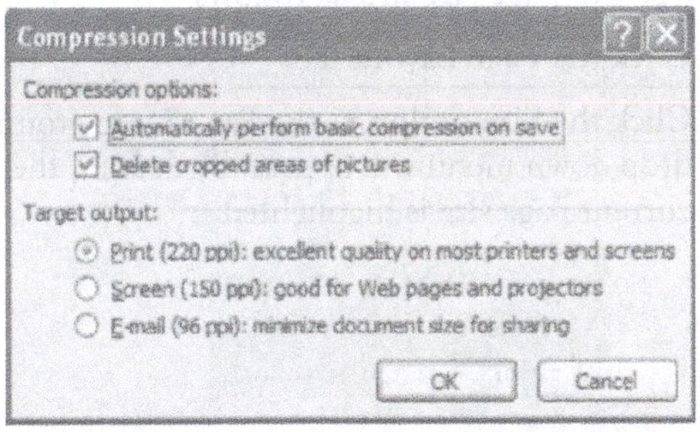

Step 5 Choose any of the **Target output** as per the requirement.

Step 6 Click on the check box(s) under the **Compression options** as per the requirement.

Step 7 Click **OK** button in the Compression Settings dialog box.

Note You need to monitor the file size of your picture and documents that include some graphics, especially if you send them *via* E-mail. Cropping and resizing the picture do not decrease the picture file size, but compression does.

Other Picture Tools

There are many other things that you can do to modify a picture. From the Picture Tools Format tab, some of the other useful features are as follows

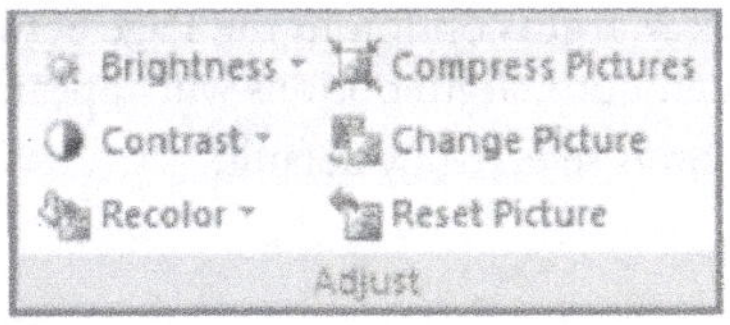

- **Brightness** Adjust the brightness of the picture.
- **Contrast** Adjust the contrast of the picture from light to dark.
- **Recolor** Modify the color in a variety of ways including black, white, sepia, pink, purple and many more.
- **Change Picture** Change to a different picture preserving the formatting and size of the current picture.
- **Reset Picture** Revert to original picture.

Change the Shape of a Picture

Steps to change the shape of a picture in a document are as follows

Step 1 Select the **picture.**

Step 2 Click the **Picture Tools Format** tab.

Step 3 Click the **Picture Shape** in the **Picture Styles** group. A Picture Shape menu will appear.

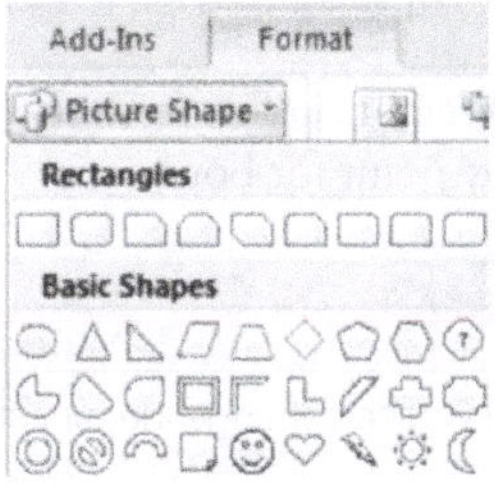

Step 4 Choose any **shape** as per the requirement.

Apply a Picture Style

Steps to apply a picture style in a document are as follows

Step 1 Select the **picture.**

Step 2 Click the **Picture Tools Format** tab.

Step 3 Click **More** drop down arrow in **Picture Styles** group to display all the Picture Styles.

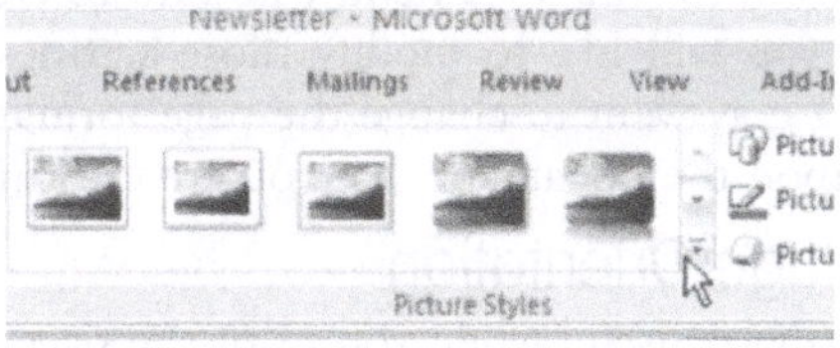

Step 4 However, when a cursor moves over different picture styles, the live preview of the style will be displayed on the picture in a document.

Step 5 Choose **any style** as per the requirement.

Add a Border to a Picture Manually

Steps to add a border to a picture manually in a document are as follows

Step 1 Select the **picture.**

Step 2 Click the **Picture Tools Format** tab.

Step 3 Click the **Picture Border** from the **Picture Styles** group. A drop down menu will appear.

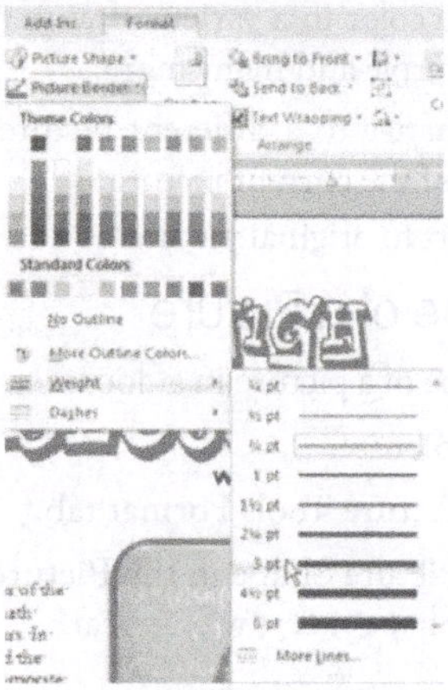

Step 4 Select **Weight** option from the list and then click any point for border.

Check Point 02

1 Using which option you can change the font style of the text in a document?

2 What is the use of Sentence case command?

3 Which alignment is used to align all the selected text equal from both the sides?

(a) Justify (b) Center
(c) Align text left (d) Align text right

4 Which option of Picture Tools Format tab helps you to modify the color in a variety of ways?

Page Setting

You may find that the default page settings in MS-Word are not sufficient for the document, you want to create, in that case you will like to modify those settings. In addition, you may want to change the page formatting depending upon the document that you are creating.

Change Page Orientation

Page orientation is useful when you print the pages. By default, MS- Word shows a page in portrait orientation and in this case, page width is less than page length. You can change page orientation from portrait to landscape orientation, in this case, page width is more than page length. Steps to change the page orientation (portrait or landscape) are as follows

Step 1 Click the **Page Layout** tab.

Step 2 Click the **Orientation** option in the **Page Setup** group, a drop down menu will appear as shown below:

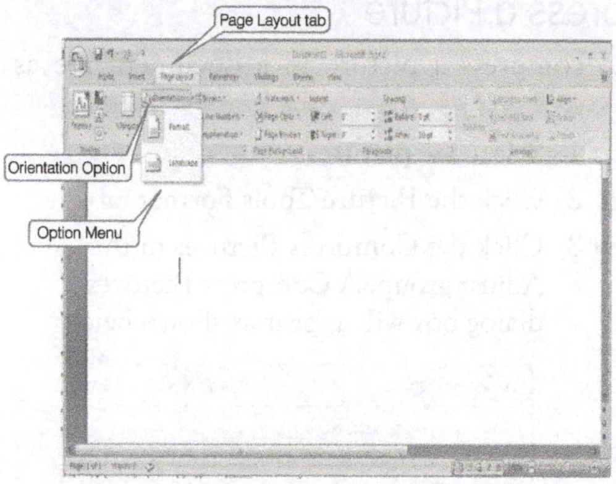

Step 3 Click either **Portrait** or **Landscape** option to change the page orientation.

Change the Page Size

Steps to change the page size are as follows

Step 1 Click the **Page Layout** tab.

Step 2 Click the **Size** option in the Page Setup group, a drop down menu will appear. By default, the current page size is highlighted.

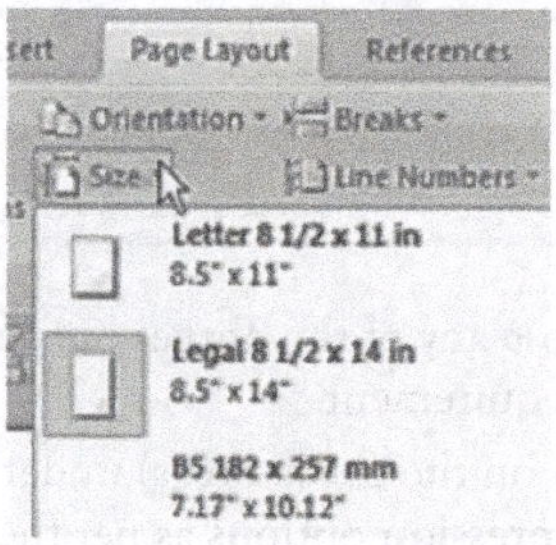

Step 3 Select the **size** as per your requirement and parallely changes will appear on a document.

Format Page Margins

Margins are the space between the edges of the paper and the text.

You can adjust right, left, top and bottom margins of your document. By default, MS-Word sets all margins (left, right, top and bottom) to 1 inch.

Steps to format the page margins are as follows

Step 1 Click the **Page Layout** tab.

Step 2 Click **Margins** option in the **Page Setup** group. A menu of margin options will appear. Normal option is selected by default.

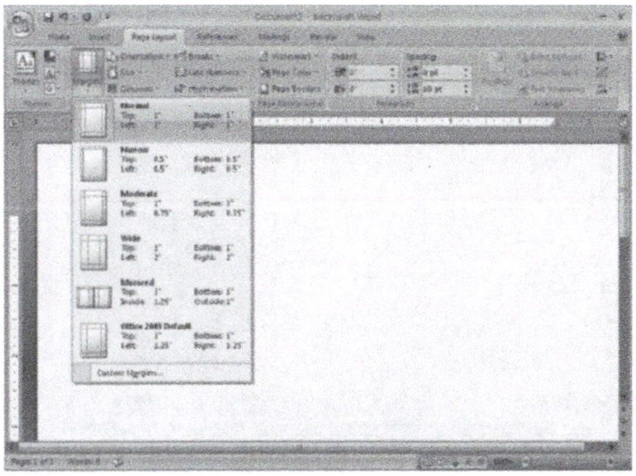

Step 3 Click the predefined margin size according to your need.

or

Select **Custom Margins...** from the menu. The **Page Setup** dialog box will appear. Enter the desired margin size in the appropriate fields.

Note You can also access the Page Setup dialog box by clicking the small arrow in the bottom-right corner of the Page Setup group.

Insert a Break

Steps to insert a break in a document are as follows

Step 1 Place your insertion point, where you want to appear the break.

Step 2 Select the **Page Layout** tab.

Step 3 Click the **Breaks** option in the **Page Setup** group. A drop down menu will appear as shown below

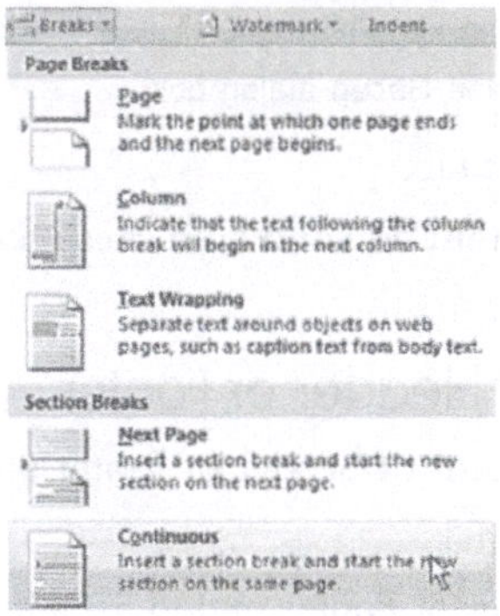

Step 4 Choose any break option as per your requirement. The break will appear in the document.

Why would you use a break?

Each type of break serves a different purpose which affects a document in different ways

Page break moves the text to a new page before reaching the end of a page and creates a barrier between parts of a document for formatting purposes.

Column break splits text in columns at a specific point.

Text Wrapping break keeps the text together with consistent formatting, which flows the rest of the document around this section.

Next Page break starts the new section on the next page. This type of section break is especially useful for starting new chapters in a document.

Continuous break starts the new section on the same page. A continuous section break is useful for creating a formatting change, such as different number of columns on a page.

Even Page or **Odd Page** break starts the new section on the next even numbered or odd numbered page respectively.

Header and Footer

You can make your documents professional and polished by utilising the header and footer sections. The header is a section of the document that appears at the top margin, while the footer is a section of the document that appears at the bottom margin.

Header and footer generally both contain information such as page number, date, document name, company logo, image etc, which are specified by page styles. Therefore, when inserted, all pages with the same page style will display same header and footer.

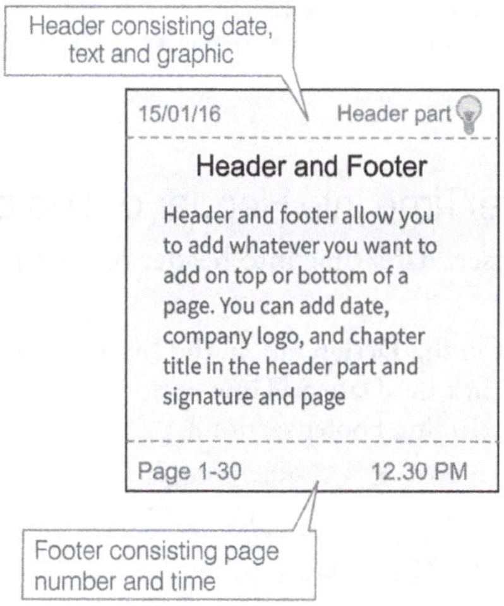

Header and Footer areas

Insert Header or Footer

Steps to insert header or footer in a document are as follows

Step 1 Click **Insert** tab.

Step 2 Select **Header** or **Footer** from **Header & Footer** group. A menu will appear with a list of Built-In options as shown below

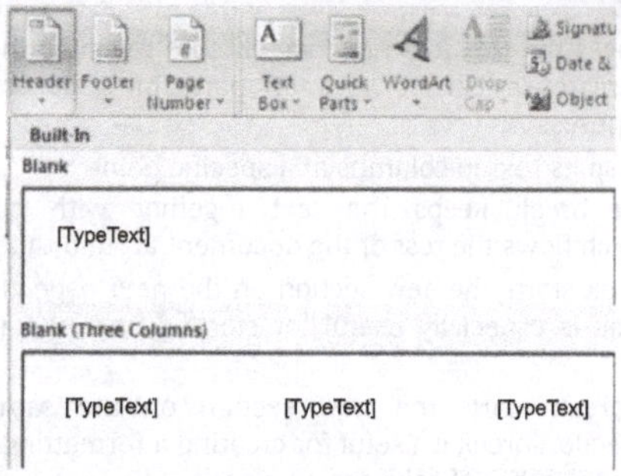

Step 3 Click one of the Built-In options as per your requirement and it will appear in the document.

Step 4 Then, Header/Footer workspace is activated on the page.

Step 5 Type information (number/text/date) or insert an image into the header or footer section.

Note Once the Header/Footer workspace is activated, the **Header & Footer Tools** with **Design** tab is displayed similar to below figure:

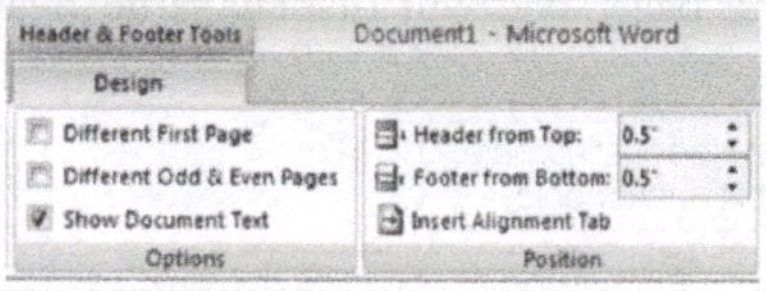

Insert Date/Time into Header or Footer

Steps to insert date/time into header or footer are as follows

Step 1 On the **Design** tab, in the **Insert** group, click the **Date & Time** option (after selecting Footer section).

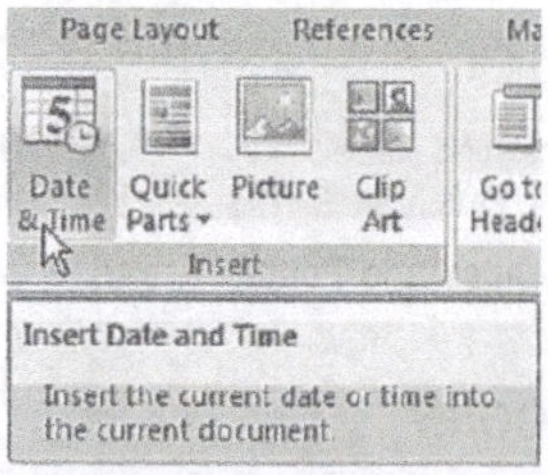

Clicking the Date & Time

Step 2 A Date and Time dialog box will appear as shown below:

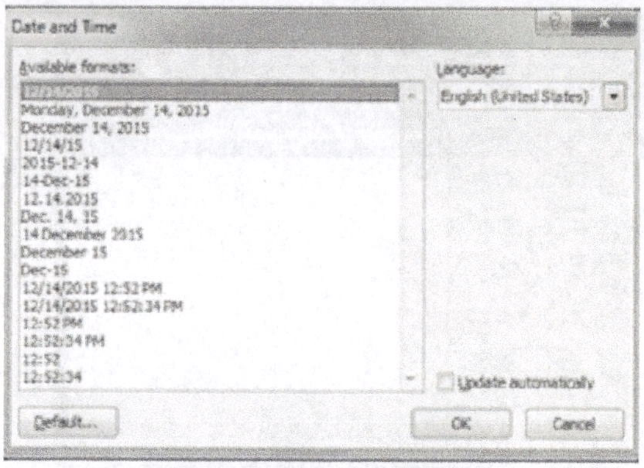

Date and Time dialog box

Step 3 Select date and time format from the **Date and Time** dialog box.

Step 4 Click **OK**.

Now, Date/Time will appear in the document.

Make the Header or Footer Different for Odd and Even Pages

Steps to make the header or footer different for odd and even pages are as follows

Step 1 Choose **Page Layout** tab.

Step 2 Click the small icon at the bottom-right of the **Page Setup** group. A **Page Setup** dialog box will appear as shown below

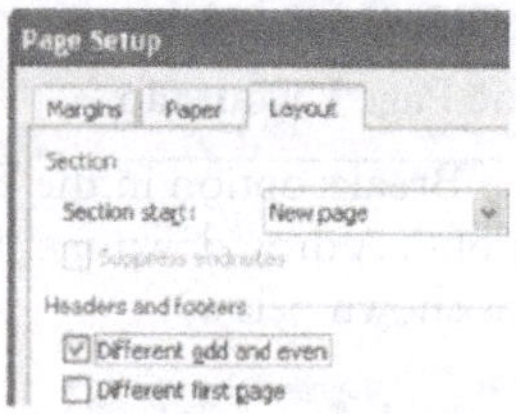

Page Setup dialog box

Step 3 Click **Layout** tab.

Step 4 Select **Different odd and even** check box.

Step 5 Click **OK**.

Edit the Content of Header or Footer

Steps to edit the content of header or footer are as follows

Step 1 Click **Insert** tab.

Step 2 Select **Header** or **Footer** option from the **Header & Footer** group.

Step 3 Click **Edit Header** or **Edit Footer**.

or

Double click on **Header** or **Footer workspace**.

Now, you can edit the content of Header or Footer.

Remove Header or Footer

Steps to remove header or footer are as follows

Step 1 Click **Insert** tab.

Step 2 Select **Header** or **Footer** option from the **Header & Footer** group.

Step 3 Click **Remove Header** or **Remove Footer.**

Now, header or footer will get removed from the document.

Numbering Pages

If your document has multiple pages, you can display the page number on each page.

Steps to insert page numbers in a document are as follows

Step 1 Click **Insert** tab.

Step 2 Click **Page Number** option from **Header & Footer** group.

Step 3 In the Page Number pop-up list, make sure that the position and alignment of the page numbers is according to your choice.

Step 4 For more page numbers options, click on the **Format Page Numbers...** option.

Step 5 The Page Number Format dialog box will appear as shown below

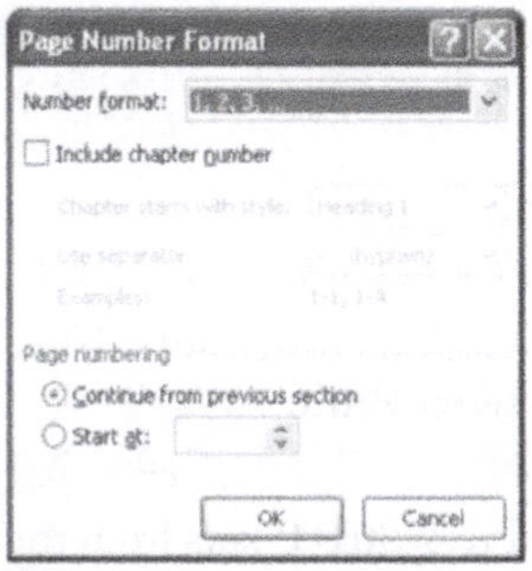

Page Number Format dialog box

Step 6 Choose **Number format.**

Step 7 Click **OK.**

Correct Spelling and Grammar

Spelling mistake is the most common type of mistakes that can occur while typing a document.

Proofing group is not used only for spelling and grammar check, but it is also used for thesaurus, translation, language setting, word count etc.

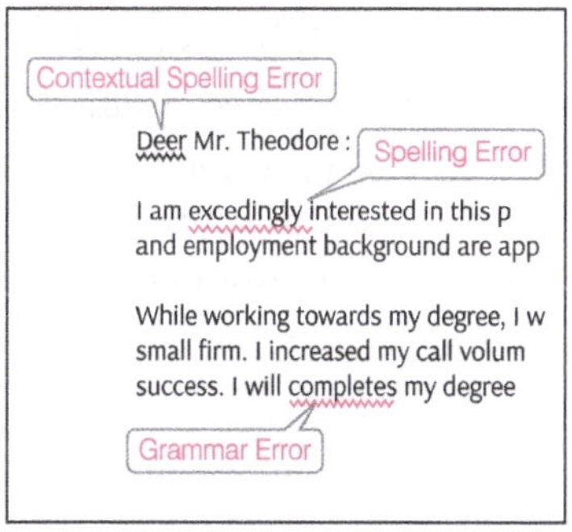

Auto spell check

By default, MS-Word automatically checks the spellings and grammatical errors in your document. These errors are indicated by different colored wavy lines, such as

- The **red wavy line** indicates a possible Spelling Error.
- The **green wavy line** indicates a possible Grammar Error.
- The **blue wavy line** indicates a possible instance of inconsistent formatting or a Contextual Spelling Error. A contextual spelling error occurs when an incorrect spelling for a word is chosen.

e.g. If someone writes, "Deer Mr. Theodore," at the beginning of a letter, Deer is a contextual spelling error because one should have used Dear.

Deer is spelled correctly, but it is used incorrectly in this context.

Using the Spelling Check Feature

Steps for using the spelling check feature are as follows

Step 1 Right click on the **word** (having wavy line). A context menu will appear.

Step 2 Select the **correct spelling** of the word from the listed suggestions.

or

To check the spell and grammar mistake, you can also **press F7** key.

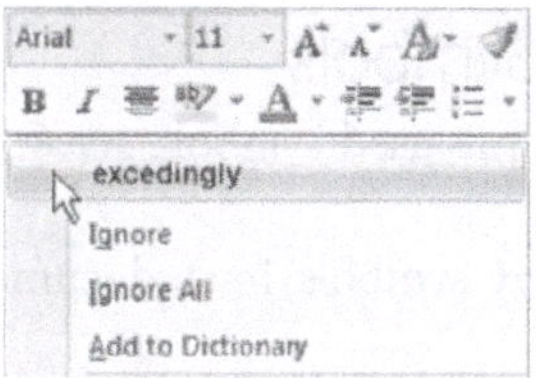

Suggested word

You can also choose **Ignore** option to ignore the word, **Add to Dictionary** or go to the **Spelling** dialog box.

Using the Grammar Check Feature

Steps for using the grammar check feature are as follows

Step 1 Right click on the **word** (having wavy line). A context menu will appear.

Step 2 Select the **correct word** from the listed suggestions.

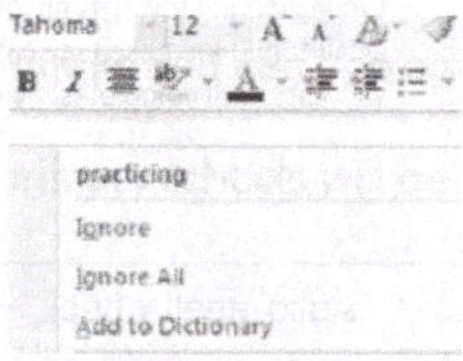

Suggested word

You can also choose **Ignore Once** option to ignore the word, go to the **Grammar...** dialog box or find out more information about the word and its usage.

Using Superscript and Subscript

A **superscript** is a number, figure or symbol that appears slightly above a word or a letter. A **subscript** is a number, figure or symbol that appears slightly below a word or a letter.

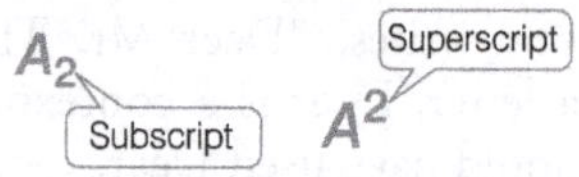

Steps to apply superscript and subscript are as follows:

Step 1 Select the **text** on which you want to apply a particular effect.

Step 2 Then, right click on the word.

Step 3 Choose **Font...** option. A Font dialog box will appear.

Step 4 Select the check box of **Superscript** or **Subscript** under the **Effects.**

Step 5 Click **OK** button.

You can also apply superscript or subscript effect to a selected text by clicking the Superscript or Subscript options in the **Font** group on **Home** tab.

Inserting Symbols

Some commonly used symbols are @, 1/2, α, β etc.

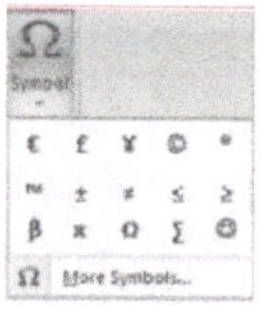

Steps to insert symbols in a document are as follows:

Step 1 Select **Insert** tab.

Step 2 Click **Symbol** option from **Symbols** group.

Step 3 Select **More Symbols...** option.

Step 4 Click on the **Symbols** tab, select the symbol that you want to insert.

Step 5 Click **Insert** button.

Check Point 03

1 It is a section of the document that appears at the top margin.
(a) Header
(b) Footer
(c) Superscript
(d) Subscript

2 Which wavy line indicates a possible Grammar error?

3 What do we call a number that appears slightly above and slightly below a word or a letter?

Printing

Once you complete all the modifications in your document, you may want to print it for various reasons. This topic covers the three basic features of printing in MS-Word including Print, Quick Print and Print Preview.

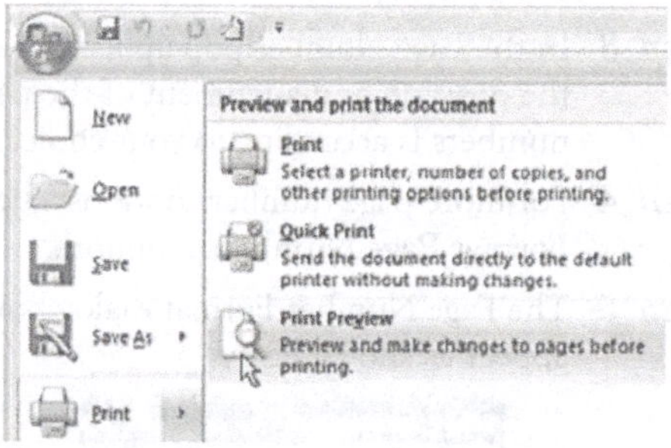

Print

Steps to print a document are as follows

Step 1 Click the **Microsoft Office** button and select **Print.**

or

Press **Ctrl+P** keys from the keyboard.

Step 2 The **Print** dialog box will appear as shown below

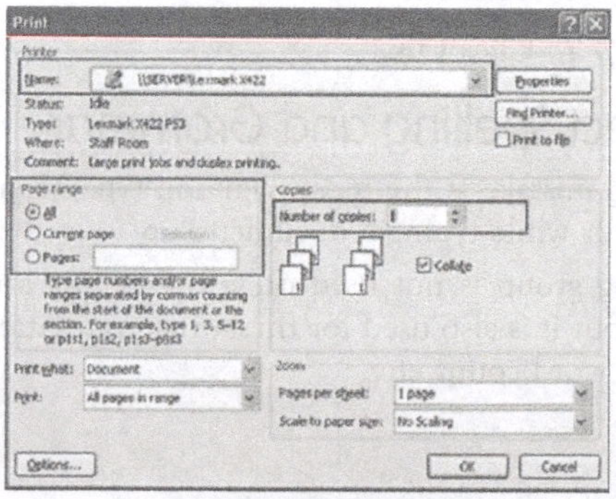

Print dialog box

Step 3 Choose the **Page range** that you would like to print either All, Current page or Pages.

Step 4 Select the **Number of copies.**

Step 5 Click the **Collate** check box, if you are printing multiple copies of a multi-page document.

Step 6 Select the printer from the **Printer Name:** drop down list.

Step 7 Click **OK.**

Print *via* Quick Print

Steps to print *via* quick print a document are as follows:

Step 1 Click the **Microsoft Office** button.

Step 2 Select **Print → Quick Print.**

The document is automatically printed by default printer.

Print *via* Print Preview

Print preview is a computing function used to display a document page, before it is produced in its final form (hard copy). Steps to preview a document before printing are as follows:

Step 1 Click the **Microsoft Office** button.

Step 2 Select **Print → Print Preview.** The document opens in Print Preview format.

Step 3 Click **Print** option in the **Print** group to print the document or click **Close Print Preview** option in the **Preview** group to exit the preview format.

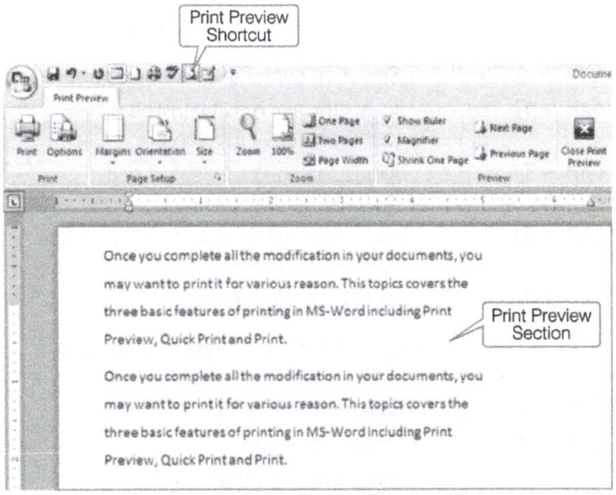

Print Preview window

In Print Preview format, you can do many tasks

(*i*) Modify the margins.

(*ii*) Change page orientation.

(*iii*) Change the page size.

(*iv*) Zoom in and Zoom out to view various parts of the document.

(*v*) View multiple pages.

(*vi*) Access Word options to change settings.

Check Point 04

1 Which option helps you to search a particular word in a document?

2 Write the name of page orientations.

3 Printing covers .... basic features of printing in MS-Word.

(a) Print (b) Quick Print

(c) Print Preview (d) All of these

Shortcut Keys for MS-Word

Working with Documents

Ctrl + N	Create a new document
Ctrl + O	Open a document
Ctrl + W	Close a document
Ctrl + S	Save a document
F12 Shift + F12	Save As

Change or Resize the Font

Ctrl + Shift + F Ctrl + D	Open the Font dialog box
Ctrl + F12	Open the Open dialog box
Ctrl + Shift + >	Increase the font size
Ctrl + Shift + <	Decrease the font size
Ctrl +]	Increase the font size by 1 point
Ctrl + [	Decrease the font size by 1 point
Ctrl + Alt + N	Normal style
Ctrl + Shift + S	Open Apply Style dialog box

Common Tasks

Ctrl + B	Make letters bold
Ctrl + I	Make letters italic
Ctrl + U	Make letters underline
Ctrl + C	Copy the selected text or object
Ctrl + X	Cut the selected text or object

Ctrl + V Shift + Insert	Paste the selected text or object
Ctrl + A	Select all contents of a document
Ctrl + E	Aligns the line or selected text to the center of the screen
Ctrl + L	Aligns the line or selected text to the left of the screen
Ctrl + R	Aligns the line or selected text to the right of the screen
Ctrl + M	Indent the paragraph
Ctrl + F F5	Open Find and Replace dialog box
Ctrl + P	Open the Print window
Ctrl + Z	Undo last action
Ctrl + ←	Moves one word to the left
Ctrl + →	Moves one word to the right
Ctrl + ↑	Moves to the beginning of the line or a paragraph
Ctrl + ↓	Moves to the end of the line or a paragraph
Ctrl + Delete	Delete word to right of cursor
Ctrl + Backspace	Delete word to left of cursor
Ctrl + End	Moves the cursor to the end of the document
Ctrl + Home	Moves the cursor to the beginning of the document
Ctrl + Spacebar	Reset highlighted text to the default font
Shift + Alt + D	Insert the current date
Shift + Alt + T	Insert the current time

SUMMARY

- A Word processor is a package that processes textual matter and creates organised and faultless documents.
- Word processor automatically fits the typed text within the specified left and right margins. This feature is called Word wrapping.
- The scroll bar contains a slider that the user can drag to scroll through the window.
- Margins refer to the distance from the text to the paper edge.
- Ruler is used to set tabs, indents and margins for a document.
- The text layout within a paragraph with respect to document margins is called text alignment.
- Line spacing is the vertical distance between lines of the text.
- Page orientation is the direction in which a document is displayed or printed.
- A header or footer is a text or graphics that is usually printed at the top or at the bottom of every page in a document.
- A superscript is a number, figure, symbol or indicator that is smaller than their normal line of type and is set slightly above it.
- A subscript is a number, figure, symbol or indicator that is smaller than their normal line of type and is set slightly below it.
- Print preview is a feature that allows you to view what a printed version of the document would look like on the screen before printing a hard copy.

Exam Practice

Multiple Choice Questions

1 Which extension is given to a document by default in MS-Word?
(a) .odt (b) .com
(c) .docx (d) None of these

Ans. (*c*) .docx is the default extension of MS-Word 2007 document.

2 The Themes group is presented on .... tab.
(a) Home (b) Page Layout
(c) References (d) Picture Tools Format

Ans. (*b*) The Themes group is presented on Page Layout tab.

3 The status of your document like current page number and number of pages are given by ....
(a) Formatting toolbar (b) Status bar
(c) Standard toolbar (d) None of these

Ans. (*b*) Status bar gives the status of your document like current page number and number of pages.

4 A new text document can be created by
(a) File → Open
(b) File → New → Blank Document → Create
(c) Open → New → Create
(d) None of the above

Ans. (*b*) Steps to create a new document are File → New → Blank Document → Create

5 The documents can be saved by using
(a) Ctrl+S (b) File → Save
(c) File → Save As (d) All of these

Ans. (*d*) Documents can be saved by clicking File → Save As, File → Save or using Ctrl+S keys.

6 The general arrangement of the text in the document is ....
(a) margin (b) text alignment
(c) clipboard (d) formatting

Ans. (*d*) Formatting is the general arrangement of the text in the document.

7 The .... alignment makes sure that none of the edges of text appear ragged.
(a) left (b) right
(c) center (d) justify

Ans. (*d*) The justify alignment makes sure that none of the edges of text appear ragged.

8 Line spacing or paragraph spacing is measured in terms of lines or points, which is known as ....
(a) text wrapping (b) PDF
(c) XPS (d) leading

Ans. (*d*) When leading is reduced, it automatically brings the lines of text closer.

9 In the .... dialog box, you can change both line and paragraph spacing.
(a) Paragraph
(b) Line
(c) Format Spacing
(d) None of the above

Ans. (*a*) The Paragraph dialog box can be used to make the document effective by using both line and paragraph spacing.

10 Which of the following features is used to revert the original picture?
(a) Recolor (b) Contrast
(c) Brightness (d) Reset picture

Ans. (*d*) Reset picture feature of Picture Tools Format is used to revert the original picture.

11 .... splits text in columns at a specific point.
(a) Column break
(b) Page break
(c) Next page
(d) Continuous

Ans. (*a*) Column break splits text in columns at a specific point.

12 It is a section of the document that appears at the bottom margin of the page.
(a) Footer
(b) Header
(c) Head
(d) Tail

Ans. (*a*) Footer is the section of the document that appears at the bottom margin of the page.

13 Spelling & Grammar option from the Proofing group comes under
(a) View tab (b) Review tab
(c) Insert tab (d) Home tab

Ans. (*b*) Spelling & Grammar option from the Proofing group comes under Review tab.

14 User can also check the spelling and .... in a document.
(a) graphic (b) text
(c) table (d) grammar

Ans. (*d*) In MS-Word, user can check the spelling and grammar in a document.

15 The .... wavy line indicates a contextual spelling error.
(a) blue (b) purple (c) red (d) green

Ans. (*a*) The blue wavy line indicates a contextual spelling error that occurs when an incorrect spelling for a word is chosen.

16 The Insert tab Symbol option from Symbols group is used to
(a) insert the footer (b) insert the header
(c) format document (d) insert symbols

Ans. (*d*) Insert tab Symbol option from Symbols group is used to insert symbols in a document.

17 In the Print dialog box, you can select the pages for printing.
(a) Even pages
(b) Odd pages
(c) All pages in range
(d) All of the above

Ans. (*d*) You can select the even, odd and all pages in range for printing.

18 Which shortcut key is used to make the selected text italic?
(a) Ctrl +I (b) Shift +I
(c) F1+I (d) None of these

Ans. (*a*) Ctrl+I is the shortcut key to make the selected text italic.

19 We can underline the text by
(a) Crl+B (b) Ctrl+I
(c) Ctrl+U (d) None of these

Ans. (*c*) Ctrl+U is the shortcut key for underlining the text.

Fill in the Blanks

1 .... is a powerful tool that you can use to create effective documents.

Ans. MS-Word 2007

2 Alignment buttons are available on the .... tab.

Ans. Home

3 Picture Shape option comes under .... tab.

Ans. Picture Tools Format

4 .... is the rectangular area of the document window, where user can type his/her content.

Ans. Work area or Work space

5 MS-Word 2007 allows you to insert .... in your documents.

Ans. pictures

6 .... and resizing the picture does not decrease the picture file size, but compression does.

Ans. Cropping

7 .... option provides a way to change the size of an image.

Ans. Compress

8 .... option is used to adjust the brightness of the picture.

Ans. Brightness

9 Portrait format changes the page orientation ....

Ans. vertically

10 .... ruler indicates the width of a document with left and right margins.

Ans. Horizontal

11 .... command is used to move the text to a new page.

Ans. Page break

12 .... and .... generally contain information such as page number, date, document name etc.

Ans. Header, Footer

13 Document writer places the page number field at the header or ....

Ans. footer

14 .... mistake is the most common type of mistakes that can occur while typing a document.

Ans. Spelling

15 .... option is used to display a document before printing.

Ans. Print Preview

True or False

1 MS-Word 2007 allows you to easily create a variety of professional looking documents using features such as Themes, Styles, SmartArt and more.

Ans. **True** MS-Word 2007 is a powerful tool that allows you to create a variety of professional looking documents because in Word 2007, all the things are replaced with a new navigation system.

2 MS-Word 2007 tool menu is packed full of lines, arrows, squares and much more.

Ans. **False** Word 2007 tool menu is not packed full of lines, arrows, squares but Word 2007 shapes menu is packed full of all these features.

3 You cannot modify your Word options and change the defined information that appears.

Ans. **False** Word options and pre-filled information can be modified by using MS-Word 2007 new features.

4 Editing text in MS-Word 2007 only involves inserting text.

Ans. **False** Editing text means making corrections as desired end results.

5 The text layout within a paragraph with respect to document margins is called text alignment.

Ans. **True** The text alignment can be horizontal or vertical.

6 Pictures can be added to Word documents and they cannot be formatted in various ways.

Ans. **False** Pictures can be formatted in various ways after adding it to the Word document like changing the shape, adding a border, modifying effects, applying a predefined style and more.

7 The distance between the text and the paper edge is called indent.

Ans. **False** The distance between the text and the paper edge is called the margin.

8 Extra spacing between paragraphs adds emphasis and makes a document easier to read.

Ans. **True** The document can be easily read, if the extra spacing is given between paragraphs, it makes the document very attractive.

9 Decreasing the leading will space the lines out, allowing for improved readability.

Ans. **False** Increasing the leading will space the lines out, allowing for improved readability.

10 After inserting a picture, a new tab appears.

Ans. **True** After inserting a picture in Word 2007 document, a new tab appears namely Picture Tools Format. This tab helps a user to edit his/her picture according to need.

11 You can insert only text as a header.

Ans. **False** You can insert any text or graphic as a header at the top of every page in the document.

12 The red wavy line indicates a possible syntax error.

Ans. **False** The red wavy line indicates a possible spelling error.

13 Proofing group in Review tab have Thesaurus option in it.

Ans. **True** MS-Word 2007 includes Proofing group from Review tab that has Thesaurus option for proofing of text.

14 X_2 is an example of subscript.

Ans. **True** A subscript is a number, figure or symbol that appears slightly below a word or letter.

15 The entire Word document can be printed by choosing Microsoft Office button → Print and OK.

Ans. **True** Steps for printing the document are Microsoft Office button → Print and OK.

Very Short Answer (VSA) Type Questions

1 How do you locate MS-Word 2007 on your computer system?

Ans. To locate MS-Word on computer system:

Click **Start** → **All Programs** → **Microsoft Office** → **Microsoft Office Word 2007**.

2 What is the use of ruler in MS-Word 2007 document?

Ans. Ruler is used to set tabs, indents and margins for a document.

3 What is formatted text?

Ans. Formatted text has styling information beyond the minimum of semantic elements: colors, styles (bold, italic), sizes and special features such as hyperlinks.

4 Write the name of alignments, which are available in MS-Word 2007.

Ans. Left, Right, Center and Justify.

5 What is the use of Crop option in MS-Word 2007?

Ans. Crop option allows a user to edit pictures (only cropping).

6 Write the steps to make the text bold.

Ans. Steps to make a text bold are as follows

Step 1 Select the text.

Step 2 Click the **Bold** button in the **Font** group on the **Home** tab.

7 Write the shortcut keys to format the text style bold, italic and underline.

Ans. **Bold** - Ctrl+B, **Italic** - Ctrl+I, **Underline** - Ctrl+U.

8 What happens, when we insert a header in Word document?

Ans. Headers are specified by page styles. Therefore, when we insert it, all the pages with the same page style will display the same header.

9 What are the basic features of printing in MS-Word 2007?

Ans. The basic features of printing in MS-Word 2007 are as follows:

(*i*) Print (*ii*) Quick Print

(*iii*) Print Preview

10 How can you print your document *via* Quick Print feature of printing?

Ans. To print a document *via* Quick Print

Click Microsoft Office button → Print → Quick Print.

Short Answer (SA) Type Questions

1 Define MS-Word 2007.

Ans. MS-Word 2007 is a Word processing software package, which allows you to easily create a variety of professional looking documents like letters, reports and other documents using features such as Themes, Styles, SmartArt and more. It is a powerful tool that you can use to create effective documents.

2 What do you mean by ruler?

Ans. Ruler appears on the top and on the left side of the document window. It allows to format the horizontal or vertical alignment of text in a document.

Two types of ruler are available in MS-Word 2007 as follows

(*i*) Horizontal ruler indicates the width of the document.

(*ii*) Vertical ruler indicates the height of the document.

3 Write the steps to create a new document.

Ans. Refer to text on Page No. 106.

4 How to save a document as a Word 97-2003?

Ans. Refer to text on Page No. 107.

5 How to save a document as a PDF document?

Ans. Refer to text on Page No. 107.

6 What is the difference between the Save and Save As option?

Ans. "Save" means the file gets saved under its current name, in whatever folder it was saved before or in the default folder of that computer, whereas "Save As" gives you the opportunity to save the file under a different name and in another folder. "Save As" allows you to name the updated version with a new name and at the same time preserving the old version.

7 How can you change the shape of a picture?

Ans. Refer to text on Page No. 111.

8 Explain Header and Footer.

Ans. The Header is a section of the document that appears on the top margin.While the Footer is a section of the document that appears on the bottom margin.

Headers and Footers generally contain information such as page number, date, document name etc.

9 Write the steps to insert date/time into Header or Footer.

Ans. Refer to text on Page No. 114.

10 What is a contextual spelling error?

Ans. A contextual spelling error occurs when an incorrect spelling of a word is chosen.

e.g. If someone writes, "Deer Mr Kumar" at the beginning of a letter, Deer is a contextual spelling error because one should have used Dear. Deer is spelled correctly, but it is used incorrectly in this context.

11 How to insert the copyright symbol into a Word document?

Ans. Steps to insert the copyright symbol into a Word document are as follows:

Step 1 Select **Insert** tab.

Step 2 Click **Symbol** option from **Symbols** group.

Step 3 Select **More Symbols...** .

Step 4 The Symbol dialog box will appear and select the **copyright** symbol.

Step 5 Click the **Insert** button.

Long Answer (LA) Type Questions

1 Explain different types of tabs available in MS-Word 2007.

Ans. Refer to text on Page No. 105.

2 Explain the text alignments with its types. Also, write the steps to change the text alignment.

Ans. Refer to text on Page No. 108-109.

3 What is the need to modify the spacing of the lines or paragraph of your text?

Ans. An important part of creating effective documents lies in the document design. Line spacing or paragraph spacing is measured in lines or points, which is referred to as leading.

As a part of designing the document and making formatting decisions, you will need to know how to modify the spacing. Just as you can format spacing between lines in your document, you can also choose spacing options between each paragraph.

Typically, extra spaces are added between paragraphs, headings or subheadings. Extra spacing between paragraphs adds emphasis and makes a document easier to read. When you reduce the leading, you automatically bring the lines of text closer together. Increasing the leading will space the lines out, allowing for improved readability.

4 Explain, how text is wrapped around a picture from Picture tools?

Ans. Refer to text on Page No. 110.

5 Write the steps to compress a picture.

Ans. Refer to text on Page No. 111.

6 Write the steps to insert header or footer.

Ans. Refer to text on Page No. 113-114.

7 Explain superscript or subscript.

Ans. Superscript or subscript refers to the number, figure or symbol that is positioned slightly higher or slightly lower than the text on the line. e.g. A footnote or endnote reference number is an example of superscript and a scientific formula might use subscript text.

X_2	X^2
Subscript	Superscript

In MS-Word, select the character that you would like to change and click the Superscript or Subscript symbol from the Font group under the Home tab.

Application Oriented Questions

1 Previous versions of Word looked similar and operated in many of the same ways. They had menus, toolbars, task pane and a 'Familiar' feeling design. In MS-Word 2007, all these things are replaced with a new navigation system and many new features.

(*i*) What is MS-Word 2007?

(*ii*) List new features of MS-Word 2007.

Ans.

(*i*) MS-Word 2007 is the Word processing software in the Microsoft Office 2007 suite.

(*ii*) Some new features of MS-Word 2007 are as follows:

(*a*) The Ribbon System (*b*) Themes
(*c*) Quick Styles (*d*) Pictures
(*e*) Live Preview (*f*) Shapes
(*g*) ClipArt (*h*) Charts
(*i*) SmartArt

2 Following are some descriptors describing some terms. Identify the terms/features these refer to.

(*i*) It is a pre-designed document that you can use to create new documents with the same formatting.

(*ii*) It is a tool that you can use to produce professional looking documents.

(*iii*) It is a new feature of 2007 Office suite that allows you to see changes in your document before you actually select an item.

Ans. (*i*) Template (*ii*) Themes (*iii*) Live Preview

3 Sona wants to add her pictures in a Word document.

(*i*) Which tab she should use?

(*ii*) Which command she should use to open Insert Picture dialog box?

(*iii*) Can she resize the image?

(*iv*) Is it possible to wrap text around an image?

Ans. (*i*) Insert tab

(*ii*) Picture command in the Illustrations group.

(*iii*) Yes

(*iv*) Yes

4 A Tablet company sells Tablets and accessories. The head of the company's marketing department has created the following leaflet by using a Word processor. The leaflet will be distributed to all the retail shops, main markets and malls.

ABC Ltd. Special Offers

To celebrate the completion of our five years in business, we are offering these special deals:

- Purchase a new mobile in June and get 50% off on MRP.
- Purchase 4 handsets and get one free.

To get more details, please contact to Mr. Naveen on 180010400.

Which of the following two options can improve the layout of the leaflet?

(*i*) Line spacing (*ii*) Search facility

(*iii*) Mail merging (*iv*) Center alignments

(*v*) Hyperlink

Ans. Line spacing, Center alignments.

5 The following figure shows a small part of a Word document. Identify different formatting features that are applied to it.

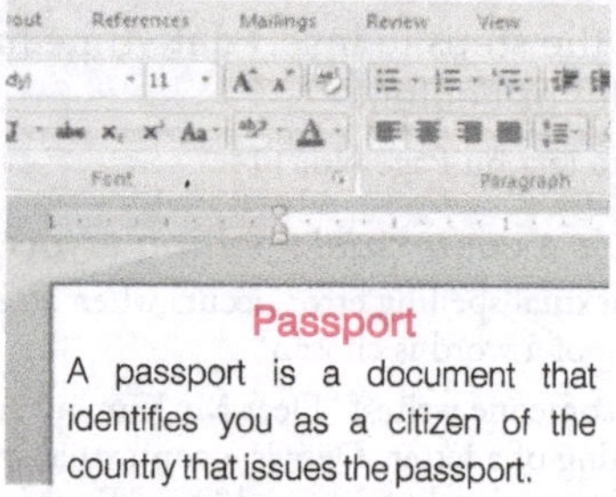

Ans.
- Center alignment of title
- Bold and color font of title
- Font type is changed for title
- Line spacing in paragraph
- Justified alignment for paragraph

6 Manu wants to replace the word 'organise' with 'organize' in a whole document.

(*i*) Name the feature which is used by Manu.

(*ii*) Write down the labels in order to show how he could replace the word?

(*a*) In **Find what** box, type organise.

(*b*) Click Home tab → Replace in the Editing group.

(*c*) Click the **Replace All** button.

(*d*) In **Replace with** box, type organize.

(*e*) **Find and Replace** dialog box with Replace tab will appear.

Ans. (*i*) Manu can replace the word using **Find and Replace** feature.

(*ii*) **Label:** b e a d c

7 You can make your documents professional and polished by utilising the header and the footer sections.

(*i*) What is a header?

(*ii*) Can you insert date or time into a header? If yes, write the procedure for doing this.

Ans. (*i*) Header is a section of the document that appears at the top margin of every page.

(*ii*) Yes, we can insert date or time into a header. Steps to insert date or time into a header are as follows:

Step 1 On the Design tab, in the Insert group, click the **Date & Time** option.

Step 2 Select a **date format** from the Date and Time dialog box that appears.

Step 3 Click **OK**. Now, Date/Time will appear in the document.

8 Rahul is using Word processor to create his chemistry coursework. He wants to insert his roll number and page numbers in the footer of a document.

(*i*) Define Footer.

(*ii*) In the text coursework, Rahul wants to insert only page numbers.

(a) Where should he insert page numbers?
In the Header, In the Footer or In the text of every page

(b) Is it possible to insert a Footer without inserting a Header?

Ans. (*i*) Footer is a section that appears at the bottom of every page. You can insert text/numbers/graphics to the footer section. Whatever is added in the footer section gets reflected on every page.

(*ii*) (*a*) In the Footer

(*b*) Yes, it is possible to insert only a footer on a page.

9 Ishanki created a document in Word. Then, suddenly she saw some wavy colored lines in her document underlining some words and sentences. Why did these lines appear? Also, tell the meaning of different colorful wavy lines.

Ans. Word automatically checks your document for spelling and grammar errors. These errors are indicated by colored wavy lines, i.e.

- Blue line indicates a contextual spelling error.
- Red line indicates a misspelled word.
- Green line indicates a grammar error.

10 Tom Hanks writes a Loan request letter to HR Manager of ABC Company as shown below:

To,

HR Manager,
ABC Company,
56-K, Maryland Street

Dear Sir,

I am writing this letter to humbly request you to grant me a loan as I am in dire need of money for my kidney stone operation. As per the doctors, I need to be operated as soon as possible to avoid any further complications. I have confirmed the estimate of expenses from the hospital and it lies somewhere around $200.

Kindly consider my situation and inform me about your decision at the earliest.

Sincerely,
Tom Hanks
Marketing Executive

Other than basic features of MS-Word, suggest any two features of the MS-Word that could be used to check the accuracy of the text used in the letter.

Ans. (*i*) Spell check (*ii*) Grammar check

CHAPTER

08

MS-Word Advanced

Chapter Checklist

- Bullets and Numbering
- Border and Shading
- Table
- Drawing Tools
- Drawing and Editing Shapes
- Insert a Picture from a File
- Insert Mathematical Symbols
- Automatic Formatting while Typing
- Comments
- Track Changes
- Reviewing Changes
- MS-Word 2010
- MS-Word 2013

We have already studied various basic features of MS-Word 2007 like creating and saving a document, formatting a document, adding headers and footers etc. Now, in this chapter, we will study more advanced features of MS-Word 2007 such as Shapes and Symbols, Drawing Tools, AutoFormat, Track Changes etc.

Bullets and Numbering

While working in a document, sometimes we need to highlight some areas of text in the form of lists for summarising key points. To achieve this purpose, we can use bullets. A bullet is an asterisk, black dot, circle or other mark that is found before the text that identifies key items or other important text. A **bulleted list** or **bullet list** is a list of items preceded with bullets instead of numbers or other objects. You can create a list within a list (nested list) in your document.

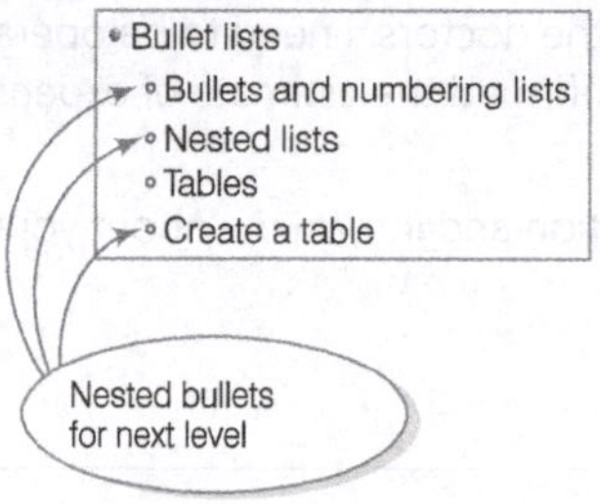

Numbering or **number list** or **order list** is a listing order that is done with numbers, often used with a checklist or a set of steps that are to be performed in a particular order. Bullets and Numbering lists can be used in your documents to arrange and format text to emphasise and to draw the attention of the viewer.

Insert Bullets or Numbering on a List

Steps to insert bullets or numbering on a list are as follows

Step 1 Select the **text** that you want to format as a list.

Step 2 Click the **Bullets** or **Numbering** option on the **Paragraph** group from the **Home** tab.

Step 3 Select the bullets or numbering style that you would like to use. Then, it will automatically appear in the document.

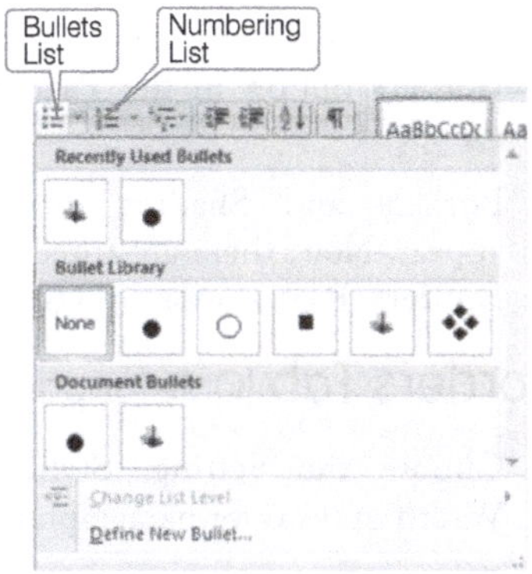

Pop-up window of bullets

Step 4 Place your cursor at the end of a list item and press **Enter** key to add bullet or number to the list.

Define New Bullets

Steps to define new bullets on a list are as follows

Step 1 Select an **existing list.**

Step 2 Click the **Bullets.**

Step 3 Select **Define New Bullet...** option from the list. The **Define New Bullet** dialog box will appear as shown below:

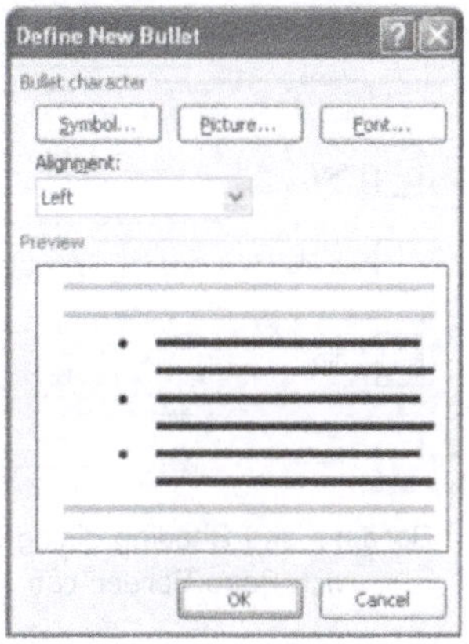

Define New Bullet dialog box

Now, there are three formats to insert bullets:

1. Using Symbol

Steps to insert a symbol as a bullet are as follows

Step 1 Click the **Symbol...** button. The Symbol dialog box will appear.

Step 2 Click the **Font** drop down box and select **font** category.

Step 3 Click a **symbol** that you want to use as a bullet.

Step 4 Click **OK.** The symbol now appears in the Preview section of the Define New Bullet dialog box.

Step 5 Click **OK** to apply the symbol to the list in the document.

2. Using Picture

Steps to insert a picture as a bullet are as follows

Step 1 Click the **Picture...** button. The Picture Bullet dialog box will appear.

Step 2 Click a **picture** that you want to use as a bullet.

Step 3 Click **OK.** The picture now appears in the Preview section of the Define New Bullet dialog box.

Step 4 Click **OK** to apply the picture to the list in the document.

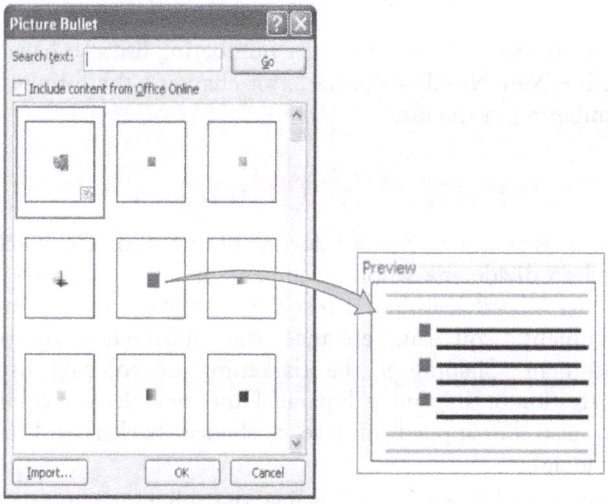

Picture Bullet dialog box

You can also insert the user defined image as a bullet by just clicking on **Import...** button of Picture Bullet dialog box.

3. Using Font

Steps to change the bullet format are as follows

Step 1 Click the **Font...** button. The Font dialog box will appear as shown below:

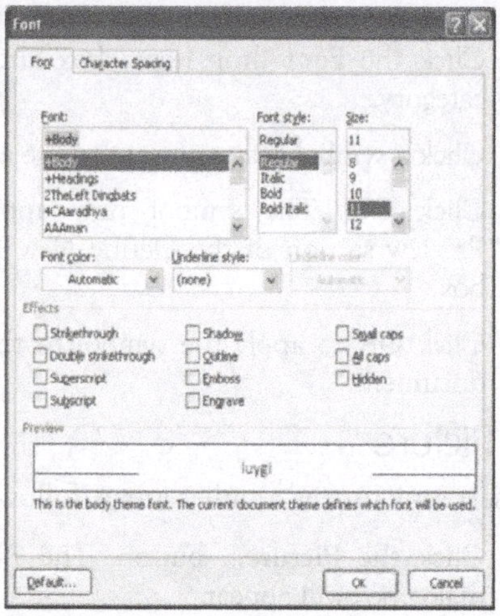

Font dialog box

Step 2 Select the **Font, Font style, Size, Font color** etc, from drop down menu.

Step 3 Click **OK**. The bullet format now appears in the Preview section.

Step 4 Click **OK** to apply the bullet format to the list in the document.

Same as Define New Bullet, the numbering list also have **Define New Number Format...** for changing the format of numbering in the list.

Border and Shading

Border is an outer edge of a document or a separator which is used to divide the whole document in several sections. By adding a border around a text box, paragraph or the entire document, you can enhance the appearance of your document. Shading is the darkening or coloring of an illustration or diagram with parallel lines or a block of color. It can also be applied to give a shaded background to a paragraph.

Borders and Shading tool makes the job much easier and neater.

Add Border and Shading on a Page or a Paragraph

Steps to add border and shading on a page or a paragraph are as follows

Step 1 Select the **page** or a **paragraph** where you want to add border and shading.

Step 2 Click **Page Layout** tab and choose **Page Borders** option in the **Page Background** group.

Step 3 Borders and Shading dialog box will appear. Now, there are three tabs available **Borders, Page Border** and **Shading.**

Using Borders Tab (Only for paragraph)

Step 1 Choose the **Setting, Style, Color** and **Width** options for paragraph border.

Step 2 Click **OK** button to apply the chosen settings.

You can also insert paragraph border using Paragraph option from Home tab.

Using Page Border Tab (For page)

Step 1 Choose the **Setting, Style, Color** and **Width** options (Art option can also be chosen) for page border.

Step 2 Click **OK** button to apply the chosen settings.

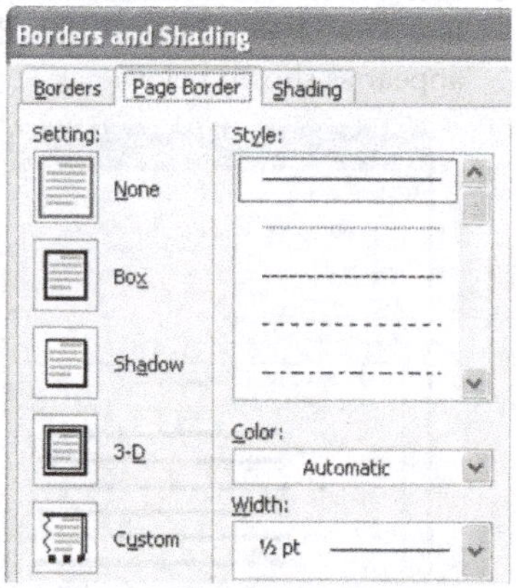

Borders and Shading dialog box with Page Border tab

Using Shading Tab (Only for paragraph or text)

Step 1 Choose **Fill, Style** per cent and **Color** of pattern.

Step 2 Click **OK** button to apply the chosen settings.

Check Point 01

1. How many options are available in Define New Bullet dialog box?
   (a) Symbol (b) Picture
   (c) Font (d) All of these
2. What is the darkening or coloring of an illustration or diagram with parallel lines or a block of color?
3. By which feature of MS-Word, you can copy a format from specific portions of your document and apply it to other document just by clicking?

Table

A table is a grid of cells arranged in rows and columns. Table can be customised which is useful for various tasks such as presenting text information and numerical data. Data in table can be arranged in any (ascending or descending) order. In MS-Word 2007, table contains 63 columns and 32767 (approx.) rows.

There is a list of operations that can be done with a table are as follows:

- Adding and deleting columns
- Adding and deleting rows
- Changing the cell size
- Aligning cell text
- Changing text direction
- Merging and splitting cells etc.

Insert a Table

Steps to insert a blank table in a document are as follows

Step 1 Place your insertion point in the document where you want to insert the table.

Step 2 Click the **Insert** tab and select the **Table** option from the **Tables** group.

Step 3 Drag your mouse over the squares to select the desired number of columns and rows into the table.

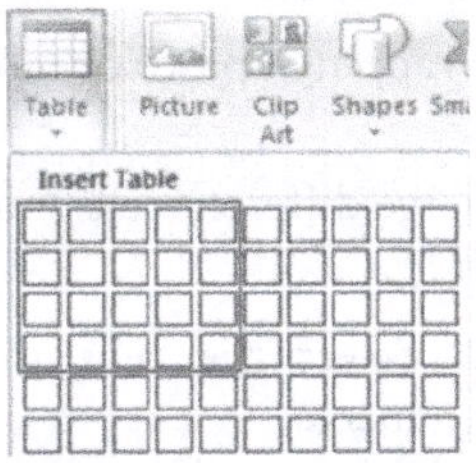

Selecting rows and columns

Step 4 Click the mouse on the squares and then, a table will appear into the document.

Now, you can enter text into the table.

Convert Existing Text into a Table

Steps to convert existing text into a table are as follows

Step 1 Select the text that you want to convert in table format.

Step 2 Click on **Insert** tab and choose **Table** option from the **Tables** group.

Step 3 Select **Convert Text to Table...** from the drop down menu. A Convert Text to Table dialog box will appear.

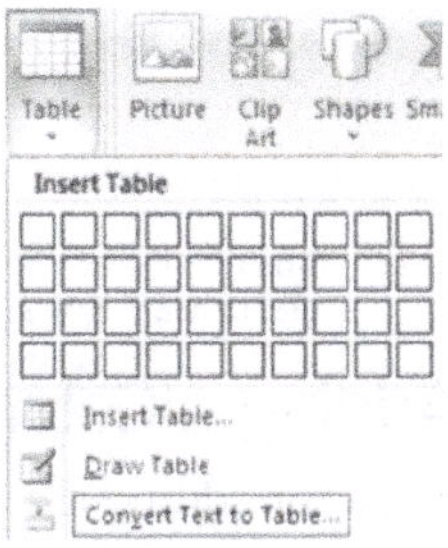

Clicking Convert Text to Table

Step 4 Choose one of the options from the **Separate text at** section.

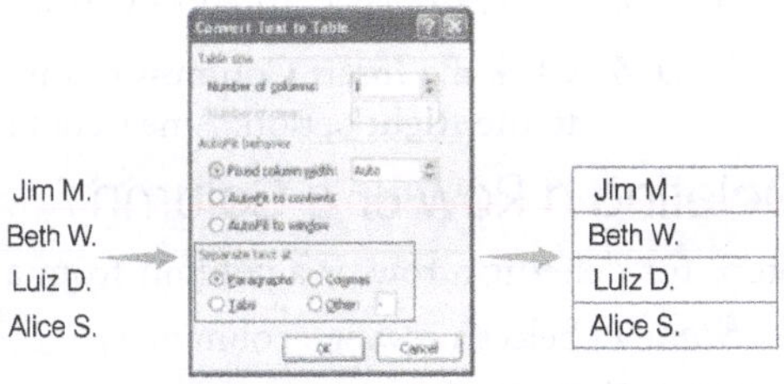

Convert Text to Table

Step 5 Click **OK**, the text will appear into a table.

Adding a Row

Steps for adding a row into a table are as follows

Step 1 Place the insertion point in a row below the location where you want to add a row.

Insertion point is in the FIRST row so we can add a new row ABOVE it.

Jim M.	$10,252
Beth W.	$5,550
Luiz D.	$8,547
Alice S.	$13,578

Sample table

Step 2 Right click the mouse, a menu will appear.

Step 3 Select **Insert**, a drop down list will appear.

Step 4 Click the **Insert Rows Above** option.

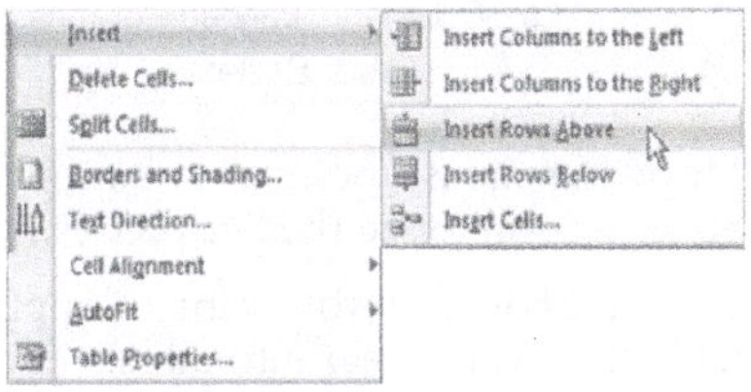

Thus, a new row appears above the insertion point.

Jim M.	$10,252
Beth W.	$5,550
Luiz D.	$8,547
Alice S.	$13,578

Sample table with new row

Note You can also add rows below the insertion point. Follow the same steps, but select **Insert Rows Below** from the menu.

Adding a Column

Steps for adding a column into a table are as follows

Step 1 Place the insertion point in a column adjacent to the location where you want to add a new column.

Step 2 Right click the mouse and a menu will appear.

Step 3 Select **Insert**, a drop down list will appear.

Step 4 Click the **Insert Columns to the Left** or **Insert Columns to the Right** option. A new column will appear.

Deleting a Row or a Column

Steps for deleting a row or a column from a table are as follows

Step 1 Select a row or a column.

Step 2 Right click the mouse and a menu will appear.

Step 3 Select **Delete Rows** or **Delete Columns.**

Apply a Table Style

Steps to apply a table style into a table are as follows

Step 1 Select the table. A **Table Tools** with **Design** tab now appears on the Ribbon.

Step 2 Select the **Design** tab to access all the Table Style Options.
The Table Style Options group sets the preferences for the table style.

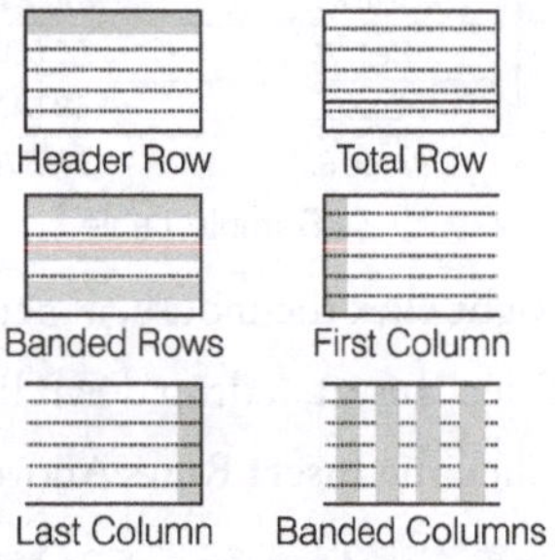

Table Styles

Step 3 Move the mouse pointer to various styles in the Table Styles section to see the live preview.

Step 4 Click a **Style** that you want to apply on the table. The table style will appear into table.

Resizing and Moving a Table

Resizing a Table

Click and drag the table's resize handle until the table appear into the desired size.

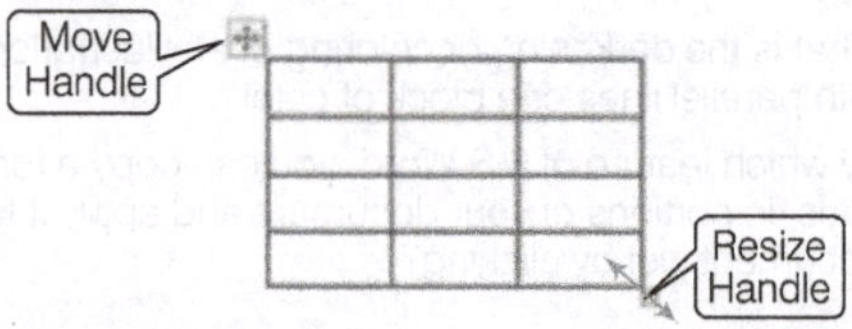

Moving a Table

Click and drag the table's move handle to a new location on the page.

Adjusting Table Alignment and Text Wrapping

Steps to adjust table alignment and text wrapping are as follows

Step 1 Select the **table.**

Step 2 Click **Layout** tab

Step 3 Select **Properties** option in **Table** group. Table Properties dialog box will appear.

Step 4 Select the **Table** tab.

Step 5 Select an **Alignment** or **Text wrapping** according to your wish.

Step 6 Click **OK.**

Note The Table Properties dialog box also includes tabs for Row, Column and Cell.

Merging and Splitting Cells

You can adjust the number of cells that appear in a table by merging and splitting cells.

Merging Cells

It means wrapping up two or more cells to form a single cell.

Steps to merge different cells into a single cell are as follows

Step 1 Select the **cells** that you want to merge.

Step 2 Select **Layout** tab.

Step 3 Click **Merge Cells** option from the **Merge** group.

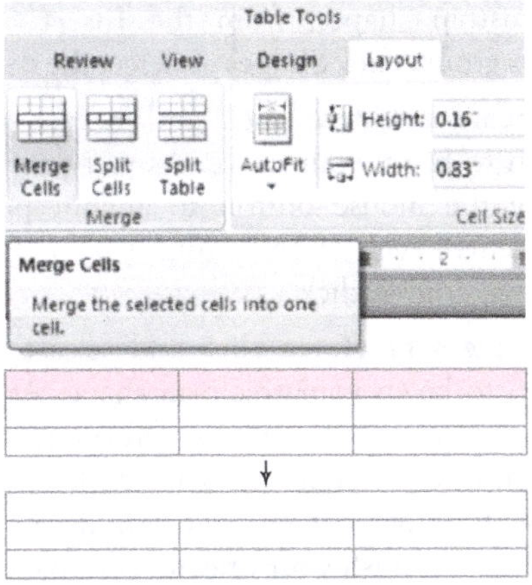

Merging cells

Splitting a Cell

It means a large cell broken up into several smaller cells. Steps to split a cell into number of rows or columns are as follows

Step 1 Select the **cell** that you want to split.

Step 2 Select **Layout** tab.

Step 3 Click **Split Cells** option from the **Merge** group. **Split Cells** dialog box will appear.

Step 4 Specify number of columns and rows in which you want to split a cell.

Step 5 Click **OK**.

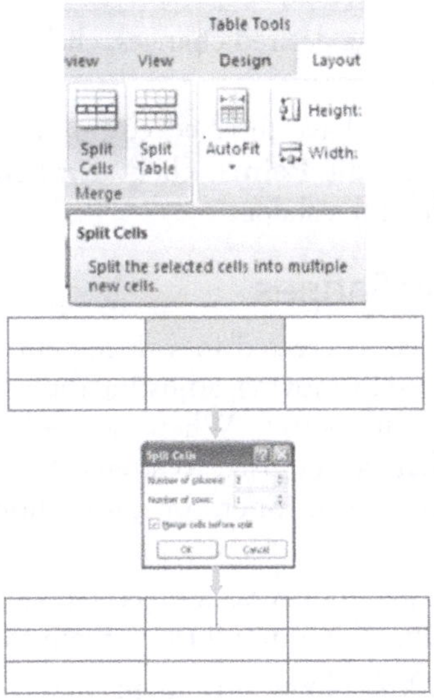

Splitting a cell

Drawing Tools

Drawing Tools are the tools used to produce your own drawings or to use the standard drawing elements provided in Microsoft Office program.

In Microsoft Office 2007, drawing tools are available in the form of ribbon. A ribbon is a graphical control element in the form of a set of toolbars placed on several tabs. This is designed to help you quickly find the commands that you need to complete a task.

Each tab relates to a type of activity, such as writing or designing a page. To reduce clutter, some tabs appear only when needed. e.g. the Drawing Tools Format tab appears only when you select a shape, line or other drawing object.

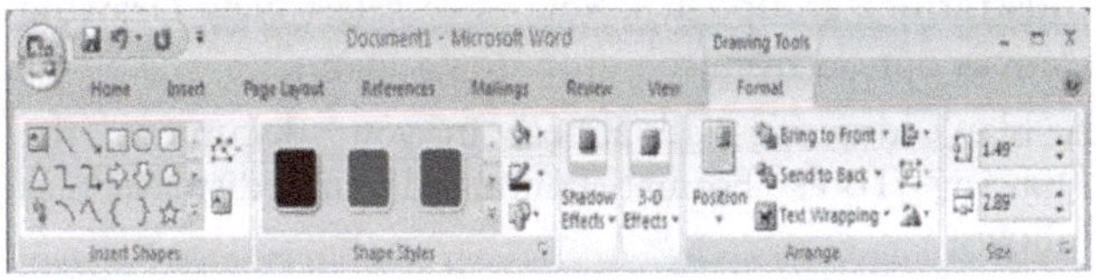

Drawing and Editing Shapes

Drawing shapes to a project can enhance or emphasize the readability and understanding of the project. You can draw your own objects or customise a number of readymade shapes by changing their colors or sizes.

You can also add text to the objects created by you. You can perform the following tasks regarding the shapes

(*i*) Drawing Shapes

(*ii*) Formatting Shapes

(*iii*) Working with Text in Shapes

(*iv*) Inserting WordArt Object

Drawing Shapes

MS-Word allows creating of simple shapes and objects with its built-in Drawing Tools, and also comes with a set of readymade shapes that can also be used in a Word document. Shape can also be combined with other shapes to make more complex shapes. Now, we are going to study about inserting autoshapes, drawing custom shapes and editing custom shapes.

Inserting Autoshapes

In the Insert tab from the Illustrations group, the Shapes option contains several categories of shapes, i.e. Lines, Basic Shapes, Block Arrows, Flowchart, Callouts, Stars and Banners that can be added very easily in the document. To insert these shapes, do the following:

(*i*) On the Ribbon, select the **Insert** tab. The Insert tab commands are visible.

(*ii*) In the **Illustrations** group, click **Shapes** option → select the desired shape.

(*iii*) Click and hold the mouse from where you want to start the shape.

(*iv*) Drag the mouse to create the desired shape. An outline indicating the size of your shape appears.

(*v*) Release the mouse button. The shape will appear in your Word document.

OPTIONAL To create a frame for several shapes, in the **Illustrations** group, click **Shapes** → select **New Drawing Canvas** option from the drop down menu.

A blank drawing will appear in your document, the Drawing Tools Format commands are displayed as follows:

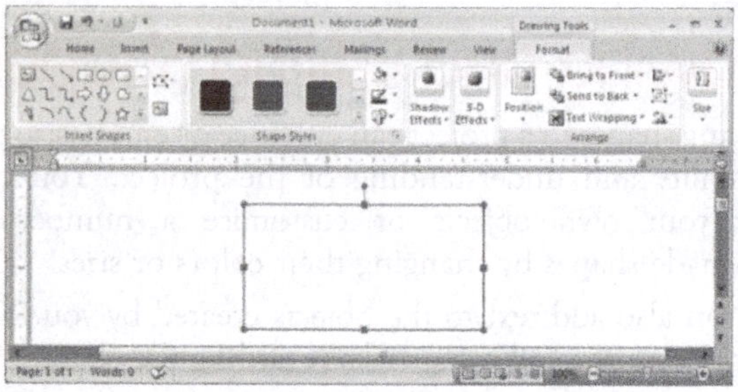

Drawing Custom Shapes

By using the three freehand drawing tools, i.e. Curve, Freeform and Scribble, desired shapes can be created.

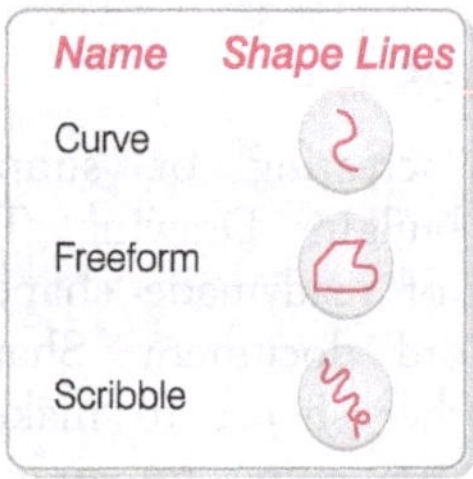

Curve lets you draw shapes that have different curves. Freeform lets you draw shapes that have both straight lines and curves. Scribble lets you draw shapes freehand with fine detail.

To draw custom shapes, from the **Insert** tab, in the **Illustrations** group, click **Shapes** → select the desired tool.

(*i*) **To create a Curve** click and release the mouse button to begin your curve. As you draw, click and release the mouse button to anchor point which your curve will form around. To finish your drawing, double click.

(*ii*) **To create a Freeform** click and release the mouse button to begin your freeform shape. As you draw, click and release the mouse button to anchor the endpoints of straight lines or click and drag the mouse to draw curves, you can do both in one drawing. To finish your drawing, double click.

(*iii*) **To create a Scribble** click and drag the mouse to draw your scribble. To finish your drawing, release the mouse button.

Editing Custom Shapes

MS-Word provides a feature called **Edit Points**, to customise the look of custom shapes. This feature allows reshaping of small segments of a drawing. For editing custom shapes, do the following

(*i*) Click the Custom Shape.

(*ii*) From the **Drawing Tools Format** tab, in the **Insert Shapes** group, click **Edit Shape** → select **Edit Points.**

Black dots, called Edit Points will appear at various places in the shape.

(*iii*) To make the desired changes, click and drag an **Edit Points.**

(*iv*) When you have finished editing of your object, to turn off **Edit Points,** click anywhere on the page outside of the shape.

Formatting Shapes

Once an object is created in a document, its appearance can be changed by moving, adjusting the size and changing the color of an object. When selected, an object has "handles" that can be used to stretch the object taller or shorter, wider or thinner, or proportionally larger or smaller.

You can also manipulate your objects in several other ways, such as shading them or adjusting them to contain text.

MS-Word 2007 allows you to preview any changes by temporarily changing the appearance of the selected shape, when your mouse hovers above a formatting option.

Working with Text in Shapes

MS-Word 2007 allows you to add text in shape without creating a text box within a shape. Working with text in shapes is done in many ways which are as follows

Adding Text

For adding text in your document, do the following

(*i*) Right click on the shape → click on **Add Text** from the drop down menu.

Note If you have already added text to this object, the Add Text option changes to Edit Text.

(*ii*) Type the text.

Note To format the font, color and size of the text, from the **Home** tab, use the various commands that are available in the **Font** group.

(*iii*) When you have done entering and formatting the text, click anywhere outside of the shape.

Editing Text

You can always go back and edit text in an existing shape. For editing text in your document, do the following

(*i*) Select the shape that contains the text which you want to edit.

(*ii*) Click on **Edit Text** from the drop down menu.

Note Depending on the chosen shape, the I-beam may appear.

(*iii*) Make the desired changes.

(*iv*) When finished, to deselect the text, click outside of the shape.

Text-Fitting Options

Several options are available to customise the text-fitting within the shape. For text-fitting in your document, do the following:

(*i*) Right click on the shape → select **Format AutoShape...** option from the drop down menu.

- The **Format AutoShape** dialog box will appear.
- Select the **Text Box** tab.

(*ii*) Select the desired option given below

Option	*Description*
Internal margin	Specifies the distance between each edge of your shape and the text contained within it.
Vertical alignment	Changes the vertical placement of your text within the shape.
Word wrap text in AutoShape	Text appears on multiple lines to fit within your AutoShape optimally.
Resize AutoShape to fit text	Resizes the AutoShape to optimally fit your text.
Format Callout...	When working with callouts (e.g. word bubbles), provides options for changing formatting.
Convert to Frame...	Changes your shape to a plain text box.

Inserting WordArt Object

WordArt can be used to make displayed text more eye-catching. It is a text modifying feature in MS-Word.

It includes effects such as shadows, outlines, colors, gradients and 3D effects that can be added to a word or phrase. To insert a WordArt object in your document, do the following

(*i*) On the **Insert** tab, in the **Text** group, click **WordArt** option. The WordArt Gallery will appear.

(*ii*) From the WordArt Gallery, select the desired style. The **Edit WordArt Text** dialog box will appear.

(*iii*) In the **Text** box, type your text.

(*iv*) To format your text, from the **Font** or **Size** pull-down list, make the desired selections.

(*v*) To change the font style, click **B**(Bold) or *I*(Italic).

(*vi*) Click **OK** button.

Insert a Picture from a File

For inserting a picture in your document, do the following

(*i*) Click where you want to insert the picture.

(*ii*) On the **Insert** tab, in the **Illustrations** group, click **Picture** option.

(*iii*) Locate the picture that you want to insert.

(*iv*) Double click on the picture that you want to insert or click the **Insert** button.

Note Drawing and picture are fundamentally different. A drawing is composed of lines and areas, whereas a picture is a fine art of colored dots (a bitmap).

Insert Mathematical Symbols

MS-Word 2007 allows insertion of mathematical symbols into equations.

To insert mathematical symbols, do the following

(*i*) On the **Insert** tab, in the **Symbols** group, click the arrow under **Equation** option and then, click **Insert New Equation**.

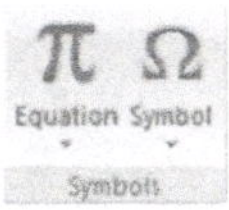

(ii) Under **Equation Tools Design** tab, select **Equation** from **Tools** group and can add more symbols from **Symbols** group, click the **More** arrow.

(iii) Click the arrow next to the name of the symbol set and then, click the name of the symbol set that you want to display.
(As you can choose operators, scripts etc.)

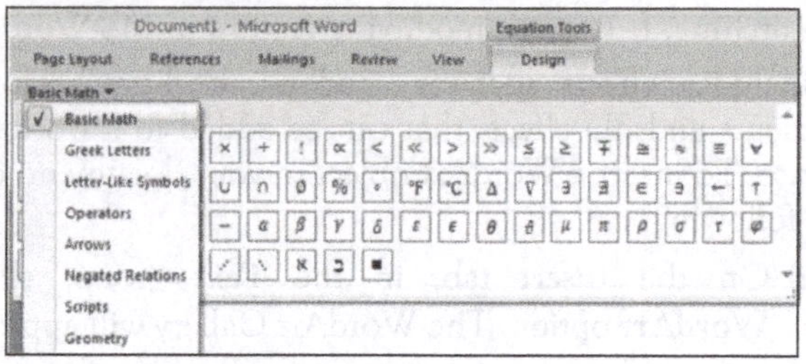

(iv) Now, click the symbol that you want to insert.

Available Symbol Sets

The mathematical symbol sets available in MS-Word 2007 are as follows

Symbol Set	*Subset*	*Definition*
Basic Math	None	Commonly used mathematical symbols, such as > and <
Greek Letters	Lowercase	Lowercase letters from the Greek alphabet
	Uppercase	Uppercase letters from the Greek alphabet
Letter-Like Symbols	None	Symbols that resemble letters
Operators	Common Binary Operators	Symbols that act on two quantities, such as + and ÷
	Common Relational Operators	Symbols that express a relationship between two expressions, such as = and ~
	Basic N-ary Operators	Operators that act across a range of variables or terms
	Advanced Binary Operators	Additional symbols that act on two quantities
	Advanced Relational Operators	Additional symbols that express a relationship between two expressions
Arrows	None	Symbols that indicate direction
Negated Relations	None	Symbols that express a negated relationship
Scripts	Scripts	The mathematical Script typeface
	Frakturs	The mathematical Fraktur typeface
	Double-Struck	The mathematical Double-Struck typeface
Geometry	None	Commonly used geometric symbols

Check Point 02

1 In MS-Word 2007, which tools are used to produce your own drawings or to improve the consistency?

2 How many options are contained in Shapes command in Insert tab?

3 Mr. Ajay wants to create a flowchart in Word document. Which features allow suitability to create flowchart in MS-Word?

4 Riya wants to write the mathematical equation in the Word document, but she is not able how to add mathematical symbol. What feature of MS-Word she should use?
(a) Equation option (b) WordArt
(c) Drawing Tool (d) Insert Picture

Automatic Formatting while Typing

Auto-formatting feature of Word processing tool allows the automatic formatting of certain kinds of text while typing. By selecting certain formatting options, the Microsoft Office 2007 system programs can automatically format certain kinds of text as you type, such as replacing a typed hyphen (-) with a dash (–).

Turn On or Off Automatic Formatting

To turn On or Off the automatic formatting, do the following

(i) Click the **Microsoft Office** button and then click **Word Options.**

(ii) Word Options window will appear.

(iii) In this window, in the left pane, click **Proofing** and then click **AutoCorrect Options...** button.

(iv) AutoCorrect: English (U.S.) dialog box will appear.

(v) In this dialog box, click the **AutoFormat As You Type** tab.

(vi) Select or clear the options that you want.

Note For including specific text or symbols, such as fractions you have to turn on AutoCorrect option and also need to set-up your own AutoCorrect entry.

(vii) Click **OK** button.

Turn On AutoCorrect

To turn on AutoCorrect option, do the following

(i) Click the **Microsoft Office** button and then click **Word Options.**

(ii) Word Options dialog box will appear.

(iii) In this dialog box, in the left pane, click on the **Proofing.**

(iv) Then, in the corresponding right pane, click **AutoCorrect Options...** button.

(*v*) AutoCorrect: English (U.S.) dialog box will appear and in this box, click AutoCorrect tab.

(*vi*) Select the **Replace text as you type** check box.

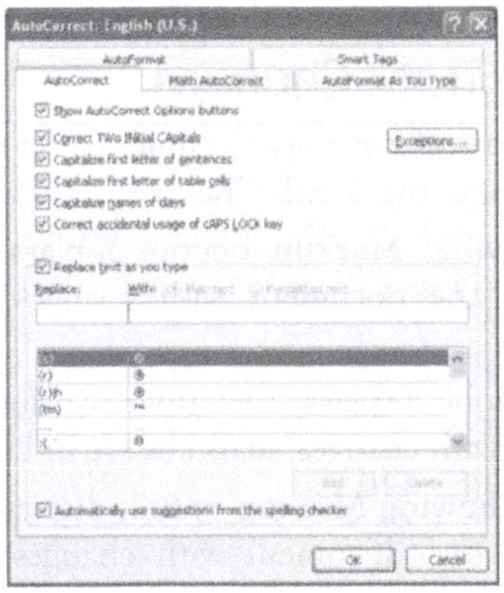

(*vii*) Click **OK** button.

Set-up your own AutoCorrect Entry

To set-up your own AutoCorrect entry, do the following

(*i*) On the **Insert** tab, in the **Symbols** group, click **Symbol** option and then, click **More Symbols...** .

(*ii*) Symbol dialog box will appear.

(*iii*) In this dialog box, click the **Symbols** tab or the **Special Characters** tab.

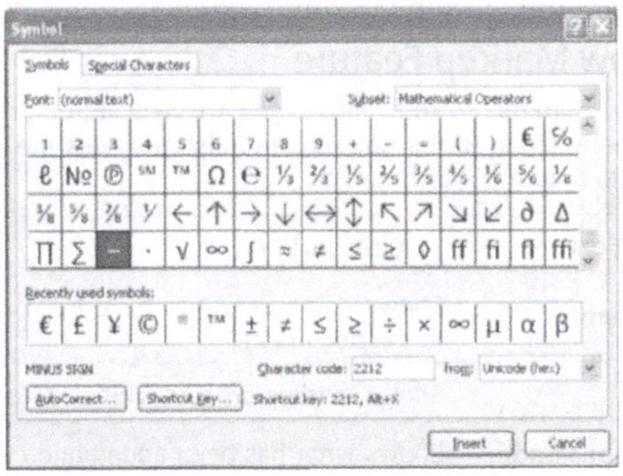

(*iv*) Click **AutoCorrect...** button.

(*v*) The symbol or character that you have selected will appear in the **With** box.

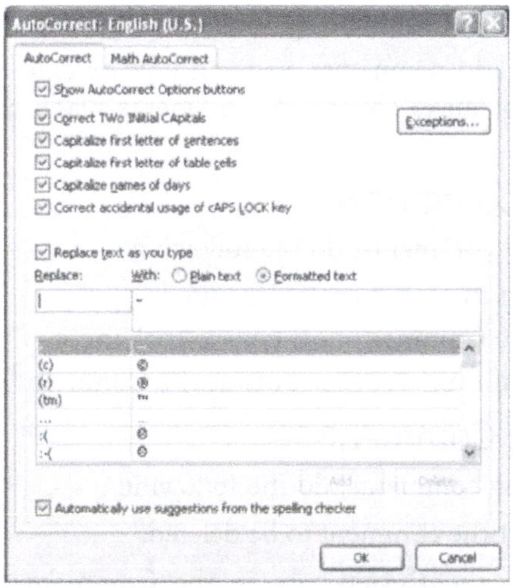

(*vi*) In the **Replace** box, type the text sequence that you want to change automatically to the symbol or character appearing in the **With** box.

(*vii*) Click **Add** button.

(*viii*) Click **OK** button.

(*ix*) Close the **Symbol** dialog box.

Comments

In MS-Word 2007, comments are very useful tool to proof-read a report. These are useful in the writing process for making notes to your own understanding, especially when you are in the flow of writing and you do not want to stop and check a fact or a resource. A note can be made for checking that fact later. Also, comments can be used to guide an author's attention to the areas where special attention is needed.

Inserting Comments

MS-Word allows users to insert comments within documents. For inserting comments in your document, do the following

(*i*) Select the text to which you want to add a comment.

(*ii*) From the **Review** tab, in the **Comments** group, click **New Comment.**

(*iii*) In the **Comment** box, type a comment.

(*iv*) When finished, click outside the **Comment** box.

Editing and Deleting Comments

Once you add comments, you can edit or delete them. You cannot make changes to comments made by other reviewers.

Editing Comments

For editing comments, do the following

(*i*) Select the comment to be edited.

(*ii*) In the **Comment** box, type your changes.

(*iii*) When finished, click outside the **Comment** box.

Deleting Comments

For deleting comments, do the following

(*i*) Select the comment to be deleted.

(*ii*) From the **Review** tab, in the **Comments** group, click **Delete** option. The comment will be deleted.

or

Right click on the comment, click **Delete Comment** from drop down box. The comment will be deleted.

Track Changes

It is used while making changes in an already created document for the purpose of keeping track of the changes that are made to original document.

Track changes is basically an editing command that permits the user to view the changes that are made to a document. You can choose to accept or reject those changes. It is a very useful tool when multiple users need to work on a single document, as it allows multiple users to make revisions without losing the context of the original document.

Track changes is also known as **redline** or **redlining.** This is because some industries traditionally draw a vertical redline in the margin to show that some text has changed.

Microsoft Office Word 2007 uses Balloons to display deletions, comments, formatting changes and content that has moved. You can also choose, how track changes and comments are displayed. e.g. in different font colors. The tools for track changes are available in the **Review** tab.

Starting Track Changes

To keep track of the changes being made to a document, do the following

(*i*) Click on the **Review** tab.

(*ii*) In the **Tracking** group, click on **Track Changes** option.

Now, all the changes made to the document can be viewed by the user.

Viewing the Track Changes

There are four ways of viewing a document after modifying the document using the **Track Changes** option

(*i*) **Final Showing Markup** option displays the final version of the document with changes noted as markups.

(*ii*) **Final** option displays the final version of the document with changes, markups are hidden.

(*iii*) **Original Showing Markup** option displays the text of the original document with changes noted as markups.

(*iv*) **Original** option displays the text of the original document.

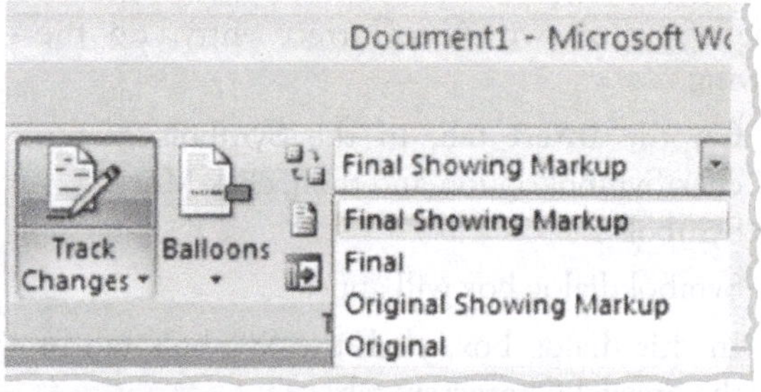

Show Markup Feature

The Show Markup Feature allows you to view different items such as comments, formatting etc, and also provides the option to view other author's comments.

Editing Feature	Description
Comments	Shows comments that have been added to the document
Ink	Shows markup created with a stylus tool
Insertions and Deletions	Shows what has been added and deleted from the original document
Formatting	Shows what formatting changes have been made to the document
Markup Area Highlight	Highlights background where changes are made
Reviewers	Shows which reviewer has made a particular edit or comment

Reviewing Changes

Accepting or rejecting changes work much like the Spell Check feature. By cycling through the changes made to a document, the author can accept or reject any or all changes.

For accepting or rejecting the changes made so far, do the following

(*i*) Open the document to be reviewed.

(*ii*) From the **Review** tab, in the **Changes** group, click **Next** option. The first change will be displayed.

(*iii*) Do one of the following

- To accept the change, click on top half of the **Accept** button.
- To accept all changes, click the ▾ on the **Accept** button → select **Accept All Changes in Document.**
- To reject the change, click on top half of the **Reject** button.
- To reject all changes, click the ▾ on the **Reject** button → select **Reject All Changes in Document.**

(*iv*) Repeat steps (*ii*) and (*iii*) until all changes have been reviewed.

(*v*) When finished, save your document.

Check Point 03

1 In MS-Word 2007, which feature is a very useful tool to proof-read a report?
(a) Track changes (b) Comments
(c) Formatting (d) Reviewers

2 Alex wants to delete a comment from own document. Suggest the tab name to Alex for this purpose.

3 Track changes is basically an editing command that permits the user to view the changes that are made to a document. In which tab, is it available?

4 How many ways are available of viewing a document after modifying the document using the Track Changes?

MS-Word 2010

It is a version of the Microsoft Office productivity suite for Microsoft Windows. It is the successor of Microsoft Office 2007 and predecessor of Microsoft Office 2013. It was released on 15th April, 2010 for manufacturing. The suite became available for retail and online purchase on 15th June, 2010. It is the last version of MS-Office with support for Windows XP, Windows Server 2003, Windows Vista and Windows Server 2008.

Some features of MS-Word 2010 are as follows

Share Documents Word 2010 lets its user to post their documents online and then access, view and edit them from almost any computer.

Add Visual Effects With Word 2010, user can apply formatting effects such as shadow, glow, reflection etc, to the document text.

Turn Text into Diagram Word 2010 offers to choose from dozen of additional SmartArt Graphics to build diagrams just by typing a bulleted list.

Image Editing New picture editing tools in Word 2010 enable a user to add special picture effects without additional photo editing software. Pictures can easily adjust with color saturation and temperature controls. Also, tools are provided for easier and more precise cropping and image correction.

Insert Screenshots User can now capture and insert screenshots directly from Word 2010 to incorporate visual illustrations in documents.

Word Translation Word 2010 helps user to work and communicate across different languages. It translates a word, phrase or document more easily than before. Also, it provides additional assistance for English as a second language with English text-to-speech playback.

MS-Word 2013

It is a version of the Microsoft Office productivity suite for Microsoft Windows. It is the successor of Microsoft Office 2010 and the predecessor of Microsoft Office 2016.

Development on this version of MS-Office started in 2010 and ended on 11th October, 2012. It was released for general availability on 29th January, 2013. This version includes new features such as integration support for online services, improved format support for Office Open XML (OOXML), Open Document Format (ODF) and Portable Document Format (PDF).

Some features of MS-Word 2013 are as follows

Edit PDF The most gratefully received new feature of Word 2013 is its ability to edit PDFs. Before 2013, user had to use PDF to Word converters for this task.

Insert youtube videos into word Word 2013 has the ability to insert Youtube videos into its documents. Word 2013 has a new command (option) on Insert tab → Online Video.

Read mode If user wants to read documents in Word 2013, read mode can be used. It automatically resizes a document to the full window.

Live layout It is a new feature that helps to position objects like pictures and charts in a document. After inserting a picture, user can drag the picture around in a document to reposition it and Word gives a real time preview of the result.

Expand and collapse Long documents become rampant to manage, especially if user is working on just a small portion of it. So, Word 2013 introduces a new feature that allows a user to expand and collapse certain parts of a document.

Alignment guides If user moves an object such as an Image, Chart or SmartArt illustration around in a document, Alignment Guides automatically appear to show where the object is lined up with other elements.

New table tools In MS-Word 2013, some new table features are included. Now, adding and deleting rows/columns from a table is much easier than previous versions. New table border tools are also included.

MICROSOFT OFFICE 2016

It is a version of the Microsoft Office productivity suite for Microsoft Windows. It is the successor of Microsoft Office 2013. It was initially released on 22nd September, 2015. As with previous versions, Office 2016 is made available in several distinct editions aimed towards different markets.

Check Point 04

1. It means a large cell broken up into several smaller cells.
   (a) Merging cells (b) Splitting a cell (c) Formatting cells (d) Adding cells
2. When was MS-Word 2010 released?
3. Name the successor and predecessor of MS-Word 2013.

Microsoft Office Word 2007 Keyboard Shortcuts

Review Documents

Alt+Ctrl+M	Insert a comment
Ctrl+Shift+E	Turn change tracking On or Off
Alt+Shift+C	Close the Reviewing Pane if it is open

SUMMARY

- Bullets (or bullet points) are small dots, squares, dashes or graphics that begin a short descriptive phrase.
- Border is a style which can be applied on page, text, paragraph, object etc.
- Using shading, you can fill background color of page, text, paragraph and objects.
- Tables are useful for various tasks such as presenting text information and numerical data.
- A merged cell is a single cell created by combining or merging two or more individual cells together.
- The splitting of cells allows you to split a cell into two or more cells.
- Drawing tools are the tools which are used to produce own drawings or to improve the consistency.
- The Drawing toolbar allows you to quickly and easily label pictures (e.g. maps) in a MS-Word file.
- Drawing objects include shapes, diagrams, curves, lines and WordArt. These objects are part of your Word document.
- WordArt is decorative text that you can add to a document.
- Microsoft Word uses the Equation Editor to produce mathematical equations, which can include fractions, integrals, matrices, mathematical symbols etc.
- The AutoFormat feature automatically formats a document as you type it by applying the associated styles to text.
- A comment is a note or annotation that an author or a reviewer can add to a document.
- Microsoft Word displays the comment in the Reviewing pane or in a balloon in the margin of the document.
- Track changes is a way for Microsoft Word to keep track of the changes that you make to a document.
- Track changes is also known as redline or redlining. This is because some industries traditionally draw a vertical redline in the margin to show that some text has changed.

Exam Practice

Multiple Choice Questions

1 Coloring of an illustration or diagram with parallel lines is known as
(a) shading (b) darkening
(c) coloring (d) bordering

Ans. (*a*) Shading is the darkening or coloring of an illustration or diagram with parallel lines or a block of color.

2 It is a grid of cells arranged in rows and columns.
(a) Row (b) Style sheet
(c) Table (d) Sheet

Ans. (*c*) Table is a grid of cells arranged in rows and columns.

3 The Table Properties dialog box includes tabs for
(a) Row (b) Column
(c) Cell (d) All of these

Ans. (*d*) The Table Properties dialog box contains four tabs namely Table, Row, Column and Cell.

4 Which tab of MS-Word contains the Shapes option?
(a) Home (b) Review
(c) Insert (d) Mailings

Ans. (*c*) Insert tab of MS-Word contains the Shapes option.

5 Which of the following is not an Autoshape?
(a) Line (b) Circle
(c) Curve (d) ClipArt

Ans. (*d*) ClipArt is not an Autoshape, because it is not found under Shapes.

6 Which of the following options is used to control the Automatic formatting that the user wants?
(a) Replace Text As You Type
(b) AutoFormat As You Type
(c) Proofing
(d) Track Changes

Ans. (*b*) For turning Automatic formatting On or Off, AutoFormat As You Type tab under Proofing is used.

7 AutoFormat settings are applied in a document
(a) as we type text (b) after we finish typing
(c) Both (a) and (b) (d) None of these

Ans. (*c*) AutoFormat settings are applied in a document as we type text or after we finish typing.

8 .... feature allows you to view different items such as comments, formatting etc, and also provides the option to view other author's comments.
(a) Display for Review (b) Track Changes
(c) Show Markup (d) Reviewing Pane

Ans. (*c*) Show Markup feature under Review tab allows you to view different items.

9 Under which tab, Comments group is present.
(a) Insert (b) Review
(c) View (d) Mailings

Ans. (*b*) Review tab contains the Comments group.

10 Which feature is used to monitor all document changes?
(a) Edit document (b) Monitor change
(c) Track changes (d) Track all

Ans. (*c*) Track changes tool is used when a document is edited or reviewed by many people.

Fill in the Blanks

1 You can also change the bullet font and formatting from the Font .... box.

Ans. dialog

2 A .... is an asterisk, black dot, circle or other mark that is found before the text that identifies key items or other important text.

Ans. bullet

3 Bulleted list can be created through ....

Ans. symbols, picture or font

4 You can add border and .... effects on tables or graphics.

Ans. shading

5 A .... is an outer edge of a document or a separator which is used to divide the whole document in several sections.

Ans. border

6 In a table, data is represented in a .... format.

Ans. tabular

7 .... can be customised that are useful for various tasks such as presenting text information and numerical data.

Ans. Tables

8 .... means wrapping up of different cells to form a single cell.

Ans. Merge cells

9 Press and hold .... of mouse while dragging for drawing a shape.

Ans. left button

10 .... are collections of information for individual items.

Ans. Records

11 The .... feature allows you to highlight and view changes made to a document.

Ans. Track Changes

True or False

1 Home tab of MS-Word contains the Object option.

Ans. **False** Insert tab of MS-Word contains the Object option.

2 The Drawing Tools Format tab appears at the bottom of the Word document window.

Ans. **False** Drawing Tools Format tab appears at the top of the Word document window.

3 To insert a symbol like © (copyright), you need to click on the special character option of the Insert tab.

Ans. **True** © is a special character which is added by Symbol option under Insert tab.

4 You cannot insert Mathematical symbols into a Word document.

Ans. **False** Word 2007 allows insertion of mathematical symbols.

5 New Comment option under Review tab helps you to insert a comment while reviewing.

Ans. **True** New Comment option helps you to insert a comment while reviewing.

6 When the Track Changes feature is enabled, track appears on the Status bar at the bottom of your documents.

Ans. **True** When the Track Changes feature is enabled, track appears on the Status bar at the bottom of your documents. When you turn Off change tracking, Track Changes is dimmed.

Very Short Answer (VSA) Type Questions

1 What is the use of bullet styles in our document?

Ans. While working in a document, sometimes we need to highlight some areas of text in the form of lists for summarising key points, so we use the option of creating bulleted and numbered lists.

2 Name the feature which is used to list the items in a document.

Ans. Using bulleted list feature, you can list the items in a document.

3 What is the use of adding border around a text?

Ans. By adding a border around a text, paragraph or the entire document, you can enhance the appearance of your document.

4 Define a table used in MS-Word.

Ans. A table is a grid of cells arranged in rows and columns. Table can be customised and useful for various tasks such as presenting text information and numerical data.

5 Under the Insert tab, which group contains the features like Shapes, ClipArt?

Ans. Under Insert tab, Illustrations group contains the features like Shapes, ClipArt etc.

6 Write down the name of the freehand drawing tools which are used when custom shapes are drawn.

Ans. Curve, Freeform and Scribble are the three freehand drawing tools which are used when custom shapes are drawn.

7 Using which option, you can create a frame for several shapes.

Ans. Insert → Illustrations → Shapes → New Drawing Canvas option is used to create a frame for several shapes.

8 How many types of Mathematical symbol sets are available in Word 2007?

Ans. 8 types of Mathematical symbol sets are available in Word 2007.

9 Which mathematical symbol set expresses a negated relationship?

Ans. Negated Relations symbols express a negated relationship.

10 State the possible purpose of adding the Comments feature in MS-Word application.

Ans. For making notes while reading the document without pen and paper, Comments feature is very useful.

Short Answer (SA) Type Questions

1 How many types of table styles are there in Table Style Options group?

Ans. There are six table styles in the Table Style Options group as follows

(*i*) Header Row (*ii*) Total Row
(*iii*) Banded Rows (*iv*) First Column
(*v*) Last Column (*vi*) Banded Columns

2 List the variety of modifications that one can make in the table.

Ans. Using commands on the Layout tab, you can make a variety of modifications to the table such as

- Adding and deleting columns
- Adding and deleting rows
- Changing the cell size
- Aligning cell text
- Changing text direction
- Merging and splitting cells and more.

3 Define Merging and Splitting cells in a table.

Ans. Refer to text on Page No. 130-131.

4 How does MS-Word 2010 differ from MS-Word 2013?

Ans. Differences between MS-Word 2010 and MS-Word 2013 are as follows

MS-Word 2010	*MS-Word 2013*
It is the successor of Microsoft Office 2007 and predecessor of Microsoft Office 2013.	It is the successor of Microsoft Office 2010 and the predecessor of Microsoft Office 2016.
It was released on 15th June, 2010 for general availability.	It was released on 29th January, 2013 for general availability.
It has no enhanced reading mode.	It has an enhanced reading mode.

5 How will you insert Mathematical symbols in your Word document?

Ans. Refer to text on Page No. 133-134.

6 Explain the feature, Track Changes of MS-Word 2007.

Ans. Track Changes is a feature in Microsoft Word which allows us to keep track of the changes that we make to a document. It allows us to accept or reject the track changes, insert or delete comments etc.

7 After modifying a document using Track Changes, in how many ways a document can be viewed?

Ans. There are four ways of viewing a document as follows

(*i*) Final Showing Markup
(*ii*) Final
(*iii*) Original Showing Markup
(*iv*) Original

8 I want to see the tracked changes in my document. How do I turn On the display of tracked changes?

Ans. In MS-Word 2007, on the Review tab, use the little menus in the Tracking group. Final Showing Markup or Original Showing Markup will show what changes you have made. But check the selected items on the Show Markup menu to be sure that Word is showing you the right things.

9 Write down the purpose and features of Show Markup option available in Review tab of Word 2007 document.

Ans. Refer to text on Page No. 136.

Long Answer (LA) Type Questions

1 Do you think, use of bulleted lists or numbered lists is more appropriate in a Word document?

Ans. The use of bulleted lists or numbered lists is an effective way to outline or list the items in a Word document.

By modifying numbered or bulleted lists, you are able to change the way of information that is displayed. Creating an outline list, which can help to organise your document for clear presentations. To customize your eye-catching bullets, Word provides many different images from which to choose.

Also, Word gives you the ways of modifying the format of your numeral list.

2 How can you add and delete a row and a column in a table?

Ans. Refer to text on Page No. 130.

3 Which feature is provided by Word to customise the look of a custom shape? Write down the steps involved.

Ans. Refer to text on Page No. 132.

4 Explain the purpose of AutoFormat feature of Word 2007. How it can be used in a Word document?

Ans. Refer to text on Page No. 134-135.

5 What do you mean by comments? How review comment is done in Word document?

Ans. Refer to text on Page No. 135-136.

6 How do I tell Word to track the changes I made to my document?

Ans. To turn On Track Changes (that is, to tell Word to track each change that you make in your document), do one of the following

- Press: Ctrl+Shift+E

or

- On the Status bar, click "Track Changes Off" to turn On track changes. If you cannot see "Track Changes" on the Status bar then right click the Status bar and click Track Changes.

or

- Click on Review Tab →in the Tracking group, click on Track Changes. When the button is highlighted, Word is tracking change.

Application Oriented Questions

1 Gunjan created a text document that contains information about records of students. Now, she wants to convert it into table format. Discuss

(*i*) What is a table?

(*ii*) Which command combination is used to convert text into table?

Ans. (*i*) Table is a grid of cells arranged in rows and columns.

(*ii*) First of all, select the text that you want to convert. Then, choose given combination **Insert tab → Table** option from Tables group → **Convert Text to Table....**

2 Mani wants to create a list as given below

- Mango
- Apple
- Orange
- Banana

Now, she wants to change the color of the bullet. Does Word allow you to change the color of the bullet. Is it possible to create the numbered list?

Ans. Yes, you can change the color of the bullet and it is also possible to create the numbered list.

3 Tick two boxes to show features of a Word processor.

	Tick two boxes
The tab key should be used to right align a heading.	
Fill series option enables you fill desired entries in a table.	
A spelling checker can be used to check whether you have used, 'there', instead of 'theire'.	
The space bar should be used to start AutoFormat.	
You can use ClipArt to illustrate the text.	

EXAM PRACTICE

Ans.

	Tick two boxes
The tab key should be used to right align a heading.	
Fill series option enables you fill desired entries in a table.	
A spelling checker can be used to check whether you have used, 'there', instead of 'theire'.	✓
The space bar should be used to start AutoFormat.	
You can use ClipArt to illustrate the text.	✓

4 Sandhya is working on her coursework of computer.

(*i*) Sandhya has copied a graphic from the Internet to put it in her document. Which method should she adopt to add this graphic in the document conveniently?

	Tick one box
Add picture from file	
Add picture from gallery	
Drag picture from Web page	
Copy and Paste	
Cut and Paste	

(*ii*) Give one example, when the AutoCorrect may not correct word when it is spelt incorrectly.

Ans. (*i*)

	Tick one box
Add picture from file	
Add picture from gallery	
Drag picture from Web page	
Copy and Paste	✓
Cut and Paste	

(*ii*) If we add a misspelt word in the dictionary then AutoCorrect cannot correct that word.

5 Following is a text document containing a letter. The line numbers are given on the right hand side of the document. Observe the following document and answer the questions (*i*) and (*ii*).

From	1
Customer Help Manager,	2
LG Corporation,	3
New Delhi	4
Date: 31st MAY, 2014	5
To,	6
Dushyant Khandelwal	7
P-125 Vasant Enclave	8
Nehru Place	9
	10
Subject : Reply to Complaint no. 52543	11
Dear Madam,	12
	13
This is with reference to your complaint no. 52543 with regard	14
to our Hair Dryer Model 978. We would like to inform	15

you the following:	16
1. The defect informed by you is not converted in our Warrant Terms.	17
2. The defective part is required to be imported from Japan.	18
3. As a privileged customer of our company will be able to give	19
50% discount on the part alongwith free replacement at your	20
premises.	21
	22
Kindly let us know your decision in the regard.	23
	24
In your best service!	25
	26
Sincerely Yours'	27
Shyam Godbole	28
Shyam Godbole.	29
	30
CustCare@LGCorp.com	31

(*i*) Name the feature used to insert the digital signature of the Customer Help Manager in line 28.
(*ii*) Identify line(s) where the text is right aligned. (Write line numbers)

Ans. (*i*) In Word processor, the digital signature is inserted using Insert →Picture option. The digital signature is a scanned image and stored in picture format.
(*ii*) The right aligned lines are 5 and 31.

CHAPTER

09

MS-PowerPoint

Chapter Checklist

- Starting PowerPoint 2007
- Concept of Slide Show
- Creating New Presentation
- Saving a Presentation
- Different Views of a Slide
- Header and Footer
- Inserting Pictures
- Creating Slide Shows
- Grouping and Ungrouping Objects

PowerPoint is a program in MS-Office package with which we can prepare presentations based on slides. PowerPoint helps us in preparing a presentation easily and quickly. Techniques we use in PowerPoint in preparing slides for making presentations are very similar to techniques used in other programs of MS-Office, such as MS-Word and MS-Excel. Besides this, we can also include information and objects prepared by other programs, such as text, chart worksheet, graphics etc, into the slides of a presentation.

PowerPoint saves us a lot of time than to write down the tips on board using chalks or pens. Using PowerPoint, audience will clearly see what's in the presentation, specially when you added some pictures and video clips.

Starting PowerPoint

In order to start working with Microsoft PowerPoint 2007, you will need to locate and open the program on your computer. To open MS-PowerPoint on your computer, do the following

Click Start button → All Programs → Microsoft Office → Microsoft Office PowerPoint 2007

MS-PowerPoint with a blank presentation will be open. By default, the name of a blank presentation is Presentation1.pptx, where .pptx is the extension of MS-PowerPoint 2007 file.

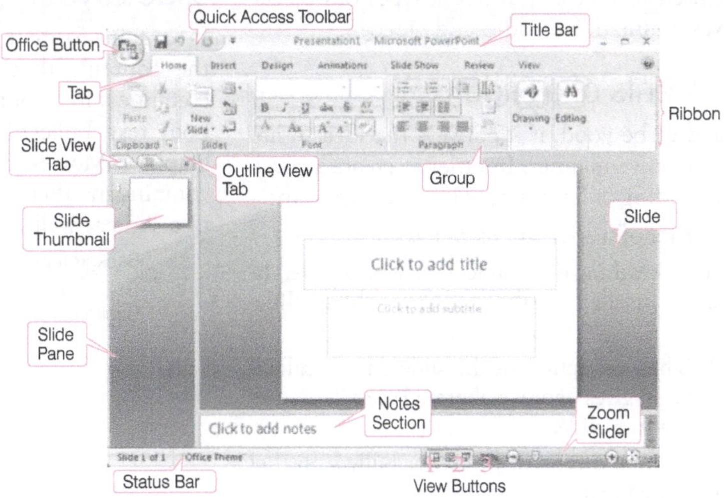

Microsoft PowerPoint window

Various components of MS-PowerPoint 2007 window are described below

(*i*) **Title bar** It contains the name of currently opened file followed by software name.

(*ii*) **Ribbon** It is same as Word and Excel, just few tabs are different like Animations, Slide Show etc.

(*iii*) **Slide** It appears in the centre of the window. You can create your presentation by adding content to the slides.

(*iv*) **Slide pane** This area of PowerPoint window displays all the slides that are added in the presentation.

(*v*) **Slide view tab** This tab displays a thumbnail view of all the slides.

(*vi*) **Outline view tab** This tab displays the text contained in the presentation in an outline format.

(*vii*) **Notes section** This can be used for creating notes.

(*viii*) **View buttons** The View buttons appear near the bottom of the screen. It is used to view the changes between Normal view, Slider Sorter view and the Slide Show view.

(*ix*) **Status bar** It displays the number of the slide that is currently being displayed, the total number of slides and the name of the design template which is in use or the name of the background.

Concept of Slide Show

A file created using PowerPoint software is known as Slide Show. Slide Show refers to the process of running a presentation. In a Slide show, you can see your presentation in full screen and also run slides in continuous series (one by one). A Slide Show consists of multiple slides. Further, a slide is a combination of graphics, stylised formatting, different types of objects like textboxes, animations, audio and video.

Basic Elements of a Slide

A slide is said to be good, if it conveys the idea in an easy and yet effective manner. In order to create a good slide, understanding of its structure is more important.

Various elements of a slide are as follows

(*i*) **Title** The heading of a slide is called a title. It represents an idea to the audience about slide contents.

(*ii*) **Subtitle** The description of the slide data is called a subtitle. It gives more elaborated detail of the central idea of a slide.

(*iii*) **Text** The entered content by user as bullets on the slide are called text.

(*iv*) **Drawing objects** The built-in shapes of MS-PowerPoint are called drawing objects.

(*v*) **ClipArt** The set of built-in pictures provided in MS-PowerPoint gallery are called ClipArt.

(*vi*) **Media clip** The set of audio, video, animated gif in MS-PowerPoint are called media clip.

(*vii*) **Pictures** The set of pictures provided in MS-PowerPoint are called pictures.

(*viii*) **Tables** The collection of rows and columns provided in MS-PowerPoint are called tables.

(*ix*) **Chart** A graphical representation of data in a slide are called chart.

(*x*) **SmartArt graphic** The quick way to convert the text in a bulleted list are called SmartArt graphic.

Slide Components used for Reference

Displaying all the information within a slide is not always possible. So, usually a presenter needs additional support like handouts, notes and outlines to display the additional information. These components are used for reference purposes so that, they can help audience to easily get the message conveyed through a presentation. The following components of a slide are used for reference purpose

(*i*) **Handouts** A smaller version of the slide is called handout. The handout of a presentation, if provided to the audience will help them in understanding the presentation easily.

(*ii*) **Speaker's notes** The small pictures of slides alongwith some description are called speaker's notes. These are used by the presenter.

(*iii*) **Outlines** The summarised version of slides in a presentation is called outlines. It consists of only titles and main text of slides and is useful for managing and organising the flow of a presentation.

Slide Layout

It contains formatting, positioning and placeholders for all of the contents that appear on a slide. Placeholders are the containers in layout that hold such content as Text (including body text, bulleted lists and titles), Tables, Charts, SmartArt graphics, Movies, Sounds, Pictures and ClipArt and a layout contains the theme (colors, fonts, effects and the background) of a slide as well.

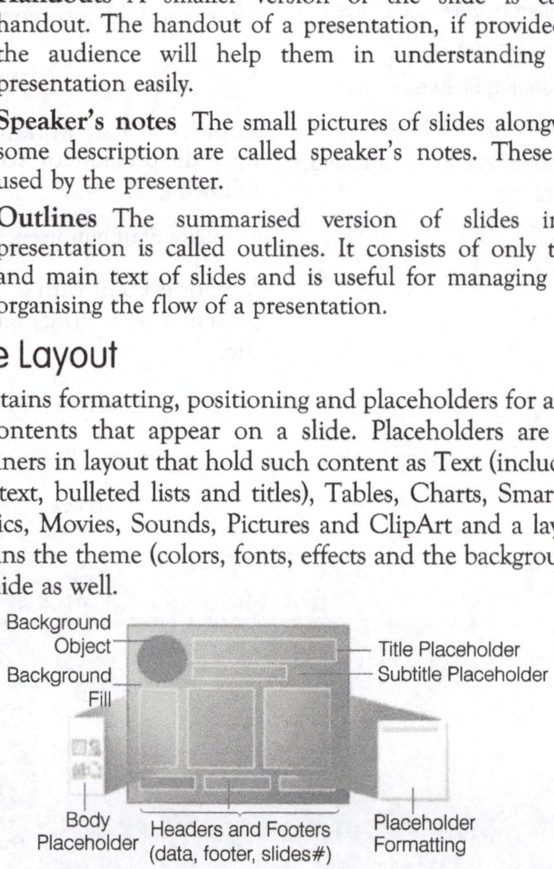

Below diagram shows all of the layout elements that you can include on a PowerPoint slide.

Different Types of Slide Layout

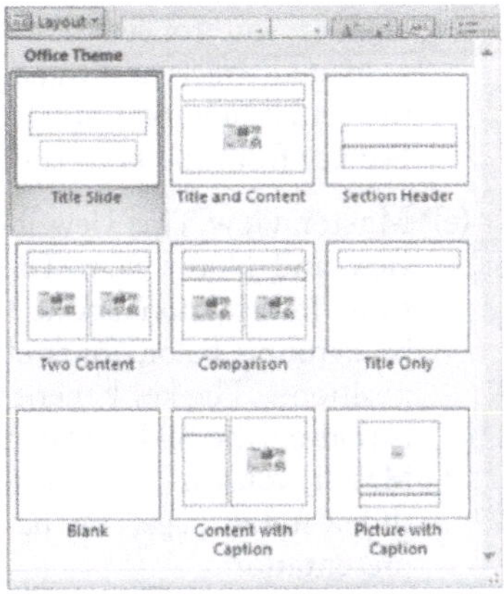

MS-PowerPoint includes **nine built-in slide layouts** (Standard layouts) or one can create one's **custom layouts** that meet the specific needs and can share them with other people, who create presentations by using MS-PowerPoint.

In this figure, each layout shows the placement of various placeholders in which you will add text or graphics.

(i) Standard Layouts

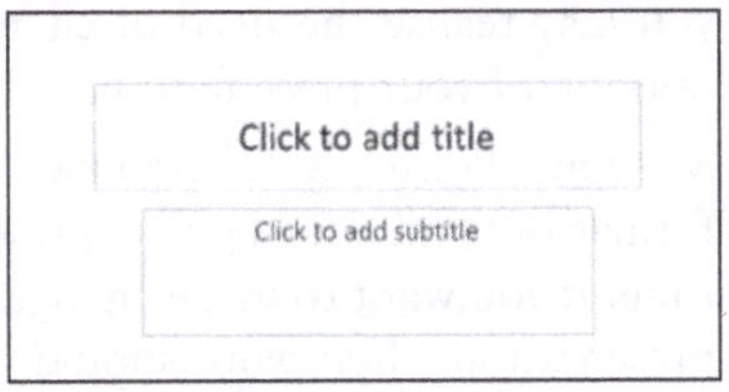

The standard, built-in layouts available in Office PowerPoint 2007 are similar to those available in PowerPoint 2003 and earlier versions. When you open a blank presentation in PowerPoint, the default layout called **Title Slide** (Shown) will appear, but there are other standard layouts that can be applied and used.

Other layouts that are present in standard layout are as follows

(*i*) Title and Content (*ii*) Section Header
(*iii*) Two Content (*iv*) Comparison
(*v*) Title Only (*vi*) Blank
(*vii*) Content with Caption (*viii*) Picture with Caption

(ii) Custom Layouts

You can create reusable custom layouts that specify the number, size, location of placeholders, background content, theme colors, fonts and effects, optional slide and placeholder level properties. You can also distribute custom layouts as part of a template, so you no longer have to waste valuable time in cutting and pasting your layouts onto new slides or deleting content on a slide that you want to use with new and different content.

Types of text and object-based placeholders that you can add to build your custom layout include as follows:

Content, Text, Pictures, SmartArt graphics, Charts, Tables, Diagrams, Media, Movies and Sound.

Creating New Presentation

For creating a new presentation in MS-PowerPoint, there are two options available to make a selection of creating new presentation

Creating Blank Presentation

For creating a blank presentation, do the following

(*i*) Click on **Microsoft Office** button and then click **New** from the menu that appears.

(*ii*) A **New Presentation** dialog box will appear.

(*iii*) Select **Blank Presentation** and click on **Create** button.

A blank presentation with one slide will be created.

Also, further slides can be added to the presentation and can change the layout of an existing slide as well.

Creating Presentation using Themes

You can quickly and easily format an entire presentation to give it a professional and modern look by applying a theme.

In MS-PowerPoint 2007, you can apply theme using these two methods which are as follows

Method 1

(*i*) Click on **Microsoft Office** button and then, click **New** from the menu that appears.

(*ii*) A **New Presentation** dialog box will appear.

(*iii*) From the left hand side page, select **Installed Themes** under **Templates**.

(*iv*) Select any one of the themes as per the user's choice.

(*v*) Click **Create** button.

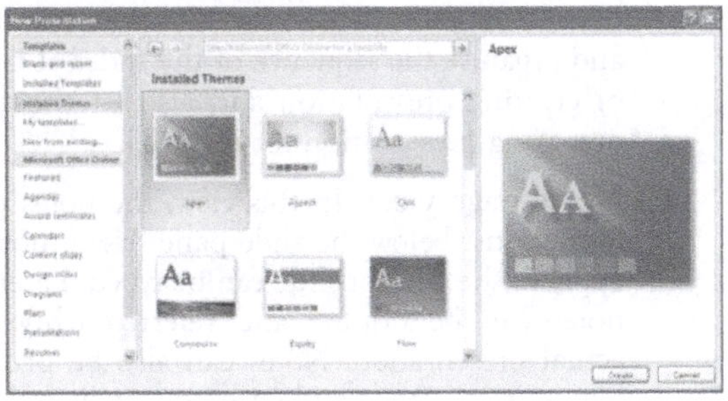

Method 2

(*i*) Select **Design** tab under the MS-PowerPoint 2007 ribbon menu system.

(*ii*) Select any one of the themes as per the user's choice under Themes group.

(*iii*) Effects will be automatically applied on all the slides.

Saving a Presentation

Procedure for saving a presentation is same as saving a MS-Word document and MS-Excel workbook. For saving your presentation, do the following

(*i*) Click on the **Microsoft Office** button and then, click **Save As** option from the menu that appears.

or

Press Ctrl+S keys from keyboard.

(*ii*) **Save As** dialog box will appear, in the **File name** box, enter a new name to save the file.

(*iii*) Then, click **Save** button.

Different Views of a Slide

In Microsoft Office PowerPoint 2007, different views of a slide are used to edit, print and deliver a presentation. PowerPoint slide views can be found in two places as follows

(*i*) On the **View** tab, in the **Presentation Views** group, where all views are available.

(*ii*) On an easy-accessible bar, at the bottom of the PowerPoint window, where the main views (Normal, Slide Sorter and Slide Show) are available.

Different types of views available in PowerPoint 2007 are explained below:

(a) **Normal view** This is the main editing view, where you write and design your presentations, i.e. actual screen which is displayed. The view is also known as slide view. A Normal view is the default view size for the screen.

(b) **Slide Sorter view** It provides a view of slides in thumbnail form. This view makes it easy to sort and organise the sequence of the slides at the time of creating presentation and also, at the time of preparing presentation for printing.

(c) **Notes page view** In this view, the notes pane is located just below the slide pane. Here, notes that apply to the current slide can be typed. Later, these notes can be printed and referred while giving actual presentation. Notes can also be printed to handout to the audience or included in a presentation that is delivered to the audience or posted on a Web page.

(d) **Slide show view** This view is used to deliver a presentation to the audience. Slide Show view takes up the full computer screen, like an actual presentation. In this view, you can see your presentation, the way audience wants. This view enables you to see how graphics, timings, movies, animated effects and transition effects will look during the actual presentation. To exit Slide Show view, press **Esc** key from the keyboard.

(e) **Master view** This view includes Slide view, Handout view and Notes view. They are the main slides that store information about the presentation, including background color, fonts effects, placeholder sizes and positions. The key benefit to working in a Master view is that on the Slide Master, Notes Master, or Handout Master, you can make universal style changes to every slide, notes page, or handout associated with the presentation.

Editing and Formatting a Slide

While developing a presentation at some point of time, you may realise the need of changing the content or the outlook of your presentation.

MS-PowerPoint 2007 provides you the flexibility of formatting and editing your presentation at any point of time. If you want to make changes in all the slides of your presentation then you should use Slide Sorter view. Otherwise, you can change outlook of individual slides as well.

1. Entering Text

Boxes within a slide layout with dotted borders that contain text and other objects are called **placeholders**. All built-in slide layouts contain content placeholders, e.g. title text placeholder, subtitle text placeholder, placeholders for pictures, charts, videos etc.

To enter text in title and subtitle placeholder, you need to click within these placeholders and enter the text. When you open PowerPoint, title slide will automatically appear. Place cursor in **Click to add title** text box and insert the derived text in it. Some layout may also have **Click to add subtitle.**

You can add textbox object in a slide anywhere and then can add text in it. For adding textbox object in your slide, do the following:

(*i*) Select the slide on which you want to insert a textbox.

(*ii*) Then, click on the **Text Box** button, under the **Insert** tab.

(*iii*) After this, draw a textbox on the slide of whatever length you want.

(*iv*) Insert the desired text in it.

2. Adding Background

Background styles are variations of background colors derived from combinations of themes, colors and background intensities in the current document theme. For changing the background of presentation, you have to choose a different background style.

For applying or changing the background of a presentation, do the following

(*i*) Click the slide or slides on which you want to add a background style.

(*ii*) To select multiple slides, click the first slide and then press and hold **Ctrl** key while you click the other slides.

(*iii*) On the **Design** tab, in the **Background** group, click the arrow next to the **Background Styles**.

(*iv*) Right-click on the background style that you want to apply and then do one of the following

- (a) To apply the background style to the selected slides, click **Apply to Selected Slides**.
- (b) To apply the background style to all of the slides in your presentation, click **Apply to All Slides**.
- (c) To replace the background style for the selected slides and any other slides in the presentation that use the same slide master, click **Apply to Matching Slides.** This option is available only when your presentation contains multiple slide masters. To create multiple slide master, click on **Slide Master view** in **View** tab, then click on **Insert Slide Master** from **Edit Master** group in **Slide Master** tab.

3. Adding Watermark

You can insert a picture, including ClipArt behind part of your slide as a watermark. By adding a picture as a watermark to one or all of your slides, can make your Microsoft Office PowerPoint 2007 presentation unique or clearly identify your presentation sponsor. You can lighten your picture, ClipArt or color so that, it does not interfere with the content of your slide. You can also use Text or WordArt as a watermark to indicate that your presentation is a draft or confidential.

Watermarks are flexible because you can change their sizes and their position on a slide. You can apply a watermark to some or all of the slides in your presentation.

Background

Watermark

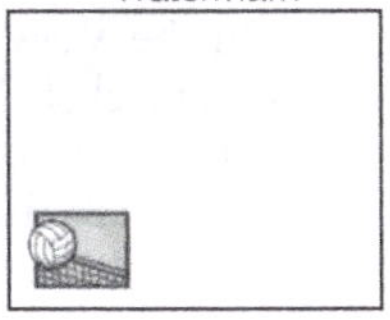

Use Picture or ClipArt as a Watermark

To use a picture or ClipArt as a watermark, do the following

(*i*) Click the slide on which you want to add a watermark. On the **View** tab, in the **Presentation Views** group, click **Slide Master.**

(*ii*) On the **Insert** tab, in the **Illustrations** group, do one of the following:

To use a picture as a watermark, click **Picture** option, locate the picture that you want to apply and then click **Insert** button.

or

To use ClipArt as a watermark, click **ClipArt.** In the **ClipArt** task pane, in the **Search for** box, either type a word or phrase that describes the clip that you want, or type all or part of the file name of the clip and then click **Go** button. Now, insert any ClipArt which you want.

(*iii*) To adjust the size of the picture or ClipArt, right-click the picture or ClipArt on the slide and then click **Size and Position...** option from the drop down menu. A **Size and Position** dialog box will appear.

(*iv*) On the **Size** tab, under **Scale,** increase or decrease the settings in the **Height** and **Width** boxes.

(*v*) To move the picture or ClipArt on the slide, click the **Position** tab under **Size and Position** dialog box and then enter the settings for the positions that you want in the **Horizontal** and **Vertical** boxes and then click on **Close** button.

(*vi*) Under **Picture Tools Format** tab, in the **Adjust** group, click **Recolor** and then under **Light Variations**, click the **color** fade that you want.

(*vii*) Under **Picture Tools Format** tab, in the **Adjust** group, click **Brightness** and then click the brightness percentage that you want.

(*viii*) When you finish editing and positioning the watermark and are satisfied with its appearance, to send the watermark to the back of the slide, under **Picture Tools Format** tab, in the **Arrange** group, click **Send to Back.**

Use of Textbox or WordArt as a Watermark

To use a textbox or WordArt as a watermark, do the following

(*i*) Click the slide that you want to add a textbox or WordArt watermark.

(*ii*) On the **Insert** tab, in the **Text** group, do one of the following:

To use a textbox, click **Text Box.**

or

To use a WordArt, click **WordArt.**

(*iii*) Enter text in the textbox or WordArt that you want to appear in the watermark.

(*iv*) If you want to reposition the watermark, click the textbox or WordArt and then when the pointer becomes a ✥, drag the textbox or WordArt to a new location.

(*v*) When you finish editing and positioning the watermark and are satisfied with its appearance, to send the textbox or WordArt to the back of the slide, under **Drawing Tools Format** tab, in the **Arrange** group, click **Send to Back**.

Check Point 01

1 The summarised version of slides in a presentation defines which term?

2 Which element of slide gives more elaborated detail of the central idea of a slide?
(a) Text (b) Title (c) Subtitle (d) ClipArt

3 What are called the main slides that store information about the presentation, including background colors, fonts effects, placeholder sizes and positions?

4 Mr.Harish wants to give your audience a collage of slides and placeholder paper copy of your presentation, which feature of MS-PowerPoint will you suggest him for this purpose?

Header and Footer

When it is required to add text (such as your presentation's title, the presenter's name, a file name, company name and many more) to the bottom of one or more slides, handouts, or notes pages in a presentation or to the top of one or more handouts or notes pages in a presentation, concept of header and footer is used.

Add a Footer to a Slide

To add a footer to a slide, do the following

(*i*) On the **Insert** tab, in the **Text** group, click **Header & Footer** option.

(*ii*) A **Header and Footer** dialog box will appear.

(*iii*) In the **Header and Footer** dialog box, on the **Slide** tab, select the **Footer** check box and then type the text that you want to appear in the centre bottom of the slide.

(*iv*) To keep the text in the footer from appearing on the title slide, select the **Don't show on title slide** check box.

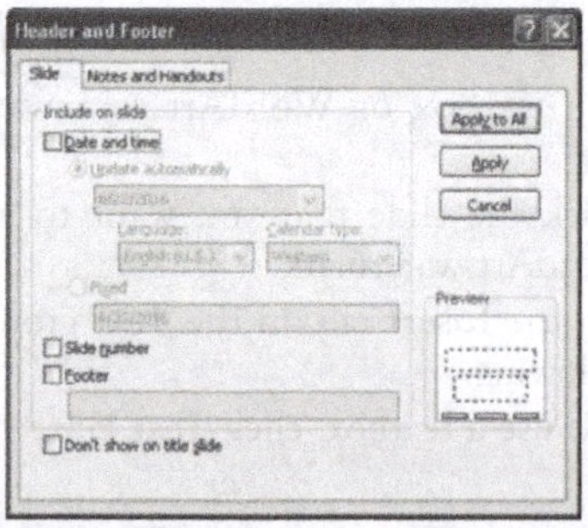

(*v*) Do one of the following:

To display footer information on the selected slide only, click **Apply**.

or

To display footer information on all the slides in your presentation, click **Apply to All**.

Add a Header, Footer or both to a Handouts or Notes Page

For adding a header and footer to a handouts or notes page, do the following

(*i*) On the **Insert** tab, in the **Text** group, click **Header & Footer** option.

(*ii*) A **Header and Footer** dialog box will appear.

(*iii*) In the **Header and Footer** dialog box, on the **Notes and Handouts** tab, select the **Header** or **Footer** check box or both and then type the text that you want to appear in the centre top (header) or centre bottom (footer) of each notes page or handouts.

(*iv*) Click **Apply to All**.

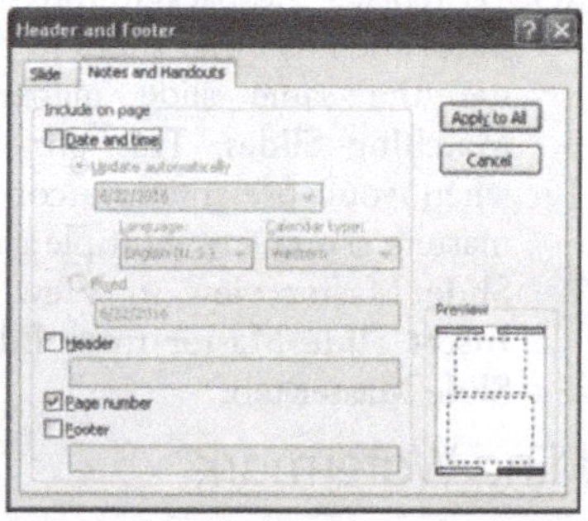

Note The Preview box, located in the Header and Footer dialog box, displays the Header and Footer information in the location that the slide, handout or notes page will display it.

Adding Slide Numbers and Date/Time to a Slide

Slide numbers, notes page numbers, handouts page numbers, the date and time can all be added to a presentation.

1. Add Slide Page Numbers

For adding page numbers to the slides of your presentation, do the following

(*i*) On the **View** tab, in the **Presentation Views** group, click **Normal** and then on the slide pane that contains the **Slides** and **Outline** tabs, click the **first slide thumbnail** in your presentation.

(*ii*) Now, click on the **Insert** tab, in the **Text** group, click **Slide Number** option.

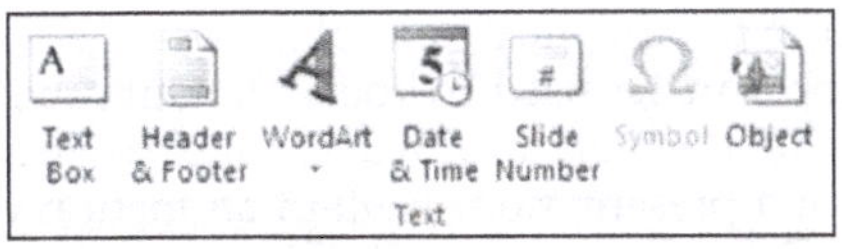

(*iii*) A **Header and Footer** dialog box will appear.

(*iv*) In the **Header and Footer** dialog box, do one of the following:

If you want to add slide numbers, click the **Slide** tab and then select the **Slide Number** check box.

or

If you want to add page numbers to notes or handouts, click the **Notes and Handouts** tab and then select the **Page number** check box.

(*v*) Click **Apply to All.**

2. Timing Text Box or Add Date and Time

For adding date and time to the slide, do the following

(*i*) On the **View** tab, in the **Presentation Views** group, click **Normal** and then on the slide pane that contains the **Slides** and **Outline** tabs, click the **first slide thumbnail** in your presentation.

(*ii*) On the **Insert** tab, in the **Text** group, click **Date & Time** option. A **Header and Footer** dialog box will appear.

(*iii*) In the **Header and Footer** dialog box, do one of the following:

If you want to add the date and time to your slides, click the **Slide** tab.

or

If you want to add the date and time to your notes pages or handouts, click the **Notes and Handouts** tab.

(*iv*) Select the **Date and time** check box and then, do one of the following:

By default the **Update automatically** radio button selected that reflect the current date and time, each time when you open or print the presentation, click **Update automatically** and then select the date and time format that you want.

or

If you want to set the date and time to a specific date, click **Fixed** radio button and then in the text box, type the date that you want.

Note By setting the date on your presentation, so that it is fixed, you can easily keep track of the last time you made changes to it.

(*v*) If you want to add the date and time to all of the slides, notes pages or handouts in your presentation, click **Apply to All.**

Inserting Pictures

Pictures and ClipArt can be inserted into a Microsoft Office PowerPoint 2007 presentation from sources such as ClipArt Website providers, Web pages or files on a computer. These pictures can be used as backgrounds for slides in a presentation.

For inserting pictures from file in your presentation, do the following

(*i*) Click where you want to insert the picture.

(*ii*) On the **Insert** tab, in the **Illustrations** group, click **Picture** option.

(*iii*) Locate the picture that you want to insert and then double click on it.

or

To add multiple pictures, press and hold **Ctrl** key while you click the pictures that you want to insert and then click **Insert** button.

Note To insert a picture into the notes pages of an Office PowerPoint 2007 presentation, switch to Notes view and then do the above same procedure.

Creating Slide Shows

Using PowerPoint, a wide range of special effects, such as transition and animation can be added in a presentation to provide visual interest to the presentation and grab the audience's attention. Points can be revealed on slides in a staggered way (i.e. one bullet displayed at a time) to keep the audience focused only on the point which is being discussed at the given time. Also, the presentation can be automated, so it runs on its own.

The slide show can be enhanced by applying the following effects

Adding Transitions to a Slide

Slide transitions are the animation-like effects that occur in Slide Show view while moving from one slide to the next during an on-screen presentation.

The speed of each slide transition effect can be controlled and sound effects can also be added to a slide. PowerPoint supports with different types of built-in transition effects like cut, dissolve, wipe down and many more.

Adding different slide transitions to the slides in your presentation, do the following

(*i*) On the left side of the slide window, in the pane that contains the **Slides** and **Outline** tabs, click the **Slides** tab and then select a slide thumbnail.

(*ii*) On the **Animations** tab, in the **Transition to This Slide** group, select any Slide Transition Effect that you want for that slide.

(*iii*) To set the slide transition speed between the current slide and the next slide, in the **Transition to This Slide** group, click the arrow next to **Transition Speed** and then select the speed that you want.

(*iv*) To add a different slide transition to another slide in your presentation, repeat steps (*i*) to (*iii*).

Adding the same slide transition to all of the slides in your presentation, do the following

(*i*) On the left side of the slide window, in the pane that contains the **Slides** and **Outline** tabs, click the **Slides** tab.

(*ii*) Select the slide thumbnail of the slides that you want to apply slide transitions.

(*iii*) On the **Animations** tab, in the **Transition to This Slide** group, select any Slide Transition Effect.

(*iv*) To set the slide transition speed between the current slide and the next slide, in the **Transition to This Slide** group, click the arrow next to **Transition Speed** and then select the speed that you want.

(*v*) In the **Transition to This Slide** group, click **Apply to All.**

Add Sound to Slide Transitions

For adding sound to the slide transitions, do the following

(*i*) On the left side of the slide window, in the pane that contains the **Slides** and **Outline** tabs, click the **Slides** tab and then select the slide thumbnails that you want to add a sound to.

(*ii*) On the **Animations** tab, in the **Transition to This Slide** group, click the arrow next to **Transition Sound** and then do one of the following:

To add a sound from the list, that you want.

or

To add a sound not found on the list, select **Other Sound,** locate the sound file from Add Sound dialog box that you want to add and then click **OK** button.

(*iii*) To add sound to a different slide transitions, repeat step (*ii*).

Animating Text and Objects

We can give sound effects or visual effects, including movement to the text or objects in a presentation. Animation can be used to focus on important points, to control the flow of information and to increase viewer interest in a presentation. Built-in animation effect can be added in Office PowerPoint 2007 presentation by doing the following

(*i*) Select the text or object that you want to animate.

(*ii*) On the **Animations** tab, in the **Animations** group, select the animation effect that you want from the **Animate** list.

To apply a custom animation effect in Office PowerPoint 2007, do the following

(*i*) Select the text or object that you want to animate.

(*ii*) On the **Animations** tab, in the **Animations** group, click **Custom Animation.**

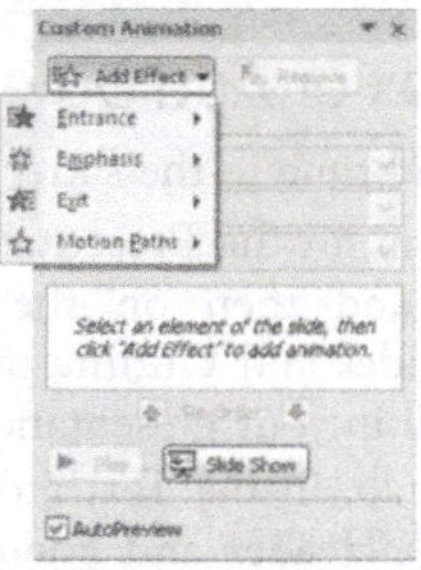

(*iii*) In the **Custom Animation** task pane, click **Add Effect** and then do one or more of the following

(a) To make the enter text or object with an effect, point to **Entrance** and then click any effect.

(b) To add an effect, such as a **Spin** effect, to text or an object that is already visible on the slide, point to **Emphasis** and then click an effect.

(c) To add an effect that makes text or an object leave the slide at some point, click to **Exit** and then click an effect.

(d) To add an effect that makes text or an object move in a specified pattern, click to **Motion Paths** and then click a path.

(*iv*) To specify how the effect is applied to your text or object, right-click any custom animation effect in the **Custom Animation** list and then click **Effect Options... .**

(*v*) Do one of the following

To specify settings for text, on the **Effect** and **Timing** tabs, click the options **Animate text** from Effect tab to use to animate the text.

or

To specify settings for an object, on the **Effect** and **Timing** tabs, click the options that you want to use to animate the object.

Note Effects appear in the Custom Animation list in the order that you add them.

Rehearse Timing

This option is used to control the speed of the transition and animation effects that have been applied to the slide. Using this feature, the amount of time you spend on each slide is recorded while rehearsing for the presentation and that timing can be used to run the Slide Show automatically in future.

For using this outstanding feature, do the following

(*i*) On the **Slide Show** tab, in the **Set Up** group, click **Rehearse Timings**.

The **Rehearsal** toolbar will appear and the **Slide Time** box begins timing the presentation.

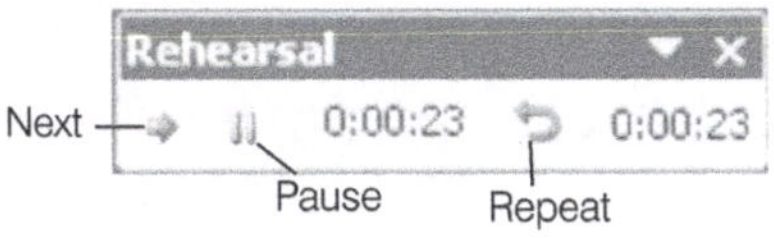

(*ii*) While you set the time in your presentation, do one or more of the following on the **Rehearsal** toolbar

(a) To move to the next slide, click **Next**.

(b) To temporarily stop recording the time, click **Pause**.

(c) To restart recording the time after pausing, click **Pause**.

(d) To restart recording the time for the current slide, click **Repeat**.

(*iii*) After you set the time for the last slide, a message box displays the total time for the presentation and prompts you to do one of the following:

To keep the recorded slide timings, click **Yes**.

or

To discard the recorded slide timings, click **No**. Slide Sorter view will appear and display the time of each slide in your presentation.

Check Point 02

1 Riya added a header while preparing her presentation on "Environment" topic. What is the use of header here?

2 Shyam wants to insert a picture in his presentation related to presentation topic. But he is not able to do this, can you help him to achieve the same?

3 Which feature of MS-PowerPoint is used to control the speed of the transition and animation effects that have been applied to the slide?

(a) Header

(b) Transition speed

(c) Transition sound

(b) Automatically after

Keyboard Shortcuts *for* MS-PowerPoint 2007

Select Text and Objects

Shift + Right Arrow	Select one character to the right.
Shift + Left Arrow	Select one character to the left.
Ctrl + Shift + Right Arrow	Select to the end of a word.
Ctrl +Shift +Left Arrow	Select to the beginning of a word.
Shift + Up Arrow	Select one line up.
Shift + Down Arrow	Select one line down.
Ctrl + A (on the Slides tab)	Select all objects.
Ctrl + A (in Slide Sorter view)	Select all slides.
Ctrl + A (on the Outline tab)	Select all text.

Delete and Copy Text and Objects

Ctrl + Backspace	Delete one word to the left.
Ctrl + Delete	Delete one word to the right.
Ctrl + X	Cut selected object.
Ctrl + C	Copy selected object.
Ctrl + V	Paste (cut or copied) object.
Ctrl + Z	Undo the last action.
Ctrl + Y	Redo the last action.
Ctrl + Shift + C	Copy formatting only.
Ctrl + Shift + V	Paste formatting only.
Ctrl + Alt + V	Paste special.

Change or Resize the Font

Ctrl + Shift + F	Open the Font dialog box to change the font.
Ctrt + Shift + P	Open the Font dialog box to change the font effects.
Ctrl + Shift + >	Increase the font size.
Ctrl + Shift + <	Decrease the font size.

Apply Character Formats

Ctrl + Equal Sign	Apply subscript formatting (automatic spacing).
Ctrl + Shift + Plus Sign	Apply superscript formatting (automatic spacing).
Ctrl + Spacebar	Remove manual character formatting, such as subscript and superscript.

Align Paragraphs

Ctrl +E	Center a paragraph.
Ctrl +J	Justify a paragraph.
Ctrl +L	Left align a paragraph.
Ctrl +R	Right align a paragraph.

Run a Presentation

F5	Start the Microsoft PowerPoint presentation from the beginning.
Number + Enter	Go to slide number.

B or Period	Display a blank black slide, or return to the presentation from a blank black slide.
W or Comma	Display a blank white slide, or return to the presentation from a blank white slide.
S	Stop or restart an automatic presentation.
Esc or Hyphen	End a Microsoft PowerPoint presentation.
E	Erase on-screen a notation.
H	Go to the next Microsoft PowerPoint slide, if the next slide is hidden.
T	Set new timings while rehearsing.
O	Use original timings while rehearsing.
M	Use a mouse click to advance while rehearsing.
Ctrl + P	Redisplay hidden pointer or change the pointer to a pen.
Ctrl + A	Redisplay hidden pointer or change the pointer to an arrow.
Ctrl + H	Hide the pointer and navigation button immediately.
Ctrl + U	Hide the pointer and navigation button in 15 seconds.
Shift + F10	Display the Microsoft PowerPoint shortcut menu.
Tab	Go to the first or next hyperlink on a slide.
Shift + Tab	Go to the last or previous hyperlink on a slide.

SUMMARY

- PowerPoint is a software package designed to create electronic presentations consisting of a series of separate pages or slides.
- A Slide Show is a presentation of a series of still images on a projection screen or electronic display device, typically in a pre-arranged sequence.
- Slide layouts contain formatting, positioning and placeholders for all of the content that appears on a slide.
- ClipArt, in the graphic arts, is pre-made images used to illustrate any medium.
- Normal view is where you'll work most frequently to create your slides.
- Slide Sorter view is a feature included in Microsoft PowerPoint software that allows the user to see all the slides in a presentation at a time.
- A watermark is any text or graphic that is printed to overlap existing text in a document, either in the background or foreground.
- A header or footer is the text that appears at the top (header) or bottom (footer) of each page in your presentation.
- Slide transitions are the animation-like effects that occur in Slide Show view when you move from one slide to the next during an on-screen presentation.
- The Rehearsal feature lets you know how long your presentation takes, and can set PowerPoint slide timings so that the slides automatically advance based on the timings you set during the rehearsal.

Exam Practice

Multiple Choice Questions

1 .... is the default file name for a PowerPoint presentation.
(a) Untitled1 (b) Book1
(c) Presentation1 (d) Document1

Ans. (*c*) The default name given to a presentation file is Presentation1.

2 File extension for a PowerPoint 2007 presentation is
(a) .ptt (b) .pptx (c) .docx (d) .clsx

Ans. (*b*) .pptx is the file extension given to all PowerPoint 2007 files.

3 The custom animation can apply
(a) Font work gallery (b) Gallery
(c) Text (d) All of these

Ans. (*d*) The custom animation can apply font work gallery, gallery and text.

4 Professional looking visual aids are prepared with the help of software called.... .
(a) DBMS (b) Multimedia
(c) Graphics software
(d) Presentation graphics software

Ans. (*d*) Professional looking visual aids are prepared with the help of software called Presentation graphics software.

5 A set of predefined formats of text or color scheme is called
(a) slide (b) presentation scheme
(c) theme (d) schema

Ans. (*c*) A set of predefined formats of text or color scheme is called theme.

6 Which of the following views is useful for representing the structure of a presentation?
(a) Notes view (b) Outline view
(c) Slide view (d) Normal view

Ans. (*b*) Outline view is useful for checking the flow or structure of a presentation.

7 The entire presentation can be seen at a time in
(a) Slide Show view (b) Outline view
(c) Normal view (d) Slide Sorter view

Ans. (*d*) Slide Sorter view enables you to view the entire presentation at a time.

8 Which among the following views allows you to give a thumbnail view of all the slides in a presentation?
(a) Normal view (b) Outline view
(c) Notes view (d) Slide Sorter view

Ans. (*d*) Slide Sorter view provides a view of slides in thumbnail form.

9 Which among the following views allows you to add some extra information to a slide which is not viewed during the presentation.
(a) Normal view (b) Outline view
(c) Notes Page view (d) Slide Sorter view

Ans. (*c*) Notes Page view allows you to add some extra information related to presentation but it is not viewed during the presentation.

10 Which file format can be added to a PowerPoint show?
(a) .jpg (b) .gif
(c) .wav (d) All of these

Ans. (*d*) .jpg and .gif are file extensions for images and .wav is an extension for video file. Hence, all of these formats are supported in PowerPoint.

11 Rama is preparing a presentation on her company's annual performance. She wants some text present on a slide to fly in from the left, when she clicks the mouse. Which of the following features should she use?
(a) Slide Show (b) Slide Transition
(c) Custom Animation (d) Text Animation

Ans. (*c*) Custom Animation can be used for the desired functionality.

12 Special effects used to introduce slides in a presentation are
(a) transitions (b) effects
(c) custom animations (d) annotations

Ans. (*a*) Special effects used to introduce slides in a presentation are known as transitions.

13 Rehearse Timings command is present on .... tab.
(a) Animations (b) Review
(c) Slide Show (d) View

Ans. (*c*) Rehearse Timings command is present on Slide Show tab.

14 To set new timing while rehearsing, ... key is pressed.
(a) Ctrl+T (b) T (c) M (d) O

Ans. (*b*) T key is used to set new timing while rehearsing.

15 What is the shortcut key to display the Microsoft PowerPoint shortcut menu?
(a) F7
(b) F8
(c) Shift+F10
(d) F11

Ans. (*c*) Shift + F10 is the shortcut key to display the PowerPoint shortcut menu.

Fill in the Blanks

1 .... is a presentation graphics software.

Ans. PowerPoint

2 An electronic page in a presentation is called ....

Ans. slide

3 A .... is a pre-designed format of text and color scheme.

Ans. template

4 .... provides a command to change the layout of your slide.

Ans. Home tab

5 New Slide button for inserting a new slide can be found on .... tab.

Ans. Home

6 A .... is a box with a dotted outline, designed for the placement of different type of content on the slide.

Ans. Placeholder

7 From .... page, it is possible for you to choose slide designs.

Ans. Layout

8 In .... view, you can see all the slides in a presentation concurrently.

Ans. Slide Sorter

9 To select slides at discrete order in the Slides Pane, you need to hold the .... on the keyboard while selecting the slides.

Ans. Ctrl key

10 .... is a special effect that allows you to specify how to navigate from one slide to other.

Ans. Transition

11 The .... Animation enhance uses the flying effect on the text and character.

Ans. Custom

12 The Custom Animation command is present on .... tab.

Ans. Animations

True or False

1 Every presentation can contain only one single slide.

Ans. **False** A presentation is a collection of multiple slides.

2 Changing a slide layout is not allowed in PowerPoint.

Ans. **False** Under Home tab by clicking at Layout button, you can change layout of a slide.

3 Microsoft Office button contains options for frequently used tasks, such as opening, saving and printing.

Ans. **True** Open, Save, Save As, Print are frequently used tasks that are available on Microsoft Office button menu.

4 We cannot insert audio recording sound in a slide.

Ans. **False** We can insert audio recording sound in a slide.

5 Objects on the slide that hold text are called placeholder.

Ans. **True** Placeholders hold the text, ClipArt, charts etc.

6 We can delete slides in Slide Sorter view.

Ans. **False** Use this view to work with a group of slides or with only one slide.

7 Special effects used to introduce slides in a presentation are called transitions.

Ans. **True** Special effects used to introduce slides in a presentation are called transitions.

8 To change the slides during the Slide Show is called Animation.

Ans. **True** Animation can be used for changing slides during the Slide Show.

9 F4 key is used to start a Slide Show.

Ans. **False** F5 key is used to start a Slide Show.

Very Short Answer (VSA) Type Questions

1 Write down the name of default view in a PowerPoint presentation.

Ans. By default, a presentation screen is always shown in Normal view.

2 Differentiate between a presentation and a slide.

Ans. A presentation is a set of slides that you present to people in a group while each page of a PowerPoint presentation is called a slide.

3 Name two ways where you can create a presentation.

Ans. You can create a presentation under Normal view and Outline view.

4 Write use of layouts in PowerPoint.

Ans. Layouts are used to define the layout of the slide, i.e. the placement of title, subtitle, components of slide etc.

5 In PowerPoint 2007 under the Insert tab, there is a button named Text Box. What is the utility of this button?

Ans. Like a title placeholder, a Text Box is used to hold the text information.

6 Is it possible to change the background of a slide at some later point of time?

Ans. Yes, we can change the background of a slide at any point of time.

7 Can graphics be inserted into the slide?

Ans. Yes, we can insert pictures, graphs, charts, SmartArt etc, into a slide.

8 Animation is a feature, which you can use in your presentation. What is the purpose of this feature?

Ans. Animations are the visual effects applied to individual items on a slide such as graphics, titles or bullet points, rather than to the slide itself.

9 Kirti wants to add sound to slide transition. Which feature of Animations tab is useful for this purpose?

Ans. On the Animations tab in the Transition to This Slide group, click the arrow next to 'Transition Sound' to add sound to slide transition.

10 What is the use of Enter and Esc key in a Slide Show?

Ans. Press Enter to move to the next slide and Esc to close the Slide Show.

11 Name any four basic elements of a slide.

Ans. The four basic elements of a slide are as follows

(*i*) Titles
(*ii*) Subtitles
(*iii*) Drawing objects
(*iv*) ClipArt

Short Answer (SA) Type Questions

EXAM PRACTICE

1 How many views of a slide PowerPoint are provided?

Ans. There are six views of a PowerPoint presentation

(*i*) Normal view
(*ii*) Outline view
(*iii*) Notes Page view
(*iv*) Slide Show
(*v*) Slide Sorter view
(*vi*) Master view

2 State three functions of the Slides Pane.

Ans. Three functions of the Slides Pane are as follows

(*i*) New slides may be added to the presentation.

(*ii*) Allows marking a slide as hidden for not showing it during a Slide Show.

(*iii*) Deleting a slide from the presentation in case it is no longer needed.

3 Write three functions that can be performed in Slide Sorter view of a presentation.

Ans. The three functions that can be performed in Slide Sorter view are as follows

(*i*) We can see the entire presentation.

(*ii*) We can move slide from one place to another using click-drag method. Also, we can rearrange the order of slides.

(*iii*) We can insert, rename and delete slides.

4 How are Header and Footer useful?

Ans. Header and Footer are very useful for displaying the similar useful information (such as presenter's name, file name, company name, presentation's title and many more) on each slide. One can change the Header and Footer details at any time in the presentation.

5 Write the steps of inserting picture in a slide.

Ans. Refer to text on Page No. 151.

6 A sales manager creates a presentation, he adds the same slide transition to all the slide. Write steps, which are followed by sales manager for slide transition?

Ans. Refer to text on Page No. 151-152.

7 What can you do if you want each slide should be shown for a specific amount of time?

Ans. Setting advance slide to one mouse click is the default and a simple setting. If you want each slide to be shown for a specific amount of time, click automatically after and enter the number of seconds. Click Apply to All slides.

8 Differentiate between Slide Transition and Custom Animation.

Ans. Differences between slide transition and Custom Animation are as follows

Slide Transition	*Custom Animation*
Slide transitions are the looks that take you from one slide to the next.	Custom Animations are the movements you put on text, pictures, objects on an individual slide.
Slide transitions are applied to slides themselves.	Custom Animations are applied to objects on a slide.

Long Answer (LA) Type Questions

1 What are the different ways in which you can start creating a new presentation? Write steps for each.

Ans. Refer to text on Page No. 147-148.

2 Explain the various views of a slide available in PowerPoint 2007.

Ans. Refer to text on Page No. 148.

3 Which tab and command let you insert animations in your slide? Write the steps for applying animations in your presentation.

Ans. Refer to text on Page No. 152.

4 PowerPoint is similar to a word processor, except that it's geared toward creating presentations rather than documents. PowerPoint presentations consist of one or more slides. Each slide can contain text, graphics and other information. You can easily rearrange the slides in a PowerPoint presentation, delete slides that you don't need, add new slides, or modify the contents of existing slides. A PowerPoint presentation can share important information such as a business plan or educational lesson, or it can be useful for entertainment purposes. You have a lot of control over customising a PowerPoint presentation and can start quickly with templates and a variety of useful tools.

(i) Presentation is the process of .... a required topic to audience.
(a) displaying (b) printing
(c) presenting (d) listening

(ii) A theme of presentation is defined as predefined combination of colors, effects and
(a) video (b) images (c) size (d) fonts

(iii) The traditional way of presenting information to people was to stand at the front of a room armed with set of ....
(a) slides (b) screen (c) camera (d) notes

(iv) To software that is used to make presentation easy and visualise is called
(a) MS-Word (b) MS-PowerPoint
(c) MS-Excel (d) WordPad

(v) Using presentation software which cannot be added to the presentations?
(a) SmartArt (b) Images
(c) Animations (d) None of these

Ans. (i) (*c*) The presentation is a process of presenting any topic to the required audience.

(ii) (*d*) A presentation theme in presentation software is a predefined combination of colors, fonts and effects that can be applied to presentation.

(iii) (*d*) A traditional way of presenting information was stand in front of the room and armed with set of notes.

(iv) (*b*) The MS-PowerPoint is software which is used to make presentation easy and more visualise.

(v) (*d*) Using presentation we can add almost everything such as : SmartArt, Animations, Images, Videos etc.

Application Oriented Questions

1 Complete the blank spaces using words from the list. You should use each word only once. Websites, slide, PowerPoint, presentation, templates, handouts, projector.

MS (*i*)............ is a (*ii*) .... program that lets you make and show slide shows. These can be viewed on the computer screen or through a multimedia (*iii*)................... . Copies of the presentation, called (*iv*)............... that can be printed out and given to the audience so that, they can make their own notes. Presentations are made up of a series of pages, called (*v*)................ as well as text , slides may incorporate graphics, animated images , sounds and video clips, graphs, charts and even links to (*vi*).................... .

Most presentation packages provide a set of themes and (*vii*)..................., which make it easy to create professional looking presentations with little skill or knowledge. They also offer the facility to add slide transition, timing and animations, which bring a presentation to life.

Ans. (*i*) PowerPoint (*ii*) presentation
(*iii*) projector (*iv*) handouts
(*v*) slide (*vi*) Websites
(*vii*) templates

2 Seema wants to give identical design to all the slides and handouts, she is going to print from her presentation.

(*i*) Which two methods can she use to accomplish her task?

(*ii*) Compare the two methods and enlist their differences.

Ans. (*i*) Seema can do this in following two ways
(a) Creating same design on each slide and handouts manually.
(b) Using slide master and handout master.

(*ii*) In the first method , the efforts are increased by many efforts and many errors in design may creep in. The second method ensures reduce efforts and identical design on each slide and handout.

3 Ketan is preparing a presentation for his new product promotion.

(*i*) The content is ready but he has no time to design backgrounds and decide on color scheme for the presentation. Name the features that will help him to create a professional presentation without devoting much time.

(*ii*) He wants to set how a slide appears and disappears on screen when he runs the slide show. Which feature should he use?

Ans. (*i*) He has to take the help of master pages from taskpane to set a suitable background which supports descent color background.

(*ii*) He must have to set some slide transition and custom animation effect from taskpane.

4 Suman is working as marketing manager in an advertising company. She has prepared a presentation on her latest product. What feature will be used for the following tasks?

(*i*) To view all slides together.

(*ii*) To set timings of the slide show while rehearsing.

(*iii*) To show the sales using a chart.

Ans. (*i*) Press the Slide Sorter view button in workspace area to view all the slides together.

(*ii*) In the Slide Transition page, set the timing in Advance slide sections Automatically after position where the slide will automatically play after a speculated time period.

(*iii*) In the layouts of tasks pane, select a chart type slide or use Insert → Chart menu option.

5 Malini has recently joined a construction company as marketing executive. She saw a presentation about the company. She however is not satisfied with it and wants to make some changes in it. Using your presentation skills, suggest the features to accomplish the following changes:

(*i*) Add the company's logo on the first slide.

(*ii*) Add audio to explain the content of the slide.

(*iii*) Add date and time on all slides.

Ans. (*i*) Insert Picture
(*ii*) Record Narration
(*iii*) Header and Footer dialog box

EXAM PRACTICE

CHAPTER

10

MS-Excel

Chapter Checklist

- Opening Microsoft Excel
- Working with a Spreadsheet
- Cut, Copy and Paste Options
- AutoFill : a Range
- Changing Font, Size and Color
- Formatting Text
- Formatting Numbers
- Inserting/Deleting Cells, Rows and Columns
- Working with Formulas and Functions
- Working with Charts
- Printing a WorkSheet/ WorkBook

Microsoft Excel is a spreadsheet application program offered in the Microsoft Office software package that runs on a personal computer. A spreadsheet is an electronic document that stores various types of data in the form of vertical columns and horizontal rows. It is very useful for storing, organising, manipulating and retrieving data. This program allows you to perform mathematical calculations quickly, use graphic tools, pivot tables, a macro programming language called VBA (Visual Basic for Applications). In addition, Excel can also be used to create charts and graphs.

The key benefit of using a Microsoft Excel is that you can make changes easily, i.e. in spelling errors or values, adding, deleting, formatting and relocating data.

Opening Microsoft Excel

In order to start working with Microsoft Excel, you need to locate and open the program on your computer. To open MS-Excel on your computer, do the following:

Click Start button → All Programs → Microsoft Office → Microsoft Office Excel 2007

It will open MS-Excel with a blank spreadsheet. By default, the name of a blank spreadsheet is Book1.xlsx, where .xlsx is the extension of MS-Excel 2007 file.

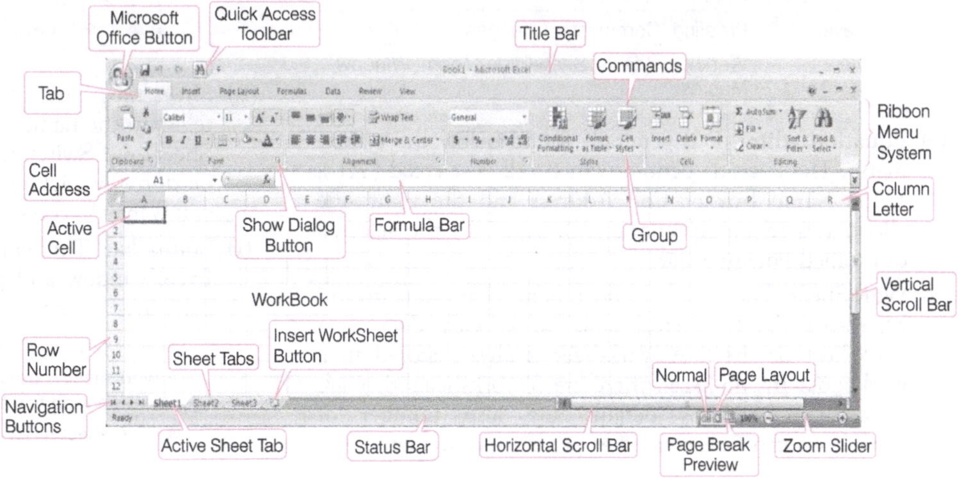

Microsoft Excel window

The major components of MS-Excel window are as follows

(i) **Office button** The Office button is found at the top-left corner of the window. When you left-click on the button, a menu will appear. From this menu, you can create a new spreadsheet, open existing files, save files in a variety of ways and print. You can also add security features, send, publish and close files.

(ii) **Quick Access toolbar** On the top-left hand side of the Title bar, you will see several little icons above the ribbon menu system. These let you perform common tasks, such as saving and undoing, without having to find them in a menu and hence is called quick access toolbar.

(iii) **Title bar** The bar located at the top of the active window is called Title bar. It contains the name of the currently open document.

(iv) **Ribbon Menu system** The ribbon is the panel at the top portion of the document. It has seven tabs and each tab is divided into various groups. These groups are logical collections of features designed to perform various functions that you will utilise in developing or editing your Excel sheets. Commonly utilised features are displayed on the Ribbon. To view additional features within each group, click the arrow at the bottom right corner of each group.

Some tabs and their groups are as follows:

Tabs	*Groups*
Home	Clipboard, Font, Alignment, Number, Styles, Cells, Editing.
Insert	Tables, Illustrations, Charts, Links, Text.
Page Layout	Themes, Page Setup, Scale to Fit, Sheet Options, Arrange.
Formulas	Function Library, Defined Names, Formula Auditing, Calculation.
Data	Get External Data, Connections, Sort & Filter, Data Tools, Outline.
Review	Proofing, Comments, Changes.
View	Workbook Views, Show/Hide, Zoom, Window, Macros.

(v) **Equation editor** It is generally found below the ribbon menu. The left side denotes which cell is selected ('A1'), called **Name Box** or **Cell Address** and the right side allows you to input equations or text into the selected cell, called **Formula Bar**.

(vi) **WorkSheet** The primary document that you use in Microsoft Excel to store and work with data is a worksheet or sheet. A worksheet is always stored in a workbook. In MS-Excel, there are 3 worksheets that are already provided by default and also number of worksheets can be increased as per the requirement.

A worksheet contains various cells formed by rows and columns. The number of rows and columns are different in each version of Excel. In MS-Excel 2007, worksheet contains 1,048,576 rows and 16,384 columns.

- **Row number** Each row is identified by row numbers starting from 1, 2, 3, 4 and so on.
- **Column letter** Each column is identified by a letter in the column. After consuming all 26 letters (i.e. A to Z) for column number, next column number starts like AA, AB, AC and so on.

(vii) **WorkBook** A spreadsheet program file that you create in MS-Excel is called a workbook. A workbook contains worksheets of rows and columns in which you can enter and calculate data. The workbook is the holder for related worksheets.

- **Cell** A box formed by the intersection of a row and a column, which gives a unique address (cell address) in a worksheet or a table, in which you enter information is called a cell. e.g. if row 3 is intersect by column E, then the address of this cell is generated as E3.
- **Active cell** An active cell (current cell) is a selected cell in which data is entered, when you start typing. Only one cell is active at a time. The active cell is bounded by a heavy black border.

(viii) **Navigation buttons** Navigation buttons or sheet tab scrolling buttons allow you to move from one worksheet to another in Microsoft Excel 2007.

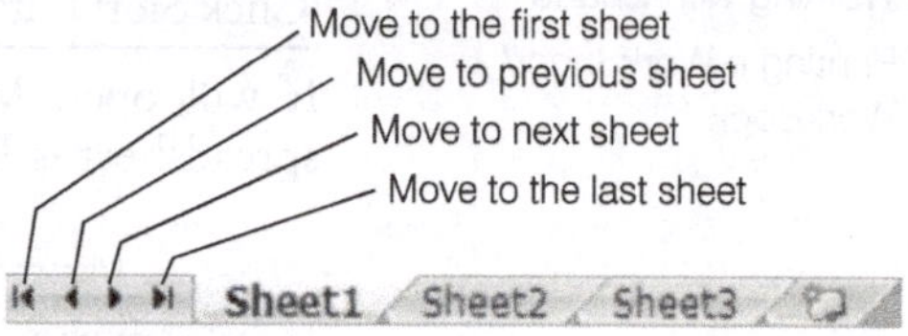

(ix) **Sheet tabs** The tab at the bottom of a worksheet tells you the name of the worksheet such as Sheet1, Sheet2 etc. Switching between these worksheets can be done by clicking on the tab of the sheet which you want to access.

(x) **Status bar** This bar appears at the bottom of the Excel window and provides such information like sum, average etc.

Note In Excel, two types of sheets are there:

- A **worksheet** is used for storing information, performing calculations and embedding charts.
- A **chart sheet** has a chart that is not embedded.

Creating a WorkSheet

By default in a workbook, there are three sheets available namely Sheet1, Sheet2 and Sheet3. You can add further sheets in a workbook. The maximum number of sheets allowed in a workbook is limited by the amount of memory available on your computer. To add a new worksheet, do one of the following:

- To quickly insert a new worksheet at the end of the existing worksheets, click the **Insert Worksheet** tab at the bottom of the screen.

or

- To insert a new worksheet in front of an existing worksheet, select that worksheet and then on the **Home** tab, in the **Cells** group, click **Insert** and then, click **Insert Sheet.**

Note You can also right-click the tab of an existing worksheet and then select Insert option from the drop down menu. The Insert dialog box will appear. On the General tab, click Worksheet and then click OK. This will insert a new sheet on the left of the selected sheet tab.

Renaming a WorkSheet

For renaming a worksheet at any point of time, do the following:

(*i*) On the **Sheet tab** bar, right-click the sheet tab that you want to rename and then, select **Rename** option from the drop down menu.

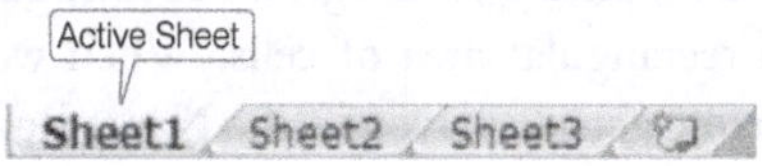

(*ii*) Sheet name will get highlighted and ready to re-type the new name and then, press Enter.

Deleting One or More WorkSheets

You can also delete more than one worksheet from a workbook by doing the following

(*i*) Select the worksheet or worksheets that you want to delete. (For selecting multiple sheets at a time, press and hold Shift key).

(*ii*) On the **Home** tab, in the **Cells** group, click the arrow below to **Delete** option and then, select **Delete Sheet**.

Note You can also right-click the sheet tab of a worksheet or a sheet tab of any selected worksheets that you want to delete and then, click Delete.

Creating a New WorkBook

To create a new workbook, do the following

(*i*) Click on **Microsoft Office** button.

(*ii*) Select **New**. The **New Workbook** dialog box will appear and Blank Workbook is highlighted by default.

(*iii*) Click **Create** button.

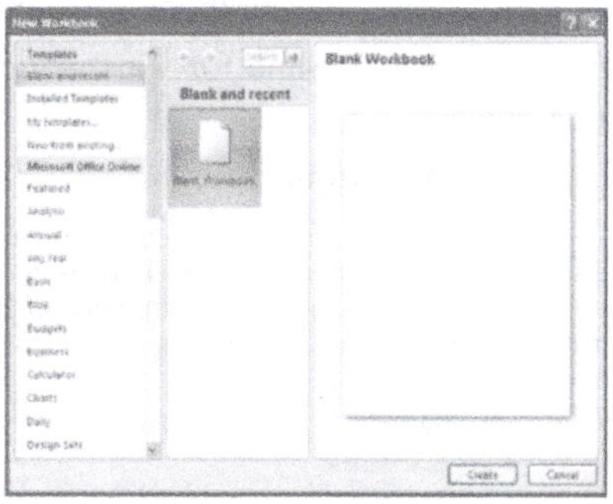

New Workbook dialog box

Opening an Existing WorkBook

To open an existing workbook, do the following

(*i*) Click on **Microsoft Office** button.

(*ii*) Select **Open**. The Open dialog box will appear.

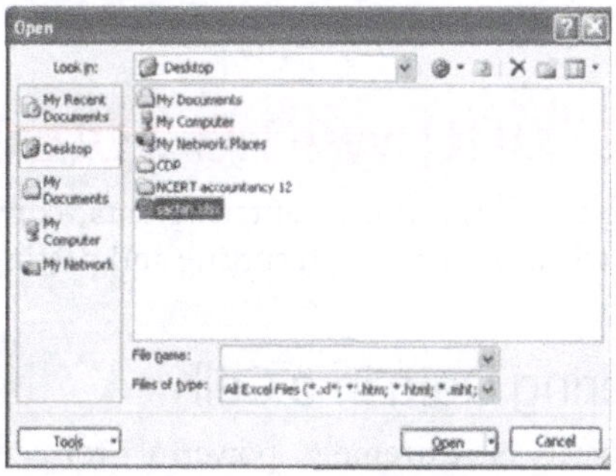

Open dialog box

(*iii*) Choose the location and select the file which you want to open.

(*iv*) Click **Open** button.

Saving a WorkBook

After creating and editing a workbook or worksheets, it needs to be saved.

Every workbook must have a different name in order to distinguish it from other workbooks created in MS-Excel 2007.

For saving a workbook, do the following

(*i*) Click on the **Microsoft Office** button, from the drop down menu select **Save As** option.

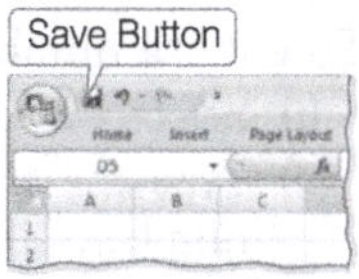

Alternatively, you can click on the **Save** icon residing on the Quick Access toolbar. This will open **Save As** dialog box, if you are saving your document for the first time. Otherwise, it simply works as the **Save** option.

(ii) In the **Save As** dialog box, first select the location where you want to save the workbook in your computer.

(iii) After that, type a name for your workbook in the **File name** box.

(iv) Click on **Save** button.

Note If you have already saved your document and now you have modified it and want to save these changes in the same workbook then select Save from the drop down menu of Microsoft Office button or directly Save icon residing on the Quick Access toolbar.

Check Point 01

1 Which is located at the top of the active window?
(a) Title bar (b) Equation Editor
(c) Sheet tabs (d) Office button

2 How many buttons are available in the Navigation buttons? Also, write their name.

3 If you have already saved your document and later you modify it then which will help you to save these changes in your document?

Working with a Spreadsheet

MS-Excel allows you to entering data, copy and paste cells and cell content through cutting and pasting or copying and pasting.

Entering Data in a Cell

MS-Excel is extremely powerful for entering, storing, displaying and manipulating different kinds of data efficiently.

There are three main types of data, i.e. text, numbers and date/time that can be entered and stored in the cells.

Entering Text in a Cell

To enter a text in a cell, do the following

(i) Select the cell in which you want to enter text.

(ii) Start typing the text.

(iii) Press the **Enter** key.

Entering Number in a Cell

To enter a number in a cell, do the following

(i) Select a cell, where you want to type a number.

(ii) Type the number. You can use %, (,), ., $ etc in the number.

(iii) Press the **Enter** key.

Entering Date/Time in a Cell

To enter date/time in a cell, do the following

(i) Select the cell, where you want to type a date/time.

(ii) Type date/time.

(iii) When you type a **date/time**, Excel converts your data to a serial number. The serial number represents the number of days from the beginning of the century until the date you type.

(iv) To format those cells in date/time format, click **Short Date** or **Long Date** or **Time Format**, respectively from the number format list.

(v) After a cell has been formatted in date or time format, date/time will be in general form, i.e. dd/mm/yy, HH : MM : SS format.

Cut, Copy and Paste Options

These options work same as they do in MS-Word 2007, we have studied earlier. But, we will look at these options in terms of cells.

Selecting a Range of Cells

A range of cells may contain a single cell or a group of cells. Basically, it is a group of contiguous cells forming a rectangular area of cells. When we select a cell, its name gets displayed in the Name Box of the Equation Editor. Similarly, the name of the selected range of cells also gets displayed in the same Name Box.

e.g. a range starting from E3 till G15 would be written as E3:G15. Here, colon (:) represents the range indicator. We can do this in two ways, through keyboard or mouse.

Using Keyboard

For selecting a range of cells using keyboard, do the following

(i) Point to the first cell that you want to be included in the range of cells.

(ii) Then, press and hold the Shift key and move to the diagonally opposite cell using arrow keys to the cells that you want to be included in the range of cells.

(iii) Lastly, release the Shift key.

Using Mouse

For selecting a range of cells using mouse, do the following

(*i*) Point to the first cell that you want to be included in the range of cells.

(*ii*) Now, press the left mouse button and drag it to the diagonally opposite last cell of the range that you want to select.

(*iii*) Release the mouse button.

Note If you want to select the cell of first row and first column to the cell of fourth row and sixth column then name of this range would be A1:F4. And, the name of the first selected cell will be displayed in the Name Box.

Copying a Range

For copying a range in Excel, we can use simple Copy and Paste option from Clipboard. For copying a cell range, do the following

(*i*) First select the range of the cell that you want to copy at other place in Excel using any of the below given methods.

(*ii*) Then, click on the **Copy** button from **Clipboard** group under **Home** tab. Alternatively, you can click on right mouse button and select **Copy** option from there or you can simply press **Ctrl+ C** through your keyboard.

(*iii*) Now, you need to select the cell where you want to copy the selected range data.

(*iv*) Click on **Paste** button from **Clipboard** group or you can simply press **Ctrl + V** through your keyboard, then the desired data will be copied.

Moving a Range

Moving means original data will be shifted to a new location, i.e. original data will be cut and pasted to the desired location. For moving a range, you need to perform the similar steps as for copying a range.

But, in place of **Copy** button for moving, you need to click on the **Cut** button. Rest everything is same.

However, there is one more yet easiest method for doing the same task using mouse. For moving a range to the desired location, do the following

(*i*) Select the range of cells that you want to move to other location.

(*ii*) Then, move the mouse pointer at the boundary of the selected cell range. Mouse pointer will convert to shape.

(*iii*) Click there and move the range to the desired target location.

AutoFill : A Range

MS-Excel supports with an excellent and time saving feature called AutoFill. Using this feature, you do not need to fill manually pattern specific data series in multiple cells in a sequence. There are two methods of using this feature:

Method 1 : Using Fill Handle

For filling a series using Fill handle, do the following

(*i*) Click the cell from where the text series is to be started.

(*ii*) Type the first entry of the text series in the selected cell. And, next entry in the adjacent cell.

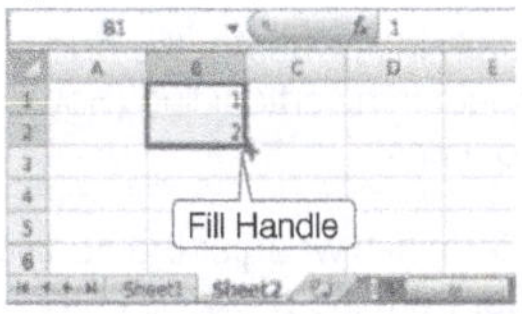

(*iii*) Select both the cells.

(*iv*) Click the Fill Handle and drag it over to the number of cells to be filled.

Method 2 : Using Fill Button of Editing Group

This option copies (repeats) the information from one cell to another. For filling a series using Fill button, do the following

(*i*) Type the information (cell contents or formula) in the first cell of the group.

(*ii*) Starting with the cell containing the contents to be copied, select the group of cells to be filled.

(*iii*) From the Ribbon, select the **Home** tab.

(*iv*) In the **Editing** group, click **Fill** Fill → select the appropriate option.

Down	Repeats the contents of the first cell throughout the selected cells below it.
Right	Repeats the contents of the first cell throughout the selected cells to the right of it.
Up	Repeats the contents of the first cell throughout the selected cells above it.
Left	Repeats the contents of the first cell throughout the selected cells to the left of it.
Across Worksheets	Repeats the contents of the selected cells in another selected worksheet.
Series...	Fills the data that is part of a pattern, rather than simply repeating the data across selected cells. This option brings up the Series dialog box, which allows you to select the type of pattern that you would like to use. e.g. if the first cell contains the day Sunday, Excel will fill the following cells with Monday, Tuesday etc.
Justify	Distributes text in the first selected cell throughout several selected rows.

Note Justify option changes the contents of these cells by moving the data to fit within the new rows.

(*v*) **Optional** If you select the Series option then in the Series dialog box, select the desired options.

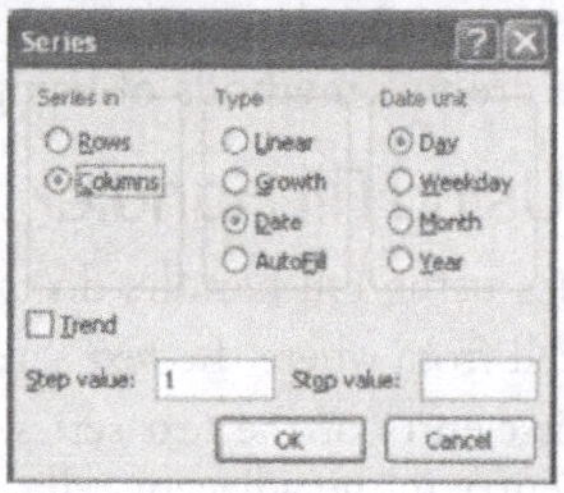

Series in	Determines whether the additional information will appear in a vertical line (Rows) or in a horizontal line (Columns).
Type	Determines whether the additional information will differ from the previous entry by a specific interval (Linear), by multiplying the previous entry by a specific value (Growth), by creating a series of dates according to the selected date format (Date) or by automatically detecting, what type of fill you would like to apply (AutoFill).
Date unit	When Date is selected as the type, determines whether numbers are listed for each day (Day), in the weekday (Weekday), for that day of every month (Month), or for that day of every year (Year).
Trend	When Linear or Growth is selected as the type, calculates the average difference between values existing in selected cells and uses that difference to calculate the fill values.
Step value	When Linear or Growth is selected as the type, determines the amount that the previous value is added to or multiplied by to come up with the results for the next cell. When Date is selected as the type, it determines how many dates should be skipped between each recorded value.
Stop value	Determines a value at which the series should no longer be continued.

(*vi*) Click **OK** button. The fill will be applied.

Changing Font, Size and Color

In Excel, you can change the font, size and color of the cell content in the same way as you have done in MS-Word 2007.

For changing the font color of the cell content, do the following:

(*i*) Select the cell or range of cells that you want to format.

(*ii*) Locate the **Font** group under the **Home** tab.

(*iii*) Click on the down-facing arrow next to the Font color menu.

(*iv*) From the list that appears, select the color that you want.

For changing the font size of the cell content, do the following

(*i*) Select the cell or range of cells that you want to format.

(*ii*) Locate the **Font** group under the **Home** tab.

(*iii*) Click on the down-facing arrow next to the Font Size menu.

(*iv*) From the list that appears, click on the **size** of the font that you want.

For changing the font type of the cell content, do the following:

(*i*) Select the cell or range of cells that you want to format.

(*ii*) Locate the **Font** group under the **Home** tab.

(*iii*) Click on the down-facing arrow next to the Font Type menu.

(*iv*) From the list that appears, click on any type of the font that you want.

Formatting Text

Formatting of text involves so many things, i.e. we can format text in terms of alignment, orientation, wrapping and merging.

Cell Alignment

By default, all cell contents are aligned to the bottom of the cell, texts are aligned to the left of a cell and numbers are aligned to the right of a cell.

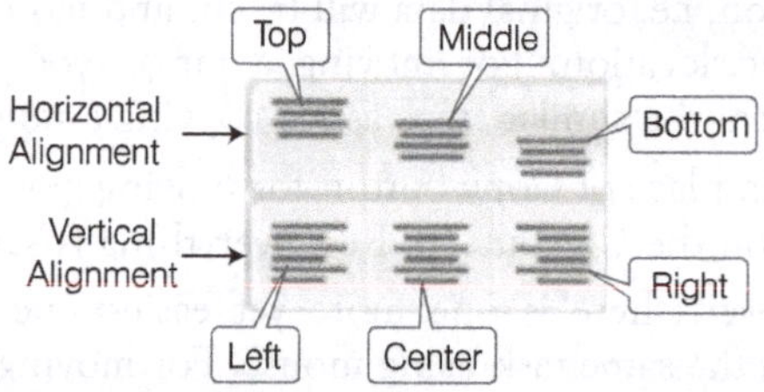

To change the alignment of the contents of a cell, do the following

(*i*) Select the cell or range of cells to be aligned.

(*ii*) Click the relevant horizontal and vertical alignment buttons from the **Alignment** group under the **Home** tab.

Cell Orientation

Cell content can be orientated to be read vertically or at an angle. This can be combined with features like merge cells and cell alignment to create effects as shown below

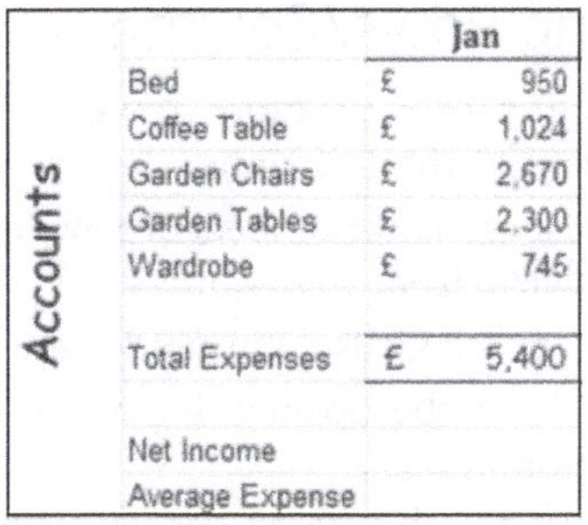

			Jan
Accounts	Bed	£	950
	Coffee Table	£	1,024
	Garden Chairs	£	2,670
	Garden Tables	£	2,300
	Wardrobe	£	745
	Total Expenses	£	5,400
	Net Income		
	Average Expense		

To change the orientation of the cell content, do the following

(*i*) Select the cell holding the text that you want to orientate.

(*ii*) Click the **Orientation** button in the **Alignment** group , under **Home** tab.

(*iii*) Select the desired orientation option from the list which will appear.

You can also orientate cell content using the **Alignment** tab of the **Format Cells** dialog box that can be opened by clicking on the small arrow in the right corner of the **Alignment** group, under the **Home** tab.

To orientate cell content, either click and drag the red diamond to the required position or enter the intended degrees in the Degrees field.

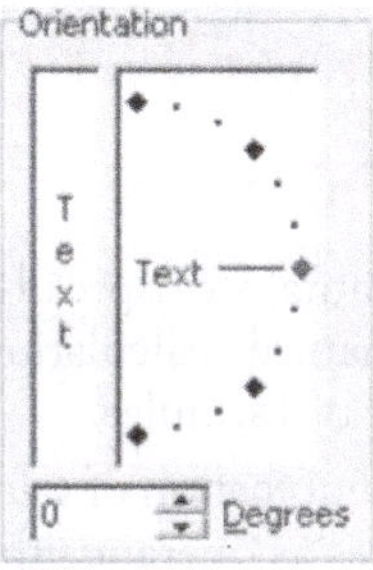

Merge Cells

Cells content can be merged and centered across multiple columns or rows making one large cell.

To merge and center cell content, do the following

(*i*) Select the range of cells to be merged and centered.

(*ii*) Click the **Merge & Center** option in the **Alignment** group, under the **Home** tab.

Note You should leave a gap between cells that have been merged and other spreadsheet content, as merging cells break up a spreadsheet's structure potentially causing problems with other Excel features.

Wrap Text

If cell content becomes too large for the column or the row, you can increase the row height or column width, i.e. to wrap the text, do the following

(*i*) Select the cell or range of cells.

(*ii*) Click the **Wrap Text** button in the **Alignment** group, under the **Home** tab.

Note You can also wrap text while entering data into the cell by pressing Alt + Enter.

Formatting Numbers

Changing the appearance of numbers comes under number formatting. For formatting numbers, do the following

(*i*) Select the cell or range of cells that you want to format.

(*ii*) Locate the **Number** group, under the **Home** tab.

(*iii*) Click on the down-facing arrow next to the **Number Format** button.

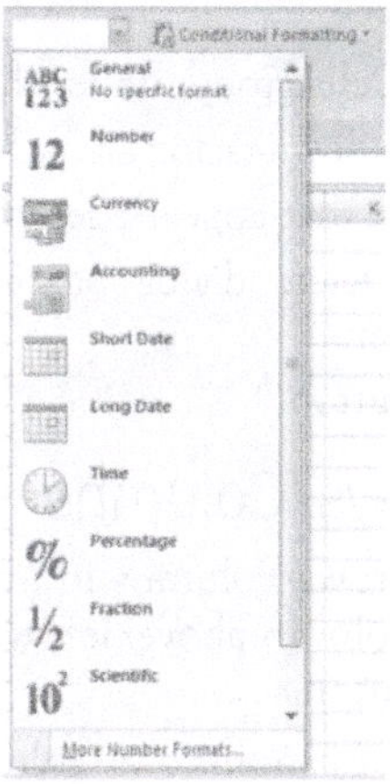

(*iv*) From the list that will appear, select the number format which you want to apply to the cell or range of cells you selected (e.g. Accounting).

Inserting/Deleting Cells, Rows and Columns

As we already know that an Excel worksheet is always in grid format, i.e. in tabular format. Still it allows you, insertion and deletion of cells, rows and columns when required.

Inserting Cell/Cells

For inserting one or more cells in your worksheet, do the following

(*i*) Select the cell or range of cells where you want the new blank cell/cells to appear.

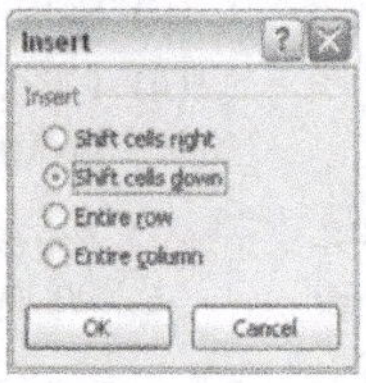

(*ii*) Locate the **Cells** group, under the **Home** tab.

(*iii*) Click on the down-facing arrow below the **Insert** button.

(*iv*) From the list that appears, select **Insert Cells.**

(*v*) From the **Insert** dialog box that appears, select the desired option.

(*vi*) Click **OK** button.

Deleting Cell/Cells

For deleting one or more cells from your worksheet, do the following

(*i*) Select as many number of cells as you want to delete from your worksheet.

(*ii*) Locate the **Cells** group, under the **Home** tab.

(*iii*) Click on the down-facing arrow below the **Delete** button.

(*iv*) From the list that appears, select **Delete Cells.**

(*v*) From the **Delete** dialog box that appears, select the desired option.

(*vi*) Click **OK** button.

Inserting Rows/Columns

Before inserting rows/columns in a worksheet, you need to select that row/column above/left where you want to insert the new row/column.

For inserting one or more rows/columns in your worksheet, do the following

(*i*) Select as many numbers of rows/columns, you want to insert in your worksheet.

(*ii*) Locate the **Cells** group under the **Home** tab.

(*iii*) Click on the down-facing arrow below the **Insert** button.

(*iv*) From the list that appears, select **Insert Sheet Rows/Columns.**

Deleting Rows/Columns

For deleting one or more rows/columns from your worksheet, do the following

(*i*) Select as many numbers of rows/columns, you want to delete from your worksheet.

(*ii*) Locate the **Cells** group under the **Home** tab.

(*iii*) Click on the down-facing arrow below the **Delete** button.

(*iv*) From the list that appears, select **Delete Sheet Rows/Columns.**

Check Point 02

1 Name the methods which are used by AutoFill.

2 Which option changes the contents of these cells by moving the data to fit within the new rows?

3 Arun is a school head and preparing the list of students with their roll no of class IX. Later on, he remembers that he forgot to add the some students' roll no in the mid of the list. Now, what feature of Excel will help him to add the roll no in the mid of the list?

(a) Insert Row (b) Insert Column

(c) Insert Cell (d) Delete Row

Working with Formulas and Functions

The biggest advantage of spreadsheet package is that it allows Mathematical calculations and makes them easier by means of formulas.

A formula is a combination of values, operators (+, –, /, *) and cell addresses as operands that perform calculation on the values contained in the cell addresses.

Entering Formula in a Cell

Any formula in Excel starts with an = (equal) sign. It means, if you do not specify = (equal) sign before a formula, either knowingly or accidentally, Excel will treat that as an ordinary text and will not perform any calculation on the contents of that cell.

Let us take an example for illustrating the concept of entering a formula in a cell.

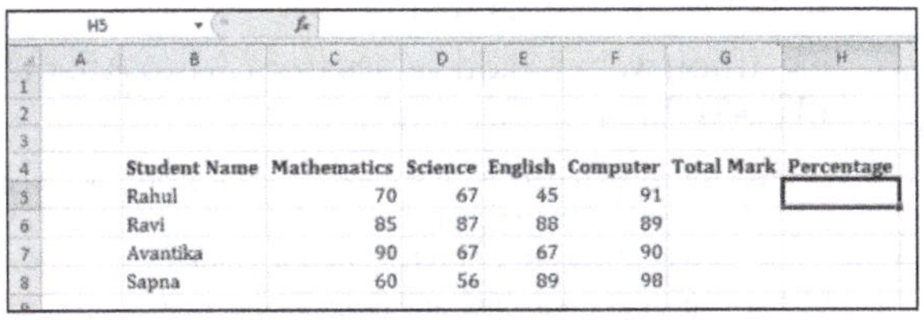

Student Name	Mathematics	Science	English	Computer	Total Mark	Percentage
Rahul	70	67	45	91		
Ravi	85	87	88	89		
Avantika	90	67	67	90		
Sapna	60	56	89	98		

The above data must be very much familiar to you as it is a simple table representing partial data of students.

Now, what you want is to calculate the total marks of individual student in column 'G' and also want to calculate percentage of each student in column 'H'.

We can write formula in cell G5 to calculate sum of data values from cells C5 to F5 in order to calculate total marks of student named Rahul. So, in cell G5 we will write like = C5 + D5 + E5 + F5 and press Enter.

As soon as you press Enter, the sum of values from cell C5 to cell F5 will be displayed in cell G5. Similarly, we can calculate the total marks of other students as well.

For calculating the percentage of student Rahul, we can write = G5*100/400 in cell H5 and press Enter. Similarly, we can calculate percentage of other students as well.

Using Operators in Formulae

The calculation that is done by a formula is defined by the operators it contains. To perform basic Mathematical operations such as addition, subtraction, multiplication or division, Excel supports following operators, which are inserted in the formulae

Arithmetic Operators	*Meaning*
+ (plus sign)	Addition
– (minus sign)	Subtraction/Negation
* (asterisk)	Multiplication
/ (forward slash)	Division

Cell Referencing

In Excel, cell is referenced by a combination of row number and column letter. Cell referencing is a method by which a cell or series of cells in a formula is referred.

Referencing a cell is beneficial in formulas because it allows your formulas to update automatically, if the value in a particular cell changes and can also update formulas as cells are copied or moved.

Three types of cell referencing are as follows

i. Relative Cell Referencing

When we want to copy a formula from one cell to another cell and also, we want to modify the cell references used in the formula according to the new cell, then it is called relative cell referencing. Consider the following example for understanding this concept:

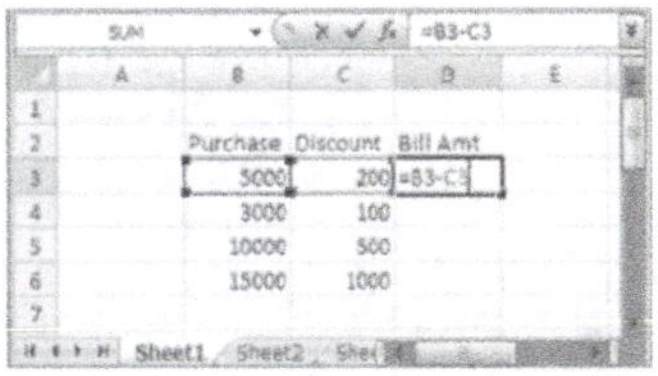

In the given screenshot, for calculating Bill Amt, we have entered formula (= B3 - C3) in cell D3.

Now, in case of relative cell referencing, if we will copy this formula in any other cell, the references used in formula B3 and C3 will change accordingly.

Let us copy this formula in cell D4. The formula will automatically become (= B4 - C4) in cell D4. Similarly, in cell D5 and D6 you can copy formula using relative referencing.

ii. Absolute Cell Referencing

When we want to copy a formula from one cell to another cell, but we do not want to modify the cell references used in the formula according to the new cell, then it is called absolute cell referencing. For making the reference of a cell absolute, we need to use '$' (dollar) sign before row number and column letter. Consider the following example for understanding this concept

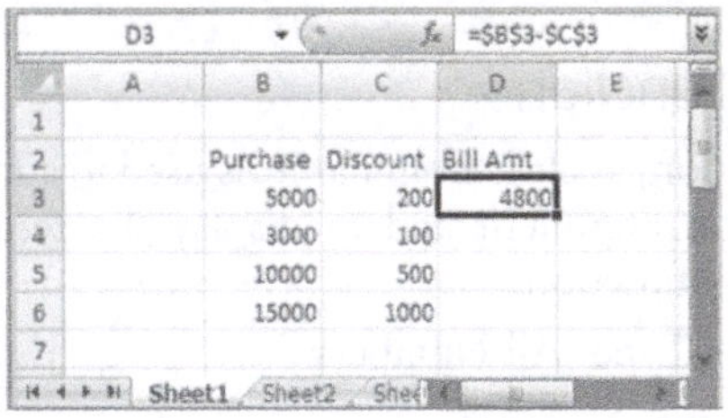

In the above example in cell D3, we have written formula = $B$3 – $C$3. Now, when we will copy this formula in cell D4, it will be copied as it is, without any change.

iii. Mixed Cell Referencing

When we use '$' sign either before row number or before column letter, then it is called mixed cell referencing. In other words, mixed referencing is a combination of both relative and absolute referencing. Consider the following example for understanding this concept

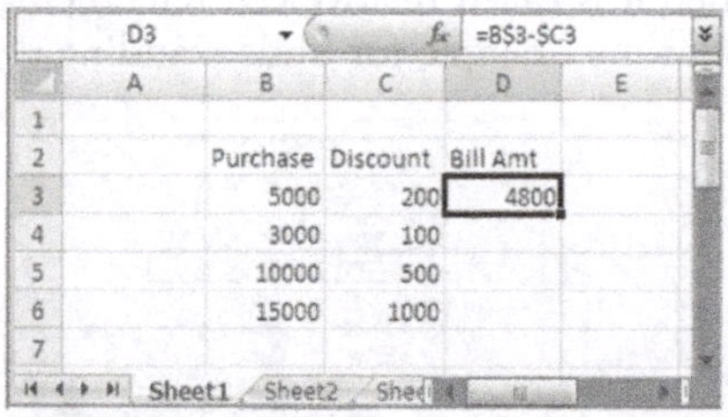

In the above example in cell D3, we have written formula =B$3 – $C3. Now, when we will copy this formula in cell D4, it will be copied as = B$3 – $C4 because of mixed referencing.

Using Functions

Predefined formulas in MS-Excel are called functions. Functions perform calculations on the values provided to them as arguments.

Two important parts of any function are arguments and structure.

Arguments refer to the values or cell references passed to a function. These are always written within parentheses and can be numbers, text, Boolean values (True or False), constants, functions or formulas.

Structure of function means the way, we write a function in a cell. It starts with function name followed by opening parentheses, then comes comma separated by argument list and finally closing parentheses. In case of formula, start it with = (equal) sign.

Some commonly used functions in MS-Excel are as follows

i. SUM Function

This function, as clear from name, is used to add all the values provided as argument and to display the result in the cell containing function.

Argument Type All Numbers

Return Type Number

Syntax = SUM(number1, number2, ...)

e.g. if you want to display the sum of values of cells A1, A2, A5 and A6 in cell A9, then you need to simply type = SUM(A1,A2,A5,A6) in cell A9 and press Enter.

The sum will be displayed in cell A9. If you want to add a values of range, then provide that range in SUM function as an argument.

e.g. if you want to add values from A1 to A5, then write like =SUM(A1:A5).

Note
- If an argument is an array or reference, only numbers in that array or reference are counted. Empty cells, logical values or text in the array or reference are ignored.
- If any arguments are error values or text that cannot be translated into numbers, Excel displays an error.

ii. AVERAGE Function

This function calculates the average of all the values provided as argument to this function.

Argument Type All Numbers

Return Type Number

Syntax = AVERAGE(number1, number2, ...)

e.g. to calculate the average of the values of range starting from A1 to A5 in cell B9, you need to write = AVERAGE(A1:A5) in cell B9.

iii. COUNT Function

This function counts the number of cells that contain numbers and numbers within the list of arguments.

Argument Type Any Type

Return Type Number

Syntax = COUNT(value1, value2, ...)

e.g. if the values contained in cells A1, A2, A3 and A4 are 5, 7, TRUE and 10 respectively,
then = COUNT(A1:A4) will return 3.

Note
- Arguments that are numbers, dates or text representation of numbers (e.g. a number enclosed in quotation marks, such as '1') are counted.
- Arguments that are error values or text that cannot be translated into numbers are not counted.
- If an argument is an array or reference, only numbers in that array or reference are counted. Empty cells, logical values, text or error values in the array or reference are not counted.

iv. COUNTA Function

This function is similar to the COUNT( ) function. The only difference is that the COUNTA( ) function also calculates the text entries even when the entries contain an empty string of length 0(zero), i.e. " ", but empty cells are ignored. The COUNTA( ) function counts the total number of values in the list of arguments.

Argument Type Any Type

Return Type Number

Syntax = COUNTA (value1, value2, ...)

e.g. if the value contained in cells A1, A2, A3 and A4 are 5, 7, TRUE and 10 respectively then = COUNTA (A1 : A4) will return 4.

v. MAX Function

This function is used to return maximum value from a list of arguments.

Argument Type All Numbers

Return Type Number

Syntax = MAX(number1, number2, ...)

e.g. if the values contained in cells A1, A2, A3 and A4 are 5, 7, 2 and 10 respectively then = MAX(A1:A4) will return 10.

Note
- MAX will consider only numeric and logical values to compute maximum.
- If an argument is an array or a reference, only numbers in that array or reference are used. Empty cells or text in the array or reference are ignored.
- If the arguments contain no numbers, MAX returns 0 (zero).
- Arguments that are error values or text that cannot be translated into numbers cause errors.

vi. MAXA Function

This function is similar to the MAX( ) function. The only difference is that the MAXA( ) function also includes the text and logical entries.

Syntax = MAXA(number1, number2, ...)

e.g. if the value contained in the cells A1, A2, A3 and A4 are PEN, ERASER, TRUE, SCALE respectively then,

= MAX(Al : A4) will return 0

= MAXA(Al : A4) will return 1

vii. MIN Function

This function is used to return minimum value from a list of arguments.

Argument Type All Numbers

Return Type Number

Syntax = MIN(number1, number2,.....)

e.g. if the values contained in cells A1, A2, A3 and A4 are 5, 7, 2 and 10 respectively then = MIN(A1:A4) will return 2.

Note
- MIN will consider only numeric and logical values to compute minimum.
- If an argument is an array or a reference, only numbers in that array or reference are used. Empty cells, or text in the array or reference are ignored.
- If the arguments contain no numbers, MIN returns 0.
- Arguments that are error values or text that cannot be translated into numbers cause errors.

viii. MINA Function

This function is similar to the MAXA( ) function. The only difference is that the MINA( ) function computes the minimum value and MAXA( ) function computes the maximum value, when Boolean values are presented in the list.

Syntax = MINA(number1, number2,...)

e.g. if the value contained in the cells A1, A2, A3 and A4 are 2, FALSE, 1, 3 respectively.

then, = MIN(A1 : A4) will return 1

= MINA(A1 : A4) will return 0

ix. IF Function

This function is used to compare two values as per some predefined condition and returns a value from them accordingly.

Syntax

= IF(logical_test, value_if_true, [value_if_false])

Where,

- **logical_test** is required, any value or expression that can be evaluated to TRUE or FALSE.
  e.g. A10=100 is a logical expression; if the value in cell A10 is equal to 100, the expression evaluates to TRUE. Otherwise, the expression evaluates to FALSE.
- **value_if_true** is required, the value that you want to be returned, if the logical_test argument evaluates to TRUE.
  e.g. if the value of the argument is the text string 'Within budget' and the logical_test argument evaluates to TRUE, the IF function returns the text 'Within budget'. If logical_test evaluates to TRUE and the value_if_true argument is omitted (that is, there is only a comma following the logical_test argument), the IF function returns 0 (zero). To display the word TRUE, use the logical value TRUE for the value_if_true argument.
- **value_if_false** is optional. The value that you want to be returned, if the logical_test argument evaluates to FALSE.
  e.g. if the value of this argument is the text string 'Over budget' and the logical_test evaluates to FALSE, the IF function returns the text 'Over budget'.

If logical_test evaluates to FALSE and the value_if_false argument is omitted, (that is, there is no comma following the value_if_true argument) the IF function returns the logical value FALSE.

- If logical_test evaluates to FALSE and the value of the value_if_false argument is blank (that is, there is only a comma following the value_if_true argument), the IF function returns the value 0 (zero).

  e.g. = IF(A10 = 100, 100, "Too small") will return 100, if cell A10 stores value 100 otherwise, it will return string "Too small".

Check Point 03

1. What is a combination of values, operators and cell addresses as operands that performs calculations on the values contained in the cell address?
2. Which referencing of cell does not modify the cell references used in the formula according to the new cell?
   (a) Relative cell referencing (b) Absolute cell referencing
   (c) Mixed cell referencing (d) All of these
3. Which group of spreadsheet allows you to move text angle clockwise?
4. If you want to find the average of numbers which are entered in cells of an Excel, which function is helpful to this situation?

Working with Charts

A chart is a tool that is used in Excel for representing data graphically.

Charts allow anyone to more easily see the meaning behind the numbers in the spreadsheet and to make showing comparisons and trends much easier. It is one of the most impressive features of MS-Excel.

Endless variations are available, allowing you to produce a chart, edit and format it, include titles and many more.

Types of Chart

Several different types of charts are available within Excel. The type to choose will depend on the data involved and what information the chart is intended to convey or highlight. Different types of chart are as follows

(i) Column	*(ii)* Line	*(iii)* Pie
(iv) Bar	*(v)* Area	*(vi)* Scatter
(vii) Stock	*(viii)* Surface	*(ix)* Doughnut
(x) Bubble	*(xi)* Radar	

The most useful types of chart and their applications are as follows:

i. Line Charts

These types of chart can be 2 or 3-dimensional. Line charts are used to compare trends over time. There are similarities with area charts but line charts tend to emphasise the rate of change rather than volume of change over time. 3-D lines appear as 'ribbons' which can be easier to see on the chart.

ii. Pie Charts

These types of chart can be 2 or 3-dimensional. They are used to compare the size of the parts with the whole. Only one data series can be plotted, making up 100%. Pie charts within their own window can be made to 'explode' by dragging or more pieces of pie away from the centre.

iii. Bar Charts

These types of chart can be 2 or 3-dimensional. They are used to show individual figures at a specific time or to compare different items. Categories are listed vertically, so that bars appear on the horizontal, thus there is less emphasis on time flow. Bars extending to the right represent positive values while those extending left represent negative values.

iv. Area Charts

These types of chart can be 2 or 3-dimensional. They are used to compare the changes in volume of a data series over time, emphasising the amount of change rather than the rate of change. Area charts show clearly, how individual data series contribute to make up the whole volume of information represented in the graph.

v. XY Scatter Charts

These types of chart are used to compare two different numeric data series and can be useful in determining whether one set of figures might be dependent on the other. They are also useful, if the data on the X-axis represents uneven intervals of time or increments of measurement.

Components of Chart

Various components or parts of chart are as follows

(i) **X-axis** Refers to a horizontal axis, which is also known as **category axis.**

(ii) **Y-axis** Refers to a vertical axis which is also known as **value axis.**

(iii) **X-axis title** Conveys the full details of the X-axis values.

(iv) **Y-axis title** Conveys the full details of the Y-axis values.

(v) **Data series** Refers to a **set of data** that you want to display in a chart.

(vi) **Chart area** Refers to the total space that is enclosed by a chart.

(*vii*) **Plot area** Refers to the main region of the chart in which your data is plotted.

(*viii*) **Chart title** Denotes the type of data plotted in a chart.

(*ix*) **Legend** In a chart showing different data series, a unique color or pattern is assigned to each data series. This unique color of pattern is known as a legend.

(*x*) **Gridlines** These are the horizontal and vertical lines within the plot area in a chart.

(*xi*) **Data label** Provides additional information about a value in the chart, that is coming from a worksheet cell.

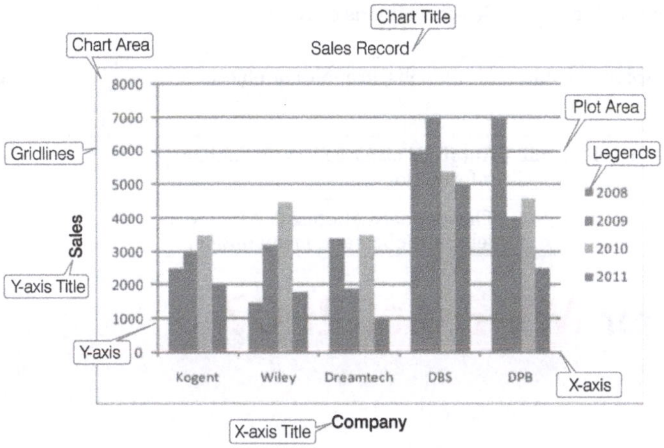

A Sample chart and its components

The chart shown in the above figure is based on the worksheet shown below

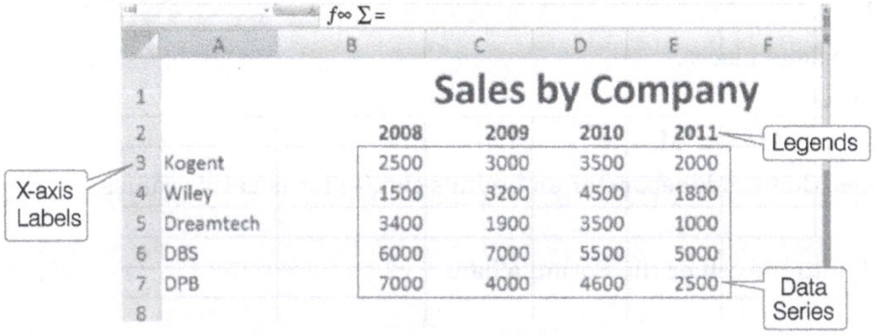

	2008	2009	2010	2011
Kogent	2500	3000	3500	2000
Wiley	1500	3200	4500	1800
Dreamtech	3400	1900	3500	1000
DBS	6000	7000	5500	5000
DPB	7000	4000	4600	2500

A Sales by Company worksheet

Creating a Chart

Here is a worksheet that shows the marks of students in a class subjectwise. To create a chart, do the following

(*i*) Select the data that you want to show, including the column titles and the row labels.

(*ii*) Then click the **Insert** tab and in the **Charts** group, click the **Column** button. You could select another chart type, but column charts are commonly used to compare items.

(*iii*) After you click **Column**, you'll see a number of column chart types to choose from. Click **Clustered Column**, the first column chart in the **2-D Column** list.

A ScreenTip displays the chart type name, when you rest the pointer over any chart type. The ScreenTip also provides a description of the chart type and gives you information about that, when to use each one.

Note If you want to change the chart type after you create your chart, click inside the chart. On the **Design** tab under **Chart Tools**, in the **Type** group, click **Change Chart Type** and select another chart type.

Printing a Worksheet/Workbook

While working on a worksheet, sometimes you may need to print the entire or partial worksheets, in order to obtain a hardcopy of the work that you have done so far.

For printing partial or entire worksheet, do the following

(*i*) Do one of the following

To print a partial worksheet, click the worksheet and then select the range of data that you want to print.

or

To print the entire **worksheet**, click the worksheet to activate it.

or

To print a workbook, click any of its worksheets.

(*ii*) Click **Microsoft Office** button and then click **Print**. Alternatively, you can also press **Ctrl** + **P** on your keyboard.

(*iii*) Under select, **Print what** an option to print the Selection, the Active sheet(s) or the Entire workbook, Table.

(*iv*) Enter the desired number of copies to be printed in the box named **Number of copies** under **Copies** section.

(*v*) Under **Print range** section, select number of pages to be printed after choosing Page(s) radio button, if you want all pages to be printed, select **All** radio button.

(*vi*) Click **OK** button to confirm.

Check Point 04

1 Which chart is used to compare the size of the parts with the whole?

(a) Bar charts (b) Area charts
(c) Pie charts (d) Line charts

2 In how many ways, can you print the worksheet?

Some Pointer Shapes in MS-Excel

Shape	Context	Action
	The default pointer shape, appears in most Excel workspace contexts	Moves cell pointer or selects a range of cells
	Appears, when the pointer is on the border of a window	Adjusts window size
	Appears, when the pointer is between a row or column divider	Adjusts height and width of rows and columns
	Appears, when you are editing cell contents	Provides a text insertion point
	Appears, when the pointer is on a column or row heading	Selects columns or rows
	Appears, when the pointer is placed over a cell border, graphic or other object	Moves cells, graphics or objects
	Appears, when the pointer is on the 'fill corner' of a cell or cell range	AutoFills other cells with similar information
	Appears, when mouse is placed over the Ribbon	The standard Microsoft Windows pointer, selects Ribbon and menu options

Keyboard Shortcuts for MS-Excel 2007

Ctrl Combination Shortcut Keys

Ctrl+Shift+(	Unhides any hidden rows within the selection.
Ctrl+Shift+)	Unhides any hidden columns within the selection.
Ctrl+Shift+~	Applies the General number format in Microsoft Excel.
Ctrl+Shift+$	Applies the Currency format with two decimal places.
Ctrl+Shift+%	Applies the Percentage format with no decimal places.
Ctrl+Shift+^	Applies the Exponential number format with two decimal places.
Ctrl+Shift+#	Applies the Date format with the day, month and year.
Ctrl+Shift+@	Applies the Time format with the hour and minute and AM or PM.
Ctrl+Shift+I	Applies the Number format with two decimal places, thousands separator and minus sign(–) for negative values.
Ctrl+Shift+:	Enters the current time.
Ctrl+Shift+	Copies the value from the cell above the active cell into the cell or the Formula bar.
Ctrl+;	Enters the current date.
Ctrl+'	Copies a formula from the cell above the active cell into the cell or the Formula bar.
Ctrl+9	Hides the selected rows.
Ctrl+0	Hides the selected columns in Microsoft Excel.
Ctrl+B	Applies or removes columns in Microsoft Excel.
Ctrl+C	Copies the selected cells. Ctrl+C followed by another Ctrl+C displays the clipboard.
Ctrl+D	Uses the Fill Down command to copy the contents and format of the topmost cell of a selected range into the cells below.
Ctrl+I	Applies or removes italic formatting in Microsoft Excel.
Ctrl+N	Creates a new blank workbook.
Ctrl+O	Displays the Open dialog box to open or find a file. Ctrl+Shift+O selects all cells containing comments.
Ctrl+P	Displays the Print dialog box.
Ctrl+R	Uses the Fill Right command to copy the contents and format of the leftmost cell of a selected range into the cells to the right.

Ctrl+S	Saves the active file with its current file name, location and file format.
Ctrl+U	Applies or removes underlining.
Ctrl+W	Closes the selected workbook window.
Ctrl+X	Cuts the selected cells.
Ctrl+Y	Repeats the last command or action, if possible in Microsoft Excel.
Ctrl+Z	Uses the Undo command to reverse the last command or to delete the last entry that you typed.

Function Keys

F1	Displays the Microsoft Office Excel Help task pane. Ctrl+F1 displays or hides the Ribbon, a component of the Microsoft Office Fluent use interface. Alt+F1 creates a chart of the data in the current range. Alt+Shift+F1 inserts a new worksheet.
F2	Edits the active cell and positions the insertion at the cell contents.
F6	Switches between the worksheet, ribbon, task pane and zoom controls.
F7	Displays the Spelling dialog box to check spelling in the active worksheet or selected range.
F11	Creates a chart of the data in the current range.
F12	Displays the Save As dialog box.

Other Useful Shortcuts Keys

Arrow Keys	Move one cell up, down, left or right in a worksheet.
Backspace	Deletes one character to the left in the formula bar.
Delete	Removes the cell contents (Data and formulas) from selected cells without affecting cell formats or comments.
Esc	Cancels an entry in the cell or formula bar.
Home	Moves to the beginning of a row in a worksheet.
Page Down	Moves one screen down in a worksheet.
Page Up	Moves one screen up in a worksheet.
Tab	Moves one cell to the right in a worksheet.

SUMMARY

- A spreadsheet is an interactive computer application for organisation, analysis and storage of data in tabular form.
- A Microsoft Office Excel workbook is a file that contains one or more worksheets that you can use to organise various kinds of related information.
- An Excel worksheet is a single spreadsheet that contains cells organised by rows and columns.
- A cell is a specific location within a spreadsheet and is defined by the intersection of a row and column.
- The cell pointer in Excel is the active cell or the selected cell and is highlighted by a bolder rectangle.
- A range is a group or block of cells in a worksheet that have been selected or highlighted.
- AutoFill allows you to identify a series of data and automatically fill cells with the appropriate text.
- Alignment means where the text is placed within the cell. Cell text can be aligned left, right, or in the center.
- WrapText is a feature that wraps the text within a cell.
- Formulas are equations that perform calculations on values in your worksheet. A formula starts with an equal sign (=).
- A cell reference refers to a cell or a range of cells on a worksheet and can be used in a formula so that Microsoft Office Excel can find the values or data which you want that formula to calculate.
- There are three types of cell references: relative, absolute and mixed.

Exam Practice

Multiple Choice Questions

1 A worksheet is a
(a) collection of workbooks
(b) processing software
(c) combination of rows and columns
(d) None of the above

Ans. (*c*) A worksheet is a combination of rows and columns.

2 By default, a workbook in Excel contains how many worksheets?
(a) 16 (b) 3 (c) 15 (d) 256

Ans. (*b*) 3 worksheets are present in every workbook by default.

3 The simplest way to move data from one location to another in Excel is
(a) by Quick Access toolbar
(b) using Cut and Paste
(c) by the drag and drop method
(d) Both (b) and (c)

Ans. (*d*) We can move data using cut and paste, and also drag and drop method is the easiest one.

4 The AutoFill can apply from
(a) left to right (b) right to left
(c) up to down (d) All of these

Ans. (*d*) AutoFill can apply from any side.

5 The default page orientation in Excel is
(a) Landscape (b) Horizontal
(c) Portrait (d) None of these

Ans. (*c*) The default page orientation in Excel is Portrait.

6 Word wrapping means
(a) the text remains in the straight line
(b) the text distributed in multiple lines
(c) displays text vertically within a cell
(d) displays the selected text in a different font style

Ans. (*b*) Word wrapping distributes the text in multiple lines.

7 A term that is used in spreadsheet which forces a line break in a cell when the cell entry is too large to fit in the cell.
(a) Wrap (b) Line Break
(c) Cell Break (d) Multiline Cell

Ans. (*a*) Wrap

8 The default alignment of text in a cell is
(a) Left (b) Right (c) Centered (d) Justified

Ans. (*a*) In Excel, by default the text is left aligned.

9 Absolute cell referencing occurs when
(a) formula is dragged but the cell references do not adjust.
(b) spreadsheet is saved with "absolute" as file name.
(c) formula is dragged and the cell reference adjusts automatically.
(d) $ symbol is automatically added with each cell value.

Ans. (*a*) Absolute cell referencing occurs when formula is dragged but the cell references do not adjust.

10 Find out the odd one
(a) Absolute (b) Relative
(c) Mixed (d) AutoFill

Ans. (*d*) Absolute, relative and mixed all three are the types of cell referencing but AutoFill is not.

11 Cell address $B$5 in a formula means
(a) it is a mixed reference
(b) it is an absolute reference
(c) it is a relative reference
(d) None of the above

Ans. (*b*) $ sign in a formula need to add before row number and column letter for absolute referencing.

12 While entering a formula, cell address B$5 represents
(a) Absolute Referencing (b) Mixed Referencing
(c) Relative Referencing (d) All of these

Ans. (*b*) It represents mixed reference because we are using $ sign before 5 only. Hence, as we will drag this, only B will change but 5 will remain same.

13 A cell range starting from first row, first column to fourth row and fifth column can be represented as
(a) [A1 : E4] (b) [A0 : E3] (c) [E4 : A1] (d) [E3 : A0]

Ans (*a*) [A1:E4] because row count starts from 1 and column count starts from A and first we write the starting cell address.

14 A cell range always has the .... symbol between the cell references.
(a) ;(semicolon) (b) .(full stop)
(c) ,(comma) (d) :(colon)

Ans. (*d*) A cell range always has the : (colon) symbol between the address of ranges.

15 If cell range A1 : A5 contains the numbers 20, 16, 5, 35 and 7 then = AVERAGE(A1 : A5, 50) will display
(a) 22.167 (b) 27.167
(c) 10 (d) 40

Ans. (*a*) 22.167

16 = COUNTA (4, 78, False, 18) will return ....
(a) 2 (b) 3 (c) 4 (d) 5

Ans. (*c*) Because the logical values and numbers directly provided as argument of COUNTA, a function will be counted.

17 If you type =2 * (6-4) in cell A1, what value will be displayed?
(a) 2 (b) 4 (c) 6 (d) 8

Ans. (*b*) = 2*(6-4) = 2*(2) = 4

18 You can place the chart legend in the chart at
(a) Bottom (b) Corner
(c) Top, Right and Left (d) All of these

Ans. (*d*) You can place the chart legend in the chart at Bottom, Corner, Top, Right and Left.

19 In Excel chart, text displayed at data points to indicate the specific category is called
(a) data point (b) data series
(c) data label (d) legends

Ans. (*c*) Text displayed at data points to indicate the specific category is called data label.

20 You have used a spreadsheet to calculate the average marks of a class in Mathematics. Which input is essential to find the average marks?
(a) Marks of each student of class in Science
(b) Marks of each student of class in Mathematics
(c) Average marks in Mathematics of each student of class
(d) Names and roll numbers of each student of class

Ans. (*b*) Marks of each student for Mathematics will be required for calculating average marks of mathematics.

21 A chart is created on the basis of values in
(a) mail merge (b) database
(c) spreadsheet (d) document

Ans. (*c*) A chart is a pictorial representation of data that created on the basis of values in a spreadsheet.

22 Which of the following charts is used for comparing the changes in data over a period of time?
(a) Bar chart (b) Area chart
(c) Scatter chart (d) Line chart

Ans. (*d*) Line chart emphasises on the rate of changes rather than volume of changes over time.

23 Which of the following charts selects only one range of the data series?
(a) Line chart (b) Pie chart
(c) Scatter Chart (d) Bar chart

Ans. (*b*) Pie chart can select only one range of the data series.

24 The another name for the XY chart is
(a) Column chart (b) Net chart
(c) Bar chart (d) Scatter chart

Ans. (*d*) XY chart is also called Scatter chart.

25 The sample of an Excel worksheet on the screen can be seen by
(a) Print preview
(b) Print
(c) Review
(d) None of the above

Ans. (*a*) Print preview enables you to view the sample of worksheet before printing it on a paper.

26 Which of the following shortcut keys brings the cursor to the last cell on the sheet that contains data?
(a) Ctrl+Home
(b) Ctrl+End
(c) Ctrl+Page down
(d) Ctrl+down arrow

Ans. (*b*) Ctrl+End shortcut key is used to bring the cursor to the last cell.

27 For selecting a non-continuous range of cells, you need to do what?
(a) Press Alt key (b) Press Shift key
(c) Press Esc key (d) Press Ctrl key

Ans. (*d*) By pressing Ctrl key and clicking on the desired cells a non-continuous cell range can be selected.

28 For selecting the entire worksheet in Excel, you need to press
(a) Alt + Shift + Spacebar
(b) Ctrl + Shift + Spacebar
(c) Shift + Spacebar
(d) None of the above

Ans. (*b*) You need to press Ctrl + Shift + Spacebar for selecting the entire worksheet in Excel.

Fill in the Blanks

1 Excel is a .... software package.
Ans. spreadsheet

2 When you .... or ...., the selected range gets surrounded by a moving border.
Ans. copy, cut

3 The .... and .... operations copy data from source range to target range and erases it from the source range.
Ans. cut, paste

4 Address of the cell at 10th column and 30th row is ....
Ans. J30

5 The cell having bold boundary is the ....
Ans. active cell

6 Any formula in Excel starts with an ....
Ans. equal (=) sign

7 The keyboard shortcut for copy is .... and for paste is ....
Ans. Ctrl + C, Ctrl + V

8 In .... referencing, the relative address of the cell gets adjusted with respect to the current cell.
Ans. relative

9 For absolute referencing, ... sign is used before the parts of formula.
Ans. $

10 If you enter 15 + 30 in a cell, Excel will display ....
Ans. 15 + 30

11 To specify the number of decimal places in a cell, the .... tab of the Format cells dialog is used.
Ans. Numbers

12 The .... tool is used in spreadsheet that creates a growth series, wherein subsequent values follow an increasing or a decreasing geometric pattern.
Ans. Fill series

13 The range of cells containing data that makes a chart is termed as .... data.
Ans. source

14 .... are text, number cell references enclosed within parentheses in a formula.
Ans. Arguments

True or False

1 You cannot open two different workbooks in Excel simultaneously.
Ans. **False** You can open two different workbooks in Excel simultaneously.

2 When a cell containing a formula is moved, the cells referring the moved cell show an error value.
Ans. **False** When a cell containing a formula is moved, the cells referring the moved cell do not show an error value.

3 A cell entry can be edited either in the cell or in the formula bar.
Ans. **True** There are two ways to edit the data which has entered in the cell, i.e. in the cell or in the formula bar.

4 If the data entered in a cell is 546Z, then Excel will treat it as a number because it starts with a digit.
Ans. **False** It will be treated as non-numeric data because it contains letters alongwith numbers.

5 We cannot enter the date/time in a cell.
Ans. **False** Date/time can be added to an Excel cell.

6 The Fill handle tool is used for labour intensive entering data in a spreadsheet.
Ans. **True** Entering data into a spreadsheet can be very labour intensive, but Fill handle tool autofills the entries and saves time.

EXAM PRACTICE

7 The Insert button is found on Cells group under Home tab.

Ans. **True** Insert button is available on Cells group under Home tab and is used to insert cells, rows and columns.

8 The title of the chart tells the type of the chart.

Ans. **False** The title of chart tells the name of the chart.

9 A chart is a graphical representation of worksheet data.

Ans. **True** A chart is a graphical representation of worksheet data.

10 The contents of a cell can be changed by pressing F2 key on keyboard.

Ans. **True** F2 is a shortcut for making cell editable.

Very Short Answer (VSA) Type Questions

1 Define the term workbook.

Ans. A workbook is a collection of worksheets. By default, there are three worksheets in every workbook.

2 Reena is new to Excel. Her instructor has asked her to open Excel on her PC and questioned about active cell. Help Reena in identifying the active cell on her screen.

Ans. An active cell is a cell with heavy black color boundary.

3 What is the default alignment of number, text and formula in a spreadsheet?

Ans. Default alignment of text or label entry is left alignment and for numbers and formula it is right alignment.

4 Elaborate the formatting necessary.

Ans. With formatting, we can make some data to be bolder, rotated or in different color. So, basically formatting provides worksheet a neater and more legible outlook.

5 Soham has clicked on the cell residing at the intersection of first row and ninth column. What will be the address of the selected cell?

Ans. First row and ninth column address will be I1.

6 How many ways are there for adding a new worksheet in an Excel workbook?

Ans. There are two methods of adding a new worksheet in an Excel workbook; Insert worksheet tab at the bottom and Insert button on Cells group under Home tab.

7 In Excel, how many ways are there to express/format a number?

Ans. Numbers in Excel can be expressed in many different formats like date, time, percentage or decimals.

8 Name the toolbar of spreadsheet which has all the options of changing the Font properties.

Ans. Formatting Toolbar

9 What do you mean by relative referencing?

Ans. Cell referencing in which the cells are referred by their relative position in the worksheet relative to a particular cell is called relative referencing.

10 How many cells would be there in the cell range [A1 : B2]?

Ans. There would be 4 cells in the given cell range.

11 The cell A1 has value Monday. If you are asked to click and drag the Fill handle of A1 downside then what will be the contents of cell A2, A3, A4 and A5?

Ans. Cells A2, A3, A4 and A5 will contain Tuesday, Wednesday, Thursday and Friday respectively.

12 If $=6-*2=6$ is entered in a cell, then what will be the cell content?

Ans. –4 will be contained in cell as a result.

13 In a spreadsheet software, the formula =A1+$A$2 was entered in cell A3 and then copied into cell B3. What is the formula copied into B3?

Ans. =B1+$A$2 will be copied into B3.

14 Write down the formula for adding values of cells A1 to A5.

Ans. Formula for adding values of cells A1 to A5 would be =SUM(A1 : A5).

15 State difference between COUNT( ) and COUNTA( ) function.

Ans. The only difference between the COUNT( ) and COUNTA( ) function is that the COUNTA( ) function computes the numbers as well as text entries, while the COUNT( ) function counts only numbers.

16 Hansika wants to apply MIN function on a cell range, but all the values in that range are of Boolean. What value will be returned by the MIN function?

Ans. MIN function will return 0(zero) in this case.

17 Why we cannot add titles to an embedded chart once chart is ready?

Ans. Titles have not been entered in chart elements step. And, these cannot be added later once chart is ready.

18 Write down the importance of legend in charts.

Ans. With the help of legend, each data series can be uniquely identified by assigning a unique color or pattern.

19 What will be the column names of the below statement?

(*i*) 26th column

(*ii*) 28th column

Ans. (*i*) Z

(*ii*) AB

Short Answer (SA) Type Questions

1 What is the difference between a workbook and a worksheet?

Ans. Differences between workbook and worksheet are as follows

Workbook	Worksheet
A workbook is an Excel file with one or more worksheets.	A worksheet is a single spreadsheet of data.
A workbook would be the entire binder, with everything in it.	A worksheet would be like one section in that binder.

2 Write down the significance of electronic spreadsheets.

Ans. Using electronic spreadsheets, large volume of data can be stored in worksheets. Worksheets can be managed, edited, viewed, retrieved and printed easily in desired format. Electronic spreadsheets support charts, which represent data pictorically.

3 Is it possible to remove a worksheet? State the process of doing it.

Ans. Yes, it is possible to remove a worksheet. To remove a worksheet, right-click on the Sheets tab of the sheet that you want to delete and choose Delete from pop-up menu, or choose Delete Sheet from the pop-up menu of Delete option on Cells group under Home tab.

4 Define the meaning of formula.

Ans. Formula plays a major role in spreadsheet making. A formula is a combination of values, operators and cell addresses as operands that perform calculation on the values contained in the addresses.

5 Suggest the appropriate functions for the following situations:

(*i*) For returning the minimum value out of a range A1 to C5.

(*ii*) For determining whether the customer is eligible for discount or not from the bill amount stored in cell D5. A customer is eligible for discount if bill amount >5,000.

Ans. (*i*) = MIN(A1 : C5)

(*ii*) = IF(D5>5,000, "Discount", "NoDiscount")

6 Suggest the appropriate function for the following situations:

(*i*) Selecting the maximum value out of a range A1 to B20.

(*ii*) Calculating average of marks entered in cells E5, F5, G5, H5 and I5.

(*iii*) Determining whether the student has passed (if scored >= 40) or not from the marks stored in cell J10.

Ans. (*i*) = MAX(A1 : B20) (*ii*) = AVG(E5: I5)

(*iii*) =IF(J10 >= 40, "Pass", "Fail")

7 Sana has entered 49+30 in a cell. The worksheet is not displaying 79 in the cell. Instead, 49+30 is getting displayed. Help Sana in rectifying the problem.

Ans. In Excel, every formula must start with an = (equal) sign. Since, Sana has not put = sign before 49+30, thus she is not able to see the desired result will be displayed if she will use = (49 + 30) formula.

8 What is the use of the COUNT( ) function in Excel?

Ans. Excel's COUNT( ) function can be used to total the number of cells in a selected range. The COUNT( ) function will add up the number of cells in a selected range that contains numbers.

9 For what purpose pie charts are useful?

Ans. Pie charts are useful for the following purposes

(*i*) They convey approximate propositional relationship at a point in time.

(*ii*) They compare part of a whole at a given point in time.

(*iii*) Exploded portion of a pie chart emphasise a small proportion of parts.

Long Answer (LA) Type Questions

1 Explain the concept of cell referencing alongwith its various types.

Ans. Excel supports three types of cell referencing, which are as follows

(*i*) **Relative** Every relative cell reference in formula automatically changes when the formula is copied down a column or across a row. As the example illustrated here shows, when the formula is entered (= B4 – C4) in cell D4 and copied in D5 then it will change into (= B5 – C5) related to cell.

(*ii*) **Absolute** This cell reference is fixed. Absolute references do not change if you copy a formula from one cell to another. Absolute references have dollar sign ($) like $S$9. e.g when the formula =C4*$D$9 is copied from row, the absolute cell reference remains as $D$9.

(*iii*) **Mixed** This cell reference has either an absolute column and a relative row, or an absolute row and a relative column. e.g. $A1 is an absolute reference to column A and a relative reference to row 1. As a mixed reference is copied from one cell to another, the absolute reference stays the same but the relative reference changes.

2 Explain any five functions that can be used in a worksheet.

Ans. Refer to text on Page No. 170-172.

3 Write down the name and purpose of various components of a chart.

Ans. Refer to text on Page No. 172-173.

4 What are the various types of charts? Explain each.

Ans. The various types of charts in Excel are given below

Line Chart Data that is arranged in columns or rows on a worksheet can be plotted in a line chart. Line charts can display continuous data over time, set against a common scale and are therefore ideal for showing trends in data at equal intervals. In a line chart, category data is distributed evenly along the horizontal axis and all value data is distributed evenly along the vertical axis.

Pie Chart Data that is arranged in one column or row only on a worksheet can be plotted in a pie chart. Pie charts show the size of items in one data series, proportional to the sum of the items. The data points in a pie chart are displayed as a percentage of the whole pie.

Scatter Chart Data that is arranged in columns and rows on a worksheet can be plotted in an XY (scatter) chart. Scatter charts show the relationships among the numeric values in several data series, or plots two groups of numbers as one series of XY coordinates.

Bar Chart Data that is arranged in columns or rows on a worksheet can be plotted in a bar chart. Bar charts illustrate comparisons among individual items.

Area Chart Data that is arranged in columns or rows on a worksheet can be plotted in an area chart. Area charts emphasise the magnitude of change over time and can be used to draw attention to the total value across a trend.

5 How are charts created in Excel? Write the steps.

Ans. Refer to text on Page No. 173.

6. The teacher has maintained a record of each student in her class in the form of an excel sheet. Each record has Rollno, Name and Marks of the students.

J24

	A	B	C	D
1	Rollno	Name	Marks	
2	1	Amit	50	
3	2	Mradul	23	
4	3	Arun	24	
5	4	Sonali	56	
6	5	Kishan	65	
7	6	Mona	58	
8				

(i) Write formula to find the sum of all marks in a class.
(a) = AVERAGE (C2:C7) (b) = SUM(C2-C7)
(c) = SUM(C2:C7) (d) = SUM(C)

(ii) Write formula to find maximum marks in the class.
(a) = MAX(C2-C7) (b) = MAX(C2:C7)
(c) = MAX(C2;C7) (d) = MAXI(C2:C7)

(iii) Find the total students in the class.
(a) COUNT(A1-A7) (b) COUNT(A2;A7)
(c) COUNT(A2:A7) (d) COUNT(A1;A7)

(iv) What is cell range of second record?
(a) A3-C3 (b) A3:C3
(c) A2-C2 (d) A2:C2

(v) Copy record 3 i.e. row 3 using shortcut keys
(a) Select A4 to C4 for copy use Ctrl+C
(b) Select Whole row and for copy use Ctrl+V
(c) Select A4 to C4 for copy use Ctrl+X
(d) Select A4 to C4 for copy use Ctrl+L

Ans. (i) (*c*) For finding the sum of all marks the cells C2 to C7 will be used in SUM( ) function as = SUM (C2 : C7).

(ii) (*b*) For finding the maximum marks in the class the cells C2 to C7 will be used in MAX() function as = MAX (C2 : C7).

(iii) (*c*) For finding the total students in the class, the cells A2 to A7 will be used in COUNT() function as = COUNT (A2 : A7).

(iv) (*b*) The second record is started from cell A3 and ends with C3.

(v) (*a*) Shortcut keys for copy is Ctrl+C and 3rd record i.e. row 3 is A4 to C4.

Application Oriented Questions

1 **In a worksheet, cell K12 has a value. A formula is to be entered in cell K15, such that if the value in cell K12 is more than 300, the value in cell K15 would be 1.33 times the value of cell K12. Otherwise, the value in cell K15 would be 1.5 times the value of cell K12. Explain the formula that you use to achieve this.**

Ans. In cell K15, enter the conditional statement = IF (K12 > 300, K12 *1.33, K12 * 1.5). Here, IF condition checks the value at K12, that is, if it is greater than 300, then calculate 1.33 of K12, otherwise 1.5 of K12.

2 **Describe, how the owner of the restaurant could use the spreadsheet for financial modelling?**

Ans. (*i*) Decide on a total purchasing need for next night/week/month/year.

(*ii*) Change figures in spreadsheet.

(*iii*) Raise/lower/add/delete any value.

(*iv*) Compare results with predicted/total needed/target results.

(*v*) For general use for budgeting like to calculate profit.

3 **Write command for the operations (*i*) to (*iii*) based on the spreadsheet below:**

	A	B	C	D	E	F	G
1	Item Code	Item Desc	Type	Unit Price	Qty	Amount	Rebate
2	101 Pen		Consumable	150	1500		
3	102 Photo Copier		Non-consumable	240000	24		
4	103 Photocopy Machine		Non-consumable	6400	70		
5	104 Eraser		Consumable	108	8400		

Sheet1 Sheet2 Sheet3

(*i*) To calculate the Amount as Unit Price*Qty for each item in Column F.

(*ii*) To calculate the Rebate as 7% of Amount if Type is consumable, else calculate Rebate as 11% of Amount in Column G.

(*iii*) To calculate total Rebate across all items in cell G6.

Ans. (*i*) At cell F2, type =D2*E2 and then copy this formula using mouse Fill handle onto range F3 : F5.

(*ii*) At cell G2, type =IF(C2="Consumable", F2*0.07, F2*0.11) and then copy this formula using mouse Fill handle onto range G3 : G5.

(*iii*) At cell G6, type =SUM(G2 : G5).

4 **Arihant stationery keeps stock of various stationeries in its shop. The proprietor wants to maintain a stock value and reorder level for following items as given in a spreadsheet. Write formulas for the operations (*i*) to (*iii*) and answer the questions (*iv*) and (*v*) based on the spreadsheet given below alongwith the relevant cell address:**

	A	B	C	D	E	F	G	H
1	Item Code	Item Name	Minimum Stock Quantity	Quantity in Stock (Unit)	Rate (₹)	Stock Value (₹)	Quantity to Order (Unit)	Order Value
2	101	P. Holder	200	500	35			
3	123	Whitner	450	150	25			
4	113	Steppler Pin	250	450	5			
5	156	Paper cutter	300	600	10			

Sheet1 Sheet2 Sheet3

EXAM PRACTICE

(*i*) To calculate the Stock Value as product of 'Quantity in Stock' and 'Rate' for each item present in the spreadsheet.

(*ii*) To calculate the 'Quantity to Order' as 'Minimum Stock Quantity'-'Quantity in Stock' for each item.

(*iii*) To calculate the 'Order Value' as product of 'Quantity to Order' and 'Rate' for the items if 'Quantity to Order'>=0, else assign the value as 0.

(*iv*) The proprietor wants to graphically represent his stationery stock. Suggest him the most appropriate feature of MS-Excel.

(*v*) If Quantity in Stock's value changes, will we have to redo all the calculations for that particular column? Explain.

Ans. (*i*) At cell F2, type = D2*E2 and then copy this formula using Fill handle in range F3 : F5.

(*ii*) At cell G2, type = C2 – D2 and then copy this formula using Fill handle in range G3 : G5.

(*iii*) At cell H2, type = IF (G2 > = 0, G2*E2, 0) and copy this formula using Fill handle in the range H3 : H5.

(*iv*) He should create chart of any type to graphically represent his data.

(*v*) No, the recalculation is not again required because the formula and functions are given changes according to the values in the cells.

5 Neha Mittal wants to store data of her monthly expenditure for a period of two years and also wants to perform some calculation and analysis. Which Microsoft application, will you suggest Neha should use for this purpose and why?

Ans. Microsoft Excel should be used because it cannot only be used for storing data, but also be used to perform calculations and analysis of the data.

Unit Test 1

Multiple Choice Questions

1 OpenOffice.org is an example of
(a) Word processor
(b) Spreadsheet
(c) Presentation
(d) None of the above

2 Which of the following font sizes is not supported by MS-Word 2007?
(a) 12
(b) 72
(c) 533
(d) None of the above

3 The Track Changes tool in MS-Word is used
(a) to edit the contents of a document
(b) to track the mistakes done while typing the documents
(c) to track the changes done by many persons reviewing the documents
(d) All of the above

Fill in the Blanks

4 .... is used to set tabs, indents and margins for a document.

5 You can use .... as a watermark to indicate that your presentation is a draft.

6 The .... symbol is used to designate an absolute cell reference.

True or False

7 There is only one type of chart in Excel.

8 A presentation can only be run in Slide Show view.

9 We cannot enter the date/time in a cell.

Very Short Answer Type Questions

10 What do you mean by column headings?

11 What is the use of UPPERCASE text case option in MS-Word 2007?

12 For what different purposes you can use Slide Sorter view?

Short Answer Type Questions

13 Differentiate between pie chart and bar chart.

14 Write steps required to accept tracked changes in a document.

15 Differentiate between Slide Sorter and Slide Show view.

Long Answer Type Questions

16 Write the steps to create a new folder and sub-folder on a desktop.

17 What are the main features of MS-Word 2007?

18 What are the different types of data that can be entered in MS-Excel?

Application Oriented Questions

19 Following are some descriptors describing some terms. Identify the terms/features these refer to
(i) It is a pre-designed document that you can use to create new documents with the same formatting.
(ii) It is a tool that you can use to produce professional looking documents.
(iii) It is a new feature of 2007 Office suite that allows you to see changes in your document before you actually select an item.

20 Sarika wants to store data of her monthly expenditure for a period of three years also wants to perform some calculation and analysis. Which Microsoft Application, will you suggest to Sarika should use for this purpose and why?

Unit Test 2

Multiple Choice Questions

1 A .... compares pieces of data using horizontal stacks.
(a) pie chart (b) scatter chart
(c) area chart (d) bar chart

2 Which of the following should be used, when you want to add a slide to an existing presentation?
(a) File, Add a new slide (b) Insert, New slide
(c) File open (d) File new

3 Which symbol set indicate direction?
(a) Scripts (b) Arrows
(c) Basic Math (d) Operators

Fill in the Blanks

4 A/An .... is a collection of styles and formatting options.

5 Clicking the .... button closes the associated application window.

6 Slide text can be edited in ....view.

True or False

7 Number + Enter short key is used to go to slide number.

8 The data source contains the text, which is common for all letters.

9 You can enter data in a cell.

Very Short Answer Type Questions

10 What do you mean by rehearse timing?

11 Name some examples of Word processing software.

12 Which Excel function is used to calculate the average of all the values?

Short Answer Type Questions

13 Write down the steps to change line spacing.

14 What is data source with reference to mail merge? Also, give advantages of Mail Merge feature.

15 What are the row headings and column headings in spreadsheet?

Long Answer Type Questions

16 How can you insert and delete cells in the spreadsheet?

17 What are comments? Write down the steps for inserting comments in your document.

18 What is presentation graphics software? Explain by giving example.

Application Oriented Questions

19 Rajat is a student and wants to make the schedule of his assignment in the form of row and column. Which feature of MS-Office will help him to do this?

20 Malini has recently joined a construction company as marketing executive. She saw a presentation about the company. She however is not satisfied with it and wants to make some changes in it. Using your presentation skills, suggest the features to accomplish the following changes:
(i) Add the company's logo on the first slide.
(ii) Add audio to explain the content of the slide.
(iii) Connect slide 2 to slide 7 directly.
(iv) Add date and time on all slides.

Unit Test 3

Multiple Choice Questions

1 A .... is a collection of buttons which represent various operations that can be carried out within an application.

(a) Button
(b) Menu
(c) Toolbar
(d) Taskbar

2 Using the Theme in the PowerPoint, we can change

(a) color (b) fonts
(c) effects (d) All of these

3 In Excel 2007, by which tab can we view and print the gridlines?

(a) Page Layout (b) Format
(c) Insert (d) Home

Fill in the Blanks

4 Page margins are indicated at each end of the .... bar by dark shading.

5 .... can be used for creating notes.

6 Test can be added in a slide using a .... or a placeholder.

True or False

7 Editing text in MS-Word 2007 only involves inserting text.

8 Ctrl + ; short key is used to enter the current date.

9 A design template can be applied to only one side.

Very Short Answer Type Questions

10 What do you mean by plot area in Excel's chart?

11 Briefly explain the AutoFill feature of Excel.

12 What is the extension of the PowerPoint presentation file?

Short Answer Type Questions

13 Explain MAX ( ) function in Excel.

14 Differentiate between Header and Footer.

15 What is the difference between single spacing and double spacing?

Long Answer Type Questions

16 Explain the role of copying and moving operations.

17 What are the different components of MS-Word 2007?

18 Design a letter in Word for thanking your parents for the efforts/pains, they take for you.

Application Oriented Questions

19 Reeva wants to give identical design to all the slides and handouts, she is going to pring from her presentation. Which two methods can she use to accomplish her task?

20 Seema's parents are planning to prepare invitation cards for 25 people for a pooja ceremony at their new house. Seema suggests to which feature of MS-Office for doing this job.

PROJECT REPORT

A project report is a written document of what the *analyser* analyses in his/her project work. The project report needs to be prepared with great care and consideration.

ELEMENTS OF THE PROJECT

Try to ensure that your report contains the following elements

Title Page

This should include the project title, name of the company/product on which you are conducting your research and name of the student. Your can also list the name of your school, class and subject teacher.

Acknowledgement

It is usual to thank those individuals, who have provided particularly useful assistance, technical or otherwise, during your project through acknowledgement.

Content Page

This should list the main sections and sub-sections of your report. Choose self-explanatory titles with their respective pages and use double spacing for clarity. Content should be impressive and explanatory, so that the reader would clearly understand the purpose of the project.

Introduction

This is one of the most important component of the project report. It should begin with a clear statement of what the project is about, so that the nature and scope of the project can be understood by the reader. It should summarise everything which you set out to achieve and provide a clear summary of the project's background, relevance and main contributions. The introduction should set the context for the project and should provide the reader with a summary of the key things to look out for, in the remainder of the report. It is useful in stating the main objectives of the project as part of the introduction.

Background

The background section of the report should set the project into action. It specifies the problem, what remedial actions are taken, what are its effects etc. It proposes the layout of the whole project.

Body of Report

The central part of the report usually consists of three or four sections detailing the technical work undertaken during the project. The structure of these sections is highly project dependent. They can reflect the chronological development of the project. It includes the detailed description regarding the matter of the project.

Evaluation

This might involve quantitative and qualitative evaluation such as expressibility, functionality, ease-of-use, etc of a product. At some point, you should also evaluate the strengths and weaknesses of what you have done. It includes certain questionnaires, sampling test, etc. which help in evaluating the result on the basis of truths and facts.

Conclusion

The conclusion should list the things, which have been learnt as a result of the work you have done. It shows the ultimate response of the project undertaken by a student. It should be expressive and impressive, so that a reader would clearly evaluate the result and rate you on the basis of your presentation.

ACKNOWLEDGEMENT

I would like to express my special thanks of gratitude to my teacher________ as well as our Principal ________ who gave me the golden opportunity to do this wonderful project.

This project helped me a lot in gaining adequate knowledge about the topic. I have completed this project after proper analysis and research and I came to know about so many new things.

I am really thankful to all of my friends, co-partners and guide, who have devoted their precious time in completing my project. Secondly, I would also like to thank my parents or guardians who helped me a lot in finishing this project within the prescribed time.

I am making this project not only for marks but also to increase my knowledge and intellect development.

Thanks again to all who helped me.

CERTIFICATE

This is to Certify that these projects work are the bonafide work of .... (Name of the student) who carried out the work under my supervision ....

Name and Signature of Teacher/Supervisor).

CONTENTS

PROJECT-1

WORD PROCESSING

Word processing software is used for the creation of text based documents. It is a GUI based software used in the windows environment. In a precise manner, it is an application that is directed by the user, performs Word processing which includes the composition, editing, formatting and sometimes printing of any sort of material. In word processor, Mail Merge feature enables you to generate a set of forms, letters etc, containing similar information that can be sent to a group of people.

Topic 1 Create Certificate for Candidates Using Mail Merge

Procedure

For creating a certificate, follow the below mentioned steps:

Step 1 Open the MS–Word 2007 document by clicking on **Start** button → **All Programs** → **Microsoft Office** > **Microsoft Office Word 2007.**

Step 2 In the MS - Word 2007 document window, under the **Mailings** tab click on **Start Mail Merge**, a dropdown menu will be opened.

Step 3 From this dropdown menu, select **Step by Step Mail Merge Wizard.**

Step 4 In Step 1 of Mail Merge Wizard, select **Letters** as the document type and click on **Next: Starting document link.**

Step 5 In Step 2, under Select starting document section, select **Use the current document** option and click on the **Next: Select recipients** link.

Step 6 In Step 3, under Select recipients, choose **Type a new list** and under Type a new list section click on **Create...**

Step 7 In the New Address List dialog box, click on **Customize Columns...** button.

Step 8 In this Customize Address List dialog box, delete all the columns. Then, add two columns, click on Add button, Type a name for your field in Text box simultaneously as. GreetingLine and AddressBlock and then click **OK** button.

Step 9 Back in the **New Address List** dialog box, type the recipient's details in the corresponding columns of the resulting table and click **OK** button .

Step 10 In the **Save Address List** dialog box, type the name of your data source in the **File name** text box and then click on **Save** button.

Step 11 In the Mail Merge Recipients dialog box, click **OK** button.

Step 12 Now, on right hand side of the screen, in the Mail Merge Wizard click on the **Next: Write your letter** link.

Step 13 And, start writing your certificate (To add GreetingLine and AddressBlock in your certificate click on particular field from Mail Merge Wizard)

Step 14 Select the content of certificate and from **Page Layout** tab, under the **Page Background** group click on **Page Borders** option.

Step 15 Borders and Shading dialog box will appear.

Step 16 In this dialog box, select the **Page Border** tab and under **Style** option, select the appropriate border for the certificate and click **OK** button.

Step 17 Click on **Next: Preview your letters.**

Step 18 And, finally click on **Next: Complete the merge** link.

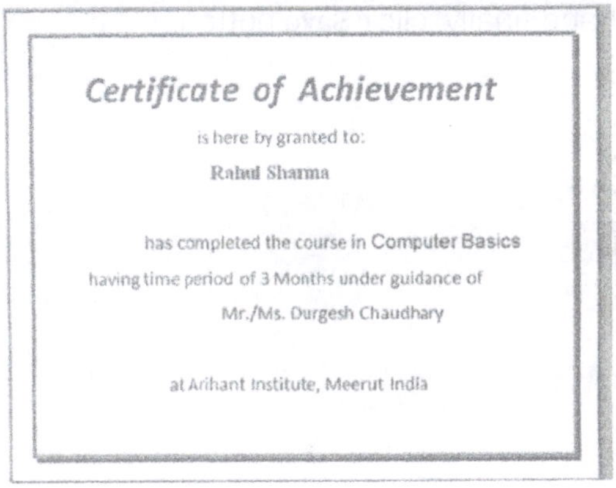

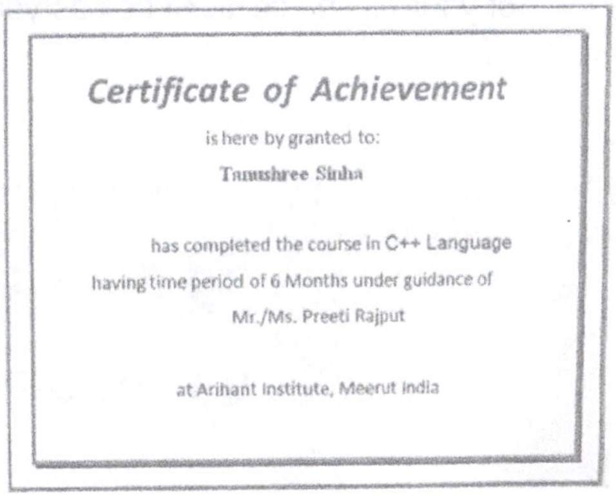

Topic 2 Create Invitation Card for Birthday Party

Procedure

For creating an Invitation card, follow the below mentioned steps:

Step 1 Open the MS- Word 2007 document by clicking on **Start** button → **All Programs** → **Microsoft Office** → **Microsoft Office Word 2007.**

Step 2 In the MS - Word 2007 document window, insert the border background from image file using command **Insert** tab → **Illustrations** group → **Picture.**

Step 3 Once the background is inserted, you need to send behind text so that you can easily type on it. For this, in the **Insert** tab from the **Text** group click on the arrow **Text Box** option. A Built-In dropdown will appear.

Step 4 From this dropdown, select **Draw Text Box** option. Now, on the image click and hold the mouse from where you want to start the text box.

Step 5 Drag the mouse to create the text box. An outline indicating the size of your text box appears.

Step 6 Release the mouse button. The text box will appear in your image.

Step 7 In the text box, enter the text according to sample card.

Step 8 After finishing your texting, under the **Text Box Tools Format** tab, from the **Text Box Styles** group, select the **Shape Outline** option.

Step 9 From this, a dropdown menu will appear. In this dropdown menu, select **No Outline** to remove the outline of the text box.

Step 10 After completing your invitation card, click **Microsoft Office** button, click **Save As** option, a dialog box will appear, select the path to save the file and give the name of your file in **File name** box as you want and finally, click **Save** button.

PROJECT REPORT

VIVA VOCE

1. ***What is Word processor?***

Ans. A Word processor is a software that enables you to create, edit, print and save document.

2. ***By which tab, you can open the Mail Merge wizard?***

Ans. Mailings tab

3. ***How many steps are there in Mail Merge Wizard?***

Ans. Six

4. ***How do you locate MS - Word 2007 on your computer system?***

Ans. Click Start button → All Programs → Microsoft Office → Microsoft Office Word 2007

5. ***Write the shortcut keys to format the text style bold, italic and underline.***

Ans. Bold - Ctrl + B Italic - Ctrl + I Underline - Ctrl + U

6. ***What is the use of ruler in MS-Word 2007 document?***

Ans. Ruler is used to set tabs, indents and margins for a document.

7. ***Under Insert tab, which group contains the features like ClipArt?***

Ans. Illustrations group

8. ***How can you open the WordArt option in your document ?***

Ans. Insert tab → Text group → WordArt

9. ***Give one advantage of mail merge.***

Ans. Mail Merge feature generates a set of forms, letters etc, containing similar information that can be sent to group of people.

10. ***How do you insert a picture in Word document?***

Ans. Insert tab → Illustrations group → Picture

11. ***Define the Page Preview feature of Word processor.***

Ans. The Page Preview feature enables us to preview a document before printing it.

12. ***What do you understand by printout?***

Ans. The printed hard copy of any electronic file is known as printout.

13. ***What is a rectangular box that is used to insert a block of text in a particular position?***

Ans. Text box

14. ***How many documents are used by Mail Merge?***

Ans. Two

15. ***Which refers to the database that stores the information, related to the name and address of the recipients in mail merge?***

Ans. Data Source

PROJECT-2

SPREADSHEET

A spreadsheet is an electronic document that stores various types of data in the form of vertical columns and horizontal rows. It is very useful for storing, organising, manipulating and retrieving data. Spreadsheets are developed as computerized simulations of paper accounting worksheets.

Topic 1 To Create a Chart of Sales made in Two Consecutive Years

Procedure

For creating a sales made in two years, follow the below mentioned steps:

Setp 1 Open the MS–Excel 2007 document by clicking on Start button → **All Programs Microsoft Office → Microsoft Office Excel 2007**

Step 2 Enter the data of two consecutive years for Sales person in the Excel worksheet in the following format:

	A	B	C	D	E
1	Sales Person	Sales 2015-2016	Sales 2016-2017		
2	Rahul	4569	7598		
3	Sahil	4579	3654		
4	Yashvardhan	2654	9842		
5	Rajvindra	7895			
6	Susmita	3654	7569		
7	Aryan	4896	4785		
8	Ayushi		3659		
9	Abhishek	8754	7895		
10					

Sheet1 Sheet2 Sheet3

Step 3 Now, to calculate total sales of year 2015-2016, click in the cell B10 and type the formula = SUM (B2:B9) and press Enter. Total sales of year 2015-2016 will be displayed in cell B10.

Step 4 Now, to calculate total sales of year 2016-2017, click in the cell C10 and type the formula = SUM (C2 : C9) and press Enter. Total sales of year 2016-2017 will be displayed in cell C10.

	A	B	C	D	E	F
1	Sales Person	Sales 2015-2016	Sales 2016-2017			
2	Rahul	4569	7598			
3	Sahil	4579	3654			
4	Yashvardhan	2654	9842			
5	Rajvindra	7895				
6	Susmita	3654	7569			
7	Aryan	4896	4785			
8	Ayushi		3659			
9	Abhishek	8754	7895			
10	Total	37001	45002			
11						

Sheet1 Sheet2 Sheet3

Step 5 Select the cell range (A1 : C9) for which we are going to create the chart.

Step 6 Now, click on the **Insert** tab and in the **Charts** group, click the arrow sign below **Line** chart and select **Stacked line with Markers** chart from the dropdown menu.

The chart will be displayed as follows:

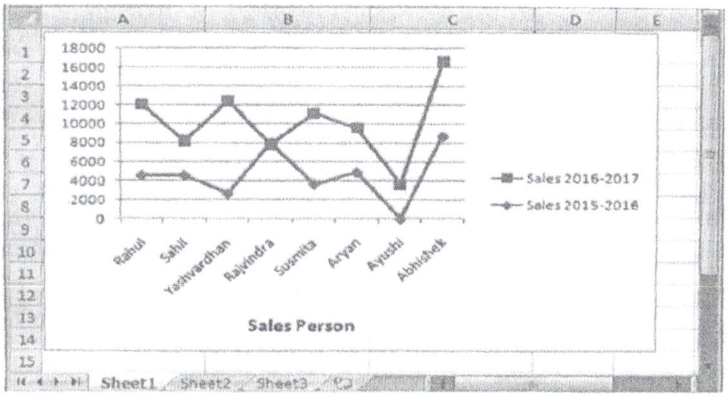

Topic 2 To Create Fruit Sales Details Report

Procedure

For creating a fruit sales report, follow the below mentioned steps:

Step 1 Open the MS-Excel 2007 document by clicking on **Start** button → **All Programs** → **Microsoft Office** → **Microsoft Office Excel 2007**

Step 2 Enter the fruit sales data in the Excel worksheet in the following format:

Fruit Sales Details					
Date	Fruit Name	Qty in Hand	Sold Qty	Price Per Unit	Total Sales Amount
11/8/2017	Mango	20	15	3	
11/9/2017	Apple	51	45	5	
11/10/2017	Banana	23	15	7	
11/11/2017	Lichi	45	35	10	
11/12/2017	Pine apple	35	28	5	
11/13/2017	Guava	14	10	10	
11/14/2017	Grapes	45	30	8	
11/15/2017	Watermelon	35	25	6	
11/16/2017	Orange	65	60	5	
11/17/2017	Papaya	55	48	12	

Step 3 Now, to calculate total sales amount of each fruit in column F, click in the cell F3 and type the formula = (D3*E3) and press Enter. The total sales amount of fruit named Mango will be displayed in cell F3.

Step 4 For calculating total sales amount of remaining fruits in consecutive cells, use AutoFill feature as it will copy the formula in cell F3 to other cells. Drag the Fill handle upto cell F12

Step 5 Now, to calculate the total of fruits which Qty in hand, click in the cell C13 and type the formula = SUM (C3 : C12) and press Enter. The total fruits which Qty in hand will be displayed in cell C13.

Step 6 To calculate the total quantity of fruits which sold, click in the cell D13 and type the formula = SUM (D3:D12) and press Enter. The total quantity of fruits which sold will be displayed in cell D13.

Step 7 To calculate the total of total sales amount of fruits, click in the cell F13 and type the formula = SUM (F3 : F12) and press Enter. The total of total sales amount of fruits will be displayed in cell F13.

Fruit Sales Details					
Date	Fruit Name	Qty in Hand	Sold Qty	Price Per Unit	Total Sales Amount
11/8/2017	Mango	20	15	3	45
11/9/2017	Apple	51	45	5	225
11/10/2017	Banana	23	15	7	105
11/11/2017	Lichi	45	35	10	350
11/12/2017	Pine apple	35	28	5	140
11/13/2017	Guava	14	10	10	100
11/14/2017	Grapes	45	30	8	240
11/15/2017	Watermelon	35	25	6	150
11/16/2017	Orange	65	60	5	300
11/17/2017	Papaya	55	48	12	576
Total		388	311		2231

VIVA VOCE

1. ***What do you understand by a worksheet?***

Ans. The primary document that you use in MS-Excel to store and work with data is a worksheet.

2. ***How many worksheets does a workbook contain, by default?***

Ans. A workbook contains three worksheets by default.

3. ***Explain the SUM () function.***

Ans. SUM () function is used to add all the values provided as argument.

4. ***What is current cell?***

Ans. The current cell refers to the cell that is currently active.

5. ***What do you mean by a group of contiguous cells?***

Ans. A group of contiguous cells is a range of cells.

6. ***Suggest the correct function for computing the total marks of the range A1 to A10.***

Ans. The correct function for computing total marks is = SUM (A1 : A10)

7. ***If a user has clicked on the cell residing at the intersection of first row and ninth column. What will be the address of the selected cell?***

Ans. I1

8. ***How many cells would be there in the cell range [A1 : B2]?***

Ans. 4 cells

9. ***Give the importance of legend in charts.***

Ans. With the help of legend, each data series can be uniquely identified by assigning a unique color or pattern.

10. ***How can you open the column chart in worksheet?***

Ans. Insert tab → Charts group → Column chart

11. ***In project 2, which formula are using in cell F5?***

Ans. = D5*E5

12. ***Write down two advantages to the project of using formulae in Spreadsheet.***

Ans. (i) Automatic Recalculation (ii) Easy calculation of totals and sums.

13. ***In project 1, name the cells in which formulae are used.***

Ans. B10 , C10

14. ***In project 1, which cells are not fill with data?***

Ans. B8, C5

15. ***In project 2, name the data type that has been used in column A.***

Ans. Date

PROJECT-3

POWERPOINT PRESENTATION

PowerPoint helps us in preparing a presentation easily and quickly. We can also include information and objects prepared by other programs such as text, chart worksheet, graphics etc, into the slides of a presentation. PowerPoint saves us a lot of time than to write down the tips on board using chalks or pens.

Topic 1 Publication Presentation

Procedure

For creating a publication presentation, follow the below mentioned steps:

Step 1 Open the MS- PowerPoint 2007 presentation by clicking on Start button → All Programs → Microsoft Office → Microsoft Office PowerPoint 2007

Step 2 Under the **Design** tab, from the **Themes** group select the **Concourse** theme for the entire presentation

For Slide 1

Step 1 Select the **Insert** tab, under the **Illustrations** group click on **Picture icon** and select the desired picture from the **Insert Picture** dialog box.

Step 2 Then, resize the picture, so that it can occupy the whole slide.

For Slide 2 and 3

Step 1 Under **Home** tab from the **Slides** group, click on **New Slide.**

Step 2 Type the title and contents according to the shown Slides 2 and 3.

For Slide 4

Step 1 Under **Home** tab, from the **Slides** group, click on **New Slide.**

Step 2 Select the **Insert** tab, under the **Illustrations** group click on **Picture** icon and select the desired picture from the **Insert Picture** dialog box.

Step 3 Then, resize the picture, so that it can occupy as bullet in slide.

Step 4 Type the title and content according to the Slide 4.

For Slide 5 and 6

Step 1 Under **Home** tab, from the **Slides** group, click on **New Slide.**

Step 2 Type the title and contents according to the shown Slides 5 and 6.

Topic 1

Slide 1
arihant
SUCCESS AND NOTHING LESS

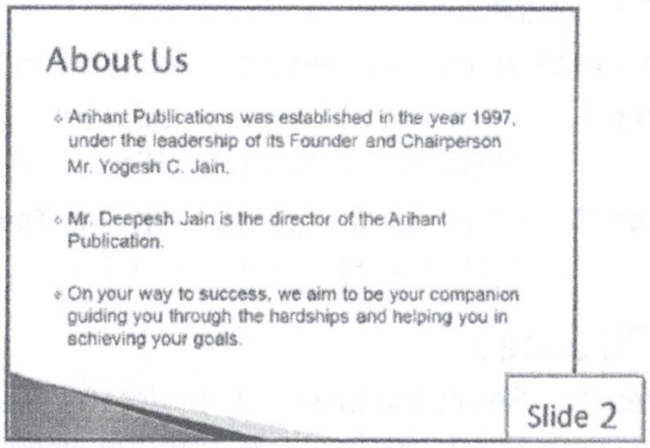
About Us
Arihant Publications was established in the year 1997, under the leadership of its Founder and Chairperson Mr. Yogesh C. Jain.
Mr. Deepesh Jain is the director of the Arihant Publication.
On your way to success, we aim to be your companion guiding you through the hardships and helping you in achieving your goals.
Slide 2

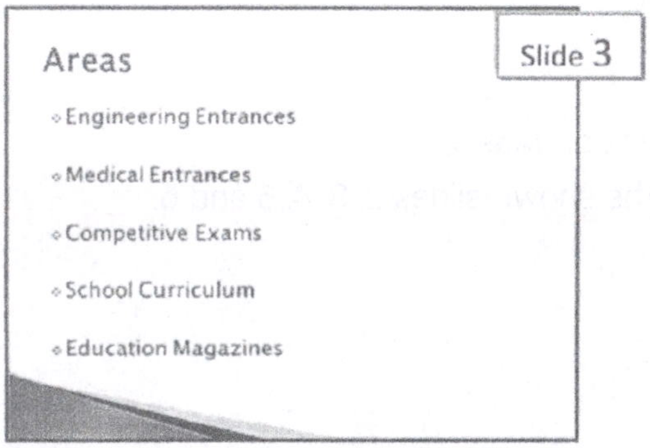
Areas
Slide 3
Engineering Entrances
Medical Entrances
Competitive Exams
School Curriculum
Education Magazines

Awards & Recognition
Received Best Publisher Award from honorable Chief Minister of Madhya Pradesh, Mr. Shivraj Singh Chauhan in Bhopal in 2017.
Received Best Publisher Award by Times of India in 2017.
Received Best Publisher Award by Delhi Pustak Vikreta Hitkari Sangh in 2016.
Received Young Publisher Award by FEPI (Federation of Education Publishers of India) in 2014.
Slide 4

Sales & support Offices
Slide 5
Agra
Ahmadabad
Bengaluru
Bhubaneswar
Bareilly
Chennai
Delhi
Guwahati
Haldwani
Hyderabad
Jaipur
Jalandhar
Jhansi
Kolkata
Kota
Lucknow
Meerut
Nagpur
Pune

Contact Us
Head Office
Kalindi, TP Nagar, Meerut (UP) - 250002
Tel: 0121 - 2401479, 2512970, 4004199
Fax: 0121 - 2401648
Corporate Office
Ramchhaya 4577/15, Agarwal Road, Darya Ganj, New Delhi - 110002
Tel. 011 - 47630600, 43518550
Fax: 011 - 23280316
Slide 6

Topic 2 Social Media Presentation

Procedure

For creating a social media presentation, follow the below mentioned steps:

Step 1 Open The MS - PowerPoint 2007 presentation by clicking on **Start** button → **All Programs** → **Microsoft Office** → **Microsoft Office PowerPoint 2007**

Step 2 Under the **Design** tab, from the **Themes** group, select the **Solstice** theme for the entire presentation.

FOR Slide 1

Step 1 Select the **Insert** tab, under the **Illustrations** group click on **Picture** icon, and select the desired picture from the **Insert Picture** dialog box.

Step 2 Then, resize the picture, so that it can occupy the whole slide.

Step 3 Type the title according to the shown Slide 1.

FOR Slide 2, 3, 4, 5 and 6

Step 1 Under **Home** tab, from the **Slides** group, click on **New Slide.**

Step 2 Type the title and contents according to the shown slides 2, 3, 4, 5 and 6.

Topic 2

Slide 1

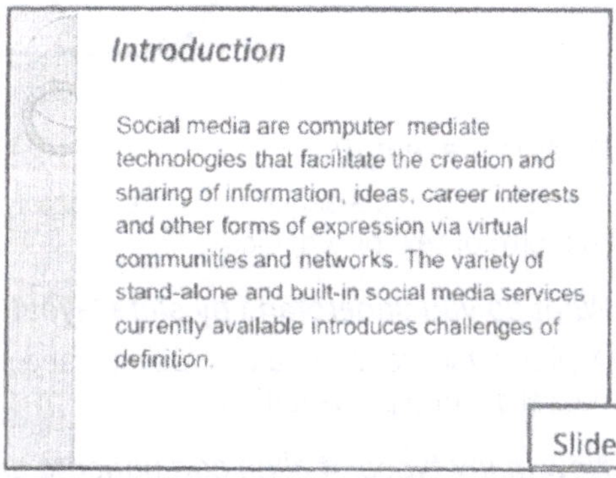

Slide 2

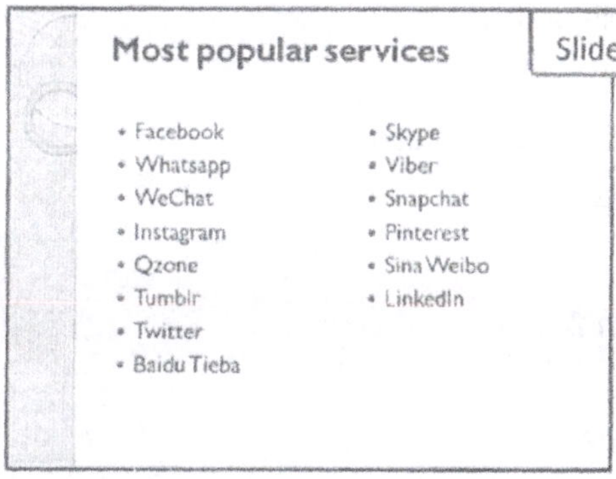

Slide 3

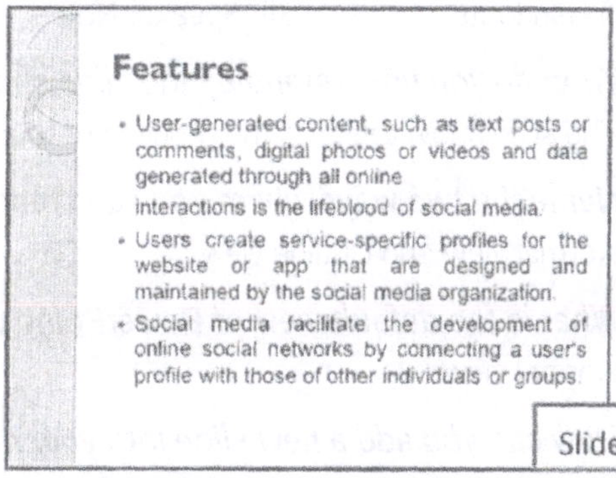

Slide 4

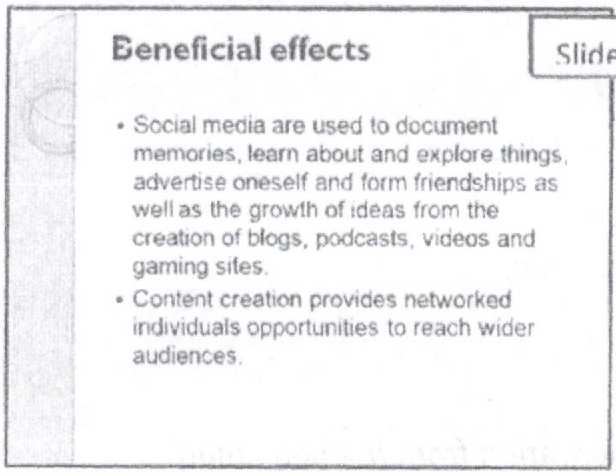

Slide 5

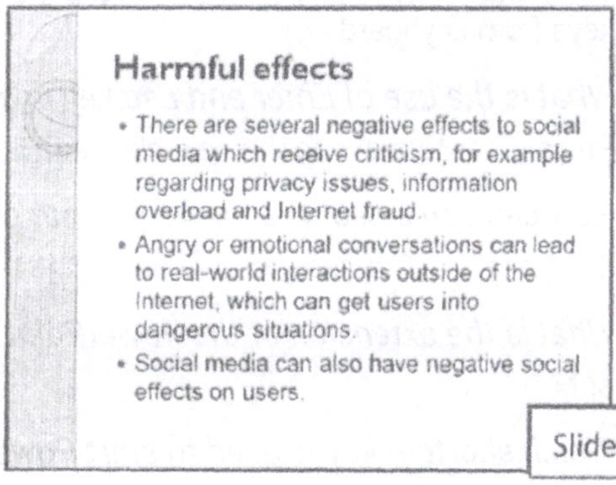

Slide 6

VIVA VOCE

1. ***What is presentation?***

Ans. A presentation is a sequential collection of slides in which each slide displays some information in the form of text or graphics.

2. ***What do you understand by slide layout?***

Ans. A slide layout refers to a pre–defined and organised set of slide elements that helps in creating a new slide for a presentation.

3. ***How many types of slide components are used for referencing purposes in PowerPoint?***

Ans. (i) Handouts (ii) Speaker Notes (iii) Outlines

4. ***What do you understand by the slide show?***

Ans. The slide show refers to the process of running an electronic presentation.

5. ***Name the two ways where you can create a presentation?***

Ans. Normal view and Outline view

6. ***What is the default view of PowerPoint presentation ?***

Ans. Normal view

7. ***How can you add a new slide into your presentation ?***

Ans. Either under **Home** tab, from the **Slides** group, click on **New Slide** option or press Ctrl+M shortcut keys from keyboard.

8. ***What is the use of Enter and Esc key in a slide show?***

Ans. Press Enter to move to the next slide and Esc to close the slide show.

9. ***How can you select the theme for your presentation ?***

Ans. Design tab → Themes group → select the theme that you want.

10. ***What is the extension of the PowerPoint presentation ?***

Ans. .pptx

11. ***Which shortcut key is used to start PowerPoint presentation from the beginning?***

Ans. F5

12. ***From which page, it is possible for you to choose slide designs?***

Ans. Layout

13. ***What is the default file name for the PowerPoint presentation ?***

Ans. Presentation1

14. ***A set of predefined formats of text or color scheme is called what ?***

Ans. Theme

15. ***The entire presentation can be seen at a time in which view ?***

Ans. Slide Sorter view

Abbreviation

ALU Arithmetic Logic Unit

AMLCD Active Matrix Liquid Crystal Display

ASCII American Standard Code for Information Interchange

ATV Associated Television

BASIC Beginner's All Purpose Symbolic Instruction Code

BCD Binary Coded Decimal

BD Blu-ray Disc

BD-R Blu-ray Disc Recordable

BD-RE Blu-ray Disc Rewritable

BD-ROM Blu-ray Disc Read Only Memory

BIOS Basic Input Output System

BOSS Bharat Operating System Solutions

CAD Computer Aided Design

CAM Computer Aided Manufacturing

CD Compact Disc

C-DAC Centre for Development of Advanced Computing

CD-R Compact Disc Recordable

CD-ROM Compact Disc Read Only Memory

CD-RW Compact Disc Rewritable

CLI Command Line Interface

CPS Characters Per Second

CPU Central Processing Unit

CRS Central/Computer Reservation System

CRT Cathode Ray Tube

CT Communication Technology

CU Control Unit

CUI Character User Interface

DBMS DataBase Management System

DDR SDRAM Double Data Rate Synchronous Dynamic Random Access Memory

DRAM Dynamic Random Access Memory

DSL Digital Subscriber Line

DTP Desktop Publishing

DVD Digital Video/Versatile Disc

DVD-R Digital Video/Versatile Disc - Recordable

DVD-ROM Digital Video/Versatile Disc - Read Only Memory

DVD-RW Digital Video/Versatile Disc - Rewritable

EB Exabyte

EDORAM Extended Data Out Random Access Memory

EEPROM Electrically Erasable Programmable Read Only Memory

E-Commerce Electronic Commerce

E-Mail Electronic Mail

EPROM Erasable Programmable Read Only Memory

FDD Floppy Disk Drive

FoIP Fax over Internet Protocol

FTP File Transmission Protocol

GB Gigabyte

Gbps Giga bits per second

GHz Giga Hertz

GNU General Public License

GUI Graphical User Interface

HDD Hard Disk Drive

HLL High Level Language

HRM Human Resource Management

IC Integrated Chip/Circuit

ICR Intelligent Character Recognition

ICT Information and Communication Technology

IP Internet Protocol

IPR Intellectual Property Right

ISP Internet Service Provider

IT Information Technology

JPEG Joint Photographic Expert Group

KB Kilobyte

KHz Kilo Hertz

LAN Local Area Network

LCD Liquid Crystal Display

LED Liquid/Light Emitting Diode

LLL Low Level Language

LSI Large Scale Integration

MAN Metropolitan Area Network

Mbps Mega bits per second

MB Megabyte

ME Millennium Edition

MHz Mega Hertz

MICR Magnetic Ink Character Recognition

MIDI Musical Instrument Digital Interface

MMS	Multimedia Messaging Service
MODEM	Modulator Demodulator
MP3	MPEG Audio Player III
MPEG	Motion Picture Expert Group
MS-DOS	Microsoft Disk Operating System
MSE	Microsoft Security Essentials
NT	New Technology
NIC	Network Interface Card
OCR	Optical Character Recognition
OMR	Optical Mark Reader/Recognition
OS	Operating System
PAN	Personal Area Network
PDAs	Personal Digital Assistance
PNG	Portable Network Graphics
PB	Petabyte
PC	Personal Computer
PDF	Portable Document Format
PPM	Pages Per Minute
PROM	Programmable Read Only Memory
RAM	Random Access Memory
ROM	Read Only Memory
RTF	Rich Text Format
SD	Super Density
SDRAM	Synchronous Dynamic Random Access Memory
SMS	Short Message Service
SRAM	Static Random Access Memory
STP	Shielded Twisted Pair
SVG	Scalable Vector Graphics
TB	Terabyte
TFT	Thin Film Transistor
URL	Uniform Resource Locator
USB	Universal Serial Bus
VDU	Visual Display Unit
VGA	Video Graphics Array
VIRUS	Vital Information Resources Under Siege
VLSI	Very Large Scale Integration
VoIP	Voice over Internet Protocol
VoWi-Fi	Voice over Wireless Fidelity
WAN	Wide Area Network
WiMax	World Wide Interoperability for Microwave Access
WLAN	Wireless Local Area Network
Wi-Fi	Wireless Fidelity
WINDOWS	Wide Interactive Network for Development Office Work Solution
WVoIP	Wireless Voice over Internet Protocol
WWW	World Wide Web
WYSIWYG	What You See Is What You Get
XP	eXPerience
YB	Yottabyte
ZB	Zettabyte

Glossary

A

Accessories A folder located in the Start menu in Windows operating environment. It contains useful mini applications.

Access time The time gap between the time stored information in computer is requested and the time it is delivered.

ALU A part of CPU that generally forms functions of (usually) two input values and produces a single output result.

ASCII Code A standard character encoding scheme introduced in 1963 is widely used on many machines. It is a 7-bit code.

Applications A program (as a Word processor or a Spreadsheet) that performs one of the major tasks for which a computer is used.

Application Software Any software that is specific to the particular role which a computer performs.

Active Cell It is a selected cell in which data is entered when you start typing. This cell is bounded by a heavy black border.

Analog Signal It is a continuous wave form that changes smoothly over time.

Attenuation During transmission, the signal strength is reduced this phenomenon is called attenuation.

B

Backup Copy of computer data (as a file or the content of a hard drive).

Bandwidth A measurement of the ability of an electronic communications device or system (such as a computer network) to send and receive information.

Barcode A group of thick and thin lines that is placed on a product.

BCD A system of writing decimal digits in their 4-digit binary equivalents.

Bluetooth It is a wireless technology standard for exchanging data over short distances.

Broadband Connection It is a high-speed Internet connection.

C

Cache Either a reserved section of main memory or an independent high-speed storage device.

Ciphertext Result of encryption performed on plaintext using an algorithm.

Commands It is a very specific instruction to a computer to perform some kind of action.

Communication Activity of exchanging information.

Compression Reduction in size of data in order to save space or transmission time.

Computer Program Sequence of instructions written to perform a specified task with a computer.

Computer Virus Program or piece of code that is loaded into your computer without your knowledge and runs against your wishes.

Cell A box formed by the intersection of a row and column which gives a unique address in a worksheet or a table, in which you enter information is called a cell.

Communication Channel A medium through which a message is transmitted to its intended receiver.

Communication Technology It is the hardware equipment, organisation structure and social values by which individual collects process and exchange information with other individuals.

Copyright It is a legal right created by the law of a country that grants the creator of an original work exclusive rights to its use and distribution, usually for a limited time.

D

Data Information in raw or unorganised form.

Database Collection of information in easily accessible manner.

Database Administrator (DBA) A person who is responsible for managing many aspects of a database including archiving, performance, security, testing and other tasks.

Deadlock A situation in which two computer programs sharing the same resource are effectively preventing each other from accessing the resource.

Device Driver A program that controls a particular type of device that is attached to your computer.

Dial-up Connection Uses a standard phone line and modem to access the Internet at data transfer rate of upto 56 Kbps.

Digital Signal It is a discrete waveform, having values 1 and 0 only.

Domain Name Unique name that identifies an Internet resource.

Domain Name System (DNS) Hierarchical distributed naming system for any resource connected to the Internet.

Download Copy from server computer over the Internet.

DTP Software Software which is used to generate layouts and produce typographic quality text and images comparable to traditional typography and printing.

E

E-Banking Method of banking in which the customer conduct transactions electronically *via* Internet.

E-Commerce Buying and selling of goods and services over an electronic network, primarily the Internet.

E-Learning Use of electronic educational technology in learning and teaching.

E-Mail Electronic method of sending and receiving messages.

E-Reservation Reservation *via* Internet.

E-Shopping Form of electronic commerce which allows consumers to directly buy goods or services from a seller over the Internet.

Ethernet Cable It is a popular type of network cable used for high speed networking between two devices.

F

Fibre-Optic Communication media which uses fibre or glass to transmit data.

File Manager A computer program that provides a user interface to manage files and folders.

Firmware Software that is written onto Read Only Memory (ROM).

FoIP Process of sending and receiving faxes *via* a VoIP network.

FTP Protocol which is used to transfer files between server and client.

Full Duplex Mode In this mode, data can flow in both directions at the same time.

G

Graphic Designer It is an art that involves a creative and systematic plan to solve a problem or achieve certain objectives with the use of images, symbols or even words.

GUI Human computer interface, that uses Windows, icons and menus which can be manipulated by a mouse.

H

Hardware Physical components that make up a computer system.

Heuristics Learning from past experiences.

HyperText Text that links to other information.

Half Duplex Mode In this mode, data can flow in both directions but only in one direction at a time.

Hard Disk Loading Installing an illegal copy of software on the hard disk of a personal computer is called hard disk loading.

Header and Footer It is a text or graphics that is usually printed at the top or bottom of every page in a document.

I

IC Sometimes called a chip or a microchip, is a semiconductor wafer on which thousands of tiny resistors, capacitors and transistors are fabricated.

ICT It refers to technologies that provide access to information through telecommunications. It is similar to Information Technology (IT), but focuses primarily on communication technologies.

Information Facts provided or learned about something or someone.

Information Technology It is broad, encompassing all forms of technology that involves any form of electronic data.

Input Something put into a system or expended in its operation to achieve output or a result.

Interface A device or a program enabling a user to communicate with a computer.

Internet Global system of interconnected computer networks.

IP address Numerical address assigned to each device participating in a computer network.

J

Job A unit of work that a computer operator gives to an operating system.

K

Kernel Central module of an operating system.

Knowledge Information after being transformed into some conceptual framework so that it can be manipulated and used cognitively is known as knowledge.

L

Laser It is used to transmit the signal similar to fibre optic link, except the beam is transmitted through free space.

Line-of-sight It is a type of propagation that can transmit and receive data only where transmit and receive stations are in view of each other without any sort of an obstacle between them.

Local Area Network (LAN) It is a computer network that spans a relatively small area. Most LANs are confined to a single building or group of building.

M

Metropolitan Area Network (MAN) It is a computer network larger than a local area network, covering an area of a few city blocks to the area of an entire city.

MODEM Combined device for modulation and demodulation.

Monitor A device that displays signals on a computer screen.

Motherboard It is a sheet of plastic that holds all the circuitry to connect the various components of a computer system.

Multimedia Combination of different media like text, image, video, graphics, audio and animation.

N

Network Group of two or more computers linked together to exchange information.

Network Administrator It is a person who manages the LAN of an organisation.

O

Operating System A software that supports a computer's basic functions, such as scheduling tasks and controlling peripherals.

Output Anything that comes out of a computer.

P

PDF A file format for capturing and sending electronic documents in exactly the intended format.

Pointing Device Used to control the movement of a cursor on a computer screen.

Process A series of actions that produce something or that led to a particular result.

Programmer A person who writes computer programs.

Presentation It is the process of presenting a topic to an audience. It is typically a demonstration, lecture or speech meant to inform, persuade or build good will.

Privacy It is related to personal information right to privacy refers to the concept that one's personal information is protected from public scrutiny.

R

Register A special, high speed storage area within the CPU.

Resolution Number of pixels contained on a display monitor.

Repeater It is a device that is used to expand boundaries of a wired or wireless LAN.

Router It is a device that forward data packets along networks. A router is connected to atleast two networks.

S

Server Computer or computer program which manages access to centralised resource or service in a network.

Smartphone A mobile phone that performs many of the functions of a computer, typically having a touchscreen interface, Internet access, and an operating system capable of running downloaded apps.

Social Networking Sites Online platforms that allow users to create a public profile and interact with other users on the Website.

Software Set of instructions or programs.

Storage A place where data is held in an electromagnetic or optical form for access by a computer processor.

Simplex Mode In this mode, data can flow in only one direction.

Slide It is a single page of presentation created with the software such as PowerPoint, OpenOffice.org Impress etc.

Switch It is a device that channels incoming data from any of multiple input ports to the specific output port that will take the data toward its intended destination.

T

Technology The application of science or knowledge into practical use to solve problems or invent useful tools.

Telecommunication Communication over a distance by cable, telegraph, telephone or broadcasting.

Text Wrapping Surrounding a picture or diagram with text.

Thread A part of program that can execute independently of other parts.

Track Changes It is used while making changes in an already created document for the purpose of keeping track of the changes that are made to that original document.

U

Uploading and Downloading Creating duplicate copies of the licensed software or uploading and downloading it from the Internet.

URL It is the global address of documents and other resources on the WWW.

User Friendly Easy to use, operate and understand.

User Interface The means by which the user and a computer system interact in particular the use of input devices and software.

Utility Auxiliary program that performs a specific, useful function to maintain or raise the efficiency of a computer system.

V

Video Conferencing Conference between two or more participants at different sites by using computer networks to transmit audio and video data.

Visual Communication Communication through a visual aid and the conveyance of ideas and information in forms that can be read or looked upon.

Visual Display Unit A device with a screen that displays characters or graphics representing data in computer memory.

VoIP It is a technology that allows you to make voice calls using a broadband connection.

W

Web Address Internet address of a Website, file or document. It is also known as URL.

Web Browser Software for retrieving, presenting and traversing information resources on WWW.

Web Page Web document that is suitable for the WWW and the Web browser.

Website Set of related Web pages typically, served from a single Web domain.

Wi-Fi It is a local area wireless technology that allows an electronic device to exchange data or connect to the Internet using radio waves.

Windows Series of operating systems developed by Microsoft.

Wireless Connection Connection establishes using wireless technology.

Word Processor Program or machine for storing, manipulating and formatting text entered from a keyboard and providing a printout.

WWW It is a system of interlinked hypertext document.

Wired (or guided or bounded) **Media** It is the transmission media in which signals are confined to a specific path wire or cable.

Wireless (or unguided or unbounded) **Media** In this media, no cables are required to guide the media.

Wisdom Capacity to choose when and how to use information.

WLAN A Wireless Local Area Network (WLAN) is a wireless distribution method for two or more devices that use high-frequency radiowave.

Workbook A spreadsheet program file that you create in Excel is called a workbook.

Worksheet It contains various cell formed by rows and columns.

Assertion & Reason Questions

CHAPTER – 1

Directions: *In the following questions, A statement of Assertion (A) is followed by a statement of Reason (R). Mark the correct choice as*

(a) Both A and R are true and R is the correct explanation of A.
(b) Both A and R are true but R is not the correct explanation of A.
(c) A is true but R is false.
(d) A is false and R is true.

1. **Assertion (A)** Memory unit is an essential component of a computer system.
Reason (R) The memory unit stores program instructions and data temporarily.

Ans. (a) Both A and R are true and R is the correct explanation of A.

2. **Assertion (A)** The Control Unit (CU) is responsible for fetching instructions from memory and interpreting them.
Reason (R) The Control Unit (CU) is the component of the CPU that manages the flow of data between the CPU and other devices in the computer.

Ans. (a) Both A and R are true and R is the correct explanation of A.

3. **Assertion (A)** The Control Unit of a computer system is responsible for controlling and coordinating the activities of all other components.
Reason (R) The Control Unit receives instructions from memory and executes them by coordinating with other components of the computer system.

Ans. (a) Both A and R are true and R is the correct explanation of A.

4. **Assertion (A)** A computer system can only understand binary language.
Reason (R) The computer hardware is designed to work with binary signals.

Ans. (a) Both A and R are true and R is the correct explanation of A.

5. **Assertion (A)** The Central Processing Unit (CPU) is the brain of the computer system.
Reason (R) The CPU performs all the arithmetic and logical operations, as well as controls the flow of data within the computer system.

Ans. (a) Both A and R are true and R is the correct explanation of A.

CHAPTER – 2

Directions *In the following questions, A statement of Assertion (A) is followed by a statement of Reason (R). Mark the correct choice as*

(a) Both A and R are true and R is the correct explanation of A.
(b) Both A and R are true but R is not the correct explanation of A.
(c) A is true but R is false.
(d) A is false and R is true.

1. **Assertion (A)** Computer software is a set of instructions that tell a computer what to do.
Reason (R) Computer hardware is useless without software.

Ans. (b) Computer software is a set of instructions or programs that are designed to run on computer hardware to perform specific tasks. Without software, hardware cannot perform any tasks, making it useless. Therefore, both the assertion and reason are true and valid.

2. **Assertion (A)** Debugging is an important step in the software development process.
Reason (R) Debugging helps to identify and remove errors in the code.

Ans. (a) Both A and R are true and R is the correct explanation of A.

3. **Assertion (A)** The primary function of computer software is to provide instructions to the computer to perform specific tasks.

Reason(R) Computer software is a set of programs, procedures, and associated documentation that tells a computer what to do.

Ans. (a) Both A and R are true and R is the correct explanation of A.

4. **Assertion (A)** The purpose of software is to enable the hardware to perform specific tasks.

Reason (R) Software consists of a set of instructions that tell the hardware what to do.

Ans. (a) Both A and R are true and R is the correct explanation of A.

CHAPTER – 3

***Directions** In the following questions, A statement of Assertion (A) is followed by a statement of Reason (R). Mark the correct choice as*

(a) Both A and R are true and R is the correct explanation of A.
(b) Both A and R are true but R is not the correct explanation of A.
(c) A is true but R is false.
(d) A is false and R is true.

1. **Assertion (A)** The operating system is the most essential software for a computer.

Reason (R) It manages all the hardware and software resources of the computer.

Ans. (b) Both A and R are true but R is not the correct explanation of A.

2. **Assertion (A)** The process management system is responsible for managing input/output operations in an operating system.

Reason (R) Input/output operations are crucial for the proper functioning of any computer system.

Ans. (d) The process management system is responsible for managing the execution of processes, allocating system resources to them, and ensuring their proper functioning. Input/output operations are managed by the input/output management system, which is a separate component of the operating system. It is responsible for managing the input/output operations of the computer system and ensuring that they are performed efficiently. Hence, A is false and R is true.

3. **Assertion (A)** An operating system is necessary to run any application on a computer.

Reason (R) An operating system provides a platform for the application to run on.

Ans. (a) Both A and R are true and R is the correct explanation of A.

4. **Assertion (A)** The file management system is an essential component of an operating system.

Reason (R) The file management system helps to store, retrieve, and manage data efficiently.

Ans. (a) Both A and R are true and R is the correct explanation of A.

5. **Assertion (A)** Multiprogramming is a technique used by operating systems to increase the CPU utilization.

Reason (R) In multiprogramming, the operating system runs multiple programs concurrently, which increases the CPU utilization.

Ans. (a) Both A and R are true and R is the correct explanation of A.

CHAPTER – 4

***Directions:** In the following questions, A statement of Assertion (A) is followed by a statement of Reason (R). Mark the correct choice as*

(a) Both A and R are true and R is the correct explanation of A.
(b) Both A and R are true but R is not the correct explanation of A.
(c) A is true but R is false.
(d) A is false and R is true.

1. **Assertion (A)** Bluetooth is a wireless communication technology used for short-range communication.

Reason (R) Bluetooth uses low-power radio waves to communicate between devices.

Ans. (a) Both A and R are true and R is the correct explanation of A.

2. **Assertion (A)** Communication technology has revolutionized the way we communicate.

   Reason (R) Communication technology has made communication faster, easier, and more accessible than ever before.

Ans. (a) Both A and R are true and R is the correct explanation of A.

3. **Assertion (A)** One of the advantages of using communication technology is that it increases efficiency in business operations.

   Reason (R) Communication technology allows for faster and more accurate transfer of information between different departments in a business.

Ans. (a) Both A and R are true and R is the correct explanation of A.

4. **Assertion (A)** Communication technology refers to the tools, systems, and applications used to exchange information and ideas between individuals or groups.

   Reason (R) Communication technology includes various forms of electronic communication such as emails, social media, instant messaging, and video conferencing.

Ans. (a) Both A and R are true and R is the correct explanation of A.

CHAPTER – 5

***Directions:** In the following questions, A statement of Assertion (A) is followed by a statement of Reason (R). Mark the correct choice as*

(a) Both A and R are true and R is the correct explanation of A.
(b) Both A and R are true but R is not the correct explanation of A.
(c) A is true but R is false.
(d) A is false and R is true.

1. **Assertion (A)** A printer is an output device.

   Reason (R) A printer converts digital data into printed format.

Ans. (a) Both A and R are true and R is the correct explanation of A.

2. **Assertion (A)** The keyboard is an input device.

   Reason (R) It is used to enter data into the computer.

Ans. (a) Both A and R are true and R is the correct explanation of A.

3. **Assertion (A)** A virus is a type of software.

   Reason (R) It is designed to damage or disrupt computer systems.

Ans. (b) Both A and R are true but R is Not the correct explanation of A

4. **Assertion (A)** The monitor is an output device.

   Reason (R) It displays the processed data.

Ans. (a) Both A and R are true and R is the correct explanation of A.

CHAPTER – 6

***Directions:** In the following questions, A statement of Assertion (A) is followed by a statement of Reason (R). Mark the correct choice as*

(a) Both A and R are true and R is the correct explanation of A.
(b) Both A and R are true but R is not the correct explanation of A.
(c) A is true but R is false.
(d) A is false and R is true.

1. **Assertion (A)** Using strong and unique passwords is an important cyber security practice.

   Reason (R) Weak passwords can be easily guessed or hacked by cyber criminals.

Ans. (a) Both A and R are true and R is the correct explanation of A.

2. **Assertion (A)** Phishing attacks are a common method used by cyber criminals to obtain sensitive information.

Reason (R) Phishing emails often appear to be legitimate emails from a trustworthy source.

Ans. (a) Both A and R are true and R is the correct explanation of A.

3. **Assertion (A)** It is important to use strong passwords to protect your online accounts.

Reason (R) Hackers can easily guess weak passwords, leaving your accounts vulnerable to attack.

Ans. (c) Strong passwords are important to protect your online accounts because hackers can easily guess weak passwords using automated tools. Hence, A is true but R is false.

4. **Assertion (A)** Using public Wi-Fi networks can be risky.

Reason (R) Cyber criminals can intercept the data you send and receive over public Wi-Fi networks.

Ans. (a) Both A and R are true and R is the correct explanation of A.

5. **Assertion (A)** You should always keep your anti-virus software up to date.

Reason (R) Anti-virus software can protect your computer from malware and other types of cyber threats.

Ans. (a) Both A and R are true and R is the correct explanation of A.

CHAPTER – 7

Directions: *In the following questions, A statement of Assertion (A) is followed by a statement of Reason (R). Mark the correct choice as*

(a) Both A and R are true and R is the correct explanation of A.
(b) Both A and R are true but R is not the correct explanation of A.
(c) A is true but R is false.
(d) A is false and R is true.

1. **Assertion (A)** The "Save As" feature in MS-Word allows users to save a document with a different name or in a different location.

Reason (R) This feature is useful when users want to create multiple versions of the same document or save a copy of the document in a different folder or on a different device.

Ans. (a) Both A and R are true and R is the correct explanation of A.

2. **Assertion (A)** In MS-Word, the shortcut key for saving a document is Ctrl+S.

Reason (R) Using the shortcut key saves time and effort.

Ans. (a) Both A and R are true and R is the correct explanation of A.

3. **Assertion (A)** Using page breaks in MS-Word allows users to control the flow of text and graphics in a document.

Reason (R) MS-Word does not allow users to insert section breaks to format different parts of a document differently.

Ans. (d) A is false and R is true because page breaks to control where a page ends and where a new page begins.

4. **Assertion (A)** The undo and redo buttons in MS-Word are used to correct mistakes made while typing a document.

Reason (R) The undo and redo buttons allow the user to undo or redo the last action performed.

Ans. (a) Both A and R are true and R is the correct explanation of A.

CHAPTER – 8

***Directions:** In the following questions, A statement of Assertion (A) is followed by a statement of Reason (R). Mark the correct choice as*

(a) Both A and R are true and R is the correct explanation of A.
(b) Both A and R are true but R is not the correct explanation of A.
(c) A is true but R is false.
(d) A is false and R is true.

1. **Assertion (A)** Bullets and numbering is used to make a list in MS-Word.
   Reason (R) Bullets and numbering helps to make the text more readable and organized.

Ans. (a) Both A and R are true and R is the correct explanation of A.

2. **Assertion (A)** MS-Word allows users to create and edit professional documents efficiently.
   Reason (R) MS-Word provides advanced formatting features, such as styles, themes, and templates.

Ans. (a) Both A and R are true and R is the correct explanation of A.

3. **Assertion (A)** Using tables in MS-Word makes it easier to organize and present information.
   Reason (R) MS-Word does not allow users to format tables or change their design.

Ans. (c) A is true but R is false because MS-Word allow users to format tables or change their design.

4. **Assertion (A)** MS-Word allows users to track changes and collaborate with others on the same document.
   Reason (R) MS-Word does not allow users to restrict editing permissions for different users.

Ans. (b) Both A and R are true but R is not the correct explanation of A.

CHAPTER – 9

***Directions:** In the following questions, A statement of Assertion (A) is followed by a statement of Reason (R). Mark the correct choice as*

(a) Both A and R are true and R is the correct explanation of A.
(b) Both A and R are true but R is not the correct explanation of A.
(c) A is true but R is false.
(d) A is false and R is true.

1. **Assertion (A)** Adding images to a PowerPoint presentation makes it more engaging and visually appealing.
   Reason (R) Images can help convey information more effectively than text alone.

Ans. (a) Both A and R are true and R is the correct explanation of A.

2. **Assertion (A)** MS-PowerPoint is a presentation software used for creating professional presentations.
   Reason (R) It provides various tools and features that make it easy to create, design, and deliver presentations.

Ans. (a) Both A and R are true and R is the correct explanation of A.

3. **Assertion (A)** MS-PowerPoint is a better tool for creating text documents than MS-Word.
   Reason (R) MS-Word provides advanced formatting features, such as styles, themes, and templates.

Ans. (d) Assertion is false and Reason is true. MS-PowerPoint is a presentation software and is not designed for creating text documents. MS-Word, on the other hand, is a word processing software and is specifically designed for creating text documents. MS-Word provides more advanced formatting options than MS-PowerPoint for text documents.

4. **Assertion (A)** MS-PowerPoint allows users to add multimedia elements to their presentations.
   Reason (R) Adding multimedia elements to a presentation makes it more engaging and interactive.

Ans. (a) Both A and R are true and R is the correct explanation of A.

CHAPTER – 10

Directions: *In the following questions, A statement of Assertion (A) is followed by a statement of Reason (R). Mark the correct choice as*

(a) Both A and R are true and R is the correct explanation of A.
(b) Both A and R are true but R is not the correct explanation of A.
(c) A is true but R is false.
(d) A is false and R is true.

1. **Assertion (A)** The use of spreadsheets in business is increasing day by day.
Reason (R) Spreadsheets provide a simple and efficient way to organize, analyze, and manipulate large amounts of data.

Ans. (a) Both A and R are true and R is the correct explanation of A.

2. **Assertion (A)** MS-Excel is a spreadsheet application used for creating and managing data.
Reason (R) MS-Excel allows users to perform complex calculations and data analysis.

Ans. (a) Both A and R are true and R is the correct explanation of A.

3. **Assertion (A)** Conditional formatting is a feature in MS-Excel that allows users to apply formatting to cells based on specific conditions.
Reason (R) Conditional formatting can be applied to any type of data in MS-Excel.

Ans. (b) Both A and R are true but R is not the correct explanation of A.

4. **Assertion (A)** MS-Excel allows users to create charts and graphs to visually represent data.
Reason (R) Charts and graphs can only be created in MS-Excel using pre-existing templates.

Ans. (c) While the assertion is true, the reason is false. Charts and graphs can be created in MS-Excel using pre-existing templates or by manually selecting and formatting the data to create a custom chart or graph.

5. **Assertion (A)** MS-Excel allows users to perform what-if analysis by changing values in a worksheet and seeing the resulting changes in calculated values.
Reason (R) What-if analysis can only be performed in MS-Excel using macros.

Ans. (c) While the assertion is true, the reason is false. What-if analysis can be performed in MS-Excel using built-in tools such as Goal Seek and Scenario Manager, and macros are not required.

ASSERTION & REASON QUESTIONS

SAMPLE QUESTION PAPER 1

A Sample Question Paper for CBSE Class 9th

Computer Applications

Instructions

1. This question paper has 5 Sections A-E.
2. All questions are compulsory. However, internal choices have been provided in some of the questions.
3. Section A has 12 questions carrying 1 mark each.
4. Section B has 7 Short Answer (SA-I) type questions carrying 2 marks each.
5. Section C has 4 Short Answer (SA-II) type questions carrying 3 marks each.
6. Section D has 1 Long Answer (LA) type question carrying 4 marks.
7. Section E has 2 Source-based/Case-based/Passage-based questions carrying 4 marks each.

Time : 2 hours ***Max. Marks : 50***

FULLY SOLVED

Section A

$(12 \times 1 = 12)$

1. Interactive combination of text, graphics, images, audio, video etc., is known as
(a) data (b) information (c) multimedia (d) internet

2. We can underline the text by
(a) Ctrl+B (b) Ctrl+I (c) Ctrl+U (d) None of these

3. _________ is responsible for dividing a file or message into very small parts, at the source computer.
(a) TCP (b) IP (c) Both (a) and (b) (d) None of these

4. It is a grid of cells arranged in rows and columns.
(a) Row (b) Style sheet (c) Table (d) Sheet

5. _________ is not an example of worm.
(a) MS-Blaster (b) Sobig (c) De bumper (d) Melissa

6. It is responsible for all numerical and logical calculations.
(a) CPU (b) CU (c) MU (d) ALU

7. The sample of an Excel worksheet on the screen can be seen by
(a) Print preview (b) Print (c) Review (d) None of these

8. Interpreter converts a high level language program into a machine language by
(a) one go mechanism (b) line-by-line mechanism
(c) group of five lines mechanism (d) None of these

9. What is the shortcut key to display the Microsoft PowerPoint shortcut menu?
(a) F7 (b) F8 (c) Shift+F10 (d) F11

10. Suppose you have bought all hardware components required for assembling a computer. After assembling the computer system, which will be the very first software to be installed?
(a) Hardware driver (b) Operating system
(c) Antivirus software (d) Word processing software

Directions *Q.Nos. 11 and 12 are Assertion and Reason Types. Each question consists of two statements, namely Assertion (A) and Reason (R). Select the must suitable option considering the Assertion and Reason.*

11. **Assertion (A)** Using strong and unique passwords is an important cyber security practice.

Reason (R) Weak passwords can be easily guessed or hacked by cyber criminals.

(a) Both A and R are true and R is the correct explanation of A.
(b) Both A and R are true but R is not the correct explanation of A.
(c) A is true but R is false.
(d) A is false and R is true.

12. **Assertion (A)** Using page breaks in MS-Word allows users to control the flow of text and graphics in a document.

Reason (R) MS-Word does not allow users to insert section breaks to format different parts of a document differently.

(a) Both A and R are true and R is the correct explanation of A.
(b) Both A and R are true but R is not the correct explanation of A.
(c) A is true but R is false.
(d) A is false and R is true.

Section B

(7 × 2 = 14)

13. Name the memory (Primary/Secondary)with the following features:
(a) If current is interrupted, data is lost.
(b) Before a program is ready to run, the program is loaded into this memory, which allows the CPU directly access the program.

14. (a) Explain the main advantage and disadvantage of an OCR.
Or (b) Write two common level of abstraction for device driver include for hardware.

15. State whether the following statements are True or False:
(a) PAN (Personal Area Network) typically covers a large geographic area, like a city or a campus.
(b) A Local Area Network (LAN) connects devices over long distances, such as between cities.
(c) Bluetooth is a wireless communication technology that can be used for connecting devices like phones and headsets over short distances.
(d) Wi-Fi is a type of wired communication technology used for local area networks.

16. (a) Name any four basic elements of a slide.
Or (b) Differentiate between a presentation and a slide.

17. What is geotagging ?

18. (a) List the different types of computer viruses.
Or (b) Privacy deals with personal information. Explain the meaning of term personal information.

19. How do you locate MS-Word 2007 on your computer system?

Section C

(4 × 3 = 12)

20. Distinguish between compiler and interpreter.

21. State three functions of the Slides Pane.

22. (a) What is the difference between the Save and Save As option?
Or (b) How to insert the copyright symbol into a Word document?

23. Compare and contrast the two wireless transmission media; bluetooth and infrared.

FULLY SOLVED

Section D

(4)

24. (a) Carefully read the following descriptions and identify what is being talked about.

(i) It consists of two insulated wires twisted around each other, which provides protection against noise and crosstalk.

(ii) Disturbance caused due to interference of one signal's electric or magnetic field into other signals.

(iii) It is an omni-directional wireless transmission media. Its range lies between 300 KHz to 10 GHz.

(iv) Communication channel that is more secure, faster, easier to set-up but expensive for longer distances and devices once configured cannot be moved.

Or

(b) Reena got an assignment on the topic Word processing software. Help her to solve the assignment.

(i) What is Word processing software?

(ii) Which type of software is Word processor?

(iii) Give some examples equivalent to type of Word processing software.

(iv) Give some examples of Word processing program.

Section E

$(2 \times 4 = 8)$

(Case Study)

25. The computer has two parts-hardware and software. Hardware needs to be operated by a set of instructions. These sets of instructions are referred to as software. It is that component of a computer system, which we cannot touch or view physically. It comprises the instructions and data to be processed using the computer hardware. The computer software and hardware complete any task together. The software comprises a set of instructions which on execution deliver the desired outcome. In other words, each software is written for some computational purpose. Some examples of software include operating systems like Ubuntu or Windows 7/10, Word processing tool like LibreOffice or Microsoft Word, video player like VLC Player, photo editors like GIMP and LibreOffice draw. A document or image stored on the hard disk or pen drive is referred to as a soft copy. Once printed, the document or an image is called a hard copy.

Based on the above information answer the following question

(i) Hardware can work only with ....

(ii) The computer software cannot be .... physically.

(iii) Any task of the computer can be completed by .... and .... together.

(iv) .... is not an operating system software.

26. Based on the following information, answer the questions which follow:

Ravi is preparing for a school presentation on environmental conservation. He uses a presentation tool to create slides, adding titles, subtitles, text, and images. He also includes a background and some animations to make his presentation engaging. However, Ravi realizes that he forgot to insert slide numbers on his slides and didn't rehearse the timings for transitions between slides.

(i) Identify the key elements Ravi should have included in his presentation to make it complete, based on the features mentioned above.

(ii) Which feature of the presentation tool can be used to add numbers to the slides, as mentioned in the scenario?

(iii) How can Ravi ensure smooth transitions between slides and make his presentation more professional?

(iv) Suggest two things Ravi could do to make sure his classmates are aware of netiquettes when presenting online.

Answers

1. (*c*) Multimedia is a interactive combination of text, animations, sounds, images etc.
2. (*c*) Ctrl+U is the shortcut key for underlining the text.
3. (*a*) TCP part breaks the messages into smaller packets which are transmitted over the Internet.
4. (*c*) Table is a grid of cells arranged in rows and columns.
5. (*c*) De bumper is a type of trojan horse.
6. (*d*)ALU is a digital circuit in which numerical and logical operations are defined.
7. (*a*) Print preview enables you to view the sample of worksheet before printing it on a paper.
8. (*b*) Interpreter is a language processor, which converts the high level language program into machine language by using line-by-line mechanism.
9. (*c*) Shift + F10 is the shortcut key to display the PowerPoint shortcut menu.
10. (*b*) Operating system will be the very first software to be installed after assembling the computer system.
11. (*a*) Both A and R are true and R is the correct explanation of A.
12. (*c*) Assertion (A) is correct because page breaks in MS Word help users control where pages start, which allows for better organization of text and graphics.
    Reason (R) is false because MS Word does allow users to insert section breaks, which help in applying different formatting (like margins, page orientation, and headers/footers) to different parts of a document.
13. The memory described with given features is Primary Memory (specifically, RAM - Random Access Memory).
    Because,
    - Primary memory, like RAM, is volatile, meaning data is lost when power is cut off, which aligns with feature (a).
    - Before a program can run, it is loaded into the primary memory, allowing the CPU to directly access and execute its instructions, matching feature (b).
14. (a) The main advantage of an OCR is the ability to scan the characters accurately.
    The disadvantage of an OCR is limited number of characters offered by it.

    Or

    (b) (i) Interfacing directly
    (ii) Using another lower level device driver
15. (a) False (b) False (c) True (d) False
16. (a) The four basic elements of a slide are as follows
    (*i*) Titles (*ii*) Subtitles
    (*iii*) Drawing objects (*iv*) ClipArt

    Or

    (b) A presentation is a set of slides that you present to people in a group while each page of a PowerPoint presentation is called a slide.
17. Geotagging automatically shows your location from your smartphone.
18. (a) (*i*) File system viruses (*ii*) Boot sector viruses
    (*iii*) Macro viruses

    Or

    (b) Personal information is the information that identifies you or could identify you. e.g. your name, address etc.
19. To locate MS-Word on computer system:
    Click Start → All Programs → Microsoft Office → Microsoft Office Word 2007.
20. Refer to text on Page No. 30.
21. Three functions of the Slides Pane are as follows
    (*i*) New slides may be added to the presentation.
    (*ii*) Allows marking a slide as hidden for not showing it during a Slide Show.
    (*iii*) Deleting a slide from the presentation in case it is no longer needed.

FULLY SOLVED

22. (a) "Save" means the file gets saved under its current name, in whatever folder it was saved before or in the default folder of that computer, whereas "Save As" gives you the opportunity to save the file under a different name and in another folder. "Save As" allows you to name the updated version with a new name and at the same time preserving the old version.

Or

(b) Steps to insert the copyright symbol into a Word document are as follows:

Step 1 Select **Insert** tab.

Step 2 Click **Symbol** option from **Symbols** group.

Step 3 Select **More Symbols...** .

Step 4 The Symbol dialog box will appear and select the **copyright** symbol.

Step 5 Click the **Insert** button.

23. Bluetooth and Infrared both are short range wireless transmission media. This is the only point at which both these data transmission technologies look similar but there is a lot of differences between the two. Infrared is mostly used in TV remotes and there must be a direct line-of-sight between the transmitter and the receiver while on the other hand bluetooth uses a radio frequency which allows transmission through walls and other objects.

24. (a) (i) Twisted pair cable

(ii) Crosstalk

(iii) Radiowave

(iv) Wired communication channel

Or

(b) (i) Word processing software is an application software that helps to create text based documents. It also processes paragraphs, pages and entire papers.

(ii) General purpose application software.

(iii) Electronic spreadsheets, database management systems, desktop publishing software, graphics, multimedia and presentation applications.

(iv) Microsoft Word, WordPerfect (Windows only), AppleWorks (Mac only) and OpenOffice.org Writer.

25. (i) Instructions (ii) Touch (iii) Hardware, software (iv) MS-Word

26. (i) Ravi should have included slide numbers and rehearsed the transition timings.

(ii) The feature to add slide numbers is the "Insert Slide Number" option.

(iii) Ravi can ensure smooth transitions by setting automatic timings and using the "Transition" feature.

(iv) Ravi should use appropriate language and avoid distractions during the presentation.

SAMPLE QUESTION PAPER 2

A Sample Question Paper for CBSE Class 9th

Computer Applications

Instructions

1. This question paper has 5 Sections A-E.
2. All questions are compulsory. However, internal choices have been provided in some of the questions.
3. Section A has 12 questions carrying 1 mark each.
4. Section B has 7 Short Answer (SA-I) type questions carrying 2 marks each.
5. Section C has 4 Short Answer (SA-II) type questions carrying 3 marks each.
6. Section D has 1 Long Answer (LA) type question carrying 4 marks.
7. Section E has 2 Source-based/Case-based/Passage-based questions carrying 4 marks each.

Time : 2 hours ***Max. Marks : 50***

UNSOLVED

Section A

(12 × 1 = 12)

1. Data by itself is not useful unless
(a) it is massive
(b) it is processed to obtain information
(c) it is collected from diverse sources
(d) it is properly stated

2. User can also check the spelling and .... in a document.
(a) graphic (b) text (c) table (d) grammar

3. A modem is connected in between a telephone line and a
(a) computer (b) serial port (c) network (d) communication adapter

4. Which tab of MS-Word contains the Shapes option?
(a) Home (b) Review (c) Insert (d) Mailings

5. ....refers to the condition in which your computer stops working.
(a) Hang (b) Virus attack (c) Hacking (d) None of these

6. .... memory is used to store large amount of information permanently.
(a) RAM (b) ROM (c) Secondary (d) Primary

7. A cell range starting from first row, first column to fourth row and fifth column can be represented as
(a) [A1 : E4] (b) [A0 : E3] (c) [E4 : A1] (d) [E3 : A0]

8. Machine language sometimes referred to as
(a) programming language that is used widely by the programmer.
(b) machine code or object code
(c) programming language that is more easily understood
(d) language that is not limited by the computer

9. Which of the following views is useful for representing the structure of a presentation?
(a) Notes view (b) Outline view (c) Slide view (d) Normal view

10. .... reduces the Kernel code size and increases the security.
(a) Micro Kernel (b) Monolithic Kernel
(c) Both (a) and (b) (d) None of these

Directions *Q.Nos. 11 and 12 are Assertion and Reason Types. Each question consists of two statements, namely Assertion (A) and Reason (R). Select the must suitable option considering the Assertion and Reason.*

11. **Assertion (A)** MS-PowerPoint is a better tool for creating text documents than MS-Word.
Reason (R) MS-Word provides advanced formatting features, such as styles, themes, and templates.
(a) Both A and R are true and R is the correct explanation of A.
(b) Both A and R are true but R is not the correct explanation of A.
(c) A is true but R is false.
(d) A is false and R is true.

12. **Assertion (A)** Phishing attacks are a common method used by cyber criminals to obtain sensitive information.
Reason (R) Phishing emails often appear to be legitimate emails from a trustworthy source.
(a) Both A and R are true and R is the correct explanation of A.
(b) Both A and R are true but R is not the correct explanation of A.
(c) A is true but R is false.
(d) A is false and R is true.

Section B

(7 × 2 = 14)

13. How is crossover Ethernet cable different from rest of the Ethernet cables?

14. (a) List down the types of computer networks.

Or

(b) Define the term byte. Differentiate between a bit and a byte.

15. State whether the following statements are True or False:
(a) Device drivers are a type of application software that allow applications to communicate with hardware devices like printers and graphics cards.
(b) Mobile applications are always considered system software because they operate on smartphones.
(c) Microsoft Windows is an example of system software that manages hardware and software interactions on a computer.
(d) Web browsers, such as Google Chrome or Mozilla Firefox, are considered system software because they provide a platform for running mobile apps.

16. (a) Define a table used in MS-Word.

Or

(b) Using which option, you can create a frame for several shapes.

17. Give some examples of computer worms.

18. (a) Explain denial of service attack.

Or

(b) Define virus.

19. State difference between COUNT( ) and COUNTA( ) function.

UNSOLVED

Section C

(4 × 3 = 12)

20. Differentiate between Slide Transition and Custom Animation.

21. When the computer network uses telephone lines as communication channel then MODEM is used as a data communication device. Now, explain the working of MODEM.

22. (a) Name the device which is used to read the barcode. Explain in short.

Or

(b) Explain LCD. Write the features of an LCD monitor.

23. What is the difference between a workbook and a worksheet?

Section D

(4)

24. (a) Some features of a specific operating system are given below:

- Free/Open source
- Virus free
- Stable, long running operating system
- Multiple work space

(i) Which operating system supports these features?

(ii) What is the meaning of multiple workspace?

Or

(b) Mr. X has recently installed a new operating system on his computer

(i) Describe the main functions of an operating system.

(ii) Name any *two* utility programs used by an operating system.

UNSOLVED

Section E

(2 × 4 = 8)

(Case Study)

25. Mobile applications which are popularly known as mobile apps, are software programs developed for mobile devices such as smartphones and tablets.

Using these apps the mobile devices becomes miniature powerhouses for completion of various function and fun. Mobile phones generally come preloaded with various mobile apps provided free by the manufacturers or the mobile service providers. But there are various apps which are available only through device specific app stores. We can categorised mobile apps in six categories– Lifestyle apps (covers dating, food, fitness, etc.), Social media apps (facebook, twitter, etc.), Utility apps (reminder, weather, calendar, calculator, etc.), Gaming apps, Productivity apps and News apps. A mobile app is always has a smaller scope in comparison to the websites, means with less functionality.

Based on the above information, answer the following questions

(i) Mobile apps are .... programs developed for mobile devices.

(ii) Mobile games apps if installed in mobile phone they make mobiles .... of various function and fun.

(iii) Some mobile apps comes with device, but there are various apps which are available only through device ....

(iv) There are .... categories of mobile apps.

26. Ananya is a student who has been given the task of creating a report using a spreadsheet for her school project. She uses various features of a spreadsheet, such as entering numbers, text, and dates, formatting cells, and applying basic functions like SUM() and AVERAGE() to calculate the total and average of the data. She also inserts a bar chart to visually represent her data.

(i) What features of a spreadsheet did Ananya use to organize and analyze her data as mentioned in the case study?

(ii) What basic functions could Ananya use in the spreadsheet to perform statistical analysis of her data?

(iii) How can Ananya visually represent her data in the spreadsheet, as described in the case study?

(iv) Suggest two ways Ananya could improve the formatting of her worksheet to make it more readable.

Answers

1. (b) 2. (d) 3. (a) 4. (c) 5. (a) 6. (c) 7. (a) 8. (b)
9. (b) 10. (a) 11. (d) 12. (a) 15. (a) False (b) False (c) True (d) False
25. (i) Software (ii) Power house (iii) Specific app stores (iv) Six

SAMPLE QUESTION PAPER 3

A Sample Question Paper for CBSE Class 9th

Computer Applications

Instructions

1. This question paper has 5 Sections A-E.
2. All questions are compulsory. However, internal choices have been provided in some of the questions.
3. Section A has 12 questions carrying 1 mark each.
4. Section B has 7 Short Answer (SA-I) type questions carrying 2 marks each.
5. Section C has 4 Short Answer (SA-II) type questions carrying 3 marks each.
6. Section D has 1 Long Answer (LA) type question carrying 4 marks.
7. Section E has 2 Source-based/Case-based/Passage-based questions carrying 4 marks each.

Time : 2 hours ***Max. Marks : 50***

UNSOLVED

Section A

(12 × 1 = 12)

1. In the .... dialog box, you can change both line and paragraph spacing.
(a) Paragraph (b) Line (c) Format Spacing (d) None of the above

2. Raw facts are called
(a) data (b) information (c) knowledge (d) wisdom

3. Which of the following uses cables to connect two or more computers?
(a) Transmission (b) Unguided (c) Guided (d) Radiowaves

4. .... feature allows you to view different items such as comments, formatting etc, and also provides the option to view other author's comments.
(a) Display for Review (b) Track Changes (c) Show Markup (d) Reviewing Pane

5. A .... is a virus that is often disguised as a useful computer program.
(a) trojan horse (b) hacker (c) worm (d) spam

6. Which type of monitor works in the same way as a television?
(a) CRT (b) LCD (c) LED (d) 3-D

7. If you type =2 * (6-4) in cell A1, what value will be displayed?
(a) 2 (b) 4 (c) 6 (d) 8

8. Which of the following is not related to a utility software?
(a) Text editor (b) Antivirus program
(c) Disk compression software (d) Railway reservation system

9. .... is the default file name for a PowerPoint presentation.
(a) Untitled1 (b) Book1
(c) Presentation1 (d) Document1

10. Which of the following is not an OS?
(a) Android (b) Windows (c) Apple (d) BOSS

Directions *Q.Nos. 11 and 12 are Assertion and Reason Types. Each question consists of two statements, namely Assertion (A) and Reason (R). Select the must suitable option considering the Assertion and Reason.*

11. **Assertion (A)** A printer is an output device.

Reason (R) A printer converts digital data into printed format.
(a) Both A and R are true and R is the correct explanation of A.
(b) Both A and R are true but R is not the correct explanation of A.
(c) A is true but R is false.
(d) A is false and R is true.

12. **Assertion (A)** It is important to use strong passwords to protect your online accounts.

Reason (R) Hackers can easily guess weak passwords, leaving your accounts vulnerable to attack.
(a) Both A and R are true and R is the correct explanation of A.
(b) Both A and R are true but R is not the correct explanation of A.
(c) A is true but R is false.
(d) A is false and R is true.

Section B

(7 × 2 = 14)

13. Give one basic difference between guided and unguided transmission channels.

14. (a) Write down the components of a computer network established between the two offices of a company across the cities.

Or

(b) What is content technology?

15. State whether the following statements are True or False:
(a) The operating system is a type of application software that helps run applications like word processors and media players.
(b) A device driver is a type of system software that enables communication between the operating system and hardware devices like printers and keyboards.
(c) Wi-Fi is a type of wireless communication used to connect devices like laptops and smartphones to the internet without using physical cables.
(d) Cloud computing refers to using remote servers over the internet to store, manage, and process data, rather than relying on local computers or personal devices.

16. (a) Differentiate between data and information.

Or

(b) "Multimedia can stimulate the eyes, ears, brain and fingertips of a person." With respect to the given statement explain the meaning of multimedia.

17. Define virus.

18. (a) Internet can affect the privacy rights of a person. Comment.

Or

(b) What do you mean by cyber stalking?

19. What will be the column names of the below statement?
(i) 26th column (ii) 28th column

UNSOLVED

Section C

(4 × 3 = 12)

20. Define a utility software.

21. Suggest the appropriate functions for the following situations:

(i) For returning the minimum value out of a range A1 to C5.

(ii) For determining whether the customer is eligible for discount or not from the bill amount stored in cell D5. A customer is eligible for discount if bill amount >5,000.

22. (a) Differentiate between CUI and GUI.

Or

(b) State any two functions of Kernel operating system.

23. How does MS-Word 2010 differ from MS-Word 2013?

Section D

(4)

24. (a) Sona wants to add her pictures in a Word document.

(i) Which tab she should use?

(ii) Which command she should use to open Insert Picture dialog box?

(iii) Can she resize the image?

(iv) Is it possible to wrap text around an image?

Or

(b) Manu wants to replace the word 'organise' with 'organize' in a whole document.

(i) Name the feature which is used by Manu.

(ii) Write down the labels in order to show how he could replace the word?

I. In **Find what** box, type organise.

II. Click Home tab → Replace in the Editing group.

III. Click the **Replace All** button.

IV. In **Replace with** box, type organize.

V. **Find and Replace** dialog box with Replace tab will appear.

Section E

(Case Study)

(2 × 4 = 8)

25. A computer is an electronic device that process data and converts into the information according to the set of instructions. This set of instructions are called as programs. Computer main advantages are

It has the ability to store, retrieve and process the data.

It is used by companies now-a-days to make documents by typing using text editors, one can send and receive E-mails and browse the Internet.

In general, computer is the combination of hardware and software. Hardware is a collection of all physical components such as scanner, keyboard, printer, monitor, CPU, etc. While, software comprises the entire set of programs, procedures, and routines associated with the operation of a computer system. There are various characteristics of computers, such as accuracy, diligence, speed, automaticity, etc.

UNSOLVED

The CPU is called as a brain of the computer. It consists with three main components – ALU, MU and CU.

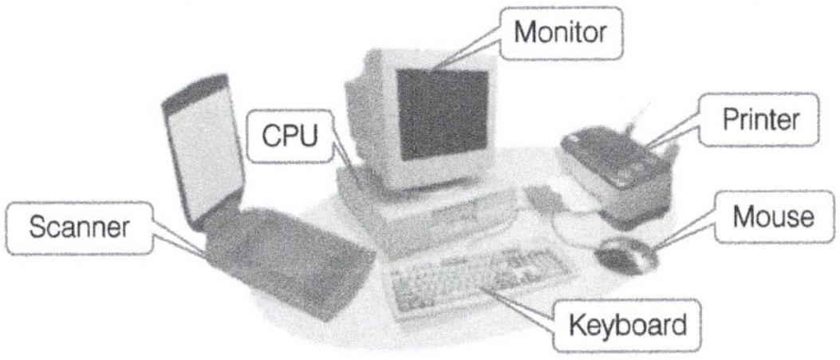

(i) Computer has an ability to .... the data.

(ii) Computer is a combination of hardware and ....

(iii) The .... is called as a brain of the computer.

(iv) Computer main task is to convert .... into ....

26. Based on the following information, answer the questions which follow:

Priya is working on a slide presentation about the history of space exploration. She uses various slide layouts, inserts relevant pictures, and adds sound effects to her slides. Priya also formats the text with headers and footers. While editing, she realizes that she forgot to add a watermark to her slides.

(i) Identify the basic elements Priya used in her slide presentation as per the features mentioned above.

(ii) What is the significance of adding a watermark in a presentation, and why might it be important in Priya's case?

(iii) How can Priya further enhance her presentation using the "slide sorter view"?

(iv) Mention two netiquettes Priya should keep in mind while sharing her presentation with her peers.

Answers

1. (a) **2.** (a) **3.** (c) **4.** (c) **5.** (a) **6.** (a) **7.** (b) **8.** (d)

9. (c) **10.** (c) **11.** (a) **12.** (c) **15.** (a) False (b) True (c) True (d) True

25. (i) Store, retrieve and process (ii) Software (iii) CPU (iv) Data, information